What can we learn about the precision, explanatory power, and empirical adequacy of the methods of community ecology by examining instances in which it is used to solve practical environmental problems? On the whole, general ecological theory has been unable, so far, to provide the precise predictions often required to direct sound preservation and conservation.

In this volume, K. S. Shrader-Frechette and E. D. McCoy discuss what practical contributions ecology can and cannot make in applied science and environmental problem-solving. In the first section, they discuss the ambiguities and inconsistencies surrounding the concepts of "balance" and "stability" that have often muddied theorizing in community ecology. Using island biogeography as an example, they also examine the ways that science (especially community ecology) is laden with ethical and methodological value judgments that impede theory building.

In the second section, however, they show that ecology can give us specific answers to practical environmental questions. Emphasizing natural history and ethical analysis, they reject several traditional norms governing statistical error and scientific decisions under uncertainty. Instead, they argue that successful conservation and preservation require both a new scientific method – that of case studies – and a new understanding of scientific rationality, one that makes an explicit appeal to ethical principles. They illustrate their new approach with a detailed case study of the endangered Florida panther. Shrader-Frechette and McCoy end by outlining a dominant role for the important, but relatively undeveloped, task of applying ecology to practical environmental problem-solving.

METHOD IN ECOLOGY

METHOD IN ECOLOGY:
STRATEGIES FOR CONSERVATION

K. S. Shrader-Frechette

Department of Philosophy
University of South Florida,
Tampa, Florida, USA

and

E. D. McCoy

Department of Biology
University of South Florida,
Tampa, Florida, USA

CAMBRIDGE
UNIVERSITY PRESS

Published by the Press Syndicate of the University of Cambridge
The Pitt Building, Trumpington Street, Cambridge CB2 1RP
40 West 20th Street, New York, NY 10011-4211, USA
10 Stamford Road, Oakleigh, Melbourne 3166, Australia

First published 1993

Printed in Great Britain at the University Press, Cambridge

A catalogue record for this book is available from the British Library

Library of Congress cataloguing in publication data
Shrader-Frechette, K. S., 1944–
Method in ecology : strategies for conservation / K.S. Shrader-
Frechette and E. D. McCoy.
p.   cm.
Includes bibliographical references and index.
ISBN 0 521 41861 5.   ISBN 0 521 44693 7 (pbk)
1. Ecology—Philosophy.   2. Nature conservation—Philosophy.
I. McCoy, Earl D.   II. Title.
QH540.5.S57   1993
574.5'01—dc20   93-9343   CIP

ISBN 0 521 41861 5 hardback
ISBN 0 521 44693 7 paperback

Contents

vii

Acknowledgments

All of the work in this volume originated as a result of research supported by the National Science Foundation under Grant BBS-86-159533, "Normative Concepts in Ecology and their Consequences for Policy," from the Ethics and Values Program. Any opinions expressed in this book, however, are ours and do not necessarily reflect the views of the National Science Foundation.

The volume is better than it might have been, thanks to the biologists and philosophers who offered constructive criticisms of the first and second drafts: Greg Cooper, Reed Noss, Michael Ruse, and Dan Simberloff. Their responses to our work have been invaluable in improving it. Whatever errors remain are our responsibility.

Dan Wigley, Heidi Adrien, and Jeannine De Bolt have done excellent work as research and editorial assistants for this book. Our greatest debt, however, is to our families. They make everything worthwhile.

University of South Florida,   *K.S.S.-F. and E.D.M.*
Tampa, Florida, USA

1 · Introduction: What ecology can't do

SCIENTISTS have long been in the business of helping to solve practical societal problems. Leonardo da Vinci helped build machines of war; Lavoisier's talents supplied gunpowder for the American Revolution, and Pasteur's experiments showed brewers and vintners how to keep their beverages from spoiling. Indeed, scientists' skills in practical problemsolving are often a barometer for the methodological sophistication of the theories that they employ. Good methods frequently lead to successful problemsolving. Failure at practical problemsolving often indicates poor scientific methods.

What can we learn about the precision, explanatory power, and empirical adequacy of the methods of community ecology – by examining the instances in which it has been used to solve practical environmental problems? This is the main question we assess in these ten chapters. Our answer is, in part, that when we wish to apply ecology in order to promote conservation or preservation, our knowledge of particular taxa is more important than our knowledge of general theory. In other words, following Kitcher's (1985b, 1989) distinction, we believe that, for practical problemsolving, "bottom-up" approaches to ecological explanation are likely to be more fruitful than "top-down," although both are needed. Top-down approaches tend to use an account of theoretical explanation to underwrite talk about fundamental mechanisms and identification of causes in particular cases. Bottom-up approaches tend to focus on specific phenomena; they emphasize our ability to see causal relations in such phenomena and then to pull together results about individual cases or events into some sort of theoretical explanation. We shall argue that, insofar as ecology is required for solving practical environmental problems, it is more a science of case studies and statistical regularities, than a science of exceptionless, general laws. Insofar as ecology is an applied endeavor, it is more a science that moves from singular to theoretical explanation, than one that proceeds from theoretical to singular explanation.

1.1 Ecology as the foundation for environmental ethics and policy

Ecologists are the gurus of the environmental movement. More than a century ago, Ralph Waldo Emerson argued in his essay, "The Uses of Natural History," that ecological science provided lessons for humans. Right, said Emerson, "is conformity to the laws of nature" (Emerson 1910, p. 208). Philosophers, scientists, and policymakers have continued to argue for the privileged position of ecology and ecologists in shaping the goals of environmental decisionmaking and in providing strategies for realizing these policy goals. Some philosophers claim, for example, that the "conceptual foundation" of environmental ethics is ecological theory (Callicott 1989, p. 22). They say that ecological stability and integrity outline norms for environmental ethics (see Taylor 1986, p. 50). "Ecological theory," they maintain, provides "a social integration of human and nonhuman nature . . . interlocked in one humming community of cooperations and competitions"; this interlocking, they say, requires each of us "to extend his or her social instincts and sympathies to all the members of the biotic community" (Callicott 1989, p. 83). It also requires us to preserve the environmental balance or homeostasis allegedly revealed by the laws of ecology (Rolston 1986, p. 18). In other words, many scholars credit ecology with supplying aesthetic, ethical, moral, and even metaphysical imperatives for environmental problems (see McIntosh 1985, p. 319; Worster 1990, pp. 1–2). Perhaps no one, more than Aldo Leopold, has emphasized the allegedly normative (as opposed to descriptive) character of ecological laws and theories. "A thing is right," according to Leopold, "when it tends to preserve the integrity, stability, and beauty of the biotic community. It is wrong when it tends otherwise." For Leopold, ecology has revealed how to preserve the integrity, stability, and beauty of the biotic community (Leopold 1949, pp. 224–225).

Even scientists themselves have not resisted the temptation to use ecology as a metaphysics, a world view, or an ethics – the foundation for environmental policy. When he was President of the Ecological Society of America, Arthur Cooper argued that there were numerous examples of the way that ecology has directed environmental ethics and policy. The best illustration, he said, has been the role that findings about estuarine ecosystems have played in stimulating government programs for coastal zone management (Cooper 1982, p. 348). Cooper also noted that ecological findings were directly responsible for environmental decisions to limit the use of DDT; to promote multispecies forests; and to publicize the problem of acid rain (Cooper 1982, pp. 348–349). In other words, Cooper appears to have said that ecological "facts" provide at least part of the basis for inferring what ethical, political, and practical "values" ought to characterize environmental decisionmaking.

Apart from the well-publicized epistemological and meta-ethical problems with attempting to use ecology ("facts") as a normative basis for rules about action or policy ("values") (see Taylor 1986, pp. 50–52), such attempts raise an interesting scientific question. Is ecology able to perform the task assigned to it by many conservationists and policy-makers? Can it provide the basis for environmental decisionmaking?

1.2 Problems with using ecology to guide environmental policy

On the whole, general ecological theory has, so far, been able to provide neither the largely descriptive, scientific conclusions often necessary for conservation decisions, nor the normative basis for policy, both of which environmentalists have sought. Ecologists have not been able, for example, to determine with confidence the number of species that a habitat can support. They have examined a number of general accounts of community structure – like the broken-stick model (see Kingsland 1985, pp. 183ff.) – only to discover that, despite their heuristic power, the models typically have been unable to provide the precise predictions often needed for environmental policymaking. Similar weaknesses have dogged other candidate general theories in community and ecosystems ecology, from log-normal distribution theories to those based on information theory and chaos. Three examples – focusing, respectively, on the passage of endangered-species legislation, on a New York utility controversy, and on the failure of the International Biological Programme of the US National Science Foundation – suggest some of the reasons why ecology, despite its many successes, has provided neither a largely descriptive general theory capable of yielding precise, conservation-related predictions nor a normative foundation for specific environmental policies.

One of the best illustrations of how, despite its heuristic power, general ecological theory has failed to provide a precise, predictive basis for sound environmental policy is that of the diversity–stability hypothesis. This hypothesis, simply put, is that more diverse communities of species are more stable, or that some "balance of nature" is maintained by promoting diverse communities of species. For many ecologists, complex *trophic systems* and diverse *communities* are more stable than less diverse, or simpler, ones. (For a discussion of stability and balance, see chapter 2). On the basis of the diversity–stability hypothesis (MacArthur 1955, pp. 533–536; Elton 1958, pp. 143–153; Hutchinson 1959, pp. 145–159; Lewontin 1969; Wilson and Bossert 1971, pp. 139–144; Futuyma 1973, pp. 443–446; Innis 1974, pp. 131–139; Wu 1974, pp. 155–165; De Angelis 1975, pp. 238–243; Goodman 1975, pp. 237–266; Worster 1977, ch. 15; McIntosh 1985, pp. 187, 252–256), preservationists have argued that we must exercise caution in altering ecosystems, so as to protect biological diversity and thus maintain the dynamic stability or balance of naturally functioning ecosystems (see Norton 1987, chs. 2–4). Merely on the grounds of its repetition over several decades, by the late 1960s the diversity–stability hypothesis achieved the status of a proposed truth, an ecological theory or paradigm. In the last ten years, however, at least in its original form, the thesis has been virtually refuted (Sagoff 1985a, pp. 107–110; Taylor 1986, p. 8).

The reasons for the disfavor attributed to the diversity–stability theory are both empirical and mathematical. Salt marshes and the rocky intertidal provide only two of many classical counterexamples to the diversity–stability view. Salt marshes are simple in species composition, but they are stable in the sense that species composition rarely changes over time. On the other hand, the rocky intertidal is a relatively diverse natural system, yet it is highly unstable, since it may be perturbed by a single change in its species composition (see, for example, Paine and Levin 1981; Sagoff 1985a, p. 109). Empirically based counterexamples of this sort have multiplied over the last 15 years, and May, Levins, Connell, and others have seriously challenged the diversity–stability thesis on both mathematical and field-based grounds (see May 1973; Levins 1974, pp. 123–138; Connell 1978, pp. 1302–1310; McIntosh 1985, pp. 142, 187–188; Sagoff 1985a, pp. 107–109; see also Paine 1969, pp. 91ff.; Goodman 1975, pp. 237–266; Lewin 1984, pp. 36–37; see also Soulé 1986a, pp. 6–7). Despite such repudiations, however, the diversity–stability theory has been, by far, the most basic and the most persuasive of the utilitarian arguments for environmental protection, perhaps because it is something that people like and want to believe (Goodman 1975). Policymakers and scientists repeatedly have trotted it out as a rationale for environmental policies designed to save species in a given area. Numerous decisionmakers, for example, have cited the diversity–stability thesis as grounds for supporting the Endangered Species Act (Commoner 1971, p. 38; US Congress 1973a, c; Myers 1983).

Admittedly, the demise of the diversity–stability hypothesis has not caused the repeal of the Endangered Species Act. This suggests that environmental legislation might not need to rely primarily on ecological findings, but could be supported instead by purely human (aesthetic, cultural, utilitarian, for example) preferences for preservation and conservation. Nevertheless, as a central tenet of general ecological theory, the diversity–stability thesis (in its original form) has been falsified. Its demise raises a question: Can general ecological theory bear the primary burden of justifying particular environmental decisions? This is one of the main questions we shall address in successive chapters.

In addition to the diversity-stability hypothesis, another interaction between general ecological theory (in this case, in the area of population ecology) and environmental policymaking occurred in the 1960s in the US, an interaction that also raised questions about the role of theorizing in ecology. In America's longest legal conflict over environmental policy, the US Environmental Protection Agency (EPA) challenged five New York utility companies to prove that their water withdrawals would not adversely affect the environment. Specifically, the disputants disagreed over the effects of withdrawals on the Hudson River striped-bass population. After spending tens of millions of dollars researching this problem, scientists still could not estimate, precisely, the ecological effects of the water withdrawals. Their failure illustrates the fact that general ecological theory was and is not precise enough to help adjudicate courtroom conflicts over environmental welfare. Unable to resolve their dispute on the basis of general ecological theory, the parties negotiated an outage schedule based on purely practical constraints (see Barnthouse *et al.* 1984, pp. 17–18; Shrader-Frechette 1989c, p. 81).

Perhaps the most spectacular interface between general ecological theory and environmental policymaking is systems ecology. In the middle 1960s, many ecologists urged a dramatic new approach to ecology, namely, the study of functional ecosystems using the methods of systems analysis and those of an international program of biological research called the "International Biological Programme" (IBP). Initially presented by a committee of the International Council of Scientific Unions (ICSU), the IBP research was funded, in the US, by the National Science Foundation and by the Atomic Energy Commission. As one scientist put it, very likely the most important event for US ecology in the last 30 years was participation in the IBP (see McIntosh 1985, p. 214). The focus of this international cooperative research in the

IBP, "big biology," was quantifying trophic effects in ecosystems and using nutrient cycles, flows of energy and matter, and systems analysis as the way to understand ecosystems. The difficulty, however, was that after a decade of millions of dollars of funding for large-scale, long-term ecosystems studies, the IBP, despite its successes (see Worthington 1975), could provide no precise theories having predictive power. Hence, the IBP provided little assistance to scientists who wished to use general ecological theories and their predictions to help justify specific environmental policies and actions. In 1974, the IBP was formally terminated (see McIntosh 1985, pp. 213ff.).

Despite the fact that ecologists had gleaned information from their ecosystems models in the decade of IBP funding, the general theory behind ecosystems ecology was unable to provide precise predictions that could be confirmed and used in the environmental courtroom. Indeed, many scientists claimed that the ecosystems approach was "unrealistic in view of the lack of valid theory" (McIntosh 1985, p. 234). Regardless of whether the predictive failures of ecosystems theory were a result of the infancy of ecology or a consequence of the inherently problematic character of the ecosystem concept, the fact remains that the ecosystems research of the IBP did not unequivocally vindicate general ecological theory. One of the concerns of this volume is to analyze the reasons for methodological failures such as the IBP. We shall also investigate alternative, practical contributions that ecological knowledge might make to applied science and to environmental problemsolving.

1.3 The argument of the chapters

In the next three chapters, we investigate some of the reasons why community ecology − so far − has been unable to arrive at a general theory having adequate explanatory power. These three chapters spell out what ecology can't do. In chapter 2, we show that ecologists have defined and used two of the concepts most basic to community ecology − "community" and "stability" − in ambiguous and often inconsistent ways. Not only have they used different terms to represent the same community and stability concepts, but ecologists have employed the same terms to stand for different concepts. Moreover, despite the fact that we are able to trace some of the ways in which the community and stability concepts appear to have changed over time, our historical and philosophical analysis reveals that there is still no clear and unambiguous meaning for these two central terms. Building a general theory of community ecology on such ambiguous, inconsistent, or unclear terms is like building a skyscraper on sand. Or, as one *Science* author put it several decades ago, "It is highly improbable that a group of individuals who cannot agree on what constitutes a community can agree to get together for international cooperative research on communities" (quoted in McIntosh 1985, p. 216). Much foundational work remains to be done.

Of course, complete agreement on the meaning of key terms and concepts is not essential for all communication in science. As Hull (1988, pp. 6–7, 513) points out, "weasel words" are important to scientists because they "buy time" while researchers develop their theories and positions. Nevertheless, although conceptual vagueness and disagreement have not brought ecology to a halt, and although they have not destroyed its heuristic power, conceptual difficulties have often prevented the formulation and evaluation of powerful, precise, general theories (in ecology) that are useful for solving specific environmental problems.

In addition to their conceptual disagreements, ecologists are likewise divided on what structures communities or holds them together. Because they do not know what, if anything, organizes communities (e.g., predation, competition) in precise ways, ecologists have not developed an uncontroversial, general theory of community ecology that is capable of providing the specific predictions often needed for environmental problemsolving. Chapter 3 discusses the most prominent of those ecological theories claiming to give such a general account, island biogeography. The chapter explains why island biogeography is still beset with controversy and, therefore, why it fails to provide a fully explanatory, complete, general theory of community ecology that is able to help resolve practical controversies over conservation decisions.

Inadequate understanding of the concepts and community structures unique to ecology are not the only reasons why community ecology, despite its heuristic power, has no general theory able to provide policy-related predictions. This area of biology has many of the same problems that make theory-building in any science difficult. One of the biggest obstacles is the fact that all empirical results, including those of ecology, are value laden. Chapter 4 examines some of the ways that science is laden with values – especially epistemic or cognitive values, but occasionally ethical values – and why it is impossible to avoid at least some of these values. It also illustrates some of the ways that cognitive or epistemic values arise in ecology. Chapter 4 further reveals that, unlike more descriptive sciences, much of ecology (especially conservation biology) is faced with developing theories that are often implicitly ethical or prescriptive. The theories are implicitly prescriptive because certain normative goals are built into specifying what is "natural" or "healthy" for the environment. In other words, because ecology is goal-directed in the way that medicine is, for example, it faces more complex epistemological and ethical problems – than other sciences do – in attempting to develop a predictive general theory. It must not only explain and predict a factual state of affairs but also help policymakers describe and defend that state as somehow healthy or normative.

The conceptual, theoretical, and evaluative problems associated with developing a precise, quantitative, and explanatory ecological science have suggested to some experts that ecology can play virtually no role in grounding environmental policy. In the last six chapters of the volume, we show why this pessimistic conclusion is unwarranted, despite the difficulties we outlined in the previous three chapters. Chapter 5 describes several things that ecology can do. It can often give precise answers to precise questions based, for example, on detailed natural-history knowledge or autecology. Ecology can also give us specific answers to practical environmental questions posed in individual case studies. As chapter 5 argues, ecology is, in part, a science of case studies, with both the assets and liabilities that the method of case studies entails.

Moreover, as a science that often emphasizes case studies, ecology is frequently able to establish where the burden of proof lies in an environmental controversy. Chapter 6 argues that, contrary to accepted scientific practice, in cases of scientific uncertainty, there are sound ethical and epistemological reasons for the ecologist to minimize type-II statistical errors. Minimizing type-II errors often is able to prevent the worst sort of environmental damage. Because chapter 6 argues for a new way to look at scientific error and for a reversal of the accepted opinion on whether to minimize type-I or type-II errors, when both cannot be avoided, the chapter is likely to raise a host of scientific, conservationist, and ethical objections. In chapter 7, we answer many of these objections and, in the process, clarify the notion of rationality underlying the application of much ecological science to environmental policy. We argue that, although ecologists in the past have frequently employed a notion of "scientific rationality," current applications of ecology to environmental problemsolving require them also to use "ethical rationality." Likewise, we explain the precise conditions under which ecological methods ought to be epistemologically conservative and ought to avoid rejecting the null hypothesis.

In order to illustrate what is perhaps our main claim about what ecology can do – namely, it can give practical advice in particular cases – in chapter 8 we present a case study. The study concerns the Florida panther, a subspecies now on the edge of extinction and reduced to about 40 individuals statewide. One question the panther poses for community ecologists is whether their discipline can provide scientific evidence relevant to the possibility of saving the subspecies in the wild. Providing a detailed analysis of specific ecological information, we show how and why ecologists can contribute to answering this question about panther preservation. Giving practical, scientific advice about particular cases, like the Florida panther, however, does not resolve all controversy about ecological methods and about how they might inform conservation policy. There are a whole host of normative, ethical, and economic questions that arise whenever one attempts to apply scientific conclusions to real-world conservation problems. In chapter 9, we discuss many of these normative questions as they arise in the panther case. Even if we could not argue effectively that ecological methods and ethical analysis have much to contribute to the future of science and conservation policy, it would be in our interest to believe so. Ecology will progress as a science only if those with the talents to make it do so also have the conviction that they will succeed. Lacking this conviction, ecologists are likely to fail. Optimism is our only scientific option.

In chapter 10, we summarize our arguments for what ecology can do, and we explain why precise concepts, theories with great explanatory power, and practical knowledge in particular cases will not resolve all the scientific difficulties facing community ecology whenever it is used to undergird environmental decisions. Perhaps more than other disciplines, ecology is beset with the difficulty of developing laws and theories about different cases, no two of which are similar in all relevant respects. Hence, compared to other scientists, ecologists face a particularly problematic task when they attempt either to move from singular to theoretical explanation (bottom-up) or to apply a general law to a specific case (top-down). They must clarify how and why the case is relevantly similar to others allegedly covered by the same law, and they must know the precise constraints on idealization in science. Of course, all scientific laws are idealized, and all particular applications of them raise questions about the required closeness of empirical fit in a given situation. Because of the difficulty of finding situations/cases in community ecology that are precisely and relevantly similar, the ecologist faces the problem of scientific idealization in an acute way. In the final chapter, we give some very preliminary suggestions for ameliorating the difficulties associated with idealizations in community ecology. Further, in the context of summarizing what ecology can and can't do, we close the volume by making several suggestions about the precise role of methodological value judgments in ecology and about the apparent inability of ecologists to follow a hypothetical-deductive model of scientific explanation. We conclude by pointing to several facts that suggest a bright future for the important, but relatively undeveloped, task of applying ecology to practical, environmental problem solving.

2 · Ecological concepts are problematic

THE QUEEN, in Lewis Carroll's *Through the Looking Glass*, claimed that she was able to believe six impossible things before breakfast. Unlike the Queen, most of us cannot believe impossible things. We, like Alice, cannot believe that inconsistent definitions of the same term or concept are both true. Often, however, we subscribe to different concepts or definitions without realizing that they are contradictory. Perhaps this occurs because we fail either to trace the logical consequences of our assent to particular beliefs or to recognize the assumptions necessary to our assent.

If community ecology, indeed, any science, is to progress, then we must learn to recognize the ways in which we, like the Queen, "believe impossible things." One way to achieve such recognition is through clarification of foundational concepts. In fact, clarification of concepts like "community" and "stability" is a necessary condition for having a science that is public, empirical, and testable. Without clarification of – and consensus about – such concepts, different ecologists will fail to make logical contact with each other. Instead, they will operate with various "private" ecologies; they will fail to provide authentic replications, confirmations, or falsifications of the findings of other scientists allegedly working on the same problem.

In the Preface to his recent philosophy of biology, *Toward a New Philosophy of Biology: Observations of an Evolutionist* (1988), and in his earlier *Growth of Biological Thought* (1982), Ernst Mayr emphasized that recent progress in evolutionary biology is a result of conceptual clarification, not a consequence of improved measurements or better scientific laws. We likewise believe that conceptual clarification is perhaps the most important key to progress in community ecology and the development of effective conservation policies. Nevertheless, we do not equate conceptual imprecision with lack of heuristic power, although we shall argue that such imprecision may hinder the application of ecological concepts to environmental problems. In this

11

chapter, we analyze two foundational concepts in ecology, "community" and "stability." We have chosen these two concepts because of their primacy throughout the history of ecology. But why should these particular concepts have achieved a predominant role in the discipline? The answer may be that, since the time of Charles Darwin, biologists have been keenly interested in what determines the number of species and in how the number of species changes. Robert May, in his Robert H. MacArthur Lecture (1986), claims that questions such as, "what factors determine number of species?" and "how is the number of species affected by perturbation?" are as fascinating and important as queries about the structure of nuclei or the large-scale composition of the universe. We share May's opinion and note that the need for precise conceptions of "community" and "stability" clearly extends well beyond the realm of theoretical ecology. Yet, we do not think that these two concepts are precise and, because they are not, human endeavors such as species conservation seem to rest on weak foundations.

In the course of examining the concepts of "community" and "stability," we trace the ways in which they are ambiguous, inconsistent, or otherwise imprecise. We argue that this imprecision is one of the reasons why community ecology has been unable to arrive at a general theory whose predictive power is adequate for many environmental applications. Although predictive power is likely too stringent an epistemic requirement for ecology, it is often precisely what is required of theories that guide environmental actions, interventions, and prohibitions. Our analysis should provide an example of some things that ecology can and cannot do with respect to environmental prediction. Whenever possible, we use exact quotations throughout our examination. While this detail may strike some readers as tedious, or perhaps even somewhat unclear and unsatisfying, we believe that our interpreting writers' claims about ecological concepts might add yet another veil of imprecision. Furthermore, our goal here is not to judge the success or failure of each individual battle in the struggle toward conceptual precision, but rather to illustrate that the war itself does not seem to be going well. We maintain that direct quotations illustrate our contention (about imprecision in ecology) admirably, and that extensive interpretation on our part either would not remove this imprecision or would misrepresent the history of ecology by camouflaging it.

2.1 The community concept

The concept of community has had considerable heuristic power as well as practical value in conservation. Because ecologists seem unable to say precisely how the community concept applies to the breadth of situations that arise in biological investigations (O'Neill et al. 1986), however, we shall argue that the practical value of the concept is somewhat limited. These limitations have arisen, in part, because examination of the stability of communities requires something we do not fully possess: a clearly defined and circumscribed conception of "community" (see Thorpe 1986; Williamson 1987). Our aim here is to provide some understanding of how the community concept has changed and developed throughout the twentieth century. Admittedly, ecologists not concerned with application of ecological concepts, as we are, might wish to take account of purely stipulative definitions of "community." Without taking a position on whether communities are natural kinds, we wish to assess the utility of various community concepts for conservation practice. Because our focus here is with application of the community concept to environmental problems, and because of space limitations, we shall not discuss any purely stipulative definitions of "community" (e.g., MacArthur 1972; Underwood 1986). Previous investigations of the concept have uncovered many interesting and intricate historical details (see, for example, Macfadyen 1963; Major 1969; MacArthur 1972; Simberloff 1980; McIntosh 1985, 1987; O'Neill et al. 1986; Taylor 1988). Later, we shall review some of these details and attempt to put them into a cohesive framework. We shall discuss how ecologists have employed various terms related to the community concept. If our account of the evolution of the community concept is correct, then it may provide both conceptual clarification and a step toward ecological consensus about the nature of communities.

2.1.1 The early community concept

A review of the community concept is largely an exercise in untangling the various attributes that have been incorporated into it over the years. Often, this exercise also involves distinguishing a series of terms that have been coined to emphasize one or another of these attributes. We begin our review in the very early years of the twentieth century.

Envision a group of species occurring in the same place at the same time. Conceptually, what attributes might be used to link these species together, such that they could be distinguished from all other similar groups? Although there is no simple answer to this question, examining the history of ecology provides several clues. Most of the early work in community ecology focused on groups of plants (see McIntosh 1985) coexisting over short periods of time – in naturally circumscribed areas such as bogs, meadows, woodlands, islands, and dunes. This early emphasis probably helped, in no small measure, to generate the appealingly simple schemes used to classify "communities" that dominated the discipline at the beginning of the century. We shall focus in particular on the influential writings of Clements (see Clements 1928, p. 140, for an outline of his classification scheme of "communities").

Clements (1905, 1928) distinguished three ways in which the "community" could be conceptualized and termed them "community," "association," and "formation." The first he defined as "a mixture of individuals of two or more [plant] species . . ." (1905, p. 316); the second as "the arrangement of individuals in vegetation" (1905, p. 315); and the third, following Griesbach, as "a group of plants which bears a definite physiognomic character" (1905, p. 3; see also Moss 1910). We think the key word in the first definition (of "community") is "mixture." By using this word, Clements (1905) conveys the impression of an entity recognized by simple juxtaposition of species in space and time, an entity that could be characterized, therefore, by a listing of the species comprising it. Likewise, we think the second definition (of "association") also has a key word, "arrangement." By using this word, Clements (1905) conveys the impression of an entity recognized by some discernible pattern among the coexisting species. This pattern appears to arise from various distributions of species within the list, such as numerical dominance of certain taxa or the relative abundance of each of the species. For example, Clements (1928, p. 129) says: ". . . [associations] are recognized chiefly by floristic differences. Associations are marked primarily by differences of species, less often by differences of genera. At the same time, their organic relation to each other . . . rests upon floristic identity to the extent of one or more dominants . . ."

Because of the phrase "physiognomic character," the definition of "formation" suggests that we recognize this entity the way we recognize a face, for example, largely in gestalt fashion. That is, we grasp it as a whole, without identifying particular components, as we might do when we recognize Clements' "community" or "association." Clements (1928, p. 127) referred to the formation as ". . . the unit of vegetation." Although he may have viewed the formation as the fundamental vegetational unit, because Clements failed to provide a clear operational definition of "formation," the term is of limited practical value. Identification of formations, as well as communities and associations, however, would seem to require specification of precise criteria for confirming their presence in nature. Yet, Clements does not provide such criteria in the definitions.

It is not surprising that these three definitions suggest quite different impressions of the entities they were meant to represent. Clements considered them to be related, either collectively or hierarchically, to one another. He (Clements 1905, pp. 296, 299) originally suggested that a community was a subdivision of an association. Likewise, he (1928, p. 140) envisioned an association as a subdivision of a formation. Both subdivisions suggest that the formation was at the top of Clements' hierarchy of community concepts. (Clements also proposed "family" and "society" as other subdivisions of the association, but we shall not deal further with these two concepts, because their related terms did not gain the widespread and long-term acceptance that "community" did.) Later, however, Clements (1928, p. 127) claimed that the community was at the top of his hierarchy, and he proposed "community" as "an inclusive term for any and all units from the formation to the family."

Some contemporaries of Clements realized that classification on the basis of community concepts was not easy in practice. For instance, Warming (1909), who was more reductionist and mechanistic than Clements (see McIntosh 1985), noted that communities, in the sense of co-occurring individuals, hardly ever are sharply separated from one another geographically. He was convinced, nonetheless, as was Clements, that plants could be grouped comprehensively on the basis of their responses to climate and soil. But even if such a comprehensive grouping were possible, and even if the formation could be shown to be the fundamental vegetational unit, all classification problems would not be solved. One reason is that the formation is specific to plants and cannot easily accommodate the other components of the environment; hence ecologists needed to devise additional classification schemes. In response to this difficulty, community ecologists resurrected the term "biome" (Carpenter 1939; Clements and Shelford 1939) to accommodate animals as well as plants. They also created the term "ecosystem" (Tansley 1935) to include non-living components of the environment. Clements and Shelford (1939, p. 20) defined "biome" as "the plant–animal formation; the basic community unit." Tansley (1935, p. 306) defined "ecosystem" as "the fundamental concept appropriate to the biome considered together with all the effective inorganic factors of its environment."

Theories of ecological organization obviously were becoming more complex in the 1930s than they had been at the time of Clements' pioneering work. These complex views brought with them a reevaluation of the way in which the natural world could be classified. The reevaluation arose, in part, because the broad variety of kinds of organisms and their ecological interactions (i.e., interrelationships among species, such as competition, parasitism, and predation) could not be classified within the proposed schemes that had been constructed for groups of plants. Ecologists could not easily and neatly arrange organisms into communities, associations, and formations. Even the writings of Clements illustrate how the presumed distinctions among these three terms were beginning to break down. In his early work (1928), Clements drew an analogy between the *formation* and the organism; but later (Clements and Shelford 1939) he drew an analogy, instead, between the *community* and the organism. (Other ecologists, with other points of view, claimed that the *association* was like an organism; see, for example, Braun-Blanquet and Furrer 1913.) Similarly, Clements (1936) equated the climax with the formation and the biome, while attributing organismal qualities to the climax, and thus to the *formation* and the *biome*. Clements' strong desire to think of the environment as a scaled-up organism seems to have fostered a tendency for him to attribute organismal properties rather indiscriminately to most of the terms created to describe and classify the environment, with the result that the terms themselves became confused.

2.1.2 Community concepts: From an idealized "type" to an interacting "group"

Despite the partially inconsistent and changing view of ecological organization, many plant ecologists were still attempting – as late as the 1940s – to classify groups of plants into fundamental vegetational units: the formations of Clements (1905) and others. Attempts at such classification were not without their critics, however, beginning with Gleason (1926, 1939, 1952) and Ramensky (1926), and including a large collection of researchers throughout the middle of the century (e.g., Cain 1947; Curtis and McIntosh 1951; Whittaker 1951, 1953, 1957; Curtis 1959). These ecologists reasoned that if the formation – or other ecological classifications, for that matter – were valid, then various "types" of formations, or communities, could be separated from one another according to objective empirical criteria, such as species composition. Their field results showed, to the contrary, that species of plants tended to be distributed independently along gradients and that community groupings such as formations usually could not be bounded in a non-arbitrary way. Several ecologists suggested that a conception of the community, a "mixture of individuals of two or more species" as any kind of idealized "type" (representing co-occurring species), probably was best relegated to duty as what Cain (1947) called a "metaphysical approximation" (also Curtis and McIntosh 1951; Ovington 1962).

One expected result of the failure to confirm the reality of an idealized community "type," as conceptualized in the formation and association, is that ecologists should be less inclined to use the terms "formation" and "association." We examined this inference by searching for explicit definitions of "association" and "formation" in sources published before 1970 and those published in 1970 or later. (We selected sources from among those in Table 2.1, at the end of the chapter.) We chose the 1970 dividing point in order to allow the results of the critical evaluations of classification schemes conducted in the 1950s to become established in the secondary literature. We used only publications containing more than one definition because we assumed that by doing so, we would restrict the resulting collection of definitions to those from the secondary literature. We assumed further that definitions from the secondary literature represent a better consensus of ecological thought than do those from the primary literature, whose purpose may be more to sway opinion than to reflect it. Our results (Figure 2.1A) suggest that explicit definitions of these two terms ("association" and "formation") were less likely to appear in ecology textbooks published after 1970 than in those published before 1970. The terms "biome," "community," and "ecosystem," however, appeared to suffer no such decline in usage (Figure 2.1B).

We speculate that failure to establish explicit criteria for traditional vegetational classification schemes, and the subsequent decline in use of terms like "association" and "formation," would have made ecologists "gun-shy." They might have become reluctant to use other terms, like "biome," "community," and "ecosystem," in any but the most vague ways possible, so that their usage could not be scrutinized too closely and subjected to criticism. We have not sought evidence to determine whether our speculation has any validity. We note, however, that such vagueness seems to have come about anyway, as a byproduct of the attack on Clements' idealized vegetational type. Some of the key players in this attack (e.g., Whittaker 1967, 1973) introduced a suite of new numerical methods into ecology that shifted emphasis away from description of "types" to quantitative surveys of the arrangement of species in space. These methods, such as multivariate analysis and ordination, rendered the term "community" less qualitative than it had been before, by establishing it as an entity to be recognized on the basis of some statistical criterion. Despite the value of quantification, however, such a definition of "community" rendered

A

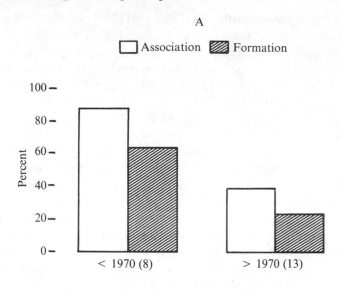

B

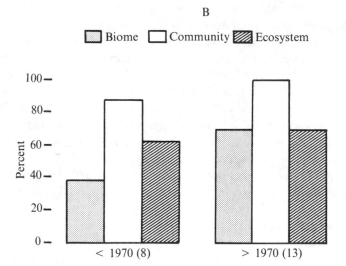

Figure 2.1. Relative representation of explicit definitions of "association" and "formation" (A) and "biome," "community," and "ecosystem" (B).

its conception less determinate, because it was based on statistical analysis (see McIntosh 1985).

The inability of ecologists to document the existence of certain vegetation "types" (representing co-occurring species) within the association or the formation framework meant that the classification schemes of Clements and others had failed to provide much insight into ecological organization. No noticeable vacuum arose in ecology as a result of this failure, however, because another way of thinking about communities, one based on internal interactions, had begun to gain broad acceptance in the 1950s. The use of interactions to delimit communities may be traced back at least to Mobius (1877), but the rising interest in interactions in the middle of the twentieth century may have had its mainspring in a paper by G. E. Hutchinson (1948). Indeed, Taylor (1988) has suggested that Hutchinson's paper may have established the "cybernetic" (i.e., self-regulating feedback system) conception of the community that predominated for the next several decades. Two of Hutchinson's students, Robert MacArthur and Howard Odum, played key roles in developing and promoting this conception of the community (see Fretwell 1975; Taylor 1988).

Other interactive conceptions of the community also came into prominence in the 1950s. Several well-known ecologists (Allee *et al.* 1949) built on the notion of feedback and developed a concept of the community as a highly structured unit. In describing this concept of the community, Kendeigh (1961, p. 18) asserts, first of all, that a community is "an aggregation of organisms which form a distinct ecological unit." He says that "major communities" are "those which, together with their habitats, form more or less complete and self-sustaining units or ecosystems, except for the indispensible input of solar energy." "Minor communities" ("societies"), on the other hand, are "secondary aggregations within a major community, and are not, therefore, completely independent units as far as circulation of energy is concerned." Although these definitions are not precise, they illustrate the burgeoning twentieth-century conception of communities as units of interacting species and habitats.

We have used the term "structure" for the first time. Ecologists widely use the term in reference to communities, but they rarely define it explicitly. Indeed, its importance as an element of "ecospeak" arose only in concert with the notion of feedback. Caswell (1976) presents an important discussion of the connection. He says (pp. 327–328):

> Function and structure (physiology and morphology, growth
> and form, operation and pattern) are dual aspects of any

system. A system, by any of the commonly encountered definitions, is (1) a collection of entities which, (2) influence each others behavior. A structural approach to the study of a system emphasizes the components, examining their nature, number, distribution, arrangement, and pattern of interaction. A functional approach, on the other hand, focuses on the dynamics of behavior and development of the system or selected subsystems. . . . Species diversity, the number and relative abundance of the constituent species, is one of the most commonly examined structural aspects of biological communities. The relationship between diversity and the dynamic functioning of communities is the subject of a large body of ecological theory. This theory has developed along three major lines. Two of these are based on very general system properties, while the third depends on more specifically biological assumptions. The three are not totally independent, but some mixture of them covers most of the commonly encountered theorizing about diversity.

The three interactive conceptions of the community that Caswell (1976) distinguished (one based on cybernetics, another on control theory, and a third on niche theory) have their roots in the middle of the twentieth century. Although he noted that these three conceptions were not independent, he constructed the following definitions for them. The cybernetic concept is that in which ". . . the state variables of a system encode all the aspects of the system's history that are relevant to its development in the future." (p. 328) The control-theoretic concept is that in which ". . . the dynamics of the system are a function of the system's current state and the environment in which it finds itself expressed through the function F $(\cdot, \cdot, \cdot)$." (p. 329) The niche-theoretic concept is that in which ". . . a species must find room in the 'niche space' [*sensu* Whittaker *et al.* 1973] of [a] community. The niche space is partly determined by abiotic features of the environment, but a considerable part of it is defined by the other members of the community." (p. 329) Both the control-theoretic and niche-theoretic concepts of the community, like the cybernetic concept, presuppose that interactions among species develop feedback loops that determine community structure (Caswell 1976).

As the middle of the twentieth century witnessed the waning of the conception of the community as an idealized "type" (representing co-occurring species) and the rising of the conception of the community as a self-regulating feedback system, it would seem worthwhile to observe what ecologists writing at the time thought about the community. We have chosen Macfadyen's (1963) thoughtful analysis for this purpose (see also Whittaker 1962). Macfadyen (1963, pp. 177–179) listed seven typical ways that ecologists supposedly thought about the community. (Although we have shortened and paraphrased his statements, we have endeavored not to alter their meanings. Hence, whatever conceptual imprecision or ambiguity existed originally still remains.) Ecologists viewed a community, according to Macfadyen, as:

1. a piece of shorthand denoting an assemblage of organisms;
2. species having mere coincidence of range;
3. species mutually linked and selected under the influence of external conditions;
4. a system that occurs under given ecological conditions and maintains in itself a dynamic balance;
5. those separate and relatively stable local elements which agree in their essential sociological characteristics, especially in their floristic composition, their aspect, and their ecological properties as determined by the local conditions;
6. an integrated organismic unit, with an ontogeny (succession) and a phylogeny (classification); and
7. a natural assemblage of organisms which is relatively independent of adjacent assemblages of equal rank, and, given radiant energy, is self-sustaining.

From these ideas, and likely because of their imprecision, Macfadyen (1963) extracted five potential properties of communities (pp. 179–180). His first is co-occurrence of populations. He points out that this was, in the view of many, the only well-established characteristic of communities. His second property is constancy of species composition, leading to the recognition of community "types." His third property is dynamic stability, such that the "normal" species composition is restored when it has been upset. Macfadyen (1963) also noted that the other two properties of communities were less frequently encountered in the literature; they are emergent properties, in which the community exhibits characteristics not predictable from its constituents, and organismal properties or analogues, in which the community is likened to plant and animal bodies. Clearly, emergent and organismal properties are connected logically; the latter comprises a subset of the former. We discuss both of these community characteristics in some detail later. In sum, Macfadyen's (1963) analysis suggests that by the early 1960s, the general conception of community was an amalgam of ideas about co-occurrence, constancy of composition, and interaction.

Our analysis suggests much the same conclusion as does Macfadyen's (1963). We have shown that the process of identification of community "types" (representing co-occurring species), although on the wane by this time, was firmly established in the literature. Large scale "type" words, however, continued to be used, perhaps because ecologists often need to typify very large-scale versions of communities like "desert," "tundra," and "deciduous forest." Ecologists appear to have settled upon the term "biome" for this purpose. We discuss the use of this term to typify communities later, in section 2.1.4. The many attempts to recognize community "types" suggests that practitioners of this art may have at least tacitly assumed that the community (when identified as a "type") had characteristics (emergent properties) beyond the collective properties of its component species. That is, the very idea of "types" seems to require some kind of metaphysical pre-suppositions or organizing force beyond mere haphazard assembly. We have also noted that some prominent ecologists likened the community to an organism by elevating it even further beyond the collective properties of its component species. Finally, we have indicated that conceptions of the community that included the property of dynamic stability (e.g., through feedback loops) were gaining acceptance.

Despite Clements' influential ideas (already discussed), Macfadyen (1963) noted that emergent and organismal properties of communities were rarely mentioned in the ecological literature written in the first half of the twentieth century. Attacks on group selection during the 1960s (e.g., Williams 1966a, b), attacks which seemed to render community ecology – of the superorganism variety – inconsistent with evolutionary theory, probably helped reduce the stock of these properties among ecologists. Interest in the emergent and organismal properties that might be associated with the community, however, increased in the second half of the century. This interest arose largely because of the conception of the community as a self-regulating feedback mechanism, with concomitant emphasis on interactions among component species and dynamic stability (Macfadyen's third property; see above). Again, the mainspring may have been Hutchinson (1948). As we already mentioned, under his cybernetic view of ecology, the community was envisioned as a self-regulating entity. Taylor (1988, p. 217) confirms the importance of Hutchinson's (1948) views in this regard: "For Hutchinson, . . . ecology was . . . united by a theoretical proposition: groups of organisms are systems having feedback loops [among species] that ensure self-regulation and persistence [of the system]." Hutchinson himself (1948, pp. 221–222) says:

When a circular causal system is described in terms of the variation in numbers of biological units or individuals . . . the mode of approach is characterized as *biodemographic*. In general, the biodemographic [approach is appropriate] to more complex cases, some of which might be regarded as involving teleological mechanisms.

Emergent characteristics, properties that are not simply collective properties (see Salt 1979; Underwood 1986), therefore, were seminal to the conception of community encompassed by this cybernetic view (see Oksanen 1988). Because of these emergent characteristics, persistence of the system could not necessarily be predicted from anything known about the component species. Eugene Odum (1977, p. 1290) provides an example of this point in his discussion of research that he and his brother Howard carried out at Eniwetok Atoll in 1954:

We theorized that the observed high rate of primary production for the [coral] reef as a whole was an emergent property resulting from the symbiotic linkages that maintain efficient energy exchange and nutrient recycling between plant and animal components.

Eventually, emergent properties began to take on attributes of a resurrected "superorganism" (see McIntosh 1976, 1980; Simberloff 1980). The organicist bent was especially evident in the blossoming field of ecosystems ecology in the 1960s (McIntosh 1985; see Evans 1956), as exemplified in a quotation from Odum (1969, pp. 262, 266):

. . . the "strategy" of long-term evolutionary development of the biosphere . . . increased control of, or homeostasis with, the physical environment in the sense of achieving maximum protection from its perturbations. . . . The intriguing question is, Do mature ecosystems age, as organisms do?

We see a very short logical path from this ecosystemic conception of nature to the currently popular idea of Gaia, perhaps the ultimate in "superorganisms" (see Rambler *et al.* 1988; Odum 1989).

Although the evolution of Hutchinson's cybernetic perspective into a revitalized organicist perspective may seem incongruous, it might have been anticipated from the fact that both perspectives so strongly embrace self-regulation. Taylor (1988, p. 220), for instance, states:

Hutchinson's self-regulating systems constituted a small step from the homeostatic communities of his contemporaries; circular causal paths were likewise a small step from groups of interspecies populations acting, reacting, and coacting to ensure coordination within the community.

The view of the community as a self-regulating feedback mechanism – as both equilibrium ecologists like Hutchinson and ecosystems ecologists like Odum emphasized – went largely unchallenged in the ecological mainstream throughout most of the 1960s and 1970s. In fact, Eugene Odum (1977) was touting this view of communities as the "new ecology" well into the 1970s – as he had done in the mid-1960s (Odum 1964). Beginning in the mid-to-late 1970s, however, a challenge began to develop, one which centered on the lack of convincing evidence in favor of some of the basic premises of the feedback view of community structure (see Dayton 1979; Simberloff 1980; Strong *et al.* 1984).

2.1.3 Community concepts: From an interacting "group" to a co-occurrence of species

One premise of the self-regulating view, that feedbacks from interactions among community components were important in maintaining the community, came under particular challenge. Critics charged that, even though interdependences clearly exist among species, ecologists have not demonstrated that communities have precise, uniform, or recognizable interactive community "structure." They said that ecologists have been no more successful in classifying groups of species by the ways in which they interact than by any other means (e.g., the "community matrix" approach; Vandermeer 1981). A second criticism is that ecologists have not shown that ecological interactions, such as competition, are responsible for whatever "structure" may be thought to exist. Ecologists have not yet settled upon a method for ferreting out the role of competition and other interactions in organizing communities. (See, for example, the "null models" debate: Connor and Simberloff 1978; Quinn and Dunham 1983; Schoener 1988). Finally, no one has established that whatever community "structure" may be thought to exist is stable in the way a self-regulating feedback system should be. (We shall address this problem later.) As a result of these failures of the feedback view, ecologists called into question foundational community concepts, particularly in the field of ecosystems ecology (see Underwood 1986).

What conception of community organization can fill the vacuum, even a partial one, left by the decline of the self-regulation view of persons like Hutchinson and Odum? Simberloff (1980) and others have suggested that a "probabilistic" account may serve this function.

Indeed, clashes between self-regulating and probabilistic approaches underlie many current controversies in ecology, for example, the "null models" debate mentioned above. Only time will reveal the outcome of these views and their impact on ecological studies (see Cody 1989; Roughgarden 1989; Vadas 1989; Ulanowicz 1990). It is interesting to note, however, that the "probabilistic" conception of ecological organization brings with it a return (some ecologists see it as a retreat) to a very simple conception of the community. The turn-of-the-century (Clements 1905, p. 316) notion of "community" as a simple "mixture of individuals" (i.e., co-occurrence of species), which was still by mid-century "the only well established . . . property [of communities]" (Macfadyen 1963, p. 179), obviously is relevant to the "probabilistic" view (see Simberloff 1980; Strong *et al.* 1984). This return to a conception of the community, as a simple co-occurrence of species in time and space, means that according to some ecologists (e.g., Gilbert and Owen 1990) the community has no structure, as we have mentioned. Whatever structure has been thought previously to exist is, in the words of Gilbert and Owen (1990, p. 33), merely ". . . a biological epiphenomenon, a statistical abstraction, a descriptive convention without true emergent properties but only collective ones . . ." Other ecologists (e.g., Hengeveld 1989) maintain that if co-occurrence of species in time and space produces no structure, in the sense of self-regulating feedback, then no community exists at all. This latter viewpoint stems, of course, from a particular conception of the community. So as not to beg any questions about how to define communities, we have chosen to include simple co-occurrence as one of the possible conceptions of the community. Hence, we cannot subscribe to the view that the community concept presupposes some kind of structure.

2.1.4 Terminology associated with the community concept

As the previous review reveals, a complete listing of the terms related to the community concept sometime during its historical development would be extensive. We have selected five terms which, because they are relatively common and long-lived, are of central importance to the development of the concept during the present century. The five terms are "association," "biome," "community," "ecosystem," and "formation." To begin to sort out the community concept, we compiled definitions of these terms from the literature. Our chronological ordering of them is in Table 2.1, at the end of the chapter.

To clarify the community concept, we attempted to employ

computer searches of databases to uncover books and articles in which definitions of the five terms appeared. This effort proved not to be workable, for three reasons. First, the most important database, BIOSIS, originated in 1969. Using it would mean that we had no information on scholarship done in the first 68 years of the century and that we were forced to focus only on work of the last 20 years. Second, even during the years 1969–1989, the number of books and articles listed in BIOSIS as specifically addressing our five terms was too large to be examined. For example, potential sources in which the word "ecosystem" appeared either in the title or in the abstract numbered 22,504. Even restricting the search to publications written in English yielded 18,140 potential sources. Similarly, potential sources for "formation" numbered 180,538, and for "community" numbered 22,504. Third, there were no database entries for terms like "community, concept of" or "community, definition of." Faced with too much material and no apparent way of circumscribing it in a wholly rational way, we compiled a list of explicit definitions of the five terms from a variety of sources. These sources include (1) ecological textbooks and dictionaries (Clements and Shelford 1939; Hanson 1962; Odum 1963; Shelford 1963; Knight 1965; Whittaker 1970; Krebs 1972 (1985); Colinvaux 1973, 1986; Collier et al. 1973; Ricklefs 1973; Pielou 1974; Pianka 1978 (1988); Brewer 1979, 1988; McNaughton and Wolf 1979; Smith 1980, 1986; Lederer 1984; Begon et al. 1986; Ehrlich and Roughgarden 1987); (2) collections of readings in ecology (Kormandy 1965; Boughey 1969; Hazen 1970; Ford and Hazen 1972); (3) "citation classics" of ecology listed by McIntosh (1989) − (These are 80 of the most highly cited publications in ecology between the years 1947 and 1977, as identified by The Institute for Scientific Information (ISI). The ISI publishes Current Contents and is a leader in developing methods to judge the impact of scientific publications on future research in their fields.); and (4) other books and papers known in advance to contain explicit definitions of one or more of the terms (Cowles 1901; Clements 1905, 1928; Tansley 1935; Gleason 1939; Cain 1947; Whittaker 1957; Curtis 1959; Strong 1983; Diamond and Case 1986a; Williamson 1987). We anticipated that this large sampling would yield an accurate representation of how the five community terms have been employed. Even so, the possibility remains that biases may have arisen as a result of data selection (see Ferson et al. 1986), as well as from our misinterpretations of what authors intended their definitions to mean – McIntosh (1985, p. 80) has noted that "ecologists . . . often used a word to mean just what they chose it to mean with little regard for what others said it meant."

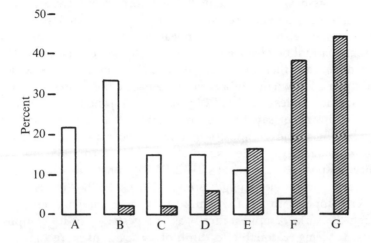

Figure 2.2. Relative frequency of appearance of categories of words in definitions of "association," "biome," and "formation" (group 1 – "type" words); and "community" and "ecosystem" (group 2 – "group" words) contained in Table 2.1. See text for an explanation of the grouping scheme. Categories each include several words which we judged to be related in emphasis: (A) "growth form," "life form," "physiognomy" (emphasize appearance but not component species); (B) "character," "characteristic," "characterized," "classification," "classified," "conception," "criterion," "type" (emphasize both appearance and component species); (C) "dominance," "dominant," "index" [species], "permanence" (emphasize prominence of certain component species); (D) "homogeneity," "similar," "similarity," "uniformity" (emphasize sameness of appearance or component species); (E) "aggregate," "arrangement," "assemblage," [uniform species] "composition," "structure" (emphasize grouping of species without clear indication of cause); (F) "co-occurrence," [spatial] "boundary" (emphasize boundedness of a group of species in time and space); (G) "complex," "dependency," "equilibrium," "integration," "interaction," "interrelation" (emphasize interconnections within a group of species).

These cautions in mind, we used the definitions as a basis for clarifying the community concept.

Based on an analysis of wording used in the definitions (Table 2.1), and ignoring the chronology of those definitions, we suggest that ecologists have two basic ways of thinking about communities. These are as types or kinds (representing co-occurring species) without precise specification of boundaries or interactions among components ("type" way), and as groups of species with quantitative boundaries and/or interactive components ("group" way) (see Figure 2.2). Definitions of three of the terms generally reflect the "type" way of thinking, and definitions of the remaining two terms the "group" way of thinking. "Association," "biome," and "formation" appear to seek typification of the biota according to a set of more-or-less specified criteria, largely related to form or appearance: their definitions suggest that some natural or idealized community "type" exists. Cain (1947), for example, says that an association is a "community type which is based upon a knowledge of a series of separate individual . . . stands which are more or less similar." Whittaker (1957) and Colinvaux (1973, 1986), for instance, say that an association is a community "unit" recognized by species composition. Many authors speak of associations being recognized by "index species" (e.g., Shelford 1963), by "uniformity of species" (e.g., Krebs 1972 (1985)), or by a "characteristic combination of species" (e.g., Brewer 1979, 1988). An association, therefore, appears to be a community type or category recognized through the form or appearance – as is a gestalt – of its composing species. It seems reasonable to think of associations as recognized in gestalt fashion because they are defined in terms of the *appearance* of a *kind*, rather than by some quantitative criterion, and in terms of *component*, rather than interacting, species. Similar conclusions can be shown to hold for the definitions of "biome" and "formation." Biomes, for example, are "units" (e.g., Clements and Shelford 1939), "kinds" (e.g., Whittaker 1970), or "types" (e.g., McNaughton and Wolf 1979; Ehrlich and Roughgarden 1987) recognized by species composition (e.g., Pianka 1978 (1988); Brewer 1979, 1988). If these definitions are representative, and we think they are, then "association," "biome," and "formation" refer to types or kinds, recognized in gestalt fashion, by means of the species composing them.

"Community" and "ecosystem," on the other hand, are defined in terms of a set of more-or-less specified biotic criteria, largely related to space, time, and interaction (i.e., interrelationships among species). Their definitions suggest that communities must have spatial and temporal boundaries and/or measurable interactions. Note that, by "spatial boundaries," we do not mean those which are obvious a priori, such as the boundaries of the "community" of a lake, an island, or a corn field (see Roughgarden and Diamond 1986). Rather, we mean those boundaries that can be set a posteriori by differentiating one group of species from another in some way. (See, for example, McCoy et al. 1986, where boundaries are identified by searching for greater and lesser than expected similarities in species composition among locations. The locations are grouped or separated according to the outcome of the similarity analysis.) Cain (1947), Collier *et al.* (1973) and Ricklefs (1973), for example, speak of communities as having definite spatial boundaries. Shelford (1963), Whittaker (1970), Collier *et al.* (1973), Ricklefs (1973), Pielou (1974), Brewer (1979, 1988), and Smith (1980, 1986) all speak of the species in a community as interacting, such as through predation or competition. Much the same can be said to be true for ecosystems. In other words, "community" and "ecosystem" appear to denote "groups" (e.g., Cowles 1901; Hanson 1962; Brewer 1979, 1988; Strong 1983) or "aggregates" (e.g., Shelford 1963; Colinvaux 1973, 1986) of species, rather than a type. These groups appear to be recognized, not primarily by the gestalt appearance of largely non-interacting component species, but by quantitatively definable *boundaries* and/or by the *interactions* of their component species.

One principal objection to this account – of two ways to think about communities – is that some of the terms we have grouped together are not as related to one another in the minds of ecologists as we have suggested they are. "Biome," in particular, seems to be problematic. Recall that previously, in section 2.1.2, we showed that "biome" did not decline in usage after 1970, as did "association" and "formation," the other two "type" terms. Rather, "biome" increased in usage, as did the "group" terms, "community" and "ecosystem." We do not think this apparent conceptual difficulty, that two "type" words decreased in usage after 1970, while a third increased, really is a problem. We suggest that the decline in usage – of "type" terms like "association" and "formation" – caused ecologists to need a term to typify very large-scale versions of communities like "desert," "tundra," and "deciduous forest." Ecologists appear to have settled on "biome" for this purpose. At least part of the reason that use of this "type" word has not become problematic, is that "biome" refers to such massive communities that their boundaries and characteristics are easy to recognize. They are typically set by major differences in the large-scale landscape. Hence, the difference in scale, presupposed by "biome," may explain its disanalogies with "formation" and "association."

We examined the definitions of terms related to the community concept (Table 2.1) for changes in emphasis over time. We chose to lump plant and animal ecology together for our analysis, in order to get a picture of the trends in the breadth of ecology, despite the fact that the two kinds of ecologies have not always viewed nature in parallel ways. Underwood (1986, p. 355), for example, has said:

> There is a certain irony that the work tending to cast such doubt on the plant ecologists' superorganisms was being

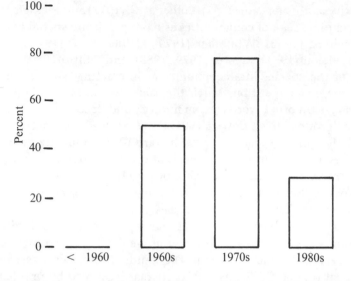

Figure 2.3. Percent of definitions of "community" contained in Table 2.1 that include the words "complex," "dependency," "equilibrium," "integration," "interaction," or "interrelation" (see Figure 2.2). Percentages are computed within four time periods.

published at about the same time as much of the work that has led to zoologists developing new definitions and conceptualizations of niche and community relationships and concurrently with a resurgence of interest in coevolved patterns of resource usage. Whilst much early plant ecology ignored animals, much of the later animal ecology appears to have ignored plant ecologists.

Analysis of the wording used in definitions of terms related to the community concept (Figure 2.3) reveals an increase in the 1960s–1970s of wording that implies interaction and then a decrease in the 1980s of the same kind of wording. We infer, albeit based upon very modest evidence, that ecologists may now be shifting emphasis to simple co-occurrence as the main idea incorporated into the community concept.

2.1.5 Conclusions: Community is a problematic concept

As our review has shown, at the beginning of the twentieth century, ecologists were concentrating on schemes to classify vegetation in great detail. They developed a suite of specific terms to accompany these schemes. Three problems, however, appear to have made detailed classification largely unworkable. The first difficulty was the inherent complexity of natural groups of species, both in their compositions and in their interactions with abiotic factors. The second problem was that attempts – to attribute organismal properties to these natural groups – muddied important distinctions among the specific terms constructed to describe them. The third problem was lack of evidence in nature that the classification schemes were realistic.

Perhaps as a result of the failure of detailed classification of natural groups of species, by the middle of the century, the community concept was a hodge-podge of ideas. Definitions derived from attempts at classification were still used by ecologists, but so were those based on considerations of the emergent and organismal properties of natural groups and on species' interactions. One researcher writing at the time (Macfadyen 1963) asserted that the main ideas embodied in the community concept of the time were three: co-occurrence, constancy of species composition, and dynamic stability.

As our review also has shown, about the middle of the century, a conception of the community as a self-regulating feedback system emerged. This conception naturally emphasized community character-istics like constancy of species composition and dynamic stability. It also encompassed previously minor aspects of the community concept, such as emergent, and even organismal, properties. Critics of this conception, like Simberloff (1980), have noted that, over 30 years, the evidence accumulated in support of communities as self-regulating feedback systems is not very strong. It remains to be seen whether or not this conception will receive evidential support in the future (see Abrahamson et al. 1989).

Analysis of definitions of the terms "association," "biome," "community," "ecosystem," and "formation" (Table 2.1) reveals that ecologists probably have two major ways of thinking about communi-ties. The first is as "types" (representing co-occurring species) recog-nized in gestalt fashion. The second is as "groups" of species defined in terms of their boundaries and/or internal interactions. By adopting either mode of thinking, ecologists assume that communities may be delimited in some fashion. We have concluded, however, that such delimitation is not easily accomplished in a way that does not beg the question. When faced with concocting a definition, suitable for conservation applications, it appears to us that ecologists seem able to say what a community *should* be. When faced with nature in all its complexity, however, they seem unable to say precisely what it *is*.

2.2 The stability concept

Ideas of community structure, discussed previously, and community stability go hand-in-hand. Precise conceptualizations of how groups of species are organized (e.g., as self-regulating feedback systems) should foster rather strict views of stability and vice versa. But are such connections between ideas of community structure and community stability readily apparent? And exactly how might a modern ecologist conceptualize stability? To answer these questions, we trace the development of the concept of "stability." In sections 2.2.1–2.2.3, we review ideas about the concepts that have predominated in the twentieth century. In section 2.2.4, we examine the development in the ecological literature of some common terms related to the concepts. (See Walker 1989 for another exercise of this sort.)

2.2.1 The early stability concept

The idea that nature maintains itself in some sort of balance is a very old one (see Egerton 1973; Goodman 1975; McIntosh 1985) and fundamental to a wide range of disciplines (see, for example, Russett 1966, Levins and Lewontin 1985). Among many traditional natural historians, "balance" in essence was synonymous with "constancy" (see Egerton 1973). Under this view, nature was in balance when no changes could be detected in the identities or population sizes of the component species of a "community." This sort of balance was thought to come about when the environment in which the community existed underwent no obvious change. The frame of reference for discerning lack of change was the period during which the community was observed, a period which usually encompassed a few years to decades. Interruptions of the balance resulted from "disturbances" (e.g., fire, timbering, cultivation) that promoted detectable changes in the environment and community. Often, such disturbances could be traced to human activities, giving rise to the common wisdom that nature would be in balance except for the meddlings of humans (see Allee *et al.* 1949 for some illustrations of this kind of thinking by relatively modern ecologists).

Some influential ecologists in the early twentieth century held that supra-organismal entities, like communities, possessed emergent and organismal properties (see section 2.1.1). Their views reinforced the impression of nature as being in some sort of balance. They ascribed balance to the inherent unity of all of the elements comprising each supra-organismal entity – the so-called "chain of being" (see Egerton

1973, McIntosh 1985). It should not be surprising, then, that "homeostasis" (= "staying the same") often was used to describe both the functioning of bodies and the functioning of communities (see section 2.2.4). Partially because nature had been viewed for so long as balanced or homeostatic, at least throughout the first half of the twentieth century (e.g., Dice 1952; Emerson 1954), the traditional, static, balance-of-nature concept refused to die.

Largely as a result of expanding the time frame of reference, a more "dynamic" perspective of nature emerged in the early twentieth century (e.g., Henderson 1913, 1917). Even so, the idea of a static balance of the community (i.e., no change in species composition or in population sizes) remained important. Clements (1905), for example, assumed that predictable groups of species replaced one another at a particular location until a "climax" was reached in which one group was self-perpetuating. Under this dynamic view, any change in the community that did occur ultimately produced a static balance, as long as the environment did not change. Some of Clements' contemporaries (e.g., Forbes 1880) also espoused a view similar to his. They claimed that species populations oscillated, but that the oscillations were kept within bounds, tending toward equilibrium (see McIntosh 1985). Although these early dynamic views are firmly within the traditional balance-of-nature camp, we see within them the seeds of two modern ideas about stability. We call these ideas "dynamic balance" and "persistence." A dynamic balance exists when change in the environment is tracked by the community, but the community returns to some "normal" condition. A community exhibits persistence when its changes seem not always to be followed by return to some "normal" condition, but it never changes so drastically as to be unrecognizable by some set of established criteria. We shall return to these ideas later.

2.2.2 Stability as dynamic balance

The idea of a static balance ultimately was doomed by the weight of evidence that was accumulating against it in ecology beginning in the early twentieth century. Elton (1930, p. 17), for example, stated:

> The balance of nature does not exist, and perhaps never has existed. The numbers of wild animals are constantly varying. . . .

And Andrewartha and Birch (1954, p. 20), in response to the ideas of Nicholson (1933) and Nicholson and Bailey (1935) – who supported the classical view of balance of nature – warned:

It is not easy to understand what precisely is meant by the word "balance."

By about the middle of the century, the idea of a dynamic balance had gained emphasis (see section 2.1.2). For example, Allee *et al.* (1949, pp. 507–508) say:

> . . . a community at the level of self-maintenance is a self-regulating assemblage in which populations of plants and animals hold each other in a state of biological equilibrium. This is an extension of the principle of biotic balance to embrace the whole community. This is not to say that communities are always in static equilibrium. Rather, they are in a condition of flux . . .

Likewise, Kendeigh (1961, p. 196) claims:

> . . . even in entirely natural communities undisturbed by man, a strict balance of nature is probably never maintained for any appreciable period of time. It is characteristic for populations to vary in size . . .

Probably because of the dated connotations of the term "balance of nature," it is rarely used any more by ecologists. The phrase virtually is never defined in recent ecological work (note the rarity of explicit definition in Table 2.2, at the end of the chapter). Indeed, the purpose of using the term in the recent ecological literature often seems to be to hold it up to ridicule (e.g., Ehrlich and Birch 1967). The analogous, but acceptable, term in modern ecology is "stability" (see Pimm 1991). Yet "stability" seems to be no more precisely defined than "balance." In fact, in the late 1960s and early 1970s, several prominent ecologists found it necessary to define and categorize the various kinds of stability that they attributed to nature, in order to increase precision. Lewontin (1969), Holling (1973), and Orians (1975), among others, reviewed stability as it had been conceptualized through the 1960s. Lewontin (1969), in probably the best known of these reviews, discussed the meaning of stability as a physicist might, in terms of particles represented in vector fields. As an illustration of the web of ideas associated with the concept of stability, this important review is worth examining in detail, even at the risk of diverging widely from a common conception of ecology. A tradition of borrowing ideas from other sciences, especially physics, and incorporating them into ecology has existed at least since the days of Lotka (1924). This tradition may be rooted in what ecologists have dubbed "physics envy": because laws are not well established in ecology, it might be judged a lesser science than physics, where laws are well established. To enhance ecology by borrowing from physics, however, requires ecologists to understand the physical foundations of ecological processes. While basic principles of physics must underlie many ecological processes, precisely how they do so is not obvious. Nevertheless, because the physico-mathematical approach is so basic to the concept of the community as a self-regulating feedback system (see section 2.1.2), its prominence in the late 1960s should not be surprising.

In his physico-mathematical approach, Lewontin (1969) used as his explanatory device ". . . the concept of the vector field in n-dimensional space" (p. 13), which he says ". . . is the most fundamental [concept] we have for dealing with the transformations of complicated dynamical systems in time" (p. 13). The vector field includes both a "position vector," which describes the succession of positions of an object (in the present case, a community), and "transformation vectors," which describe the direction that the object would move at every point in hyperspace and the magnitude of the motion. Lewontin defined "neighborhood stability" as the kind of stability in which all of the vectors that are very near a "stationary point" (point at which the magnitude of the transformation vector is zero) aim toward that point (thus making it a "stable point"). He defined "global stability" as the kind of stability in which all of the vectors aim toward the stable point from all other points in the dynamical space. Neighborhood stability, therefore ". . . is a simple yes or no test for the behavior of a system at a point, i.e., for arbitrarily small perturbations" (p. 16), while global stability is a test for ". . . how . . . the system [will] behave for large perturbations" (p. 16) (see also Wu 1977; Pimm 1982). From Lewontin's (1969) discussion, it appears that "perturbation" involves movement of the object in hyperspace in violation of the transformation vectors. Neighborhood stability, Lewontin (1969) says, is mathematically more tractable than global stability. Also, as our previous remarks have shown, because a study of neighborhood stability does not necessarily give information about global stability, it follows that neighborhood stability is understood better than global stability. Global stability, however, is likely to be the kind of stability of interest to ecologists, because they typically study the ramifications (for the community) of relatively large changes in the environment. Lewontin (1969) also says that realistic considerations such as random perturbations may hamper detection of global stability, even if it really exists. Or, they may actually prevent stability. He notes that stability may be absent, yet species may persist, when a system is "dynamically bounded." Using the terminology of physics, he says that (p. 19):

> . . . a system is "dynamically bounded" in some interior set S if at all points in the neighborhood of the boundary set B the transformation vectors point into the interior set S.

A simple way to illustrate dynamic boundedness is to assume that the environment varies randomly in such a way that one species is favored on the average but a second species is very strongly favored occasionally. In this case, no stable equilibrium abundance of the two species (relative to each other) will be reached, but neither species will be eliminated. If nothing else, Lewontin's (1969) review makes it clear that classical mathematical stability, which does not incorporate ideas of global stability and random variation, probably is not an ecologically relevant kind of stability.

Holling (1973), in particular, emphasized the dichotomy between classical mathematical and ecologically relevant stability. He says (p. 5):

> the sense one gains . . . of the behavior of the traditional models [of stability] is that they are either globally unstable or globally stable . . . [and] that neutral stability [what Lewontin (1969) termed "dynamic boundedness"] is very unlikely . . .

Holling (1973) notes, however, that under numerous realistic environmental conditions, systems may not show much evidence of typical point (neighborhood) stability. Rather, he claims that they may display a capacity simply to persist, a capacity that Holling (1973) terms "resilience." Specifically, he says that (p. 17):

> resilience determines the persistence of relationships within a system and is a measure of the ability of these systems to absorb changes of state variables, driving variables, and parameters, and still persist.

"Stability," on the other hand, he defines (p. 17) as:

> . . . the ability of a system to return to an equilibrium state after a temporary disturbance.

We made this same contrast (between stability and resilience) earlier in this section, but we used the terms "dynamic balance" and "persistence" rather than Holling's (1973) terms.

Recognizing further variants of the concept, Orians (1975, pp. 141–143 and figure 1) identified seven conceptions of "stability" as applied to ecological systems:

1. "constancy": lack of change in some parameter (e.g., number of species, taxonomic composition) of a system;
2. "persistence": survival time of a system or some component of it;
3. "inertia": ability of a system to resist external perturbations;
4. "elasticity": speed with which the system returns to its former state (e.g., number of species, taxonomic composition) following a perturbation;
5. "amplitude": area over which a system is stable;
6. "cyclic stability": property of a system to cycle or oscillate around some central point or zone; and
7. "trajectory stability": property of a system to move towards some final end point or zone despite differences in starting points.

Note that these seven conceptions of stability identified by Orians (1975) are neither mutually exclusive nor comparable in terms of having the same referent. Further evidence of the ambiguities surrounding the concept of stability is the fact that not all seven conceptions (listed by Orians) are operationalizable.

These reviews of Lewontin (1969), Holling (1973) and Orians (1975) suggest that in the late 1960s and early 1970s a wide range of concepts, with a variety of applications, could be found under the umbrella of "ecological stability." At least two of the authors who reviewed the stability concept realized that this state of affairs did not bode well for conservation and that, because ecologists lack a solid understanding of what constitutes ecological stability, they cannot advise resource managers on how best to ensure the long-term survival of ecological systems. Holling (1973), for example, points out the consequences of adopting either his "stability" view or his "resilience" view. The stability view, he says (p. 21):

> . . . emphasizes the equilibrium, the maintenance of a predictable world, and the harvesting of nature's excess production with as little fluctuation as possible.

On the other hand, the resilience view:

> . . . emphasizes domains of attraction and the need for persistence.

Holling (1973) suggests that resilience could be reduced or lost if ecologists tried to assure a stable maximum yield that might change the deterministic conditions of an ecological system. This is because previously innocuous chance events might trigger a sudden dramatic change in the system. Orians (1975), waxing equally pessimistic, warns (pp. 147–148):

currently, ecological advice on matters relating to community stabilities is highly intuitive and is not very different from Aldo Leopold's dictum that the first rule of intelligent tampering is to save all the pieces.

He also says that (p. 148):

scientific ecology should be able to provide better advice to decision makers who are responsible for difficult choices in matters relating to preservation . . .

Once we have finished our review of the stability concept, we shall return later to the difficult task of applying ecological concepts like stability to real environmental problems.

Despite the vagueness and variation in stability concepts that we have just outlined, ecologists firmly believed that as a community became more diverse, in terms of number of component species (the so-called "richness" component of diversity), it also became more stable in relation to perturbation (e.g. Clements and Shelford 1939; Odum 1953; Colinvaux 1973; Collier *et al.* 1973). In part because of this belief, ecologists during the late 1960s and early 1970s became absorbed with the link between community structure and stability. Hence, Paine (1966), MacArthur (1971, 1972), May (1972, 1973), van Emden and Williams (1974), Levins (1974, 1975), Goodman (1975), and others examined the supposed causal relationship between species diversity and community stability (see chapter 3). Their pioneering work and subsequent mathematical analyses failed to demonstrate any causal link between species diversity and community stability, however, as had generally been assumed to be true (see Pimm 1984).

One outcome of these failures was a shift of emphasis away from diversity–stability relationships to complexity–stability relationships (e.g., Pimm 1984), a shift that seems actually to have been a return to earlier ideas about what attributes – like interaction among community components – might enhance community stability (see Goodman 1975). But what is complexity? The complexity of a community encompasses more than just its diversity. While species richness and species evenness (how near a relative abundance distribution of species comes to equal representation of all species; evenness and richness together comprise diversity) are components of complexity, so are, for example, "interaction strength" and "connectance." Pimm (1984, table 1) defines "interaction strength" as "the mean magnitude of interspecific interaction: the size of the effect of one species' density on the growth rate of another species." He defines "connectance" as "the number of actual interspecific interactions divided by the number of possible interspecific interactions" (see also Levins 1974). As Pimm's definitions reveal, emphasis on complexity compels one to examine precisely the connections between community structure and some measure of stability. It may not be the mere number of species that is important but the species' identities. For example, as Pimm (1991, p. 356) hypothesizes,

> Complex communities should be most sensitive to the loss of species from the top of the food web, because secondary extinctions propagate more widely in complex than in simple communities. Simple communities should be more sensitive to the loss of plant species than complex communities, because, in simple communities, the consumers are dependent on only a few species and cannot survive their loss. . . . trophically generalized species should have profound effects on community composition. . . . Specialized species should produce fewer changes.

As Pimm (1991) admits, however, the evidence for his hypotheses regarding complexity is anecdotal, at present.

Apart from whether particular hypotheses about complexity turn out to be true, the general shift in emphasis from diversity–stability relationships to complexity–stability relationships is, in a sense, a liberal move for ecological theorizing. This is because complexity–stability relationships seem compatible with any of the various accounts of the community (see sections 2.1.1–2.1.3). Consider, for example, how complexity–stability relationships might mesh with the probabilistic conception of the community. According to this conception, interactions among the component species of a community may simply be the result of species' being in the same place at the same time. Even though, under the probabilistic conception, interactions may be fortuitous and temporary, they still can convey stability, by "spreading the risk" of extinction (see Reddingius and den Boer 1970; Hengeveld 1988, 1989). Hengeveld (1989, p. 129) says risk spreading occurs when:

> the variance of fluctuation [of population] is kept within bounds purely statistically: The greater the number of mutually dependent variables affecting a species, the smaller the variance.

That is, the larger the number of connections among the component species of a community, no matter how those connections come about, the greater the stability of the community. Hengeveld (1989, p. 129) also says:

in risk spreading, unlike regulation theory, relationships between species are thought to be non-specific and communities, consequently, to be non-existent.

We interpret this statement to mean, in our terminology, that a conception of the community as a self-regulating feedback mechanism (with its resulting deterministic species composition) is incompatible with a statistical account of stability based on risk spreading. Currently, some researchers (e.g., O'Neill *et al.* 1986, Maurer 1987, Moore and Hunt 1988) propose that complexity is related to community stability, but in a different way than simply by risk spreading. They think that complexity derives from the arrangement of species into community subunits such as "sink" and "source" food webs (Cohen 1978), and that stability derives from the interconnections among these subunits. Their proposal requires further examination (see Winemiller 1989), however, and there is no consensus regarding it.

2.2.3 Stability as persistence

Despite numerous attempts to link some measure of complexity with stability, the matter remains poorly resolved at present. Several problems contribute to the poor resolution. One is understanding how stability at the population level relates to stability at the community level. Pimm (1984, 1991) suggests some possible relationships, and Strong (1986a) reviews regulation at the population level. Another problem is measuring stability. Goodman (1975), Pimm (1984, 1991), and Williamson (1987) discuss methods of measuring stability, appropriate for various situations, and some problems in their use. We shall not deal further with these two difficulties because they have been reviewed recently and ably. Instead, we shall concentrate on two other problems that are conceptual rather than practical, difficulties that have been addressed less frequently in discussions of complexity and stability.

Perhaps the most important of these problems is conceptual vagueness. The term "stability" appears to be as vaguely defined currently as it was when Orians reviewed its meanings in 1975 (see Rutledge *et al.* 1976; Santos and Bloom 1980; Connell and Sousa 1983; Chesson and Case 1986). Pimm (1984, p. 322; see also Pimm and Redfern 1988; Pimm 1991), for example, lists five meanings of the term. Compare the meanings of "stability" listed by Pimm (1984) to those listed by Orians (1975) a decade earlier, and note how modestly the vagueness has been reduced. Pimm's (1984) list of meanings is:

1. "stability": the variables (his list of "variables" includes individual species abundances, species composition, and trophic level abundance) all return to the initial equilibrium (he seems to mean the conditions of variables before perturbation, although he does not say so explicitly) following perturbation;
2. "resilience": how fast the variables return towards their equilibrium following a perturbation;
3. "persistence": the time a variable has a particular value before it is changed to a new value;
4. "resistance": the degree to which a variable is changed, following a perturbation; and
5. "variability": the variance ((animals)^2/unit area) of population densities over time, or allied measures.

One gains the impression from reviews of the stability concept, such as those written by Orians (1975) and Pimm (1984, 1991), that a major impediment in understanding the concept is the large collection of meanings ascribed to it. We shall explore this matter further in the next section of this chapter.

The final problem contributing to poor resolution of the question of linkage between complexity and stability is determining the scale, both temporal and spatial, over which stability is to be judged. Virtually every modern author, writing about stability at any level of organization, includes some mention of scale (e.g., Shugart and West 1981; Pimm 1984; Berryman 1987; Blondel 1987; Ricklefs 1987; Williamson 1987; Morris 1988). Particular examples of the importance of scale in understanding the stability of communities may be found in Davis (1986) and Graham (1986). Connell and Sousa (1983) also detail how scale may influence perceptions of stability in natural communities. They conclude from their review of previous studies of stability that virtually no evidence exists for conceiving of ecological stability as some variable remaining at equilibrium (what we have termed "static balance") or returning to equilibrium after perturbation (what we have termed "dynamic balance"), once difficulties such as inadequacies of scale are resolved. They say (p. 808):

> There is no clear demarcation between assemblages that may exist in an equilibrium state and those that do not. Only a few examples of what might be stable limit cycles were found. There was no evidence of multiple stable states in unexploited natural populations or communities. Previously published claims for their existence either have used inappropriate scales in time or space, or have compared populations or communities

living in very different physical environments, or have simply misconstrued the evidence.

Connell and Sousa (1983, p. 808) conclude:

> rather than the physicist's classical ideas of stability, the concept of persistence within stochastically defined bounds is . . . more applicable to real ecological systems. [Recall that this conclusion was also reached by Holling (1973) and Lewontin (1969).]

By "persistence within stochastically defined bounds," Connell and Sousa (1983) mean without extinction, or with extinction and rapid recolonization, within those bounds. They note that judgments of "persistence" are themselves dependent upon the scale of observation. For example, if a "community" is viewed on a relatively large scale, it may be easy to judge its persistence, because the criterion may be as obvious as determining, say, whether a grassland persists or gives way to a forest. If, instead, a "community" is viewed on a relatively small scale, it may be more difficult to judge persistence, because the focus is on detailed changes, such as in the composition and relative abundances of species. Judgments of "persistence" also are dependent upon the time scale imposed by the organisms that make up the community. They are much more difficult for long-lived species because, to draw meaningful conclusions, observations must be made over at least one complete turnover of individuals. Problems of scale thus exist no matter what conception of stability one employs.

In sum, it appears that the modern conception of stability, like the modern conception of community, is imprecise. This imprecision probably derives in part from historical arguments about the relative importance in ecology of what we have termed "dynamic balance" (change in the environment is tracked by the community, but the community returns to some "normal" condition) and "persistence" (changes in the community are not always followed by return to some "normal" condition; communities possessing persistence never change so drastically as to be unrecognizable by some set of established criteria). Currently, most ecologists appear to favor the persistence viewpoint. Part of the imprecision also probably derives from the variety of meanings ascribed to "stability." These many meanings are specifically tailored to the wide variety of ecological situations that can arise. Finally, part of the imprecision likely comes from the fact that stability may be judged on a variety of scales, some of which lend themselves to precise measurement, and some of which do not.

2.2.4 Terminology associated with stability concept

Table 2.2 (at the end of the chapter) contains a chronological ordering of definitions of four relatively common and long-lived terms related to the concept of stability: "balance of nature," "equilibrium," "homeostasis," and "stability." These definitions were taken from the same sources (see section 2.1.2) used to construct Table 2.1, with one exception. Recall that several of the sources were chosen specifically because they were known in advance to contain definitions of terms related to the community concept. Because we could not guarantee that these sources would also contain definitions of terms related to the stability concept, we sought replacements for them. Fortuitously, two of the original sources did contain terms related to the stability concept (Tansley 1935; Williamson 1987), and we used them. We searched for additional sources containing one or more of the appropriate terms, sources that also were chronologically close to the original ones, and we were successful in five instances (Lotka 1924; MacArthur 1955; Oosting 1958; Connell and Sousa 1983; Chesson and Case 1986). We could not, however, find appropriate new sources to replace most of the early original ones (target dates of 1901, 1905, 1939, and 1947); instead, we chose two recent sources (Grant 1986; Hubbell and Foster 1986). We chose only two recent sources because we had obtained two more "citation classics" for examining the stability concept than for examining the community concept.

The scarcity of items in the table (relative to the number of items in Table 2.1) reflects, we think, a reluctance on the part of authors to be pinned down to specific definitions of stability terms, especially recently (see, for example, Begon *et al.* 1986, Pianka 1988). Table 2.2 does help us trace the development of the stability concept, however, because it provides tantalizing hints that the concept has changed recently, and in the manner that we suggested in section 2.2.3: namely, ecologists currently appear to favor the "persistence" viewpoint over the "dynamic balance" viewpoint.

Based on the wording they employed, the definitions seemed to fall naturally into three categories. The first category includes definitions whose wording suggests that the community is in balance, that some attribute of the community (e.g., species composition, relative abundances) does not change in the face of disturbance or returns to initial conditions after disturbance (e.g., "constancy," "dampened oscillations," "recovery," "resistance"). The second category includes definitions whose wording suggests persistence of some attribute of the

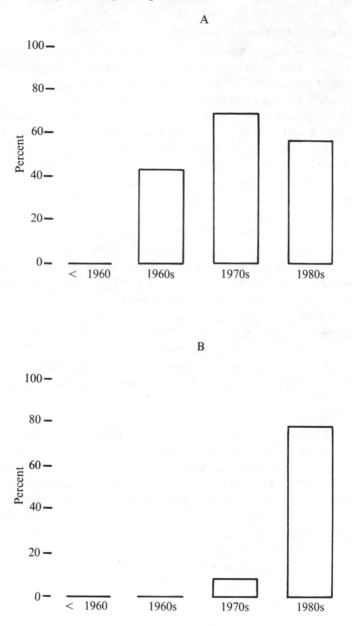

Figure 2.4. Percent of definitions contained in Table 2.2 that fall into each of three categories of wording, balance (A), persistence (B), and interaction among components (C) (see text for an explanation of these categories), during four time periods.

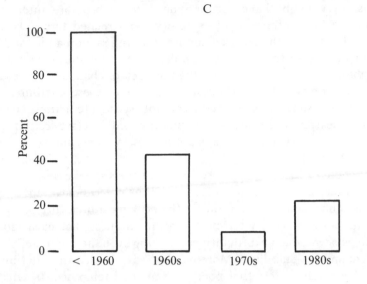

community (e.g., "bounded," "low chance of extinction," "persistence"). The third category includes definitions whose wording suggests interaction among components (usually species) of the community (e.g., "assembly," "checks and balances," "integration," "partitioning"). The percents of definitions contained in Table 2.2 that fall into each category, when displayed chronologically (Figure 2.4), suggest a recent decline in emphasis on lack of change in community attributes or on return to initial conditions of these attributes after disturbance. The percents also suggest a recent substantial increase in emphasis on persistence.

Figure 2.4 also suggests that the use of definitions implying interaction among community components was greater before and during the 1960s than after the 1960s. Emphasis on interaction was least during the 1970s. We have no explanation for the apparent modest increase in use of such wording in the 1980s. Perhaps our sample size is not large enough and representative enough to have revealed a real pattern. If it was large enough and representative enough, then one possible reason for the decline in emphasis on interaction after the 1960s might be the general acceptance, at that time, of the importance of interactions in structuring communities (see section 2.1.2). If ecologists supposed that interactions were integral to community structure, then they might also have supposed that interactions were integral to community stability.

Thus, they might have seen no need to incorporate interactions explicitly into definitions of "stability" and related terms. We also think that part of the reduced emphasis on interaction after the 1960s could be due to the increased emphasis on community persistence. Emphasis on persistence, rather than on lack of change in community attributes or on return to initial conditions of these attributes after disturbance, simultaneously reduces emphasis on interaction of components, at least in the sense of self-regulating feedback (see section 2.1.3). This is because such feedback is not necessary to promote persistence (see section 2.2.3).

We noted in section 2.2.3 that much of the vagueness surrounding the stability concept seems to come from the myriad meanings applied to "stability" and related terms in the ecological literature of the last two decades. Indeed, we would venture to guess that most modern ecologists would have difficulty verbalizing even their own definitions of "community stability." Moreover, we suspect that their definitions are likely to include rather poorly formulated references to what we have called "static balance," "dynamic balance," and "persistence," as well as interactions among components of the community. Some ecologists have realized this problem, and they have attempted to attach specific definitions to often confused terms, such as "stability," "stationarity," and "equilibrium" (e.g., Williamson 1987).

2.2.5 Conclusion: The stability concept is problematic

Our review has shown that the stability concept originally reflected a view of communities as unchanging. Later, most ecologists rejected this view. They distinguished among static balance (i.e., lack of change in community attributes), dynamic balance (i.e., return to initial conditions of community attributes after disturbance), and persistence (no drastic change in community attributes). Their notions about communities formed the basis for modern concepts of stability. The idea that communities are dynamic (= resilient), rather than static (= resistant), entities naturally accompanied the conception of communities as self-regulating feedback mechanisms (because of interactions among their component species). This probabilistic conception of communities allows one to place emphasis on the idea that communities are persistent, rather than either resistant or resilient, because persistence does not require invocation of self-regulating feedback.

Analysis of definitions of the terms "balance of nature," "equilibrium," "homeostasis," and "stability" (Table 2.2) reinforces the conclusions that we have drawn about communities. The definitions fall into three categories, based on the wording they employ: "balance," "persistence," and "interaction among components." "Balance" refers to a lack of change in community attributes or a return to initial conditions of these attributes after disturbance. Definitions in the "balance" category accommodate both "static balance" and "dynamic balance" views of stability. The "interaction among components" category accommodates mostly the "dynamic balance" view of stability. If our sample size was large enough and representative enough, then we were able to document an apparent reduction, during the last decade, in the relative number of definitions falling into the first category, and an apparent reduction, during the last two decades, in the relative number of definitions falling into the third category. Also, if our sample size was large enough and representative enough, then we were able to document an increase, during the last two decades, in the relative number of definitions falling into the second category.

We conclude that the concept of community stability, as persistence of some specified community attributes, has moved to the fore in recent years (see Steele 1985; Chesson and Case 1986; Strong 1986a, b). On the one hand, a major problem in applying this concept to actual communities is the choice of appropriate spatial and temporal scales of examination (see Connell and Sousa 1983). On the other hand, persistence is compatible with all of the community concepts we have discussed (see sections 2.1.1–2.1.3), including the probabilistic view. Persistence also meshes well with modern ideas about how communities can be sustained for relatively long periods of time (see chapter 3).

2.3 Ecological concepts and environmental policy

We have argued that "community" and "stability," two of the concepts most fundamental to community ecology and most central to applications of ecological theory to environmental policymaking, are saddled with uncertainties. Evidence for the lack of clarity in the community and stability concepts, as our analysis has shown, are (1) the vagueness and imprecision of many ecologists' discussions of the concepts; (2) the variety of different terms used to represent the concepts; and (3) the inconsistent usages of these terms, both by the same authors and by different ones, throughout different periods of ecological history.

Despite the ambiguities surrounding both of these concepts, we have been able to trace some apparent trends in the terms used to represent the concepts and in the properties associated with them. Such trends, however, even if they are correct, reveal only how community ecologists have used community and stability concepts and terms, not how they ought to have used them. Our analysis has suggested the evolution of a *descriptive consensus* about ecological thinking on community and stability, rather than a *normative justification* for such thinking. This suggests that there are at least two constraints likely to limit our applying these imprecise ecological concepts to controversies over environmental policy. *First*, our application of ecological concepts gives, at best, a consensus, rather than a rational justification for particular environmental policies. That is, ecologists are able to give advice, but not unassailable evidence, for the community and stability concepts relevant to environmental policy. *Second*, given the apparent community and stability concepts dominant during different historical periods, it seems unlikely that environmental policies based on the concepts of one era might be consistent with those based on the concepts of another era. In subsequent paragraphs, we shall suggest how different interpretations of the two concepts lead logically to divergent consequences regarding the goals and methods of conservation.

Connell and Sousa (1983, p. 808) claim that "if a balance of nature exists, it has proven exceedingly difficult to demonstrate" (but, see Silvertown 1987). By "balance of nature," they mean a lack of change in community attributes or return to initial conditions of these attributes after perturbation. Yet, this idea of balance of nature is well rooted in the conservation movement (e.g., Leopold and Leopold 1953; Poirot 1964; see also Watt 1968). In fact, it still holds great sway there (see, for example, Lewin 1986). Goodman (1975, p. 238) pointed out that the deep interest in balance among ecologists probably derived tit-for-tat from its potential importance to conservation. He states in reference to diversity–stability relationships:

> the particular appeal of such ideas in ecology was, no doubt, reinforced by subliminal realization that the developing science of ecology might serve as the intellectual foundation for the normative judgments of the conservation movement . . .

Diversity–stability relationships offer strong justification for conservation efforts because they suggest that simplification of the species composition of a community not only reduces its stability (what we have termed "static balance" and "dynamic balance"), but also enhances its susceptibility to invasion (see Howard 1931; Elton 1958; Pimentel 1961). In either case, if conservationists were convinced of the reality of diversity–stability relationships, they could maintain that loss of individual component species would push a community to the brink of collapse. Their rationale could be that, while naturally simple communities (e.g., salt marsh, tundra) may persist for exceedingly long periods of time, those simplified (or enriched) by human activities may not.

The prevalence of belief in diversity–stability relationships among environmentalists is illustrated well by a review of the important symposium "Conservation 2100," held in 1986 (Lewin 1986). One participant, Brian Walker, identified a two-part problem in managing nature reserves. The first part is that managers attempt to maintain high species richness by stabilizing the ecosystems concerned. The second part is that managers judge stability by lack of fluctuations in component populations. Diversity–stability arguments aside, one should realize from sections 2.2.1–2.2.3 that lack of fluctuations in component populations is only one way to judge community stability, and a rigid one at that. Walker points out that populations tend to fluctuate in "natural" systems, and that attempts to maintain constant population sizes on reserves may well endanger the very diversity a manager hopes to protect (Lewin 1986 relates an example of this situation, acacia woodlands in Chobe National Park, Botswana).

Walker's ideas about population fluctuations are new neither to ecology nor to conservation (see, for example, Holling 1973; White and Bratton 1980), but their importance may have been underestimated until recently. Goodman (1987a, b) suggested that when populations are broken up into subpopulations connected only by occasional movements of individuals, they are better buffered against environmental variation than when they are not. (This idea is elaborated in chapter 8.) Under this scheme, various fluctuations occur: some subpopulations may decline and even go extinct, while others remain constant or increase. Colonization from prosperous subpopulations may renew failed ones. The result is that species persist over the entire landscape, even though they do not persist locally (see Wiens and Rotenberry 1981; Pulliam 1988). All of this suggests that the relevant scale for judging community stability may be larger than surmised in the past, and that stability does not preclude fluctuations. That is, the relevant spatial scale may encompass collections of subpopulations of all species, rather than single ones. It follows that conservationists may need to give at least equal attention to multiplicity as to size of individual components in reserve design (see Soulé and Simberloff 1986). Further, it may also be crucial for them to know the natural histories of the reserve's residents, in order to spot unusual population changes (see Williamson 1987; Morris 1988).

Just as stability has been erroneously associated with fluctuations, so also it has been linked with resistance to invasion. Indeed, we noted earlier that simplification of the species composition of a community has been thought to result in increased susceptibility of that community to invasion. Elton (1958), for instance, proposed that islands were particularly prone to invasion because the paucity of species in island communities reduced their ability to resist invaders. Likewise, resistance to invasion has long been considered one attribute of a stable community (e.g., Elton 1958; see also Crawley 1987) and therefore an important goal of conservation. In this respect, islands once again have been used as the paradigm for conservation efforts because many of the well-documented cases of invasion come from islands (see Mooney and Drake 1986).

Using island data about population fluctuations and resistance to invasions, ecologists have drawn inferences about how to stabilize nature reserves as well as about how to defend the diversity–stability relationship (e.g., Elton 1958; Pimentel 1961). Such data do not provide an unassailable defense of the diversity–stability relationship, however. It may be true that communities with many species generally are less likely to be colonized than those with few species (Pimm 1984, 1991; Moulton and Pimm 1986). Likewise, it may be that island systems in general are the most vulnerable to invasion (Loope et al. 1988; Usher 1988). Nevertheless, it does not necessarily follow that islands are relatively easily invaded because they are depauperate (see Goodman 1975; Simberloff 1981, 1986a; Drake 1988). They may be more easily invaded because they have a particular species composition, or because they have special physical habitat features, or for some other reason. Hence, there is no clear evidence that depauperate communities, whether on islands or in nature reserves, are less stable.

By logic similar to that applied to islands, it could be argued (1) that unstable communities – such as those strongly affected by grazing, fire, and other similar "disturbances" – should be relatively prone to invasion (Elton 1958; see also Orians 1986), and hence (2) that conservation managers ought to minimize disturbances in reserves. Numerous examples of a correlation between level of human influence and propensity for invasion are available. See, for example, chapters by Simberloff (insects), Moyle (fish), Dobson and May (pathogens and parasites), Pimentel (agricultural pests), Mack (plants), and others in Mooney and Drake (1986). Yet, there is little evidence that disturbance alone is a sufficient condition for an increase in invasibility, as suggested by Elton (1958) and others (see Simberloff 1986a; Crawley 1987). Further, similar sorts of disturbance can promote invasion in some situations but not in others, as Macdonald and Frame (1988) show.

Savanna reserves in Africa apparently are less prone to invasion by large mammals than reserves in Java and Australia that are subjected to similar types and degrees of disturbance. Macdonald and Frame (1988) suggest that differences in the composition of reserve faunas in the two locations, in particular the relative paucity of carnivores equipped to deal with large prey in Java and Australia, promote the greater invasibility of reserves there. Hence, there is no clear mandate, based on diversity–stability, for avoiding all disturbances in reserves.

Based upon a small number of cases in which the consequences of invasions are known, Simberloff (1981) concluded that when species do invade a community, their most common effect is to produce no discernible change (but, see Herbold and Moyle 1986; Pimm 1991). Likewise, Williamson (1987) presented arguments which indicate that invasion of a species of diatom into the waters of Britain caused the native community simply to shift from one stable (= persistent) state to another. Documentation of the consequences of most invasions is poor (see Diamond and Case 1986b; Usher 1988), but observations like those of Simberloff (1981) and Williamson (1987) suggest that many communities have substantial abilities to persist, even though their species compositions and other attributes may vary from time to time. The apparent human influence on invasibility and the relative ease of invasion of islands (discussed previously) indicate, however, that these abilities may be taxed in some circumstances. That is, when individuals, which make up populations, which in turn make up a community, are disturbed (*sensu* Pickett *et al.* 1989; see also Petraitis *et al.* 1989) or confined, they may be less able to make the demographic, behavioral, or other sorts of adjustments necessary to survive and reproduce at rates that will prevent population decline.

Other ideas about community stability, also discussed previously, have consequences for conservation goals. One such idea is that a population broken up into semi-isolated subpopulations is better buffered against environmental variation than if it were not broken up. This idea may offer some insight into the reasons why certain communities have the ability to persist and also why other communities appear to lack it. Assuming that a community has been identified in some way, consider a situation in which each of the component populations is broken into a mosaic of variously isolated subpopulations. These subpopulations may be conceived of as either relatively fixed in space or as variable in space. On the one hand, if they are relatively fixed in space, then the entire population is in some sort of "equilibrium" (see Blondel 1987; also selected chapters in Pickett and White 1985). In such a situation, persistence of spatially fixed subpopulations is a balance between extinction and colonization of those subpopulations. On the other hand, if the subpopulations are conceived of as variable in space, then the entire population is "nonequilibrium" (see Hengeveld 1988, 1989). Regardless of whether the entire population is "equilibrium" or "nonequilibrium," an important point is that it persists at a spatial scale that encompasses all of the subpopulations; any reduction of scale, such as by creation of a reserve, may concomitantly lessen persistence. If reduction of scale does lessen persistence, then the construction of a reduced-scale nature refuge qualifies as a disturbance, as defined by Pickett *et al.* (1989). Further, if the reduction of scale affects many populations, then community persistence also may be lessened.

Usher (1988) uses an example (from Gerell 1985, pers. comm.) which clearly illustrates how a mosaic of subpopulations buffers the entire population from disturbances which could potentially lead to its demise. Invading mink (*Mustela vison*) destroyed breeding colonies of common eider (*Somateria mollissima*) so widely in southern Sweden that the ducks only nested successfully on islands without minks. Subsequently, however, ducks have begun to nest on islands with minks. It appears that ducks and minks are able to coexist there. This experience suggests that if mink-free islands had not been available when the ducks were under severe pressure, then the ducks would have been exterminated. If, for example, the ducks had been confined to a single location naturally or by design (as might be true of a nature reserve), they may well not have recovered from the initial pressure applied by the minks.

What consequences does all of this discussion have for conservation? The obvious result is that ecologists' or conservationists' conceptions of communities and stability in great part determine their views of what constitutes an appropriate conservation strategy. To illustrate how different conservation strategies might be linked to different views of ecological concepts, we use an exercise in logic. First, we construct five hypothetical, but realistic, scenarios – different combinations of concepts about community organization and stability. Next, we suggest the conservation strategies that might follow from each of these scenarios. The different ecological concepts we use deal with the ways in which the populations that make up a community may be arranged in space and how a community may respond to disturbance.

First, one could construct a scenario based on two assumptions. One is that populations generally are homogeneous units (i.e., they are not broken up into semi-isolated subpopulations, as described earlier, in this section). The other assumption is that community "stability" is the result of self-regulating feedback or risk-spreading probabilistic mechanisms (as described earlier, in section 2.2.2). The conservation strategy that might follow from these two assumptions is one that endeavors to damp population fluctuations of all resident species within some arbitrarily circumscribed area. This strategy could be termed the "balance-of-nature strategy."

Second, one could assume, as before, that community "stability" is the result of self-regulating feedback or risk-spreading probabilistic mechanisms, but that populations are broken up into semi-isolated subpopulations. Further, one could assume that these subpopulations are fixed in space, so that some equilibrium interchange of individuals is established among them (as described earlier in this section). The conservation strategy that follows from these ideas is likely to be one that endeavors to damp population fluctuations of all resident species, but one that does so by promoting movement of individuals among subpopulations, by use of corridors and the like. This strategy could be termed the "island-biogeographic strategy."

Third, one could assume that populations are not broken up into semi-isolated subpopulations, and that community "stability" is the result of resilience of species to disturbance. Recall that "resilience" implies no feedback among components of the community, as might be conveyed by self-regulating feedback or risk-spreading probabilistic mechanisms, but rather simple persistence of those components. The conservation strategy likely to follow from these ideas is one that endeavors to ensure persistence of all resident species, even while allowing considerable fluctuation of populations, for some specified period of time, within some arbitrarily circumscribed area. This strategy, as well as the next two, appear to have no obvious ecological epithets, so we have chosen terms that relate the manipulation of organisms in conservation efforts to the manipulation of objects in various games. We have termed the present strategy the "chess strategy."

Fourth, one could assume, once again, that community "stability" is the result of resilience, but that populations are broken up into semi-isolated subpopulations that are fixed in space. Recall that, under these assumptions, the subpopulations could be expected eventually to establish an equilibrium interchange of individuals. The conservation strategy likely to follow from such assumptions is one that endeavors to ensure persistence of all resident species, even while allowing considerable fluctuation of populations. The strategy provides persistence, despite fluctuation, by promoting movement of individuals among subpopulations for some specified period of time. Such a strategy could be termed "the pinball strategy."

Finally, one could assume that community "stability" is the result of resilience, and that populations are broken up into semi-isolated subpopulations, just as in the fourth case, but that the subpopulations are variable in space. Recall that such subpopulations were termed "nonequilibrium" to distinguish them from subpopulations that are fixed in space. In this case, the conservation strategy that is likely to follow from this fifth set of assumptions is one that endeavors to ensure persistence of all resident species, even while allowing considerable fluctuation of populations, just as does "the pinball strategy." Unlike "the pinball strategy," however, this strategy provides persistence within an area circumscribed by the temporal and spatial dynamics of the component species, for some specified period of time. Such a strategy could be termed "the space-invaders strategy."

We do not maintain that our distinguishing among these five cases makes the tasks of applied ecology – developing strategies for dealing with particular conservation problems – any easier. Nor was it our intention even to attempt such a daunting task here. Indeed, realistic scenarios could embody elements of several of these strategies. Our primary concern is not with presenting actual conservation strategies but to emphasize the epistemological point that different conservation strategies are based on different ecological concepts. (Conservation strategies also are based on ecological theories. We discuss this relationship in chapter 3.) Moreover, just as different interpretations of those concepts (and theories) lead to different conservation strategies, so also they lead to different environmental consequences. To the degree that ecological concepts (and theories) differ, to that same extent do the strategies and conclusions of applied ecology differ. If our ecological concepts (and theories) are uncertain, then so are our applications.

Ecological concepts (and theories) do not affect only strategies for conservation, but also the cost, and even the feasibility, of conservation efforts. Why should this be so? The more a particular conservation strategy attempts to incorporate natural variability (e.g., resilience and nonequilibrium subpopulations), the larger the scope and the cost of the environmental undertaking becomes. The scope and the cost become larger because the strategy must allow the time and space for fluctuations of populations to occur. Such fluctuations, in turn, require enough area to ensure that failed subpopulations are replaced by newly founded ones. In the face of considerable environmental fluctuation, the area and the financial resources necessary to implement any conservation strategy could be quite large.

2.4 Ecological concepts and their epistemological status

Despite the fact that the uncertainty surrounding the ecological concepts of community and stability typically results in uncertainty regarding various conservation strategies, there are good reasons for believing that the two concepts nevertheless may have some heuristic value for future ecological theorizing. To see the precise ways in which some of the conceptual problems we have outlined may lead to progress in ecology, we need to have an account of when a conceptual difficulty is useful, versus when it is useless.

Following Wimsatt's (1987; see also Wimsatt 1980) analysis of how and why some false models can often help us to find better ones, we might argue that some uncertain concepts in community ecology, like community and stability, can often help us to find more certain or precise ones. In other words, we might argue that, just as there are epistemological roles for false models, so also there are epistemological roles for imprecise concepts. After all, every science is uncertain, and neither the concepts nor the evidence in community ecology (or anywhere else) are unassailable. Given this unavoidable uncertainty, it may be that the problems we have uncovered in community and stability concepts are not so much evidence of obstacles to scientific theorizing but, instead, are somehow heuristically useful for the progress of community ecology.

On Wimsatt's (1987) scheme, there are at least seven ways in which models can be false, four of which sometimes produce useful insights for error-correcting activity and three of which are rarely helpful in such situations. Useful types of falsity, for Wimsatt, are cases in which the model may be: Only locally applicable; an idealization never realized in nature; incomplete in leaving out causally relevant variables; or misdescriptive of the interactions of some variables. Rarely useful or not useful types of model falsity, for Wimsatt, are those in which the model is: a totally wrong-headed picture of nature; purely phenomenological; or erroneous in its predictions, that is, consistent with any of the preceding states of affairs. If one assumes (as seems reasonable) both that Wimsatt's (1987; see also Wimsatt 1980) categorization of "useful" and "rarely useful" false models is approximately correct and that this categorization yields analogous insights for distinguishing between "useful" and "rarely useful" conceptual imprecision in science, then his analysis provides one vehicle for interpreting the epistemological significance of the problems with the community and stability concepts. Following these two assumptions, do the problems associated with the community and stability concepts fit into analogous categories of useful or rarely useful instances of imprecision?

In order to answer this question, we must have a clear idea of the main difficulties with the community and stability concepts. These are (a) problems associated with measuring community properties and with measuring stability, (b) problems with determining the temporal and spatial scale over which a community and stability are to be judged, and (c) problems with the variety of meanings ecologists attribute to community and stability terms. What is the epistemological significance of these difficulties with the ecological concepts of community and stability?

The problem (a) that community properties and stability are difficult to measure appears to be one that may be epistemologically useful. Although measurement difficulties may be indicative of conceptual problems of varying degrees of seriousness, the measurement problems associated with the community and stability concepts appear to be difficulties related to idealization in science. In the case of the community concept, we have idealized notions of the concept associated either with particular community "types" or with groups of species that either interact or are merely within a spatial or temporal boundary. By searching for ways to group species in some non-arbitrary way (see, for example, Whittaker 1967, 1973; Legendre *et al.* 1985; McCoy *et al.* 1986), we can attempt to set community boundaries a posteriori. That is, we can remove some of the problems associated with the idealization of the community concept by operationalizing community terms through use of techniques such as ordination and comparison of species' similarities. Hence, despite the measurement problems associated with the community concepts, the difficulties suggest ways to operationalize use of community terms.

In the case of stability, the conditions of applicability of the concept vary from situation to situation because alternative measures of stability, for example, are appropriate for different situations in nature (Goodman 1975; Pimm 1984, 1991; Williamson 1987). Hence the concept itself is idealized. But, because a variety of measures for the concept are apparently applicable in alternative situations, it appears possible to localize problems of idealization, given different ecological communities. For example, different temporal measures for stability-related concepts may be applicable to marine, as opposed to terrestrial, communities, because of the longer cycles of many processes in marine communities. Because it appears possible to localize measurement problems and hence to modify, correct, or make more precise the idealized concept by working with the unrealistic parts – such as temporal measures that are too short – the typical sorts of difficulties associated with measuring stability seem to be of the "useful" type for theorizing. Hence, problem (a) does not appear to be a prima-facie obstacle to theorizing in ecology.

Problem (b) – that stability or a community may be judged present or absent, depending on the chosen spatial and temporal scales – is arguably an instance of conceptual imprecision that could be useful in achieving greater precision. This difficulty is, in large part, that the concept alleged applicable at one level or scale is not clearly applicable at another level. Wimsatt appears correct, that such problems of applicability are problems that can provide a basis for further scientific progress, because we can localize applicability problems, and hence we can use what he calls "piecemeal engineering" to improve the concept or model. For example, one could look for density independence or density dependence at different spatial scales and then use the findings to determine the precise concepts that were applicable or inapplicable to different communities. Hence, problem (b) does not appear to be a prima-facie obstacle to theorizing in community ecology; indeed, it may well aid it because we are able, at least, to pinpoint the precise areas in which applicability of a particular concept of community or stability is problematic.

The variety of meanings attributed to stability and community terms, problem (c) discussed earlier, however, appears to be a difficulty that is unlikely to be useful for further theorizing in community ecology. First, the meaning variability of both terms is a manifestation of conceptual incoherence and perhaps even inconsistency. The five meanings attached to the concept of stability, for example, as outlined by Pimm (1984), do not even all describe alleged characteristics of communities; some of the meanings refer to the time during which community changes take place, rather than to the change itself, and some of the concepts presuppose different spatial and temporal scales than other ones. Likewise, the various meanings associated with the community concept are inconsistent; sometimes communities are said to be identifiable on the basis of interaction or on the basis of how similar they are, a priori, to some idealized grouping, or on the basis of mere co-occurrence of species. Indeed, just as some scholars have argued about the species concept (see, for example, Ghiselin 1969, 1974; Hull 1976b, 1978; Gould 1982; Rosenberg 1985; see also Kitcher 1985c), there is no universally applicable specification of the characteristics that describe either stability or a community, no set of necessary and sufficient conditions for defining a community or for a community's being stable. What, in practice, is often described as "stability" or as a "community" is a disjunction of relationships, none of which is essential for all instances of stability. There is no homogeneous class of processes or relationships that exhibit stability or that define a community, and there is no single, adequate account of what either community or stability is. Hence, the conceptual incoherence surrounding community and stability terms and meanings appear more to block heuristic power and scientific progress rather than to aid it, because the more plausible meanings associated with the concept do not appear to be isolable. Hence, it is difficult to pinpoint problematic meanings and to correct them.

Second, the meaning variability associated with stability and community concepts seems unlikely to aid future theorizing in that, at some minimal level, scientists' meaning the same things when they talk about the same concepts appears to be a necessary condition for progress in clarifying those concepts. Scientific progress seems to presuppose the ability to isolate semantic from non-semantic problems, and such isolation does not appear possible, given the degree of variability of meanings associated with the community and stability concepts.

Third, because the apparently dominant meaning associated with stability concepts, that of persistence, is compatible with all models of community structure – from mere species coexistence to feedback models – the concept of stability does not appear to provide useful information for theorizing. The concept seems to have little "cash value" for explaining community processes. Indeed, because the current concept of stability – emphasizing persistence – appears compatible with incompatible community models, it appears consistent with almost any state of affairs and hence seems incapable of explaining any of them. Thus, to the degree that the stability concept focuses only on persistence, it appears to have little epistemological or theoretical utility for progress in community ecology. Given the absence of potential explanatory power or theoretical utility and the presence of conceptual incoherence already mentioned, it is arguable that ecologists might do better not to employ stability terms (such as "balance," "equilibrium," "homeostasis," or "stability") at all. The one precise sense in which ecologists use the term "stability" refers to "dynamic equilibrium" (Pimm 1984), but dynamic equilibrium is highly questionable and has largely been abandoned, as we argued earlier. As we explained in preceding paragraphs, it is a relationship supportable only if one misrepresents the ecological evidence (Connell and Sousa 1983). The alternative to employing an imprecise general concept of stability, or to using a precise but discredited term, "stability" (dynamic equilibrium), might be to abandon use of the concept and term altogether. Following our discussion of the various terms allegedly related to the stability concept (see Orians 1975; Pimm 1984, for instance), community ecologists might do better to employ, analyze, and refine such specific terms as "persistence," "resistance," and "variability" (see Williamson 1987). For example, we might do better to clarify the temporal and spatial scales or applicability of such terms and to abandon, for the most part, use of stability terms such as "equilibrium."

In the case of the community concept, the apparently dominant meaning, that of mere species co-occurrence, is compatible with virtually any model for the possible structures underlying the community. Nevertheless, by operationalizing the concept in terms of techniques such as ordination, for example, it may be possible to infer some of the reasons (if any) for the co-occurrence of species and for their being in a particular temporal and spatial location. The exercise of determining, a posteriori, the boundaries of a community may have heuristic power for uncovering any structures underlying such communities, if indeed there are any. If there are no operational ways to specify community terms such as "association" and "formation," however, then ecologists are probably justified in not using them, just as we have suggested they ought not use the term "stability" in ecology.

Fourth, even if we abandon use of stability concepts and terms, such as "equilibrium" and "homeostasis," and use of community concepts and terms, such as "association" and "formation," it is not clear that pursuing the alternative – of employing precise stability terms such as "persistence," "resistance," and "variability" or of using community concepts that can be operationalized – will necessarily get us "home free" in community ecology. Such alternatives merely appear less undesirable than to continue to use vague, or discredited concepts. Indeed, the apparent evolution of the community and stability concepts, away from emphasis on interactions among component species and toward emphasis on *persistence* or co-occurrence of species, may provide little basis for explaining patterns of communities or stability. It appears merely to focus on presence/absence or co-occurrence/non-co-occurrence of species, independent of mechanisms that might account for such presence or absence, co-occurrence or non-co-occurrence. Hence, this evolution in meanings – toward the current emphasis on persistence and co-occurrence – does not seem to provide a fertile ground for theorizing about what explains possible community characteristics. The most recent problems with the stability concept, for example, appear to indicate that it may be approaching heuristic bankruptcy and that its problems may not lead us to greater conceptual clarification in community ecology. Because of the operational potential of community concepts, however, the heuristic prognosis for them may be brighter. But regardless of the optimistic prognosis, if the arguments of this chapter are correct, then foundational concepts (like community and stability) in community ecology may not be able to give us, at present, the precise predictions we need to justify environmental actions, prohibitions, and interventions. And if not, then despite the scientific status of community ecology, it may fail us at some of the times that we most need it, at times of application to conservation problems.

Table 2.1. *Definitions of the terms "association," "biome," "community," "ecosystem," and "formation" taken from representative twentieth-century ecological literature (see section 2.1.4 for discussion of these definitions)*

	ASSOCIATION
Clements (1905, 1928)	The arrangement of individuals in vegetation.
Cain (1947)	A conception of the *community* type which is based upon a knowledge of a series of separate individual *community* stands which are more or less similar.
Whittaker (1957)	Occurrence together of species populations to form *community* units which may be recognized by species composition.
Hanson (1962)	A group of organisms characterized by a definite floristic composition, presenting uniformity in physiognomy and structure and growing under uniform habitat conditions. A group of *communities* classified together because they meet certain standards of similarity.
Shelford (1963)	The largest distinct subdivision of a *biome*, identified by the presence of characteristic climax dominant or index species.
Knight (1965)	A transitional type of entity, partially abstract and partly concrete, based on ecological criteria.
Krebs (1972, 1985)	Major unit in *community* ecology, characterized by essential uniformity of species composition.
Colinvaux (1973, 1986)	Plant *community* unit; variously, often subjectively defined. A *community* type.
Ricklefs (1973)	A group of species occurring in the same place.
Brewer (1979, 1988)	A subdivision of the *formation*, with a characteristic combination of species.
Smith (1980, 1986)	A natural unit of vegetation characterized by a relatively uniform species composition and often dominated by a particular species.
	BIOME
Clements and Shelford (1939)	The plant–animal *formation*; the basic *community* unit.
Hanson (1962)	A major biotic *community* composed of all the plants and animals and *communities*, including the successional stages of an area; the *communities* possess certain similarities in physiognomy and in environmental conditions.
Shelford (1963)	The largest *community*; recognized by the character of the climax but includes seral stages. Plant *formations* with the animal constituents integrated.
Whittaker (1970)	A major kind of *community*, conceived in terms of physiognomy, on a given continent. *Formation* is used when the concern is with plant *communities* only.
Colinvaux (1973, 1986)	*Ecosystem* of a large geographic area in which plants are of one *formation* and for which climate sets the limits.

Table 2.1. (*cont.*)

Pianka (1978, 1988)	Major *communities* of characteristic plants and animals.
Brewer (1979, 1988)	A *community* of geographical extent characterized by a distinctive landscape based on the life forms of the climax dominants.
McNaughton and Wolf (1979)	A regional *ecosystem* type with similar *communities*.
Smith (1980, 1986)	Major regional ecological *community* of plants and animals; usually corresponds to plant ecologists' and European ecologists' classification of plant *formations* and classification of life zones.
Lederer (1984)	One or more large *ecosystems* that are similar in form and function.
Begon *et al.* (1986)	A biotic *community* of geographical extent characterized by a distinctive physiognomy based on the climax dominants.
Ehrlich and Roughgarden (1987)	A major ecological *community* type.

COMMUNITY

Cowles (1901)	A group of plants living together in a common habitat and subjected to similar site conditions (= habitat group).
Clements (1905, 1928)	A mixture of individuals of two or more species; a group of families.
Gleason (1939)	A piece of vegetation which maintains a reasonable degree of homogeneity over an appreciable area and a reasonable permanence over a considerable time.
Cain (1947)	A single, specific entity of aggregate character, with limited spatial boundaries and a rather completely describable composition and structure.
Curtis (1959)	A more or less homogeneous set of species which is found distributed more or less uniformly throughout the area of a province.
Hanson (1962)	A group of one or more populations of plants and animals in a common spatial arrangement; an ecological unit used in a broad sense to include groups of various sizes and degrees of integration.
Patten (1962)	Any aggregation of mixed taxa.
Odum (1963)	All of the populations of a given area.
Shelford (1963)	Aggregations of plants and animals of all sizes that have dynamic interrelations and dependencies.
Knight (1965)	Primarily concerned with the plant and animal life in an area.
Wilhm and Dorris (1968)	(. . . STRUCTURE) The complex of individuals belonging to the different species in the *ecosystem*.
Whittaker (1970)	An assemblage of populations of plants, animals, bacteria, and fungi that live in an environment and interact with one another, forming together a distinctive living system with its own composition, structure, environmental relations, development, and function.

Table 2.1. (*cont.*)

Krebs (1972, 1985)	Same as Hanson (1962), above.
Colinvaux (1973, 1986)	Aggregation of living plants having mutual relations among themselves and to the environment.
Collier *et al.* (1973)	The group of species populations occurring together and interacting with one another in a small region of space.
Ricklefs (1973)	An association of interacting populations usually delimited by their interactions or by spatial occurrence.
Pielou (1974)	Several or many species-populations occurring together and interacting with one another in a small region of space.
Pianka (1978, 1988)	The biotic components of an *ecosystem*, or all of the organisms living in it, taken together.
Brewer (1979, 1988)	A group of organisms occupying a particular area; the connotation is of a coacting system.
McNaughton and Wolf (1979)	A group of populations co-occurring in space and time.
Smith (1980, 1986)	A group of interacting plants and animals inhabiting a given area.
Strong (1983)	A group of species living closely enough together for the potential of local interaction.
Lederer (1984)	All the living organisms of an area.
Begon *et al.* (1986)	Assemblage of species populations which occur together in space and time.
Diamond and Case (1986a)	The populations of some or all species coexisting at a site or in a region.
Ehrlich and Roughgarden (1987)	All of the organisms that live in a given area (sometimes more restricted).
Williamson (1987)	The populations that are found in a defined region.

ECOSYSTEM

Tansley (1935)	The fundamental concept appropriate to the *biome* considered together with all the effective inorganic factors of its environment. In an ecosystem, the organisms and the inorganic factors alike are components which are in relatively stable dynamic equilibrium.
Hanson (1962)	The *community*, including all the component organisms together with the abiotic environment, forming an interacting system.
Odum (1963)	The *community* and the non-living environment functioning together.
Shelford (1963)	Habitat and *community* as an interacting unit.
Knight (1965)	Includes all of the living and non-living components of the environment, so that the entire world could be considered a giant ecosystem.
Wilhm and Dorris (1968)	Natural unit composed of abiotic and biotic elements interacting to produce an exchange of materials.
Whittaker (1970)	A *community* and its environment treated together as a functional system of complementary relationships, and transfer and circulation of energy and matter.

Table 2.1. (*cont.*)

Krebs (1972, 1985)	Biotic *community* and its abiotic environment; the whole earth can be considered as one large ecosystem.
Pianka (1978, 1988)	The climate, soils, bacteria, fungi, plants, and animals at any particular place together.
Brewer (1979, 1988)	The *community* plus its habitat; the connotation is of an interacting system.
McNaughton and Wolf (1979)	All the organisms and environments in a single location.
Smith (1980, 1986)	Same as Tansley (1935), above.
Lederer (1984)	All organisms, the surrounding environment, and their interactions in a stable situation.
Begon *et al.* (1986)	Comprises the biological *community* together with its physical environment.
Ehrlich and Roughgarden (1987)	The biological *community* in an area and the physical environment with which it interacts.

FORMATION

Clements (1905, 1928)	A group of plants which bears a definite physiognomic character.
Whittaker (1957)	A great regional unit of vegetation characterized by its dominant growth form.
Hanson (1962)	One of the largest subdivisions of the vegetation of the earth, usually of great geographical extent, composed of *communities* that are similar in physiognomy and broad environmental relations.
Knight (1965)	Synonymous with *biome*.
Whittaker (1970)	See definition for *biome*, above.
Brewer (1979, 1988)	One of the great subdivisions of the earth's vegetation having a distinctive physiognomy based on the life forms of the climax dominants.
Smith (1980, 1986)	Classification of vegetation based on dominant life form.

Table 2.2. *Definitions of the terms "balance of nature," "equilibrium," "homeostasis," and "stability" taken from representative twentieth-century ecological literature (see section 2.2.4 for discussion of these definitions)*

	BALANCE OF NATURE
Hanson (1962)	The state in an ecosystem when the interrelationships of organisms to one another and to their environment are harmonious or integrated to a considerable degree.
	EQUILIBRIUM
Lotka (1924)	(TRUE...) – All forces are balanced; a "stationary state." (QUASI...) – States maintained constant or approximately so with a continual expenditure of energy; a "steady state."
Oosting (1958)	(DYNAMIC...) – A continuing steady state, in which the ecosystem is at the peak of productivity.
Hanson (1962)	(COMMUNITY...) – The condition in which a community is maintained with only minor fluctuations in its composition within a certain time period. (DYNAMIC...) – A system that is maintained in approximately the same condition because of the action of opposing processes or activities proceeding at about equal rates.
Patten (1962)	(BIOCOENOSE...) – An aggregation of mutually exclusive species occupying mutually exclusive niches in a perfectly partitioned biotope.
Whittaker (1970)	(DYNAMIC...) – Constancy in a system, based on a balancing of income and outgo.
Colinvaux (1973)	(...SPECIES) – Populations are relatively *stable*.
Ricklefs (1973)	(...MODEL) – Any hypothetical or actual representation of a system in which two balancing forces act to maintain *stability* in the system.
Smith (1980, 1986)	(...SPECIES) – Species whose population exists in equilibrium with resources and at a *stable* density.
Connell and Sousa (1983)	(STABLE...) – Particular state of a characteristic at which a system will remain, or if moved away from it, to which the system will return.
Colinvaux (1986)	(...SPECIES) – Species adapted to persist; K-strategist.
Grant (1986)	A state of balance, not constancy; a fixed relationship between numbers or biomass of consumers and numbers or biomass of resources, not fixed numbers of consumers and resources.
Hubbell and Foster (1986)	(...COMMUNITY) – A community in which there is *stability* as well as persistence of a particular taxonomic assemblage of species in a defined area.
Williamson (1987)	Return of a system to an initial state after perturbation.

Table 2.2. (*cont.*)

	HOMEOSTASIS
Hanson (1962)	The maintenance of constancy or a high degree of uniformity in functions of an organism or interactions of individuals in a population or community under changing conditions, because of the capabilities of organisms to make adjustments.
Odum (1963)	See definition for *stability*, below.
Krebs (1972, 1985)	Same as Hanson (1962), above.
Collier *et al.* (1973)	Ability to reestablish a normal state following disturbance.
Ricklefs (1973)	Maintenance of constant internal conditions in the face of a varying external environment.
Brewer (1979, 1988)	Keeping certain important aspects of the organism's internal environment constant despite the changing external environment.
Smith (1980, 1986)	Maintenance of nearly constant conditions in function of an organism or in interaction among individuals in a population.
Colinvaux (1986)	Maintenance of constancy or near-uniformity in organism, community or other entity.

	STABILITY
Tansley (1935)	Property of the dynamic *equilibrium*, in which the system is relatively separate and autonomous, and highly integrated.
MacArthur (1955)	The effect of the abnormal abundance of one species on all the other species of the community is small.
Oosting (1958)	The complex of species is so adjusted to each other that they are capable of reproducing within the community and of excluding new species.
Hanson (1962)	The state in the interrelationships of organisms in which integration and adjustment between the organisms and between them and the prevailing environment is being attained; maximum stabilization occurs in climax communities, usually.
Odum (1963)	Operation of *homeostatic* mechanisms, which we may define as checks and balances (or forces and counterforces), to dampen oscillations.
Hall *et al.* (1970)	Related to the manner in which functional properties are partitioned between the species or species groups.
Whittaker (1970)	Interactions among species in their different niche roles, tending in various ways to limit and stabilize [= reduce fluctuations] one another's populations.
Jordan *et al.* (1972)	Return monotonically or with decreasing oscillations toward the steady state.
Krebs (1972, 1985)	Absence of fluctuations in populations; ability to withstand perturbations without large changes in composition.
Colinvaux (1973)	The number of individual living things are roughly constant from year to year without being given to sudden changes.

Table 2.2. (*cont.*)

Ricklefs (1973)	Inherent capacity of any system to resist change.
Pielou (1974)	The tendency of a community's composition to remain constant.
Brewer (1979, 1988)	(RESISTENCE) – Tendency to remain unchanged in the face of perturbations. (RESILIENCE) – Tendency to return to the former state.
Smith (1980, 1986)	Ability of a system to resist change or to recover rapidly after a disturbance.
Connell and Sousa (1983)	The existence of one or more equilibrium points or limit cycles at which the system remains when faced with a disturbing force or to which it returns if perturbed by the force.
Chesson and Case (1986)	(COMMUNITY . . .) – Exhibiting the properties of "conservation" [= little tendency to lose species], "recovery" [from events causing low density of any species], "assembly" [= built up by immigration], and "historical irrelevance" [= no effect of past abundances of species].
Colinvaux (1986)	The chance of extinction is low.
Williamson (1987)	A system is bounded.

3 · Ecological theory is problematic

APPLICATIONS OF COMMUNITY ECOLOGY are not uncertain merely because of the imprecision and vagueness of some of its central concepts. They are also uncertain because the fundamental theories that tie ecological concepts and principles together are ambiguous, value laden, and often untestable. In this chapter, we shall outline and illustrate some of the ways in which ecological theory fails to provide a firm basis for environmental problemsolving.

We have argued (Shrader-Frechette and McCoy 1990) that the imprecision of current ecological theories, such as diversity and succession, prevents ecologists from employing the powerful philosophical tool of theory reduction. That is, imprecision in ecological concepts and their interrelationships prevents our interpreting "higher level phenomena," such as diversity and succession, in terms of "lower level processes" or mechanisms, as some (e.g., Loehle 1988) have suggested they can. This imprecision likewise provides grounds for different interpretations of the same theory and for theoretical dissent. We have also argued that, in ecology and in science generally, theoretical units (theories + definitions + principles + auxiliary assumptions) can be evaluated only as units. As a result, ecologists are rarely able conclusively to reject a single thesis, such as one of Loehle's (1988) alleged "laws." This is because each law is tied definitionally to the theory in terms of which it is interpreted. The existence of such value-laden theoretical units not only helps to generate theoretical dissent in ecology but also forces ecologists to pursue the path of theoretical pluralism. Ecologists must compare whole theoretical units to each other and not merely search for the traditional "crucial experiment" (Shrader-Frechette and McCoy 1990). We have argued (Shrader-Frechette and McCoy 1990), likewise, that candidates advanced by some ecologists (e.g., Murray 1979, 1986; Loehle 1988) as ecological laws are, in fact, non-empirical and uninformative. Many of them are also untestable, but philosophers of science and ecologists disagree as to whether, and the extent to which, this lack of testability is a fundamental theoretical flaw. In our opinion, the best candidates for ecological laws are statistical laws. If our conclusions about theory reduction and ecological regularities are justified, then they illustrate well our contention that both the theoretical and empirical underpinnings of ecology are not strong.

To see how theoretical problems limit the applications of community ecology to environmental problemsolving, we consider one of the most important of all such theories, that of island biogeography. We discuss island biogeography because it has been one of the leading contenders for a general theory of community ecology, because no other general theories, at present, appear to be more conceptually developed, and because it has obvious applications to problems of conservation.

3.1 The theory of island biogeography

The theory of island biogeography was developed by MacArthur and Wilson (1963, 1967; but see Brown and Lomolino 1989) to explain how the number of species on an island could remain roughly constant over time while the taxonomic composition changed. MacArthur and Wilson (1967) suggested that organisms on islands were in a "dynamic equilibrium" such that while some populations were colonizing the island, others were going extinct. Under their scheme, colonization occurred at a rate dependent largely on distance from the island to a "source pool" of potential colonists, usually the mainland. In other words, an island nearer the source pool would exhibit a higher rate of colonization than an island farther away, all else being equal. Extinction occurred at a rate largely dependent on the size of the island. That is, a smaller island would exhibit a higher rate of extinction than a larger one, all else being equal. Why did they believe that the rate of extinction would be higher on the smaller island? They maintained that the smaller island would, in general, support smaller population sizes of resident organisms than the larger island and that, as a result, more organisms would be expected, simply as the result of demographic stochasticity, to go extinct per unit time on the smaller island. MacArthur and Wilson (1967) also showed that rate of colonization and rate of extinction, considered simultaneously, would yield both a predictable "equilibrium number of species" that is maintained over time and a predictable "turnover rate" of species that also is maintained over time.

Since its original exposition, the theory of island biogeography has undergone some modifications of its basic premises. Whitehead and

Jones (1969) proposed that the rate of colonization depends on an island's size, as well as on its distance from a source pool of potential colonists, because larger islands present larger "targets" for colonists than do smaller islands. Similarly, Brown and Kodric-Brown (1977) proposed the so-called "rescue effect," in which distance from an island to a source pool of potential colonists affects the rate of extinction as well as the rate of colonization. They hypothesized that the "rescue effect" occurs because immigration of individuals of taxa already resident on the island slows the rate of extinction of those taxa by keeping population sizes higher than they would be in the absence of immigration.

What must be done to test the theory of island biogeography? A brief discussion of the theory that we have just presented makes it clear that four separate determinations are necessary to infer that it has validity: (1) a constant number of taxa, (2) a change in taxonomic composition, (3) a colonization rate related to distance from the island to the source pool of potential colonists, and (4) an extinction rate related to the size of the island (see Gilbert 1980). These are not easy determinations to make, and they require detailed and long-term study of the island in question. It should not be surprising, then, that very few of these sorts of studies have been done. Instead, the theory of island biogeography often has been "validated" by short-cut methods, such as by use of species–area relationships. We shall outline two rigorous tests of the theory of island biogeography and present the conclusions that they support. We shall then review some of the short-cut methods and detail some criticisms that have been leveled against them. Finally, we shall comment on the scientific and epistemological status of the theory and on its consequences for conservation decisionmaking.

The first test of island biogeographic theory was that of Simberloff and Wilson (1969, 1970; Wilson and Simberloff 1969; Simberloff 1976a). They employed small (11–25 m in diameter) red mangrove (*Rhizophora mangle*) islands in the Florida Keys for their experiment. They censused these islands exhaustively for terrestrial arthropods and then fumigated some of them (experimental islands) with methyl bromide to kill the arthropods. Periodically thereafter, they censused all islands, experimental and control, for several years. By 250 days after defaunation, colonization had restored the species number to near its original value on all islands except the most distant one. They observed extinction, as well as colonization, but the rate at which either process occurred was impossible to estimate from the data, because the periodic nature of sampling meant that a large proportion (Simberloff and Wilson (1969) estimate perhaps two-thirds) of colonizations and extinctions went undetected. The data did indicate, however, that colonization rates were higher on nearer (to a source of potential colonists) islands during the first 150 days after defaunation. The data also showed that the nearest island (2 m from a source of potential colonists) supported more than twice as many species as the comparably sized farthest island (533 m).

Another test of the theory of island biogeography was carried out by Rey (1981, 1985). He employed census and defaunation techniques, similar to those described for the red mangrove islands, on cordgrass (*Spartina alterniflora*) islands in north Florida. Colonization restored species numbers to predefaunation levels in about 140 days. Neither rate of colonization nor rate of extinction could be shown to be related to distances of islands from a source pool of potential colonists. Both rates were related, however, to the sizes of islands (islands ranged in size from 56 m² to 1023 m²); rate of colonization was related positively and rate of extinction was related inversely. Data collected after predefaunation species numbers had been restored indicated that a change in taxonomic composition (turnover) did occur, at a rate of about 0.14 species per island per week.

What can be said about the results of these Florida tests of the theory of island biogeography? The researchers who carried out the tests were cautious in their comments about their results, because they were not as straightforward as one might have hoped. Some predictions of the theory, such as a constant number of taxa and a change in taxonomic composition (turnover), were validated. But the rate of turnover was unexpectedly low, and sometimes rates of extinction and colonization, respectively, could not be related convincingly to size of an island and distance from the island to a source pool of potential colonists. Simberloff (1976a, pp. 577–578) noted that the inferences about movements of individuals among islands permitted by his use of empty islands were not possible in most other examples given as evidence for the validity of the theory. He concluded that "until . . . observations [of dispersal rates] have been made on a number of systems, the . . . theory of island biogeography must be considered a hypothesis, and one which is difficult to test." As Simberloff (1976a) warned, measuring dispersal rates has proved exceedingly difficult, and the difficulty largely has been responsible for the use of short-cut methods for "validating" the theory of island biogeography.

There are at least three such short-cut methods. One relies on employing artificial substrates to represent various "islands" (e.g.,

Maguire 1963, 1971; Schoener 1974a, b). For example, tiles of various sizes might be placed in the marine intertidal zone to be colonized by barnacles and other fouling organisms. These "tests" typically confirm two of the predictions of the theory of island biogeography: that a constant ("equilibrium") number of taxa will become established on the tiles/islands and that change in taxonomic composition (turnover) will occur over time. Often the short-cut tests can show that the number of taxa on a particular "island" of substrate is related positively to the size of the "island," as would be expected if the rate of extinction were a function of the size of the "island." However, rate of extinction and rate of colonization usually cannot be observed directly, mostly because of the length of time between observations, but also because the exact source of colonists cannot be determined, particularly in aquatic studies. Furthermore, the use of artificial substrates calls into question the significance of the results of such short-cut "tests" for real situations.

The second major short-cut method is to compare lists of taxa resident on an island at different times (e.g., Diamond 1971; Abbott and Grant 1976). An inference about rate of change of taxonomic composition (turnover) can be drawn from such a comparison, as well as a determination of whether or not a constant ("equilibrium") number of taxa can be found on the island. In addition, if lists are available for several islands, and if those islands differ in size and/or distance to a source pool of potential colonists, then further inferences can be drawn about the relationship between size and distance and rates of extinction and colonization. For most of the "tests" of this sort, however, lists are available for only two times, and the interval between compilation of lists is long, typically decades. Moreover, lists from different times may be compiled by different persons employing different methods and devoting different amounts of effort to the project. For these and other reasons (see Lynch and Johnson 1974; Simberloff 1976b), the results derived from comparisons of lists must be viewed with extreme caution.

The final short-cut method for "validating" the theory of island biogeography is to employ species–area relationships. To show how species–area relationships have been used in this fashion, we present a hypothetical example. Assume that the theory is relevant to the taxa found, for example, on a particular archipelago of islands of various sizes, and assume that the islands all contain similar habitats for the taxa and are at the same distance from a source pool of potential colonists. If all three assumptions are granted, and if rates of colonization are identical for all islands, while rates of extinction are related inversely to the sizes of the islands, then the short-cut method dictates that the ("equilibrium") number of taxa found on each island should be related positively to its size. Because the species–area relationship appears to follow directly from predictions of the theory of island biogeography, some researchers have inferred that the observed species–area relationship indicates the operation of island-biogeographic processes. Such an inference is not justified, however (see Simberloff 1974; Connor and McCoy 1979; McGuinness 1984), because a species–area relationship can result from other processes, such as an increase in numbers of habitats with area, or even from random sampling of the pool of available species.

The practical difficulties in testing the theory of island biogeography in a rigorous way and the inadequacies of the short-cut methods have left the theory in much the same position as Simberloff observed in 1976: a largely unconfirmed hypothesis (see also Gilbert 1980). For this reason, researchers in a wide variety of ecological fields have questioned the importance of the theory (e.g., Raab 1980 (paleoecology); Rey and McCoy 1979, Simberloff 1986c (agricultural pest control); Strong 1979 (insect–plant interactions)). Ecologists have debated vigorously the significance of the theory for conservation, and we shall review this debate in the next section.

3.2 Applying the theory of island biogeography to conservation

Because of the largely hypothetical status of the theory of island biogeography, owing largely to difficulties involved with testing it, our analysis has shown that the theory enjoys a *descriptive consensus*, but not a *normative justification* among ecologists. In other words, like the community and stability concepts, island-biogeographical theory, despite its potential heuristic value, provides little evidence to support ecologists' advice regarding environmental policy. As a consequence, the uncertainties surrounding this ecological theory, like those surrounding ecological concepts, often render environmental/conservation conclusions correspondingly uncertain. To understand why an uncertain ecological theory leads to uncertain environmental policy, we must examine in more detail the specific relationship between ecology and policy. Let us investigate what happens when we try to apply purely hypothetical theories, like island biogeography, to actual environmental controversies.

Shortly after the appearance of the theory of island biogeography, ecologists recognized its potential application to conservation (e.g., Terborgh 1974; Diamond 1975; May 1975a; Wilson and Willis 1975; see Willis 1984). Using the theory as a basis, Diamond (1975) proposed that nature reserves, which may be thought of as "islands," possessed predictable extinction rates. He also hypothesized that those extinction rates could be lowered by designing reserves according to certain island-biogeographic principles. Specifically, he suggested that to lower extinction rates: (1) larger reserves are preferable to smaller ones; (2) single reserves are preferable to subdivided ones of equal cumulative size; (3) nearby reserves are preferable to more widely separated ones; (4) reserves grouped in clumps are preferable to ones arranged linearly; (5) circular reserves are preferable to elongate ones; and (6) reserves connected by "corridors" are preferable to unconnected ones.

These six suggestions were quickly criticized. One of the first criticisms was by Simberloff and Abele (1976), who maintained that the theory did not directly justify designing a reserve to encompass the largest possible single area. Nor, they said, was such a design even an appropriate action, given a number of realistic ecological conditions. Other ecologists quickly and vociferously challenged the critics' iconoclastic position (e.g., Diamond 1976; Terborgh 1976; Whitcomb *et al.* 1976). Not much was resolved in these early debates, but they initiated a continuing controversy over the role of island-biogeographic principles in designing nature reserves.

Three of Diamond's (1975; see also Wilson and Willis 1975; Diamond and May 1976) suggestions – about how extinction rates in nature reserves may be lowered – have been more hotly contested than the others (see Simberloff 1986b). The most controversial suggestion has proved to be the one questioned early on by Simberloff and Abele (1976). This is that island-biogeographic theory dictates that single large reserves are preferable to groups of small ones of equal total area. The debate generated by this suggestion has been termed the "SLOSS (single-large-or-several-small) debate." Another highly controversial suggestion is that circular reserves are preferable to elongated ones. Because no popular parallel acronym to SLOSS has been created for the controversy over shape, we should like to term it the "CONC (circular-or-not-circular) debate" (but see Usher 1991, who terms it the "SION (shape-important-or-not?) debate"). The final highly controversial suggestion is that reserves connected by corridors are preferable to unconnected ones. Because ecologists have ably and frequently monitored all three debates, we shall revisit only the SLOSS controversy here. For detailed discussion of the CONC debate, we refer interested persons to the writings of Game (1980); Blouin and Connor (1985); Simberloff (1986b); and Usher (1991). We shall address the corridors debate later.

The SLOSS debate has arisen as a supposed consequence of island-biogeographic principles, and it has occupied many journal pages. We start our discussion of the controversy with a précis of the arguments presented by Simberloff and Abele (1976). This summary demonstrates that the theory of island biogeography does not unequivocally predict that single large reserves are preferable to groups of small ones having equal total area.

Simberloff and Abele (1976) consider the common form of the species–area relationship (see Connor and McCoy 1979), $S = kA^z$ (where S is the number of species on an "island," A is the area of the "island," and k and z are constants). This relationship is an essential premise of the arguments presented in favor of single large reserves because, according to the theory of island biogeography, extinction rates (and therefore numbers of species) are determined entirely by area either when colonization is absent or when colonization is equal among "islands." Simberloff and Abele (1976) contrast a single reserve of size A_1 with a reserve subdivided into two components, each of size $A_2 = A_1/2$. Letting z take on a value for log-normal distributed population sizes (the exact value of z is unimportant to the outcome), they find $S_1 = kA_1^{0.263} = k(2A)^{0.263} = 1.200S_2$. This value is less than the expected number in the subdivided reserve ($2S_2 - S_2^2/P$, where P is the number of species in the pool) for $S_1/P < 0.96$. Simberloff and Abele (1976) also show, by similar calculations, that the more a reserve is subdivided, the more likely it is that it will contain more species than a single large reserve of equal total area. This finding counters the assertion of Diamond (1975) that the theory of island biogeography dictates a preference for single reserves to subdivided ones of equal cumulative area.

Subsequent empirical analyses also seem to counter Diamond's (1975) assertion. These studies consist, typically, of grouping small sites together, counting the cumulative number of species at these sites, and then comparing the cumulative number with the number observed at a single site of area equal to the cumulative area of the small sites. For a wide range of organisms, the analyses show either that there is no consistent difference in species richness between a single large site and several small sites combined, or that several small sites have a greater combined species richness (Simberloff and Abele 1982; Simberloff and Gotelli 1984; Simberloff 1986b). Moreover, little evidence has been mustered in support of the premise underlying a preference for single large reserves, namely that subdivision automatically increases rates of extinction for the components (Gilbert 1980; Margules *et al.* 1982; Reed 1983; Boecklen and Gotelli 1984). Admittedly, however, a given habitat could be subdivided into such small reserves that rates of extinction for them would be unacceptably high. Although Simberloff and Abele (1976) made the point explicitly, we suggest that the failure – to distinguish this sort of pathologically small subdivision from subdivision in general – still underlies the SLOSS debate (see, for example, Jarvinen 1984, Simberloff and Abele 1984 vs. Willis 1984; Lahti 1986 vs. Murphy and Wilcox 1986). The debate may also be continuing because of the beneficial consequences (for conservation) following from belief in the desirability of large reserves.

To know when a habitat has been subdivided so finely that rates of extinction for the components have risen to unacceptable levels, one must possess a great deal of knowledge about the organisms with which one is concerned. It may turn out for some organisms, such as large vertebrates, that subdivision into massive components will cause rates of extinction to surpass acceptable levels (e.g., Newmark 1987, but see Glenn and Nudds 1989), while for other organisms, subdivision of the habitat into the same-sized, or finer, components will not cause rates of extinction to rise (but see Quinn *et al.* 1989). Strangely, however, determining exactly how levels of subdivision affect suites of organisms has received little theoretical (see McCoy 1983) or practical (see Simberloff 1986b) attention. Ecologists may have ignored the effects of subdivision because the information needed to deal with the problem is very difficult to obtain. The difficulty in obtaining needed information, in turn, has caused some ecologists to suggest that, by the time they can secure this information, most options for designing reserves will have disappeared (e.g., Soulé 1980; East and Williams 1984). While the difficulty of obtaining information is a point well taken, an unfortunate consequence of anxiety over the imminence of the extinction threat is to retreat to the comfortable fortress of theory, even though island biogeographic theory lacks credibility (e.g., East and Williams 1984; Harris 1984; Kent 1987).

One problem with this retreat to theory is that it permits complacency about our abilities to develop conservation strategies. If ecologists are not careful, they can allow themselves to believe that any theory (even a poor one) is better than no theory – that because certain strategies have theoretical underpinnings, they must be better than alternative strategies which lack theoretical underpinnings. Yet, strategies based upon the theory of island biogeography, to the exclusion of other kinds of ecological information, may prove ill-founded (see, for example, Pickett and Thompson 1978; Zimmerman and Bierregaard 1986). This retreat to theory is also questionable because it focuses primary conservation efforts on diversity. That is, because the theory of island biogeography deals exclusively with numbers of species, so too do the suggestions about design of reserves that are thought to follow from the theory. Design and choice of reserves, however, is a much more complicated process than the emphasis on diversity would seem to indicate. It actually involves many other important considerations, such as rarity of the species and typicalness of the habitat (see Usher 1986b).

Because of problems such as the retreat to theory and the overemphasis on diversity, the SLOSS debate is, at best, a difference of opinion among ecologists that seems to have no resolution. At worst, it is irrelevant to discussions about the optimal size of nature reserves (see Soulé and Simberloff 1986). In either case, the theory of island biogeography has not provided a sound foundation for answering the important questions about reserve design that are bound up in the SLOSS debate. The theory also appears to have failed to resolve debates over other aspects of reserve design that we did not choose to discuss, like the CONC debate (see Simberloff 1986b). For all these reasons, if we take theories like island biogeography as paradigmatic, then general ecological theories provide conservationists with limited help in formulating conservation policies and in adjudicating environmental controversies. Ecological theories provide little predictive power in real-world applications.

3.3 Ecological theory and its epistemological status

Despite the repeated claims of ecologists that island biogeography is of considerable importance for an enlightened approach to nature conservation (see, for example, Begon et al. 1986, pp. 735, 761), our discussion of the SLOSS debate and of island biogeography reveals that, even though the theory gives us some rough rules of thumb, it is unable to answer the questions that conservationists most want answered. Island biogeography is able to give us insights, such as that larger islands (or nature reserves) closer to the mainland (or to sources of colonists) typically have greater numbers of species. However, the theory is able neither to tell us much about the size and shape of nature reserves in particular areas, for example, nor about all the factors that are able to predict greater or lesser species numbers. For these more specific questions, we need detailed knowledge of individual species' ecologies. As Peters (1991, p.189) puts it, island biogeography is relevant to reserve design only when "all else is equal," when preservation is concerned with species numbers and not with particular species, and when all areas are homogeneous. Because all things are never equal, however, and because species and regions differ in ways that are essential to reserve design, most of the theory of island biogeography is not relevant to environmental practice.

Although the theory of island biogeography does not appear to be able to give conservationists the predictions they need to accomplish their goals, there are several reasons for believing that the theory may have some heuristic value for future ecological theorizing. Perhaps the main source of its heuristic value is that island biogeography, like other top-down theories (see Kitcher 1989, pp. 430ff.), attempts to provide a systematic, unified framework for explaining some fundamental mechanisms of ecology. On the top-down view, explanation is tied more to theoretical unification than to testability or predictive power. Given its unifying value, island biogeography has considerable heuristic power in directing us, for example, to obtain data on immigration and extinction; to determine if, when, and where species number is constant through time; to investigate whether species number declines with increasing remoteness of an island; to assess whether habitat diversity – as opposed to area *per se* – determines numbers of species; and so on. In particular, as Gilbert (1980) points out, island biogeography has considerable heuristic power in that it has stimulated a great deal of valuable research, such as Janzen's (1968, 1973) on the colonization of plants by phytophagous insects.

Admittedly, there are serious problems with some variants of island biogeography – such as Lack's (1969, 1976) habitat diversity theory and MacArthur and Wilson's (1967) equilibrium theory. Neither takes account of the fact that a community on an island may reflect evolution that may have occurred on the island itself. Indeed, on some oceanic islands, evolution of species may be faster than immigration (Williamson 1981). Also, as was already admitted, the theory is oversimplified and fails to take adequate account of the internal (island), genetic, or geographical diversity that may characterize communities. Regardless of these specific theoretical deficiencies, even if island biogeography is false, it might help us to find better ecological theories.

Just as we argued in the last chapter that there are epistemological roles for uncertain concepts, despite their disutility for predictive environmental applications, so also there are epistemological roles for simplified theories like that of island biogeography. Following Wimsatt's (1987; see also 1980) analysis of how and why some false models can help us to find better ones, island biogeography offers some avenues for future ecological progress. Useful types of falsity, for Wimsatt, are cases in which the model or theory may be only locally applicable; an idealization never realized in nature; incomplete in leaving out causally relevant variables; and misdescriptive of the interactions of some variables. Let us assume, as in the previous chapter, both that Wimsatt's categorization of "useful" and "rarely useful" models is approximately correct and that it yields insights for determining the epistemological status of the theory of island biogeography. If we grant these two assumptions, then the theory, even as an idealization never realized in nature or even as incomplete in leaving out causally relevant variables, may be heuristically useful, just as was suggested in the next to last paragraph. Hence, island biogeography has significant epistemological status, largely by virtue of the investigations it has prompted.

Apart from whether island biogeography is good or bad science – and we think that it is a help toward the former – it is clearly an inadequate foundation for applying ecology to environmental problems. As Underwood (1990, p. 386) correctly noted, "any statement about management of habitats or pollutants, or any prediction about harvesting or conservation of populations can easily be seen to be a predictive hypothesis." Environmental management requires statements about probable consequences of our actions. Hence, island biogeography fails us, as a conservation aid, because it cannot guarantee the accuracy of such consequences and because it is not predictive. Later we shall suggest some ways in which ecology may better serve us.

4 · Ecological science is value laden

COMMUNITY ECOLOGY currently has neither unambiguous definitions of basic concepts (see chapter 2), nor a precise, testable general
theory capable of providing specific predictions in environmental
applications (see chapter 3). Indeed, there may never be a confirmed
general theory of ecology, despite the heuristic power of a number of
candidate theories. As one ecologist put it, "the search for general
theories languishes" (Murray 1986, p. 146). This search is in trouble, in
part for the reason that Schoener (1972) recognized two decades ago;
ecology has a "constipating accumulation of untested models," most of
which are untestable. Models have other virtues besides testability, of
course, but the fact that so few models in ecology are testable suggests
that Woodwell (1978) may have been right when he spoke of ecology's
being in a state of "paradigms lost."

4.1 Will hypothesis deduction solve most problems of ecology?

Cognizant of the conceptual and theoretical difficulties besetting their
discipline, a number of ecologists have claimed that it is beginning to
get on track. They have argued that community ecology is becoming
more of a predictive science (Kolata 1974; see McIntosh in Saarinen
1982), and that it is developing and ought to develop along hypothetico-deductive (H-D) lines (Fretwell 1975; see Haines-Young and Petch
1980; Romesburg 1981). Cody and Diamond (1975; see McIntosh 1982,
p. 27) have boldly proclaimed that, largely because of the work of
MacArthur, ecology is becoming more predictive and quantitative and
hence is progressing along H-D lines. Some ecologists (for example,
Murray 1986, pp. 145–158) have even claimed to have constructed H-D
theories for competitive interactions in communities. If such optimists
about H-D in ecology are correct, then is the discipline "home free"? Is
it beginning to become predictively successful and therefore able to
provide a precise foundation for environmental policy? Will use of H-D

resolve the major problems associated with applying ecological theory to environmental policy? In this chapter, we shall argue that the answer to all these questions is "no." Using H-D in ecology is not alone sufficient to resolve the methodological problems in the science, in part because (1) the lawlike status of ecological hypotheses is often questionable; (2) it is difficult to construct uncontroversial null models to test hypotheses; and (3) cognitive or methodological value judgments in ecology often determine the relationship between evidence and theory.

In order for ecology to produce H-D theories, we need a clear account of ecological laws. Yet, one of the problems with alleged ecological "laws" is that, as McIntosh (1982; see Goudge 1961; Smart 1963) has noted, they are frequently not generalizable and are indistinguishable from mere principles. Moreover, ecologists do not agree on what the basic principles or laws are (McIntosh 1982). Often the "laws" are trivial, tautological, or not testable (Shrader-Frechette and McCoy 1990). Obviously an alleged test of an hypothesis that is tautological or definitionally true will not contribute to an H-D account of the predictive power or the general theory of ecology. Hence, H-D testing is limited by the nature of the hypotheses and regularities in ecology. Indeed, Van Valen and Pitelka (1974) stated flatly that "ecology has no known regularities." Even if there are regularities in ecology (and we think there are), however, it is doubtful that the science will progress along classical H-D lines. There are still fundamental difficulties – arising largely because of unavoidable methodological value judgments (evaluative assumptions) – that block an uncontroversial move to general theory, both in ecology and in other sciences. To understand these problems, recall the discussion (in the previous chapter) of island biogeography. Although there are many general theories, it is perhaps the leading contender for the title of "general theory" in community ecology, and at least four separate determinations are necessary to test it. Because of the difficulty of testing island biogeography, ecologists have used several short-cut methods to do so, as we explained in the previous chapter. Because each of the short-cut methods relies on controversial evaluative assumptions – for example, that artificial substrates are analogous to islands; that lists of various taxa are comparable; that species–area relationships indicate island-biogeographic processes – there is disagreement in ecology about the extent to which each of the short-cut methods really provides a valuable "test" of island biogeography. Some ecologists make the methodological value judgment (i.e., the evaluative assumption) that the short-cut methods provide an important test of the theory (Diamond 1971; Abbott and

Grant 1976), whereas others claim that the alleged tests yield no increased confirmation (Lynch and Johnson 1974; Simberloff 1976b). In other words, given ambiguous ways of interpreting the test data, ecologists have been forced to make methodological value judgments about whether the data confirm the theory. The result is that different groups of scientists cannot agree on which null models would even constitute a legitimate test of their hypotheses. Their methodological value judgments about the null model are themselves controversial (see, for example, Connor and Simberloff 1984; Gilpin and Diamond 1984; May 1984). Hence, although null hypotheses are, *in theory*, a way to "get around" the lack of sameness in ecological phenomena, as Strong (1982a, p. 255) points out, *in practice*, controversial methodological value judgments (evaluative assumptions) undercut the significance of null models. Indeed, in the case of competition theory, the random colonization and competition hypotheses may not be formulable in ways that exclude each other (see Sloep 1990).

Although the status of alleged "confirmations" in ecology is especially problematic, in part because of inadequate understanding of basic ecological processes, no science can avoid completely the difficulty of methodological value judgments associated with interpretations of confirmation. As Longino (1990) has argued, any alleged confirmation, in any science, in any H-D account, is rendered somewhat questionable because of the methodological value judgments necessary for interpreting the data. (Admittedly, however, the degree to which these value judgments are controversial may be a function of how developed the theory and its empirical bases are. There may be more scientific justification for, and more consensus about, specific methodological value judgments in more developed sciences.) But if such value judgments are unavoidable, even in the most sophisticated of sciences, then H-D may not be the unambiguous savior of ecology that many theoreticians suppose it to be. To see how value judgments in ecology may limit the utility of various methodological approaches, including hypothesis deduction, we consider the role of values, both in science generally and in ecology specifically.

4.2 All scientific facts are laden with values

On Longino's classification, values can be divided into three basic types: bias values, contextual values, and constitutive or methodological values – a classification (she admits) that is neither mutually exclusive nor exhaustive (Longino 1982, 1990). Bias values occur in science whenever researchers deliberately misinterpret or omit data, so as to serve their own purposes. These types of values obviously can be avoided in science, although many famous scientists have fallen victim to them. Robert Millikan, for example, who won the 1923 Nobel Prize, in part for his studies of electronic charge, likely employed bias values in some of his work. In 1913 he published a major paper on the electronic charge, a paper based on experiments on liquid droplets. In the paper, he claimed that "this is not a selected group of drops but represents all of the drops experimented upon during 60 consecutive days." More than half a century later, however, investigators studying his laboratory notebooks discovered that the 58 observations presented in his 1913 article were selected from a total of 140. Even if Millikan was correct in making the judgment to exclude some of the data, he was certainly incorrect in asserting that he had not done so. Hence, his claim seems to reveal a bias value in his work (Jackson 1986, pp. 12–13). Less dramatic cases of bias values occur throughout the practice of science; Hull, for example, presents a compelling account of bias values that apparently influenced refereeing of papers by cladists, as opposed to non-cladists, for the journal *Systematic Zoology* (Hull 1988, pp. 322–353).

Contextual values are even more difficult to avoid in research than are bias values. Scientists subscribe to particular contextual values whenever they include personal, social, cultural, ethical, or philosophical emphases in their judgments. For instance, they may make evaluative judgments that presuppose metaphysical assumptions. Likewise, scientists employ contextual (philosophical) values if they assume that ecological data can or cannot be interpreted in the light of Aristotelian teleological notions – such as an ecological "strategy" that implicitly posits some goal, like the global feedback mechanism of the Gaia hypothesis. Although in principle it might be possible to avoid contextual values, in practice it would be almost impossible to do so in science, because even science is done in some context. It is influenced by cultural, metaphysical, ethical, and financial considerations. For example, as Longino points out, industrial microbiology, as practiced by small firms of biochemists, has been heavily influenced by cultural and financial (contextual) values, such as the profit motive (Longino 1982, pp. 6–7, 1990). Money, in fact, appears to be a crucial contextual value influencing scientific research. For example, when the Scientific Research Society, Sigma Xi, asked respondents in 1987 to choose the most important issue facing the scientific community, the top vote-getter was "interruption of funding." This suggests that the need for funding might drive some of what is done in the name of science (Erman and Pister 1989, p. 5). One reason why contextual values, like obtaining funding, have played such a large role in many areas of scientific activity is that any research is hampered by some type of incomplete information. Scientists use contextual values to fill the gaps in their knowledge and to help determine scientific procedures and assumptions.

Constitutive or methodological values are even more difficult to avoid in science than are contextual and bias values. Indeed, it is impossible to avoid them, because scientists make methodological value judgments whenever they follow one methodological rule, rather than another. For example, whenever one uses a particular research design, because of available computer software, one is making a methodological value judgment that the research design is adequate. The methodological value judgment may be particularly problematic when the software is not produced by researchers for their own use but is instead supplied to them. By virtue of their value judgment, the researchers may rely on computer results without understanding all the associated hypotheses and assumptions built into the software design (see Jackson 1986, pp. 12–13). Even collecting data requires use of methodological value judgments because one must make evaluative assumptions about what data to collect and what to ignore, how to interpret the data, and how to avoid erroneous interpretations. For example, one must always simplify any scientific problem, in order to make it tractable. Ecologists using the short-cut methods of confirming island biogeography, for example, simplify their task so as to make it tractable. Which simplifications are legitimate, however, is in part a matter of methodological value judgments. Indeed, we make a methodological value judgment if we assert that the simplifications are so inappropriate as to represent bias values rather than methodological values. In his 1830 book, *Reflections on the Decline of Science in England*, Charles Babbage described two such types of methodological value judgments. He called them "trimming" and "cooking." In trimming, the scientist smooths irregularities to make the data look accurate and precise. In cooking, the scientist retains only those results that fit the theory and discards other results (see Jackson 1986, p. 11). Admittedly, of course, "trimming" and "cooking" could easily slip into bias value judgments.

In one recent controversy in ecology over species extinction, deforestation, and reserve design, at least part of the disagreement was over contextual and methodological value judgments. One ecologist, Kangas (1987, p. 160), argued that his conclusion (that tropical deforestation would cause only minimal species losses) provided evidence for using the conservation dollar in the most effective ways. More interested in the contextual value of conservation, rather than that of economic efficiency, another ecologist, Noss (1986, p. 279), supported quite different contextual values and claimed that Kangas' conclusions erred because they encouraged "the deforestation of the tropics." Kangas also made a number of controversial methodological value judgments, such as that one needed only to use species presence/absence data in order to draw conclusions about rates of extinction in the tropics (Kangas 1987, p. 159). Denying the plausibility of this methodological value judgment, Noss said that Kangas ought to have included data on minimum sustainable/viable populations (Noss 1986, p. 278).

As the Kangas–Noss controversy shows, methodological value judgments, as well as facts, are important in science. Not only may the validity of a particular conclusion turn on such judgments, but also they often are not recognized by scientists. Methodological value judgments are unavoidable even in "pure" science, because they bridge the gap between hypotheses and evidence. Perception does not provide us with pure facts. Knowledge, beliefs, values, and theories we already hold play a key part in determining what and how we perceive, and some beliefs and values are more reliable determiners of perception than others. Different background assumptions and evaluative assumptions (methodological value judgments) enable us to assess the evidence differently. But how do we assess our methodological value judgments? How do we know which are more reliable? In part, we assess them on the basis of our training. High-energy physicists, for example, do not count all the marks on cloud-chamber photographs as observations of pions, but only those streaks that their training and theories indicate are pions. Likewise, community ecologists do not count all instances of co-occurring or non-co-occurring species as cases of competition, but only those cases that their training and theories indicate are likely to be examples of competition. Even in the allegedly clear case of observational "facts" contradicting a particular interpretation of theory, researchers need not reject the theory (laden with interpretational values); they could instead reject the interpretational value judgments. Or they could reject the "facts" and hold on to the theory, thus implicitly affirming that the facts (as well as the theory) are value laden. In general, we assess our methodological value judgments in some of the same ways that we assess our theories: on the basis of their heuristic power, explanatory fertility, simplicity, and so on.

Earlier in this century, when beta decay was observed, it was not taken as a counterinstance to the theory of conservation of energy and momentum. Rather, the value-laden conservation theory was accepted, and beta decay was treated, not as a hard-and-fast "fact," but as a "problem" that scientists needed to solve on the basis of methodological value judgments. All this suggests that methodological values structure not only theories but also scientific experiments and determine the meaning of observations (see Brown 1977, pp. 97–100, 147; Shrader-Frechette 1980, pp. 302ff.). The rise and fall of the "broken-stick" model of species abundance provides a salient ecological example (see MacArthur 1957, 1966; Hairston 1969; May 1975b; Pielou 1981). Likewise, when one looks at controversies in ecology, it is especially clear that different methodological values structure scientific experiments and determine the meaning of observational data. We shall consider, for example, the controversies surrounding choosing the size and shape of a reserve design; deciding between preservation and development; between hunters' and animal-rights goals; and between chemical and biological pest control. We shall illustrate that all of the cases involve evaluative, methodological conflicts over ecological evidence for appropriate environmental policy. Because they do involve such conflicts, we shall argue that ecology, alone, is not sufficient to ground environmental policy and that we need epistemological and ethical analyses as well.

4.2.1 Ecology and value conflicts over wildlife-reserve design

One important case – that illustrates the role of methodological values – concerns how to design wildlife reserves, given ecological information about the relationship between reserve size and species losses. Brazil, for example, seeking to curb tropical deforestation, requires that when any area of virgin forest is cleared, 50 percent of the initial stand must be left in forest. This law, however, does not solve the problem of how many, and what size, forest reserves to create. To address this question, the World Wildlife Fund and Brazil's National Institute for Amazon Research have recently begun long-term (more than 20 years) research called the "Minimum Critical Size of Ecosystems Project" (Lovejoy et al. 1986, pp. 257-285; see also Janzen 1973; Lamb 1977; Mares 1986; see Alyanak 1989; Sawyer 1989). The Amazon forest research is interesting both because it is based on certain methodological value judgments concerning the nature of ecological stability, and because the results of the research are almost certain to be used in setting policy about the optimal design for reserves. Consider first the methodological value judgments. The research is premised, at least in part, on one of the most discussed theories of modern ecology, the MacArthur–Wilson theory of island biogeography (MacArthur and Wilson 1967; see chapter 3 of this volume), which attempts to explain the numbers of species found on islands.

One of the methodological value judgments that is most crucial and essential in order for the theory of island biogeography to "work" is that the number of species on an island tends toward equilibrium, toward a sort of balance of nature. According to the theory, the equilibrium results from a dynamic balance between species coming onto the island and those leaving the island. The rates of immigration and emigration for these species are functions of the island's area and position and, at equilibrium, there are equal numbers of species coming and going. The central equilibrium or balance notion imbedded in the theory of island biogeography, however, is empirically underdetermined – not uncontroversially confirmed – and "fuzzy" in its meaning, as Ruse points out (1984, p. 10). A number of ecologists have claimed that the notion of balance or equilibrium has little supporting evidence, relies upon imprecise notions of immigrant and emigrant species, and is only tenuously connected with reality (see, for example, Gilbert 1980, pp. 209–235). MacArthur and Wilson, however, defend the notion on the grounds that it allows them to go beyond a purely descriptive account of species behaviour (MacArthur and Wilson 1967, pp. 20–21). In defending equilibrium, its proponents appear to make a number of judgments about *methodological* values; for example, one ought to posit equilibrium, because doing so makes biogeographic computations possible, and such computations are important to the practice of ecology. When proponents of biogeography apply their results to conservation problems, they likewise make unavoidable *contextual* value judgments, for example, that extinction is bad, or that minimizing loss of species is ethically or aesthetically desirable.

Those who employ equilibrium notions and their associated value judgments, in order to study the ecological effects of different designs for clearing Brazilian forests, for example, are very likely to use these notions to support specific types of environmental policy recommendations. They are likely, for instance, to come up with a reserve design which (they believe) minimizes loss of species, based on their assumptions about equilibrium, reserve size, and species loss (see Diamond 1975; Diamond and May 1976; Simberloff and Abele 1976; Soulé and Wilcox 1980; Begon *et al.* 1986, pp. 759–761). More specifically, they likely generate certain reserve designs, in part, because of their contextual value judgment that there are compelling ethical or aesthetic reasons, for example, for minimizing species losses. Particular reserve designs also presuppose various methodological value judgments about how to minimize species losses. In such cases, the methodological value judgments amount to assessments of instrumental value: that a given design is probably the best *means* to a particular *end*, species preservation. However, even if one is able to make these contextual and methodological value judgments, the best course of action regarding reserve designs is not clear because the relevant ecology – in part, because of island biogeography – is underdetermined. Moreover, although all science is empirically underdetermined, the magnitude of the ecological underdetermination is the problem here. In the absence of an uncontroversial general theory of ecology – or in the absence of a careful study of the species or community whose conservation is desired – ecologists are forced to "fill in" the gaps of their scientific knowledge. They fill in the gaps with methodological or contextual value judgments like those just mentioned. We believe that it makes sense to call what they fill in, "methodological value judgments," because such judgments require one to make a choice, among different options, for how to practice science, and such choices are never wholly determined by the data. Some of the factors responsible for scientific gaps and for the need to make methodological value judgments about the island biogeographic theory underlying reserve designs are the following:

1. Ecologists must decide whether ethical and conservation priorities require protecting an individual species, an ecosystem, or biodiversity, when not all can be protected at once. Different actions are likely required to protect a particular species of interest, as opposed to preserving entire functioning ecosystems, as opposed to preserving biotic diversity (Margules *et al.* 1982, p. 116; Soulé and Simberloff 1986; see Zimmerman and Bierregaard 1986, p. 134; Williamson 1987, p. 367).

2. Ecologists often must choose between maximizing present and future biodiversity. Currently they are able only to determine which types of reserves contain the most species at present, not which ones will contain the most over the long term (Soulé and Simberloff 1986, pp. 24ff.).

3. In the absence of adequate empirical data, ecologists frequently must decide how to evaluate the worth of general theory. The preferred reserve design does not depend on any general ecological theory, but on a practical, specific knowledge of taxa and their habitats. It depends on empirical rather than theoretical matters (Margules *et al.* 1982, p. 124; Soulé and Simberloff 1986, pp. 25ff.;

Boecklen and Simberloff 1987, pp. 250–252, 272; Simberloff and Cox 1987; see Zimmerman and Bierregaard 1986, p. 135).

4. Ecologists sometimes must rely on subjective estimates and values whenever "minimum viable population" sizes are not known in a precise area (Soulé and Simberloff 1986, pp. 26–32; Boecklen and Simberloff 1987, pp. 252–255; see Orians et al. 1986, p. 231).

5. Ecologists often are forced to assess subjectively the value of different reserve shapes. Moreover, reserve shape, as such, may not explain variation in species number (Blouin and Connor 1985).

6. The island-biogeographical theory underlying current paradigms regarding reserve design has rarely been tested (see Margules et al. 1982, p. 117; Zimmerman and Bierregaard 1986, p. 134) and is dependent primarily on ornithological data (see Zimmerman and Bierregaard 1986, p. 135), on correlations rather than causal explanations (see Zimmerman and Bierregaard 1986, pp. 130–139), on assumptions about homogeneous habitats (Margules et al. 1982, p. 117), and on unsubstantiated turnover rates and extinction rates (Boecklen and Simberloff 1987, pp. 248–249, 257). Hence, ecologists who use the theory must make a variety of methodological value judgments about its applicability.

7. Factors other than those dominant in island biogeography (e.g. maximum breeding habitat) often have been shown to be superior predictors of species number (Boecklen and Simberloff 1987, p. 272; see Margules et al. 1982, p. 120; Zimmerman and Bierregaard 1986, pp. 136ff.; Simberloff and Cox 1987, pp. 63–71). As a consequence, ecologists must assess the value of such factors even before they have been tested extensively.

8. Islands are disanalogous in important ways with nature reserves (Margules et al. 1982, p. 118). As a result, ecologists who apply data about islands to problems of reserve design must make a number of value judgments about their representativeness and importance.

9. Corridors (an essential part of island-biogeographic theory) have questionable overall value for species preservation in particular cases (Simberloff and Cox 1987; see Orians et al. 1986, p. 32; Salwasser 1986, pp. 227–247). Hence, recommending use of corridors requires ecologists to evaluate their effectiveness subjectively.

10. Island biogeography often yields predictions that cannot be tested, owing to their imprecision, for example, because of large variance about species–area relationships (Connor and McCoy 1979; Boecklen and Simberloff 1987, pp. 261–272; see also McCoy 1982, 1983). Those who use the theory are often forced to make subjective evaluations of non-testable predictions.

Because of scientific and conceptual difficulties such as these ten, it is uncertain how successful (environmentally speaking) a potential nature-reserve design might be. As the Chair of a recent National Academy of Sciences group phrased the problem, when speaking of the difficulty of preventing/delaying species extinction: "Even if we had control over habitat destruction, we would be far from understanding how to protect these species. Theoretical research in meta-population management is in its infancy, and the data needed for emerging models are difficult to acquire and are lacking for most species" (Orians *et al.* 1986, pp. 245–246). But if so, then scientists faced with the need to provide ecological evidence for particular reserve designs are forced to make methodological value judgments about the theory and data they use as evidence. Hence, it is not always clear whether ecologists ought to accept or reject a particular design or a particular evaluative interpretation of the relevant data or theory (see Chase 1986, especially pp. 253–254). For example, as was already mentioned earlier in this chapter, in 1986–1987 a number of ecologists were involved in a dispute over design of wildlife refuges and over species losses resulting from deforestation. The battle was played out largely in the pages of the *Bulletin of the Ecological Society of America.* The most focused aspect of the controversy began in August 1986 when P. C. Kangas gave a paper at the meeting of the Fourth International Congress of Ecology, held in Syracuse, New York.

Using data on trees in Costa Rica, and the "objective approach" of species–area curves, Kangas argued that extinction rates due to deforestation in the tropics are actually much lower than most other researchers have alleged (Kangas 1986, p. 194). Alarmed at Kangas' claim, ecologists in the audience demanded to be heard. They disagreed with Kangas' assertion that extinction rates were indeed lower, complained that his questionable results would be used to justify more rapid and widespread deforestation, and claimed to have "sharply trounced his [Kangas'] arguments" (Noss 1986, pp. 278–279). In the next issue of the *Bulletin,* R. F. Noss accused Kangas not only of "bad science," but of "encouraging the deforestation of the tropics . . . a serious breach of ethics" (Noss 1986, p. 279). Criticizing Kangas for concluding, at the August meeting, that "you can deforest an area for a long time before you have a decline in species" (Noss 1986, p. 278), Noss argued that Kangas' conclusion was fallacious, for at least five reasons. Moreover, although Noss did not mention it, each of these five difficulties represented Kangas making a methodological value judgment about the validity of some ecological technique, hypothesis, or simplifying assumption. The five alleged problems were the following. (1) The flatness of Kangas' species–area curve is an artifact of his extrapolation technique. (2) Kangas considered only presence/absence of tree species, not minimum viable population sizes of trees. (3) Kangas ignored the importance of animal mutualists. (4) Kangas ignored the diversity of insects in the forest canopy. (5) Finally, Kangas assumed that tropical forests are close to equilibrium (Noss 1986, p. 278).

Other ecologists, in subsequent issues of the *Bulletin*, criticized Noss' suggestion (a contextual value judgment about the importance of conservation) "that scientists should shade their results to make sure that they come down on the 'right' side of ecologically important issues." Instead, they argued for an alternative contextual value, the "open expression of alternative points of view" as critical in maintaining the credibility of any scientific policy (Waide 1987, p. 485). They criticized Noss for having a "moral stance" that was "myopic," for assuming that only "dire predictions of extinction" would encourage conservation (Simberloff 1987, p. 156), and for ignoring the fact that such dire predictions could lead to loss of scientific credibility and to subsequent problems for anyone defending conservation (Simberloff 1987, p. 156). Rather than take part in the ethical arguments, still other ecologists made a methodological value judgment, claiming that the philosophical discussion of Kangas' actions was premature, since the content of his remarks was never refereed and was highly questionable (McCoy 1987, p. 535).

Kangas defended himself by claiming that he was taking about species extinctions, not refuge design, as was alleged. He also responded that his species–area curves, like any models, were simplifications of reality. Arguing that he was not encouraging deforestation of the tropics, Kangas said that he was merely arguing for using the limited "conservation dollar" most effectively, rather than in ways that would not, in effect, conserve the most species (Kangas 1987, pp. 158–160). In other words, Kangas claimed to be supporting the contextual value of economic efficiency in making conservation decisions, whereas his opponents, like Noss, claimed to be affirming the contextual value of conserving the greatest number of species. In addition, both sides in the dispute disagreed over the methodological value judgments (see the five problems noted earlier) used to draw Kangas' conclusion about deforestation. Noss asserted that he was not criticizing Kangas' right to present his views, but rather Kangas' failure to see that his "simplistic study" could lead to "potentially dangerous conclusions." In other words, careless methodological value judgments (such as the judgment to ignore the size of minimum viable populations) could help justify ethically, scientifically, and politically questionable conservation policies. Noss argued not for censorship but for prudence in the presentation of results (Noss 1988, pp. 4–5). In the end, neither Noss' nor Kangas' arguments, nor any others, appear to have been judged the scientific winner. In this situation of ecological uncertainty about species–area relationships and reserve design, some scientists made methodological value judgments about the acceptability of certain simplifying assumptions, for example, while other scientists rejected those simplifying assumptions and hence made quite different methodological value judgments. The particulars of this controversy make it clear that different methodological value judgments structured the opposed interpretations of Kangas' scientific experiments and determined the meaning of his observational data. Moreover, the value judgments were unavoidable. Different models, based on different methodological value judgments, undergirded different environmental policies.

4.2.2 Ecology and value conflicts over preservation and development

Different methodological value judgments likewise support different environmental policies in disputes between developers and preservationists. Hutchinson's account of the feedback processes structuring communities (1959, 1975), for example, affirms the importance of maintaining the existence of a hypothetical balance of nature. If one accepts this account, then Hutchinson's ecological conclusions (along with his associated methodological value judgments) can easily be used to support the position of preservationists rather than developers.

But suppose one follows a different account of the balance of nature, one unlike that of Hutchinson and others who presuppose causal regularities. This is an account that argues that it is necessary to show departure from random assemblages (which proponents of the "balance" allegedly have not done) before positing biological mechanisms to explain presumed departures (see Strong *et al.* 1979, 1984; Strong 1982a; Simberloff 1983; Chase 1986, pp. 319–125). If one subscribes to this account, then (although Strong, Simberloff, and others probably would not want their ecological conclusions used in this way) their skeptical response, to those postulating a "balance of nature," could be used to support policies of commercial development of wilderness areas. After all, if there were no conclusive ecological evidence for a "balance of nature" preserved in pristine wilderness, then postulating such a balance would require making contextual and methodological value judgments. But if positing some "balance" were dependent upon such value judgments, then it would be more difficult for environmentalists to argue against development on the grounds that it might destroy some inherent "balance." This case illustrates that, again, because of the magnitude of the empirical underdetermination of ecological theory (regarding balance or stability), scientists have been forced to make methodological value judgments about which, if any, account of balance or stability to pursue. Different value judgments, in turn, have different consequences for environmental policy.

4.2.3 Ecology and value conflicts over hunting versus animal rights

Much the same situation faces ecologists confronting the conflict between hunters or ranchers (interested in human control of predators) and preservationists. For some time, a number of ecologists have claimed that predators control their prey populations; they have based this claim on a famous account of an eruption of the deer population on the Kaibab Plateau (a wilderness area near the Grand Canyon) after predators were removed (see Leopold 1933; Chase 1986, pp. 24–26, 69). A number of ecologists also subscribe to the "world is green" thesis and posit that herbivores in general are regulated by predation, and that herbivores could never be regulated from below (see, for example, Hutchinson 1959; Hairston et al. 1960).

If one makes the methodological value judgment, for example, that the Kaibab case is paradigmatic for explaining structure in all biotic communities, then one will likely accept an account which claims that predators structure herbivore communities of species and keep them "in balance." As a consequence, one might be likely to accept the ethical and policy position of some persons in the US Department of the Interior and the US Department of Agriculture. Proponents of this position maintain that, since predators control deer populations, for example, and since predators are often killed by hunters and by ranchers protecting their livestock, therefore prey populations need to be kept in check artificially, through hunting. Thus, the ecological findings and methodological value judgments supporting a predation account of community can be used by those who favor hunting as a wildlife-management policy. Admittedly, other ecological findings and methodological value judgments, also supporting a predation account of community structure, can be used by those who are opposed to hunting as a wildlife-management policy. For example, groups like Defenders of Wildlife and the National Audubon Society might claim that predators regulate their prey in a more natural or efficient manner than hunters do. They support the view that human hunting – focusing on trophy animals – and natural predation are very different types of selective pressure. Therefore, even though members of such groups believe that predation structures communities, they remain opposed to hunting.

On the other side, one might reject the "world is green hypothesis" (see, for example, Murdoch 1966). In this case, if one claims, for example, that species populations are not kept in check in any regular way, or that they are kept in check, not by predation, but by competition or by some other factor accounting for the "balance," then one might argue that prey should not be controlled. Indeed, to support their position, preservationists have argued both that there was no Kaibab deer eruption, and that a reduction in predators does not necessarily cause an increase in the prey populations (see Caughley 1970). Obviously, the preservationists who might use such arguments employ methodological value judgments quite different from those of the hunters, who also claim to be interpreting the same observational data.

If the preceding analyses are plausible, then it appears possible that ethical commitments (e.g., to hunting or to predator control) might influence methodological value judgments used to interpret data about species eruptions and the role of predators. Such methodological value judgments, in turn, might influence whether one subscribes to a belief in some thesis about ecological stability. These beliefs about whether or not some balance or stability exists, in turn, support particular environmental policies designed either to maintain or to disregard the alleged balance. While there is no necessary connection between adherence to a particular account of stability or ecological balance and consequent environmental policy, belief in the balance does appear to increase the probability of environmental action designed to safeguard that balance. Hence, this controversy – over hunting versus preservation – tends to illustrate not only that policy conflicts often cannot be adjudicated by appeal to the scientific facts of the matter, because the ecology is underdetermined, but also that methodological and ethical value judgments might guide interpretation of the data.

4.2.4 Ecology and value conflicts over pest control

Scientific or factual underdetermination, with resultant methodological value judgments, is also often a problem in conflicts over chemical, versus biological, forms of pest control. According to Strong, Simberloff, Abele, and others (see chapter 2, this volume, and Strong *et al.* 1984, for example), no deterministic community structures ought to be posited until one has shown departure from random assemblages. On this view, if one cannot provide strong evidence for deterministic community structures, then one ought not posit an interactive notion of balance or stability. And if not, goes the argument, then one ought not argue that chemical pest control destroys some balance of nature. Indeed, according to the argument, one cannot destroy something whose existence is in question and which cannot be defined operationally. The judgment that no interactive balance or stability exists, however, is dependent upon a number of methodological value judgments, for example, regarding the nature of random behavior and the evidence that is sufficient to reveal the presence of community structures.

On the other hand, one might reject the conclusions of Strong, Simberloff, Abele, and others (see Gilpin and Diamond 1984) and therefore accept an interactive view of the balance of nature. For example, if one adopts an account of the balance of nature that presupposes causal regularities, an account based on the importance of predators, then one would have grounds for supporting biological pest management. One might claim that biological control was less likely to disturb some sort of stability or balance of nature. In either case, the fact that the science itself admits of alternative, plausible interpretations of the alleged "balance" data means that (in this case) ecology cannot provide us with clear guidelines for actions that are in accord with environmental welfare. And if not, then ecology provides little help in adjudicating conflicts over environmental well-being (for other examples, see Hughson and Popper 1983; Popper and Hughson 1983). Again, in the pest-control example, as in the previous three, the reason for the lack of ecological conclusiveness is the same as in many other areas of science: the reason is that ecologists interpreting observational data are always forced to make methodological value judgments. In ecology the problem with such value judgments may be more acute than in other sciences, however, simply because the empirical underdetermination is so great.

Not all methodological values are created equal, however. Some are more problematic than others. That is, they may be more *ad hoc*, or they may be based on more gratuitous assumptions, or they may contribute less to heuristic power than other judgments. Hence, the ecological conclusions founded on more questionable value judgments are likewise more problematic. For this reason, it is important for scientists to distinguish different types of methodological value judgments, to assess their respective reliability, and to determine the degree to which controversies in ecology – and in science generally – turn on specific methodological value judgments. Indeed, this is one of the points illustrated by the previous four examples (reserve design, preservation, hunting, and pest control).

4.3 Categorical value judgments are more problematic than others

Among methodological value judgments, different degrees of reliability are often a function of the types of judgments involved. For example, one can distinguish *instrumental value judgments* from *categorical value judgments*. On the one hand, we can make a largely factual, instrumental judgment about the extent to which a particular thing possesses a characteristic value. For example, we can make an instrumental value judgment about the extent to which an ecological theory about community structure possesses the value of explanatory or predictive power. Or we can make such a judgment about the extent to which a community is stable through time. On the other hand, we can make a largely subjective, categorical judgment about whether an alleged property, such as falsifiability, is really a value for a particular scientific theory. Or we can make a categorical judgment of value about whether a characteristic, such as stability, is really a value/goal for communities or ecosystems (Scriven 1982; McMullin 1983).

Instrumental value judgments posit that, if a specified value or goal (e.g., community stability) is to be obtained, then a certain action (e.g., promoting species diversity) is good because it is a means to the value or goal. Categorical value judgments state that a certain goal, for example, community stability, is prima-facie good, independent of particular circumstances (Hempel 1965, 1979, 1982, 1983; Scriven 1982; McMullin 1983). McMullin, Scriven, and other critics of positivism/hypothesis deduction (H-D) accept both types (instrumental and categorical) of methodological value judgments in science. Hempel, Carnap, and some other classical proponents of H-D, however, believe that categorical value judgments have no place in science. Their complaint against them is that, because they cannot be confirmed empirically, they are subjective (Hempel 1965, 1979, pp. 45–66, 1982, p. 263, 1983, pp. 73–100; see Nagel 1961, p. 492; Scriven 1982).

Apart from whether Hempel and other H-D proponents are right to reject categorical value judgments about methods, their presence in a scientific decision does render it more controversial than would the presence of an instrumental value judgment. This is because instrumental value judgments can be assessed on the basis of some methodological goal, or end, whereas the criterion for a categorical value judgment is, by definition, no particular methodological goal. Moreover, one cannot empirically confirm the success of a categorical value judgment, because it has no empirical criterion for success. At least in some cases, however, one can empirically confirm the success of an instrumental value judgment about method by comparing its results to those of other such value judgments. For example, one might compare the results of theory A to those of theory B with respect to predictive success regarding some phenomenon. Hence, categorical judgments are likely to be more controversial than instrumental value judgments, both in ecology and in science generally.

This controversy becomes clearer if we examine why Hempel and other hypothetico-deductivists are wrong to exclude categorical judgments about methodological values from science. That accomplished, it will be easy to argue later that certain categorical judgments in ecology are both defensible and unavoidable. In making empirical confirmability a criterion for judgments in science and thereby excluding categorical judgments about methodological values, naive positivists and hypothetico-deductivists like Hempel and Carnap appear to err, because they demand assurance inappropriate to much scientific investigation. They demand an inappropriate level of assurance because their requirement of empirical confirmability would not allow those who do pure science (if there is such a thing) to decide on criteria for theory choice, gathering and interpreting data, or rejecting hypotheses, because such judgments could not be empirically confirmed. (And they could not be empirically confirmed because each of them relies on at least one categorical judgment about methodological values, that is, each relies on an assumption about the prima-facie importance of some criterion – e.g., testability, explanatory power, simplicity – for theory/ hypothesis choice.) Yet, as examples such as beta decay and wildlife-reserve design (cited earlier) indicate, scientists do make judgments about weighting criteria for evaluation of theories, observations, and hypotheses. They do so all the time. All theories are evaluated in the light of some goal, like testability, and that goal is articulated in terms of a categorical judgment of value. But if theory evaluation requires categorical judgments of value, then scientific practice does not confirm the H-D denial of categorical value judgments in science. Hence, because H-D fails to represent the importance of such value judgments in ecology, it fails to represent an adequate account of ecological method (see Shrader-Frechette 1989c, pp. 74–80). (This does not mean, of course, that one ought to reject H-D. Testing remains a goal in science, even if it cannot be realized perfectly. The more ecological theories/hypotheses can be tested, the better for the science. Our criticisms of H-D do mean, however, that one ought not claim that most of the methodological problems with community ecology could be solved, and the discipline easily used to guide environmental policymakers, if only ecologists would use H-D. This claim is wrong because methodological value judgments would always render H-D science, and especially ecology, problematic.)

If all judgments in science had to be empirically confirmed, as the hypothetico-deductivists and naive positivists claim, and if there were no methodological value judgments in science, then community ecology would come to a halt. Ecologists could never make judgments about theory choice, because such choices rely in part on unconfirmable categorical judgments about methodological values. Moreover, if ecology were as value free as H-D proponents claim science ought to be (see, for example, Nagel 1961, p. 492), then it would never need to progress. Obviously, however, ecology does need to progress, and impotent hypotheses ought to be discarded. Hence, ecology needs methodological value judgments – both instrumental and categorical. Cases like island biogeography (see chapter 3) make it obvious, both that some judgments in ecology *are not* empirically confirmed, and they *cannot* be, if ecology is to progress. For ecology to progress, we need attention to empirical evidence and epistemological assessment of its assumptions and hypotheses via conceptual criticism. As we shall argue in later chapters, this conceptual criticism – and not allegedly infallible, value-free H-D methods – safeguards the objectivity of science (see Longino 1990, p. 74).

As one object of conceptual criticism, categorical value judgments have an especially significant role in ecological theorizing. This is because ecology cannot typically tell us, in a non-question-begging way, how to preserve the health of the biosphere. It cannot do so because ecology alone cannot provide conclusive grounds for making categorical judgments of value. (Categorical value judgments can tell us what things, for example, maintaining alleged biotic equilibrium, are valuable as such, valuable apart from whether they are the means to some other end.) Ecology alone cannot provide grounds for such value judgments because, like all sciences, its focus is descriptive/empirical, and value judgments must be justified via logical and conceptual analyses, not on descriptive/empirical grounds alone. Because ecological science cannot provide uncontroversial, categorical judgments of value, yet because such judgments are essential to practical, environmental applications of ecology, ecologists themselves are forced to make value judgments about the interpretation and adequacy of their scientific goals, methods, hypotheses, and conclusions. Because of these methodological value judgments, ecologists' scientific findings do not always bear up under epistemological and ethical scrutiny. Hence, if one attempts to base environmental policy on ecologists' value-laden scientific conclusions (about the value of stability, for example), then one might be in a situation analogous to that of Kant, who attempted to ground his metaphysics on a false physics (McClure 1989, p. 60). Environmental policy is uncertain, not only because much of ecology is empirically underdetermined and dynamic, but also because, in the face of this underdetermination, ecologists are forced to make a number of methodological value judgments about their data and conclusions. For example, if ecologists argue that a particular form of chemical pest control destroys the balance or stability of a given community, then their conclusion relies in part on the methodological value judgment that certain community phenomena are not merely random and hence reveal stable community structures. To the degree that this value judgment is uncertain, the policy conclusion could likewise be uncertain.

It is important to discuss the role of methodological values in ecology because many experts forget that all scientists are forced to make value judgments. They forget that science is never completely neutral with respect either to methodological values or ethical consequences. Yet, as the director of Sigma Xi, the Scientific Research Society, recently pointed out: "Scientific problems such as the structure of DNA or the origin of submarine canyons are investigated by scientists, who may be all-too-human in their capacity to make mistakes, to miss or misinterpret critical pieces of evidence and, on occasion, deliberately to fake research results. Science may be morally neutral, but so is a traffic light; car drivers and scientists are not" (Jackson 1986, pp. 1–2). Let us examine more closely why science, including ecology, is not value neutral and, hence, why ecological theorizing, even at its best, is beset with uncertainty as a result of ecologists' commitments to particular methodological values.

4.4 Scientists often ignore methodological values

Why have many scientists ignored the methodological value judgments of their own work? Why have they erroneously believed that it was possible to make value-free judgments about scientific data, theories, and methods? One reason is that they may subscribe to the fact–value dichotomy, a famous tenet held by hypothetico-deductivists and naive positivists (Hanson 1958; Polanyi 1959, 1964; Toulmin 1961; Kuhn 1970). This is the belief that facts and values are completely separable, and that there are facts that are not value laden. Applied to community ecology, this claim is that accounts of community structure ought to consist of *factual* and neutral observations, although the interpretations of these observations, and the environmental policy decisions made as a consequence of them, may be *evaluative* (US Congress 1976, pp. 66, 200, 220; Foell 1978, p. 196; see Lovins 1977, p. 940). Apparently, many scientists and hypothetico-deductivists fail to see the problems associated with their belief in purely factual (non-evaluative) science. Belief in the fact–value dichotomy, however, is incompatible with formulation of any scientific theory or analysis to explain causal connections among phenomena. This is because formulation of any theory requires one to make methodological value judgments, including categorical value judgments. Also, presenting alternative accounts of one's theoretical or methodological options can never be a purely descriptive or factual enterprise. This is because one has to use evaluative criteria to select which options to present, and these normative criteria are outside the scope of purely empirical inquiry (see Tool 1979, p. 280). Also, to subscribe to the fact–value dichotomy is to hold the belief that there can be pure facts and presuppositionless research. As the earlier discussion of bias, contextual, and methodological values indicates, there is no presuppositionless research. Ecologists and other scientists, however, often erroneously believe that ecology is more factual than it is. They sometimes appear to think that their work is presuppositionless. They fail to see the ways in which methodological values structure their allegedly "objective" methods. One ecologist in a controversial, value-laden case claimed, for example, that he had "an objective approach to quantifying extinction rates . . . based on species–area curves" (Kangas 1986, p. 194). Or, sometimes ecologists recognize the methodological value judgments in their work, but then claim that their scientific conclusions are not highly sensitive to them. The analysis of island biogeography in chapter 3 suggests that some ecologists minimize the potential of their methodological value judgments for causing false confirmations of the theory. The solution to both of these errors involving value judgments (either failing to see them or minimizing their significance) is quite simple, according to one ecologist: "In conservation biology, the interpretation of results involves values, whether or not we choose (or are able) to recognize these values explicitly. When sensitive issues are at stake [like justifying deforestation on the basis of value-laden scientific conclusions], we might do best by putting our values, biases, and assumptions 'up front'" (Noss 1988, p. 4).

Admittedly, the traditional positivist and hypothetico-deductivist motivation behind denying the presence of certain methodological values in science and behind belief in the fact–value dichotomy is a noble and important ideal. It is noble because value-free observations, if they existed, would guarantee the complete objectivity of one's scientific research. Values threaten objectivity, however, only if they *alone* determine the facts. They do not. Both our values and the action of the external world on our senses are responsible for our perceptions, observations, and facts. Just because facts are value laden, this does not mean that there is no sufficient reason for accepting one theory over another. One theory may have more explanatory or predictive power, or unify more facts, for example. Quark theory provides a dramatic example of this point. Isolated quarks are in principle unobservable, yet there are numerous good reasons (simplicity, external consistency, explanatory power) for accepting quark theory. Hence, the value-ladenness of facts, even in science, does not mean that science is completely subjective or relative. This is because observation of value-free data, *alone*, does not provide the only reason for accepting one theory, or one value judgment, rather than another. Because there are other good reasons for acceptance of theories and value judgments, science is not wholly subjective. These other good reasons, however, because they are not based solely on observation, are never compelling in the way the naive positivists and hypothetico-deductivists thought that science was conclusive and empirically confirmed. Because they are not compelling, perhaps we should not expect the science of ecology to have a clear, uncontroversial, general theory capable of providing specific predictions to guide environmental practice. Nor should we expect ecology to give clear, uncontroversial responses to questions about what will promote environmental welfare. Ecology can provide a basis for environmental ethics/policy, but what policy it supports will be a function of which methodological value judgments ecologists accept.

4.5 Ecology cannot dictate ends or goals

Ecology alone cannot provide us with goals or values for environmental policy, but it can often guide us regarding the means to attain these ends or goals. For example, *if* we make a categorical value judgment that stability and diversity are good, *then* indeed ecology can give us help in policymaking. It often can tell us what means or interventions in communities are likely to achieve or to thwart diversity. Because ecology (as a science) cannot provide us with a general definition of an end or goal, however, we ourselves must make the relevant categorical judgment of value.

Unlike ecology, medicine does have an obvious goal. This goal is the health of the individual patient. Human health is a fairly easy value to posit, both because there are many clinical norms for what is normal or healthy, and because there is general agreement regarding the categorical value judgment about the goal of patient health. Unfortunately, analogous value judgments in ecology are more controversial. Some researchers have argued that one can measure biotic health by means of factors such as the ability of ecosystems to recover their equilibria after a disturbance; their not losing sensitive species; or their resistance to disease (Rapport 1989). Using such factors as indicators of health, however, presupposes accounts of equilibrium or stability that are question-begging and unconfirmed (see Worster 1990, pp. 8ff.). Ecology has no clear, unambiguous norms for when a community is normal or healthy and, as a consequence, positing a goal for ecological practice is quite difficult. Likewise, ecologists and laypersons often do not share the same uncontroversial, unambiguous ecological goals because ecological practice affects different persons differently, for example, depending on whether they are land developers, conservationists, scientists, or manufacturers. In ecology, unlike medicine, there is no single individual whose health is the goal of activity. Thus, even if ecology could unambiguously define a goal for ecological activity, it would still face the problem of which species' and which individuals' welfares to aim at optimizing. If we humans want to focus on efficiency, for example, and to maximize production of rockfish in a particular area (see Sagoff 1985a, p. 101), then ecologists can often tell us how to do this, just as they can tell us how to maximize long-run production of certain natural goods and services. Ecology alone cannot, however, tell us what our values or goals, for example, maintaining stability, ought to be.

4.6 Ecology cannot tell us what is "natural"

One of the most common goals of ecologists is the attempt to specify and sustain what is natural. This goal often fails to provide directives for environmental policy because ecologists cannot always specify what is "natural" or when human actions are in accord with nature. Knowing that one is acting in accord with nature is difficult, for example, because "natural" is often defined as a condition in existence before the activities of humans who perturbed the system (Jorling 1976, p. 141). The definition is flawed, however, both because it excludes humans, a key part of nature, and because there are probably no fully natural environments or ecosystems anywhere. As Sober points out, there are likely no "natural states" in biology anyway; humans merely confuse what moral philosophers call "natural" with what biologists call "natural" (1986, pp. 179–184). Also, if natural systems are those that existed prior to human influence, then it would be difficult to know precisely what sorts of natural systems existed prior to human influence. Moreover, short of removing all humans, or at least radically reducing their numbers and changing their lives, it would be impossible to have a "natural system" unperturbed by humans. Likewise, because natural systems continually change, it is difficult to specify a situation at one particular time, rather than another time, as natural. For all these reasons, we are forced to define "natural" environments in a highly stipulative and question-begging way. In other words, we are unable to define "natural" in a way free of categorical values. We are unable to define it in a way recognized by hypothetico-deductivists as part of science. Yet, it is part of science.

On the view that what is "natural" is what exists prior to human disturbance, even destructive events not caused by humans may be said to be natural. As the controversy over the summer 1988 fires in Yellowstone Park revealed, however, the extent to which such large-scale disturbances are natural is both controversial and of relatively recent origin. From approximately 1920 to 1965, Clements' theories of what was "natural" shaped the attitudes of park managers towards wilderness. On this early account, disturbances such as fires, even when not caused by humans, altered the structure of ecosystems and made the landscape less habitable. Following the advice of Smokey the Bear, we attempted to suppress all forest fires, not only those caused by humans. More recent research, however, has taught us that Clements' views are simplistic, if not incorrect. We now view many "disturbances," such as fires, as essential to diversity and to preserving some wilderness ecosystems (see, for example, Knight and Wallace 1989; Romme and Despain 1989a). The objects of preservation at places like Yellowstone are now more likely to be, not *climax communities* as they existed in the past, but the ecological *processes* that maintain various species, communities, and ecosystems (see Chase 1989, p. 55; Christensen 1989, pp. 46–48; see Elfring 1989; Schullery 1989).

Although ecologists' attitudes toward whether fires are natural and whether they ought to be suppressed or managed, have changed, there is little agreement on the range, frequency, and behavior of allegedly natural fires. Different agencies, administrative regions, and individual parks use different prescriptions for designating "natural fires"; they employ different monitoring requirements for the fires, and they have different standards for the number and size of fires that are allowed to burn at one time (see Chase 1989, p. 56; Nichols 1989, p. 52). Hence, our understanding of what is natural is inadequate, ambiguous, and provides little basis for environmental policy (see Christensen *et al.* 1989; Romme and Despain 1989b; Tolba 1989). We are not sure precisely what is natural and, therefore, whether we ought simply to watch a disturbance or intervene (see Christensen 1989; Omi 1989, p. 44). Either way, our action is not neutral. Fire suppression achieves some goals (see Minshall *et al.* 1989; Singer *et al.* 1989), but it does not preserve ecosystems completely, since they change by having fire withheld, just as they change by burning (see Pyne 1989, p. 33). This means that any methodological or policy judgment about the naturalness of some ecological process or event is, in part, a categorical value judgment, a value judgment that some "natural" thing is good.

4.7 Conclusion

If ecology cannot tell us, uncontroversially, what is natural, or what our goals ought to be, or which categorical value judgments are correct, then ecology cannot deliver uncontroversial conclusions. Because it presupposes methodological value judgments, either categorical or instrumental, ecology relies on presuppositions that are more or less questionable. And because it presupposes value judgments that are at least somewhat controversial, ecology itself delivers controversial conclusions. Hence, ecological conclusions (even those confirmed by hypothesis deduction) are not alone sufficient to ground environmental policy in an uncontroversial way. For help in both tasks, we need epistemological, ethical, and methodological analyses. We have a special need for such analyses in ecology, because neither good science nor good policy can be the result of simple-minded application of an algorithm, and because ecology is such a new and empirically underdetermined science. Perhaps ecologists in the past have not achieved more because they thought that theorizing and conceptual analysis were too easy. Or, perhaps, they thought there were algorithms, general theories, or H-D methods that would preclude the necessity for tough-minded, situation-specific, methodological analysis in ecology and for sophisticated knowledge of individual taxa. What we have tried to show, so far, is that there is no easy ecology. As we shall argue, however, ecology is both possible and necessary. In subsequent chapters of the volume, we shall illustrate how methodological and epistemological analyses might be helpful in ecology, and how they can enhance the accuracy, objectivity, and utility of ecological methods. Even though ecology is not value free, we shall show that it can be objective and rational. To understand what ecology can do, and why it can be objective and rational, we shall examine a new account of ecological rationality and a new approach to methods of applied science.

5 · What ecology can do: The logic of case studies

IN *The Evolution of Physics* (1947), Albert Einstein claimed that physical concepts are free creations of the human mind and not uniquely determined by the external world. Much of our argument in the previous four chapters has been to show that, at least in contemporary community ecology, Einstein is in part correct. Ecological concepts and theories, as partially free creations of the human mind, are not uniquely determined by the external world. If they were, they would not be so riddled with ambiguity, imprecision, and unavoidable methodological value judgments.

Having illustrated the difficulties associated with various ecological concepts, theories, and value judgments, it may seem that we have "pulled the rug" out from under ecology. If ecology is beset with conceptual and methodological problems, how can it provide a scientific foundation for environmental policymaking? In this and the four subsequent chapters, we argue that, despite our pessimism about the predictive power of general ecological theory in specific environmental applications, we nevertheless believe (1) that general theories do have significant heuristic power, (2) that numerous lower-level theories aid us in environmental management, and (3) that, in particular, natural-history information has much to contribute to practical problemsolving in conservation and preservation. Therefore, we believe that pessimistic conclusions about the importance and utility of current ecology are not warranted. First, we examine the arguments of two prominent pessimists, biologist Robert Henry Peters and philosopher Mark Sagoff. Next, we examine some of the problems with ecological laws and theories and show how we might re-conceptualize laws in ecology so as to make them more defensible and more accurate. Third, following the advice given in a recent US National Academy of Sciences (NAS) committee report, we suggest specific ways that ecology can inform environmental policy, despite the problems outlined in our earlier chapters. Fourth, we provide a new account of rationality and explana-

106

tion in ecology. This new account is based on the method of case studies, a method that will help ecology to ground environmental policy. Finally, in chapter 8 we provide a case study that exemplifies one of the main points of the volume: that, although ecology has little general theory able to provide accurate predictions in environmental applications, it can provide a wealth of lower-level theories and natural-history knowledge that is both useful to environmental problemsolving and illustrative of the significance of case studies.

5.1 Peters and Sagoff: Pessimists about ecology

Using ecology for environmental problemsolving is rarely easy. In earlier chapters, we have discussed some of the reasons for this difficulty. Applying ecology is so difficult that some authors, like Robert Henry Peters and Mark Sagoff, are pessimistic about the contributions contemporary ecology is making to environmental policy and practice. Both Sagoff (1985a) and Peters (1991) diagnose ecology as an unhealthy science unable to provide firm foundations for environmental problemsolving. Peters' prescription, in the main, is to restore ecology to health by making it more predictive. Sagoff's prescription is closer to letting the patient die; he argues for having ethical, cultural, and aesthetic arguments take over the role often played by ecology in grounding environmental decisionmaking. Although we are more sympathetic with Peters' analysis than with Sagoff's, it is important to assess the views of each of them regarding what ecology can do. We believe that Sagoff asks too little of ecology and therefore concludes that it can do almost nothing to address environmental problems. On the other hand, we believe that Peters asks too much of ecology and therefore urges ecologists to do what is almost impossible. Let us see where each of these views goes wrong.

In an analysis that is both tough-minded and controversial, Peters argues that ecology is a "weak science" (1991, p. 10). He claims that the primary way to correct this weakness is to judge every ecological theory "on the basis of its ability to predict" (1991, p. 290). Peters' main arguments for the weakness of ecology are:

1. that ecologists confuse predictive theories with non-predictive constructs and hence fail to use hypothetical-deductive methods (1991, pp. 17–37);
2. that ecological papers are cited less frequently than non-ecological papers (1991, pp. 6–10);
3. that the environmental "problems that ecology should solve are not being solved" by ecologists (1991, pp. 10–14);

4. that reputable ecologists believe ecology to be weak and, therefore, they have engaged in "scientific criticism" of the discipline (1991, pp. 4–6);

5. that many theories in ecology are merely tautological (1991, pp. 38–73); and

6. that many central ecological concepts are vague and incapable of being operationalized (1991, pp. 74–104).

Because Peters has pointed out some of the same difficulties with ecological concepts and methods as we have, we agree with much of his analysis. In fact, we believe that his arguments (4), (5), and (6) are largely correct assessments of some of the scientific problems facing ecology. Indeed, we have argued for several theses similar to his. Our discussion of some of the weaknesses of general ecological theory in chapter 3 of this volume reflects several of the same points as his argument (4). Likewise, our earlier analysis, Shrader-Frechette and McCoy (1990), criticizes trivial and tautological claims in ecology, just as does his argument (5). Finally, our chapter 2 in this volume substantiates many of the same points as his argument (6), that many ecological concepts are vague and cannot be operationalized. We also agree with Peters that, "once the problems of a science are identified, the science can grow around them" (1991, xii). The main question, however, is how ecology ought to grow around the difficulties that we have discovered. This is where we disagree, in part, with Peters.

Peters' first three arguments, presuppose, respectively, (1) that ecology ought to become a hypothetico-deductive and predictive science, (2) that other scientists citing ecological articles less than ecologists cite nonecological articles reveals that ecology is weak, and (3) that ecology as a science can be blamed for the failure to solve environmental problems. Although we believe that prediction is a good thing in science, that increased citations to ecological work would likewise be beneficial, and that ecologists could do more to solve environmental problems, nevertheless we have fundamental disagreements with the presuppositions and arguments (1) through (3). Let us consider the strengths and weaknesses of each of these arguments.

Peters' argument (1), that the main criterion for ecological theorizing ought to be its predictive power, is somewhat correct in at least two senses. Prediction is often needed for applying ecology to environmental problemsolving, as we have argued throughout this volume. When ecologists cannot predict precisely, policymaking is typically more difficult. We also believe that Peters is correct to emphasize prediction, because it is clearly an important goal for science. Moreover, one can only attain predictive theories by consistently seeking the goal of prediction.

In spite of these areas of agreement, we believe that Peters' argument (1) is misguided in at least four ways. For one thing, (1.1) Peters is wrong to use prediction as a *criterion for*, rather than a *goal of*, ecological theorizing, because not all sciences are equally predictive. Geology, economics, and sociology, for example, are all more explanatory than predictive, yet it is not obvious that they are non-scientific by virtue of being more explanatory than predictive. By their very nature, some scientific phenomena appear to be incapable of precise prediction. Because of the demise of uniformitarianism in geology, for example, many geological phenomena are not susceptible to precise, long-term prediction. We conclude from this, not that geology is weak, and not that we should reject the goal of precise geological prediction, but that geology probably deals with phenomena that are less deterministic than those in some other sciences. In overemphasizing the importance of *prediction* in ecology and science generally, Peters has erred in underemphasizing the role of *explanation*. (1.2) Peters' overemphasis on prediction and hypothesis deduction is also highly questionable in the light of the last three decades of research in philosophy of science, much of which has identified fundamental flaws in the positivistic, hypothetico-deductive paradigm for science; with Kuhn (1970) and other critics of the positivist paradigm, we believe that science is likely based more on retroduction and conceptual analysis than on deduction alone. (1.3) One of the fundamental reasons why not all sciences are deductive in method is that they depend on methodological value judgments. As we argued in chapter 4, such value judgments render validation/confirmation through strict hypothesis deduction impossible. Moreover, although all sciences depend on such value judgments, this dependence is particularly acute for ecology. It is a special problem for ecology because this science is more empirically and theoretically underdetermined than many other sciences. Indeed, in section 4.2.1, for example, we listed ten areas of underdetermination in island-biogeographical theory. The greater this underdetermination, the more ecologists are forced to make methodological value judgments to "fill in the gaps." Therefore, because ecology appears to be more dependent upon methodological value judgments than other sciences, it likewise appears to be much less amenable to hypothesis deduction than they are. (1.4) Moreover, as we shall argue in subsequent sections of this chapter, overemphasizing the hypothetico-deductive component of ecological method ignores the recent National Academy of Sciences'

(NAS) emphasis on a bottom-up, case-study approach in ecological method, rather than a top-down, hypothetico-deductive approach (see Orians *et al*. 1986). The NAS panel emphasized the case-study approach in part, because of the uniqueness and historical character of many ecological phenomena. Later in the chapter, we shall spell out the need for, and the components of, case-study and natural-history methods. We shall explain why they are often more appropriate for ecological theorizing, especially in applied areas, than is hypothesis deduction alone.

Apart from our differences over the centrality of hypothesis deduction, we also disagree in part with Peters' (1991, pp. 6–10) argument (2), that other scientists citing ecological articles less than ecologists cite nonecological articles reveals that ecology is weak. While Peters is correct to emphasize the importance of citations, and while we use citation information ourselves, especially in chapter 2 of this volume, we believe that he overstates the case for citation, just as he has overstated the importance of hypothesis deduction. Peters errs because he assumes that nothing but (or primarily) the weakness of ecology could explain why ecological articles are cited less frequently than those in other sciences. However, a number of other reasons could explain this phenomenon: (a) the newness of the science of ecology; (b) the fact that ecology receives less funding than other, more established sciences; (c) the fact that, because ecology deals with unique phenomena, among which connections are not readily apparent, its articles are less cited; and (d) the fact that, because ecology is more holistic than other sciences, it therefore employs the findings of other sciences more than other sciences employ its findings. Moreover, the fact that ecological articles might be cited less than those of other sciences does not show, unequivocally, that ecology is weak. It could also show that other scientists are not paying attention to an important field, and that they err in not doing so. In other words, Peters' argument (2) is merely sociological, not prescriptive or confirmatory. At best, it establishes that scientists do not cite ecology; it does not establish that they are correct in not citing ecology or that they ought not cite ecology. It also does not establish that there is a causal link between the lack of citation and the alleged weakness of ecology. Hence, Peters' argument (2) is quite dependent on a number of highly questionable methodological value judgments.

Finally, although we recognize the importance of environmental problemsolving, and although this volume is addressed to improving ecological methods for precisely the purpose of grounding environmental practice and theory, we have a number of disagreements with Peters'

(1991, pp. 10–14) argument (3). Here he presupposes that ecology as a science can be blamed for the failure to solve environmental problems. Like his argument (2), this argument also errs because it presupposes that nothing but (or primarily) weak ecological science explains the continuing failure to solve environmental problems. However, a great many other reasons could be causally responsible, more responsible than ecology, for our failures in environmental problemsolving. One of the reasons for this failure might be: (a) the fact that government does not regulate polluters and resource depleters on the basis of the best ecological knowledge – in other words, the problem is not ecological knowledge but our failure to act on it. Other reasons might be (b) the fact that industry often lobbies against environmental reforms; and (c) the fact that we are frequently unwilling to spend the money necessary to achieve environmental progress. Peters' argument (3) also is questionable because he blames *weak ecological science* for flawed environmental decisionmaking, yet it is clear that his solution to this problem is in part political and not merely scientific. He says that "ecologists could influence policy by entering the public arena with essentially political arguments" (Peters 1991, p. 12). Hence, in argument (3), Peters' own words reveal that he has confused *improving ecological methods* with *increasing ecologists' environmental activism*. In aligning scientific method and environmental activism, and in postulating incomplete or questionable causes for environmental deterioration, Peters has again made a number of problematic methodological value judgments. Hence, his argument (3) docs not provide hypothetico-deductive grounds for his conclusion. We do not believe, of course, that all reasonable arguments ought to be hypothetico-deductive. Our point is merely that, just as ecology nceds to emphasize other methods in addition to hypothesis deduction, so also ecologists (like Peters) need to recognize that hypothesis deduction cannot be the primary criterion for acceptance or rejection of a scientific theory. Indeed, it does not appear to be the primary criterion used by Peters.

Unlike Peters, Sagoff does not argue for more hypothesis deduction in ecology. His rejection of ecology is more sweeping, because he believes that most ecological arguments for environmental protection are misguided. Sagoff begins his analysis by summarizing several hypotheses that are now questioned (in their original formulation) by ecologists. Given the failure of the stability–diversity hypothesis, for example, Sagoff asks whether ecologists ought to "blow the whistle" on ecologically misguided arguments for environmental protection based on this hypothesis. Or, ought ecologists simply to go about their work and ignore such arguments? Sagoff's answer, in general, is that ecologists ought to use ethical, cultural, and aesthetic arguments to protect the environment. He says that they ought not rely on utilitarian–prudential arguments based on ecological concepts and theories associated with environmental health or with balance-of-nature theses (Sagoff 1985a, pp. 111–112). Sagoff also argues that ecologists ought to attempt to identify *un*healthy states of the environment and ecosystems, and not to place so much emphasis on defining some balance of nature or community structure (Sagoff 1985a, pp. 113–116). In other words, Sagoff's two responses to problems with ecological concepts and theories are (1) to ignore the possible ecological/scientific foundations for judgments about environmental welfare, since they are uncertain, and (2) to focus on obvious, uncontroversial cases of what is environmentally unhealthy.

While Sagoff's two responses do provide a way out of the dilemmas facing ecologists who must make professional judgments about environmental issues, they have a number of disadvantages. For one thing if we ignore the alleged ecological/scientific foundations for judgments about environmental well-being, as Sagoff suggests, then we shall lose the ability to use policy needs to drive scientific progress. If necessity is the mother of invention, then the necessity to ground environmental policy on a firm scientific foundation could possibly speed the invention/development of scientific theory in ecology (see Lubchenko *et al.* 1991). By arguing that we should ignore possible scientific foundations for judgments about environmental well-being, Sagoff commits himself to a self-fulfilling prophecy: that we shall not discover firm foundations for ecology, and that we shall not rid the science of many of its current uncertainties. Sagoff also begs the question of whether or not ecology will ever be able to develop such foundations. His begging the question makes this development less likely.

Likewise, in eschewing the scientific foundations of environmentalism, in favor of ethical and aesthetic arguments, Sagoff would require environmentalists and developers/industrialists to change their strategies for winning policy conflicts. Developers and industrialists, in particular, however, are unlikely to do so. If there are minimal ecological grounds for supporting a particular move, then developers and industrialists are likely to capitalize on this fact, not merely to ignore ecological arguments. They know that, in the absence of the ability to demonstrate conclusively that some environment-related action will cause clear, ecologically definable harm, they are innocent until proved guilty. Hence, although environmentalists may try to avoid ecological arguments related to environmental protection, because of the uncertainty involved, it is questionable whether their opponents will allow them to do so. This is both because ecological uncertainties benefit the opponents of environmentalism, and because scientific data or the lack of them typically trump other arguments. Moreover, even if it were possible to avoid ecological arguments in discussing environmental protection, it is not clear that it would be desirable to do so, for reasons already spelled out in the first response. Avoiding difficulties rarely makes them go away.

Another problem with Sagoff's arguments, against using ecological claims for environmental protection, is that it may not be possible to determine what is environmentally *un*healthy, as Sagoff suggests. Indeed, as we argued in the last chapter, we cannot be sure of the ecological foundations for such judgments. Admittedly, the most egregious sorts of environmental harm may be obvious, and we can avoid them, as Sagoff recommends. Obvious harm, however, is usually not the source of the policy conflict. Controversy typically surrounds, not cases of obvious harm, but boundary cases where the harm is uncertain/unknown. If so, then focusing on obvious harm may not be of much help in resolving environmental policy disputes. Hence, Sagoff's suggestion may be useful, but not in the situations (borderline cases where harm is uncertain/unknown) where we most need help.

Most importantly, Sagoff's remarks do not address the essential ethical, epistemological, and professional difficulties facing scientists who must interpret their results (see chapter 4). Even if ecologists take Sagoff's advice and do not try to use ecology for environmental policymaking, they must be able to interpret their results. They must know how to deal with problematic ecological concepts, theories, evidence, and value judgments. Interpretation of results is unavoidable if ecology or any other science is to have any meaning. Moreover, given numerous scientific, environmental, and policy controversies whose resolution often relies on such interpretations, we need to provide some guidance for ecologists and other scientists who repeatedly must decide how to present/interpret their findings, in the face of empirical underdetermination and epistemic value judgments. Hence, the real issue is not whether ecology can help policymakers. It must. The real issue is how ecologists can interpret their results in the most desirable way. They cannot avoid interpretations, even if they are problematic. Because they cannot, we must at least try to assess the extent to which, in particular cases, ecology can help ground environmental policy. For pragmatic reasons, we ought not follow Sagoff in assuming, a priori, that ecology has nothing to offer policymakers. There are also scientific reasons, as we shall argue shortly, for believing that the discipline has much to give to environmental policymaking.

5.2 New directions for ecological laws and theories

The point of our discussing (in chapters 2 and 3) some of the problems with ecological concepts and theories has not been to argue for the futility of trying to use ecology to ground environmental policy. Rather, our point is to establish the fact that ecology must be applied in extremely complex and probabilistic ways if it is to support policy, and to warn that often the application of general ecological theory is premature (see Walters 1991, p. 520). Later, we shall spell out what some of these complex and probabilistic applications – of lower-level ecological theories and regularities – might be like.

Although there are rough generalizations that can aid problemsolving in specific situations, it is unlikely that we shall be able to find many (if any) simple, deterministic laws that we can easily apply to a variety of particular communities or species. One reason why such laws are unlikely is that, as we argued in chapter 2, fundamental ecological terms (like "community" and "stability") are imprecise and vague, and therefore unable to support precise empirical laws. A related reason why such laws are unlikely is that, although the term "species" has a commonly accepted meaning, and although evolutionary theory gives a precise technical sense to the term, there is no general agreement in biology on an explicit definition of "species." Likewise there is agreement neither on what counts as causally sufficient or necessary conditions for a set of organisms to be a species, nor on whether species are individuals. Phenetic taxonomy has failed to generate a workable taxonomy, perhaps because species are not natural kinds, and perhaps because facts cannot be carved up and rearranged in accord with the hopes of numerical taxonomists (Rosenberg 1985, pp. 182–187; see Sokal and Sneath 1963; Hull 1988, pp. 102ff.).

Moreover, there are at least four prominent definitions of species – the biological, the evolutionary, the ecological, and the phylogenetic. These four are neither mutually exclusive nor exhaustive; they have different conceptual emphases. Each of them is fundamentally flawed. The *biological species notion*, grounded on reproductive isolation, is problematic, for example, because there is typically no operation that will tell us whether interbreeding is possible. Also, the biological species notion is difficult to reconcile with the existence of asexual species, and the notion seems incompatible with gradual interspecies anagenesis. The *evolutionary species notion*, stressing the response of a unitary lineage to selection, is likewise problematic, for example, because of its apparent inability to deal with anagenesis. Also, it appears ultimately to need to appeal to morphological differences (as does the biological species concept) and hence to renounce a strictly evolutionary notion of species. The *ecological species notion*, based on species' positions in an ecosystem, fails largely because there seems to be no non-circular way to identify niches or adaptive zones, independent of their inhabitants. Finally, the *phylogenetic species notion*, one type of evolutionary species concept, is based on parental patterns of ancestry and descent (Cracraft 1983, pp. 169 170). This species notion is problematic because it is sometimes difficult to infer different parental patterns of ancestry and descent and therefore difficult to separate lineages on the basis of shared, derived characteristics. The phylogenetic species concept is likewise controversial, in some circles, because its mathematical models place more emphasis on questionable inferences about phylogeny rather than on morphology or on fossil evidence (Kitcher 1985c; Rosenberg 1985, pp. 187–200; Hull 1988, pp. 131–157; see also Mayr 1942, p. 120, 1963, p. 28, 1982, pp. 273–275; Simpson 1961; Ghiselin 1969; Hull 1974, 1976b, 1978, 1988; Van Valen 1976; Gould 1981; Sober 1981).

Admittedly, what is correct about each of these four accounts of the species concept is that they are anti-essentialist. They recognize that, if there is an evolution of species then, for each species, there is no non-trivial set of properties of organisms that are distinctive of them and necessary and sufficient for membership in that species. In other words, what is correct about the four anti-essentialist accounts of the species concept is that they recognize the constraints set by the theory of evolution. Or, as Darwin put it, the most significant characteristic about a given species is the variation among its members. What happens in systematics is that each of these four definitions of "species" is employed, but in different contexts and because of different reasons and different needs. The upshot, as Rosenberg (1985, pp. 200–202) observes, is that the notion of a species is nothing like the physicists' notion of an element. There is no universal specification of the species concept that fixes the properties that determine species membership, no link between general theory in biology and taxonomy. And if not, then there can be no homogeneous class of items called "species." (For discussion of arguments that species are individuals, see Rosenberg 1985, pp. 204–212.) Species are not natural kinds, like elements. Elements have a common atomic structure that justifies their taxonomy in the periodic table; they have differences in atomic structure that account for chemical and physical variations. Because it is not clear that species labels represent real biological kinds, it is unlikely that ecology can give us general, deterministic laws about species. From a logical point of view, if taxa are individuals (see Hull 1978; Ghiselin 1987; Mayr 1987), then statements that mention *particular species* cannot be laws of nature (see Van Der Steen and Kamminga 1991). Hence, there cannot be deterministic laws about individual species.

Instead, what ecology often gives us is mathematical models, like the Lotka–Volterra equations that provide us, for example, with an hypothesized relationship between predator and prey species. Such models do not express a general, empirical law, but rather a more-or-less accurate fact about a particular situation. Hence, despite the professed aims of many ecologists for "general mechanisms" (Underwood and Denley 1984, pp. 151ff.) to account for ecological phenomena, it seems unlikely that such goals will generate general, deterministic, ecological laws that have no exceptions. Such laws and theory appear unlikely in ecology because the apparent biological patterns keep changing, both because of heritable variations and because of evolution. Moreover, particular communities do not recur, at different times and places, and particular species do not recur, at different times and places. Both the communities and the species that comprise them are *unique* (see, for example, Norse 1990, pp. 17ff. and Wilcove 1990, p. 83). In other words, no environment or community is ever the same, ever exactly like another. Hence, although ecologists' mathematical models may have substantial heuristic power, it may be unrealistic to think that they will ever develop into general laws that are universally applicable and able to provide precise predictions for environmental applications.

Whether or not there are exceptionless general laws and deterministic general theory in ecology, however, is in part a question of whether ecology is an historical science; whether historical sciences differ from non-historical ones in any important respects; and whether prediction and explanation are possible in historical sciences. We shall not address all these issues here, both because they would take us too far afield from our practical and ecological concerns, and because other philosophers and scientists already have done so (see, for example, Simpson1964; Ruse 1971, 1989; Hull 1974; Fetzer 1975; Grene and Mendelsohn 1976; Mayr 1982; Rosenberg 1985; Sattler 1986, pp. 186ff.; Sober 1988a). Apart from what we believe about historical explanation, however, as we have already suggested in earlier chapters, there are strong reasons for believing that hypothetical-deductive explanation (see Ruse 1971) will not enable ecology to attain deterministic general theory. There are problems with methodological value judgments (ch.4), with basic concepts like "community" and "species," and with the uniqueness of ecological events.

Of course, every event is unique in some respects (see Stent 1978, p. 219). And, as Hull (1974, p. 98) points out, repetition of unique events is in principle impossible. Unique events, such as "the extinction of the Florida panther" (see chapter 8), however, can be described in terms of general concepts, such as "extinction" and "panther." Hence, one cannot categorically exclude the possibility that we may one day come up with general laws concerning panthers and extinctions. If we did so, then some aspects of a unique event could be explained in terms of the covering-law model. (Perhaps the most persuasive explanations of particular occurrences, often in the context of practical applications, come from the causal accounts of persons such as Fetzer (1974a, b; 1975), Railton (1980, 1981), Humphreys (1981, 1982, 1991), Scriven (1982), Salmon (1984, 1989) or Cartwright (1989a, b). Later, we shall discuss the causal account of scientific explanation more carefully). When we refer to unique events in their uniqueness, however, explanation in terms of the covering-law model is probably not possible because, at the experimental level, unique events cannot be conceptualized fully; they are unique (see Sattler 1986, pp. 188ff.). In theory, however, initial conditions might be able to capture some of the uniqueness of the event. As Van Der Steen and Kamminga (1991; see Ruse 1973, pp. 65–66) point out, that is why one needs both initial conditions and laws in explanatory premises. Consider a law of the following form: "if an entity of type E is subjected to stimulus S at [time] t, it will show behavior B at $t + 1$. If one adds the information that a *particular* entity of type E gets S at a *particular* time (initial condition), one can infer that this entity will show B at a particular time (one time unit later)." This amounts to the explanation of a unique event on the basis of law (Van Der Steen and Kamminga 1991). If the event is unique, however, it is typically difficult to specify the relevant initial conditions and to know what counts as behavior B. Often one must have extensive historical information in order to do so (see Kiester 1982, pp. 355ff.; see Fetzer 1975). Hence, from an empirical point of view, complexity and uniqueness hamper elaboration of general, deterministic laws in ecology. One alternative, as Gorovitz and MacIntyre (1976) agree, is to deemphasize general, theoretical laws and to emphasize natural history.

Admittedly, an ecologist may try to discover laws by applying useful findings about a particular model system to another situation or to another species or community. Often models have applications beyond their original domains. Nevertheless, these models are unlikely to help us develop general, exceptionless laws. Their components – for example, species – do not appear to be natural or biological kinds. Indeed, biology does not appear to have deterministic laws governing particular species (Van Der Steen and Kamminga 1991). Yet, to carve up the world by means of general, deterministic laws, we need to know the natural kinds. And if so, then perhaps the best paradigms of laws in ecology do not mention the species category at all. Eldredge (1985; see also Brandon 1990, pp. 72ff.), for example, argues that because species are members of a genealogical hierarchy only, they do not take part in biological processes. If Eldredge and others are correct, and if models about species are the best that we can have in ecology, then although laws about the species *category* are possible, ecology is likely to be characterized by empirical generalizations that admit of exceptions – natural history – or, alternatively, by statistical regularities.

Moreover, the ultimate units of ecological theory, for example, organisms, are few in number as compared with the ultimate units in other scientific theories. These other units, for example, molecules or subatomic particles, can easily be replicated; those of ecology cannot. This means that ecologists can rarely discount the random or purely statistical nature of events or changes; one disturbance in one key environment may be enough to wipe out a species. The random nature of many ecological events, the problem of replication, and the importance of disturbance all suggest that perhaps the best candidates for ecological laws are statistical. One example that comes to mind is Rosen's (1978) method of historical biogeographical analysis, which relies mostly on phylogenetic inference rather than on the more usual interpretation of geographic distributions. The method searches for improbable levels of concordance when phylogenies (cladograms) of several taxa are superimposed upon locations (so-called "areagrams"). Simberloff *et al.* (1981) and Savage (1983) discuss ways to calculate probabilities of concordance. Moreover, because statistical laws arguably have the characteristics essential to scientific laws, for example, universality (Schlick 1949; Hempel 1965, pp. 376–386; Achinstein 1971; Van Valen 1976; Earman 1978; Kitts and Kitts 1979; Wilson 1979), it could easily be argued that statistical laws constitute evidence for the claim that ecology provides genuine scientific explanations (Shrader-Frechette and McCoy 1990). Of course, none of these considerations establishes that it is *impossible* to formulate valid, deterministic, ecological laws. The point is that organisms which are similar at some level of organization may have different subsystems. Although all properties of all subsystems are never necessary in explaining a particular phenomenon, the uniqueness and complexity of such properties are so pervasive, among organisms, that deterministic ecological laws appear unlikely. It is not clear how one could demonstrate that such laws are impossible (see Van Der Steen and Kamminga 1991).

5.3 Insights from the National Academy report

Because of the problems associated with ecological concepts, deterministic laws, and proposed general theories in ecology, it is unlikely that theoretical arguments alone (such as the one just given for using statistical laws in ecology) would convince many persons of how community ecology might be applied in environmental problemsolving. Instead, what is needed is to demonstrate the utility of ecology in one or more particular case studies that illustrate concretely how ecological information might be used in specific situations. Of course, all our case-specific knowledge presupposes some lower-level ecological theory, such as demographic theory or population genetics. Such theoretical presuppositions, however, tend to be close to empirical regularities and therefore less inferential, less general, and more testable than the general theories we criticized in chapter 3. Hence, although we cannot avoid theory in using the case-study method, we can avoid the more questionable uses of general theory that we criticized earlier.

The case-history approach is exactly the one taken by a recent committee of the US National Academy of Sciences (NAS) and the National Research Council (Orians *et al.* 1986), when the committee was asked to assess the applications of ecological theory. The committee's rationale for the assessment was similar to our own; there are overwhelming problems with applying general ecological theory, given that species are not obviously natural, biological kinds, and given that each individual in a population is unique. Likewise, the committee's conclusion was similar to our own: We need to illustrate how case-specific ecological *knowledge*, rather than general ecological *theory*, might be used in environmental problemsolving (see Orians *et al.* 1986, pp. 1, 5).

As the US National Academy committee also recognized, ecology's greatest predictive success occurs in cases that involve only one or two species, perhaps because ecological generalizations are most fully developed for relatively simple systems. This is why, for example, ecological management of game and fish populations through regulation of hunting and fishing can often be successful (Orians *et al.* 1986, p. 8). Applying this insight to our discussion of what ecology can do, we conclude that ecology might be most helpful when it does not try to predict complex interactions among many species, but instead attempts to predict what will happen for only one or two taxa in a particular case. Predictions for one or two taxa are often successful, in spite of the fact that general ecological theory is weak. The success occurs in part because, despite the problems with general ecological theory, there are numerous lower-level theories in ecology that provide reliable predictions. Application of lower-level theory about the evolution of cooperative breeding, for example, has provided many successes in managing red-cockaded woodpeckers (Walters 1991, p. 518). Such cases suggest that the practical and predictive successes might be coming from a source other than the general theory. In the case of the red-cockaded woodpecker, for instance, successful management and predictions also appear to have come from natural-history information, for example, about the presence of cavities in trees that serve as habitat (Walters 1991, pp. 506ff.). Likewise, if the case studies used in the National Academy committee report are representative, then some of the most successful ecological applications arise when (and because) scientists have a great deal of knowledge about the natural history of the specific organisms investigated in a particular case study (see Orians *et al.* 1986, p. 13). As the authors of the National Academy report put it, "the success of the cases described . . . depended on such [natural-history] information" (Orians *et al.* 1986, p. 16).

The vampire-bat case study, for instance, is an excellent example of the value of specific natural-history information when ecologists are interested in practical problemsolving (see Orians *et al.* 1986, p. 28). The goal in the bat study was to find a control agent that affected only the "pest" species of concern, the vampire bat. The specific natural-history information that was useful in finding and using a control, diphenadione, included the facts that the bats are much more susceptible than cattle to the action of anticoagulants; that they roost extremely closely to each other; that they groom each other; that their rate of reproduction is low; that they do not migrate; and that they forage only in the absence of moonlight (Mitchell in Orians *et al.* 1986, pp. 151–164). Using this natural-history information, ecologists were able to provide a firm foundation for policy about controlling vampire bats. Rather than attempting to apply some general ecological theory, "top-down," they scrutinized a particular case, "bottom-up," in order to gain explanatory insights. Their explanation is local in the sense that it shows how particular occurrences come about. It explains specific phenomena in terms of collections of causal processes and interactions. Their explanation does not mean, moreover, that general laws play no role in ecological explanations, because the mechanisms discussed in the vampire-bat study operate in accord with general laws of nature. Likewise their explanation does not mean that all explanations are of particular occurrences, since we can often provide causal accounts of regularities. Rather, their explanation, like the account we wish to emphasize, is "bottom-up" in that it appeals to the underlying microstructure of the phenomena being explained. "Top-down" explanation, however, appeals to the construction of a coherent world picture and to fitting particular facts into this unified picture (Salmon 1989, pp. 182–184).

The success of the NAS case study, with its "bottom-up" approach to scientific explanation, suggests that ecological method often might be characterized as a method of case studies. Such a method is particularly needed in unique situations, like most of those in community ecology, where we cannot replicate singular events. Paradoxically, however, as Hull (1988, p. 28) points out, many experts are suspicious of scientific research that focuses on detailed case studies (see Kazdin 1980, pp. 9–32, 1981, 1982; Edelson 1988, p. 255), even though case studies are widely used in teaching science and philosophy of science (see Kitcher 1977). We shall argue that these suspicions are frequently misplaced. If we can use the vampire-bat study as a model for future ecological research, and if the National Academy Committee is correct, then both suggest that accounts of ecological method might do well to focus on practical applications of the science. Moreover, if ecology turns out to be a science of case studies and practical applications, it is not obvious that this is a defect. Ecology may not be flawed because it must sacrifice universality for utility and practicality, or because it must sacrifice generality for the precision gained through case studies.

5.4 The method of case studies

But what is the case-study method? In subsequent paragraphs, we shall define and characterize the method, using examples from the NAS analysis of how to conserve the spotted owl in the Pacific Northwest. Various authors have identified the method of case studies with techniques associated with fieldwork, ethnography, participant observation, qualitative research, exploratory research, and hypothesis generation (see Merriam 1988, p. 5). Campbell (1984, p. 8) claims that the method of case studies is "quasi-experimental" – an interesting choice of terms, since ecologists (see Parker 1989, pp. 199ff.) sometimes classify their methods as "classical experimental," "quasi-experimental," and "observational." Classical experimental methods involve manipulation, a control, replicated observations, and randomization. Observational methods may not include any of the four components (randomization, and so on). Between these two methodological extremes lie quasi-experimental methods, like the method of case studies, that embody some manipulations but which lack one or more of the four features of classical experiments (Parker 1989, p. 199).

The method of case studies is (in part) "experimental" – as opposed to merely observational or descriptive – in that its goal is specification of cause-and-effect relationships by means of manipulating some of the variables of interest (Merriam 1988, pp. 6–7). It is "quasi"-experimental, however, in that control of these variables often is difficult, if not impossible. Because the method, at best, controls for only a few, but "explicitly specified," rival hypotheses, Campbell (1984, p. 8) says that it is closer to the classical or "older paradigm" of the experimental method, rather than to the newer one. The older paradigm, he says, is epitomized by experimental isolation and laboratory control. Within this paradigm, for example, scientists shield their apparatus from radiation and control for temperature and moisture. Which hypotheses are controlled for is typically a function of the current disputations in science. The newer paradigm of the experimental method, however, "purports to control an infinite number of 'rival hypotheses' without specifying what any of them are. This newer approach is epitomized by the randomized trials of medical and pharmaceutical research and by statisticians' mathematical models" (Campbell 1984, p. 8). Admittedly, randomized trials usually are not possible in community ecology, as they are in medical and pharmaceutical research. In ecology, quasi-experimental methods often involve some manipulation and some partially replicated observations. The interactions are so complex (see, for example, Levins 1968a, pp. 5ff.; McEvoy 1986, p. 83), however, with uncertainties typically existing regarding (1) subject and target systems, (2) unknowable boundary conditions, (3) unknown bias in the results, (4) the nature of the underlying phenomena, and (5) poor data, that it is impossible to do classical experimentation or even to specify an uncontroversial null hypothesis. Indeed, such difficulties mean that quasi-experimental methods often are quite limited in ecological studies, particularly long-term investigations (Parker 1989, pp. 199–200).

In addition to being quasi-experimental, the method of case studies is also partially descriptive, as the natural-history component illustrated in the vampire-bat study. Generally speaking, the method likewise tends to be *particularistic* (focusing on a specific process or phenomenon), *heuristic* (encouraging further discovery and investigation, rather than confirmation of hypotheses), and *inductive* (rather than deductive). It is a method that also employs multiple sources and kinds of evidence (Yin 1981a, b, 1984; Merriam 1988, pp. 12–21). Finally, the method of case studies is *wholistic* in that it "investigates a contemporary phenomenon within its real-life context" (Yin 1984, p. 23).

5.4.1 General characteristics of the method of case studies

In general, the case-study method aims at testing, clarifying, amending, and evaluating examples or cases. Unfortunately, in investigating certain examples or cases – such as whether the $-3/2$ power thinning law is actually an "ecological law" in plant ecology (see, for example, Pahor 1985) – there is no simple algorithm that one can follow. In using the consequentialist method, one follows principles of hypothesis deduction. In using a case study, however, one must confront the facts of a particular situation, and then look for a way to make sense of them. Often one knows neither the relevant variables nor whether the situation can be replicated. Indeed, in some of the best case studies ever performed – those cited in the recent National Academy of Sciences report (see Orians *et al.* 1986) – ecologists performing the studies remain divided on the issue of the relevant variables. In the case study on how to conserve the regional spotted-owl population in the Pacific Northwest (Salwasser 1986; Thomas *et al.* 1990), for example, some theorists claimed that limiting genetic deterioration is the most critical variable in preserving the owl and determining minimal population sizes. Other researchers, however, maintained that demographic (not genetic) factors are the most critical variables. As a consequence of such uncertainties, those who use the method of case studies are often forced to eschew precise, quantitative methods of analysis and instead "to analyze, evaluate, and make recommendations" about events (Donaldson 1990, p. 14).

In order to analyze, evaluate, and make recommendations about the component events or relationships in a particular study, one typically makes a number of inferences about the most significant phenomena; about what caused the events/relationships to occur; and how typical they are. In other words, one typically uses informal causal, inductive, retroductive, and consequentialist inferences in order to "make sense" of a particular example or situation (see Grunbaum 1984, 1988, pp. 624ff.; Gini 1985; Carson 1986, p. 36; Edelson 1988, pp. xxxi–xxxii, 237–251). To make sense of a particular situation, one might construct models that appeal to some theory having heuristic power. In the case of ecology, however, such an appeal does not presuppose that *general theories* in ecology have significant predictive power in practical environmental problemsolving. In the famous spotted-owl case study from the NAS volume (Orians *et al.* 1986), for example, ecologists "made sense" of the situation by means of a number of inductive inferences. These inferences were based on observations about reproductive ecology, dispersal, and foraging behavior. As such, the inductive inferences in the spotted-owl case might be said to be "quantitative natural history" (Salwasser 1986, p. 227; see Ervin 1989, pp. 86ff., 205ff.; Norse 1990, pp. 73ff.).

Making sense of a case study, however, does not stop with causal, inductive, retroductive, or consequentialist inferences. It also requires practical insight into the situation (Donaldson 1990, p. 17). Practical reasoning aims at action or at guiding scientific behavior, unlike the theoretical reasoning that aims at rules or concepts. (Some scholars identify the "practical reasoning" of the case-study method as "casuistry," a non-pejorative sixteenth and seventeenth-century term meaning "discerning judgment" (Carson 1986, p. 36).) Although proponents of the casuistical method adhered to no particular theory about the norms governing actions, they did employ the tools of Aristotelian rhetoric: using examples and maxims to reason about recommended actions (Jonsen 1986).

In the practical reasoning that characterizes use of the case-study method, one moves from the informal, non-deductive inference that a particular scientific phenomenon is analogous to another, to the recognition that this analogy is a *means* for reaching an *end*, ideally, causal explanation of the phenomenon (see Adelman 1974, p. 215; de Vries 1986, p. 199; Donaldson 1990, p. 17). In evaluating alternative means to the same end, namely, providing a causal account of a particular phenomenon, the case-study analyst's main objectives are twofold: To pose and to assess competing explanations for the same phenomenon or set of events, and to try to discover whether (and if so, how) such explanations might apply to other situations (see Yin 1984, pp. 16ff.). When they wrote *All the President's Men* (1974), for example, Bernstein and Woodward used a popular, journalistic version of the method of case studies. They posed and assessed competing explanations for how and why the Watergate coverup occurred. They also suggested, if only briefly, how their explanations might apply to other situations of political power and coverup (see Yin 1984, p. 24).

5.4.2 Five components of case studies

In order to pose and assess competing explanations of the same case, scientists need to consider at least five factors (See Edelson 1988, pp. 278–308; Merriam 1988):

1. the research design of the case study;
2. the characteristics of the investigator;
3. the types of evidence accepted;
4. the analysis of the evidence;
5. the evaluation of the case study.

The research design, the first component of the case study, is a blueprint. It is a plan for assembling, organizing, and evaluating information according to a particular problem definition and specific goals for how to use the research findings (Merriam 1988, p. 6; see Edelson 1988, pp. 231ff.). The research design is what links the data to be collected and the resulting conclusions to the initial questions of the study. Because the use of case studies is so new, as Yin (1984, p. 27) points out, there is no "catalog" of alternative research designs that has been developed for the method. There are not even textbooks like the well-known volume by Cook and Campbell (1979) that summarizes the various research designs for quasi-experimental situations. Nevertheless, most research designs have at least five distinct components (see Yin 1984, pp. 29ff.; Merriam 1988, pp. 36ff.):

1. the questions to be investigated;
2. the hypotheses;
3. the units of analysis;
4. the logic linking data to hypotheses;
5. the criteria for interpreting the findings.

Later, in chapter 8, we shall illustrate the case-study method and its components, including its research design, by examining the question whether it is possible to save the Florida panther, an endangered subspecies, in the wild. In the spotted-owl case study from the NAS volume (see Orians *et al.* 1986), the research design focused on two main *questions*: First, what are the minimal regional population sizes of owls that are necessary to insure long-term survival? Second, what are the amounts and distribution of old-growth forests (the owls' habitat) necessary to insure their survival (Salwasser 1986, p. 231)? Although a given research design involves multiple *hypotheses*, one hypothesis in the spotted-owl case was the following: "This particular spotted-owl management area (SOMA) is supporting as many pairs of owls as expected on the basis of calculations of N_e, effective population size" (Salwasser 1986, p. 242). The *unit of analysis* in the research design of the spotted-owl case study was the existing population of individual owls. The northwestern regional spotted-owl population is currently estimated at approximately 2,000 in the US (Salwasser 1986, p. 240). In other case studies, of course, the unit of analysis could be an individual organism, for example, or there could be multiple units of analysis.

The most problematic aspect of the research design of a case study is the fourth component, the logic linking the data to the hypotheses. Essentially this "logic" is a way to assess whether the data tend to confirm the hypotheses. Because the auxiliary assumptions, methodological value judgments, and controlling parameters in a case study frequently are not clear, and because a case study often represents a unique situation, scientists typically are unable to use hypothetico-deductive means of employing case-study data to confirm an hypothesis. Instead, they are often forced to use informal means of inference, or what Kaplan (1964, pp. 333–335) calls "pattern" models of inference. Deductive models give us predictive power, whereas pattern models of inference enable us merely to fill in and extend data, so as to formulate some hypotheses or patterns. Discussing the relationship between the annual number of traffic fatalities and automobile speed limit in the state of Connecticut, Campbell (1975) provided an example of the informal inferences he called "pattern matching." Each of his two hypotheses corresponded to a different pattern of fatalities. These hypotheses were that the speed limit had no effect on number of fatalities, and that it had an effect. Although he was not able to formulate an uncontroversial null hypothesis and to test it in a statistically reliable way, Campbell was able to conclude that, apparently, there was a pattern of "no effects" (Campbell 1969; see Yin 1984, pp. 33–35). He simply looked at the number of fatalities, over time, and determined that there was no systematic trend.

In using informal inferences to examine whether data are patterned, however, one can always question whether an actual inference is correct. In the spotted-owl case study, for instance, the ecologists used a number of "patterns" from theoretical population genetics and ecology, including specific formulae for factors such as F, the inbreeding coefficient. Because some of the variables in the formula for F, for example, cannot be measured in wild populations, the ecologists' informal inferences about actual F are questionable (Salwasser 1986, p. 236).

The issue of the correctness of informal inferences raises the question of the fifth component of research designs: the criteria for interpreting a study's findings. Campbell (1969) claimed, for example, that his data matched one pattern (no effect) much better than another, but it is not clear how close data have to be, in order to be considered a "match." He admitted that his interrupted time series, showing annual traffic fatalities over nine years, exhibited an apparent "statistically signifi-cant downward shift in the series after the crackdown [lower speed limits]." Nevertheless, he concluded that an "alternative explanation" of this significant effect exists (Campbell 1969, p. 413). Part of this alternative explanation is that there is no control (in the traffic-fatality data) for the effects of other potential change agents. One important agent of potential change was increased enforcement of speed limits, a factor that could also explain the lower traffic fatalities (Campbell 1969, p. 416). Also, because his time series show great instability, Campbell points out that any subsequent year would, on average, show fewer traffic fatalities "purely as a function of that instability" (Campbell 1969, p. 414). In other words, he claims that if we examine any time series with variability, then pick a point that is "highest so far," on average the next point will be lower. Moreover, while in principle the degree of expected regression can be computed from auto-correlation of series like Campbell's, he notes that the data are not extensive enough to do this with any confidence (1969, p. 414). He had five data points prior to the reduced speed limit, and four data points after it. These are an insufficient basis for reliable statistical testing. Campbell's problems, in interpreting his patterns, point up exactly the difficulty with deciding whether data fit a pattern or hypothesis in a case study: the case is unique, so it is difficult to determine the correctness of the inference from data to hypothesis. The inference is difficult because it rests on a number of methodological value judgments, for example, that there are no other potential change agents that explain the data. As we noted in chapter 4, cognitive or methodological value judgments occur through-out science, even hypothetico-deductive science. The same criteria for making reasonable methodological value judgments – criteria such as explanatory power and simplicity – likewise apply in making judg-ments about the research design of case studies. Later, we shall discuss some Wittgensteinian means for evaluating the informal inferences that characterize the method of case studies.

If one analyzes the social-scientific literature on case studies, one can discover a number of criteria for assessing the quality of research designs. Kidder (1981) and Yin (1984 pp. 35ff.), for example, both discuss four tests for research design: construct validity; internal validity of the causal inferences; external validity or applicability of the case study; and reliability. One tests for *construct validity* of the research design by employing multiple sources of evidence; by attempting to establish chains of evidence; and by having experts review the draft of the case-study report. One tests for the *internal validity* or causal validity of the research design by doing pattern matching, as exemplified in the Campbell case already noted, and by attempting to provide alternative explanations, other than those included in the research design (see Grunbaum 1984, 1988). One tests for *external applicability* of the research design by attempting to replicate the case-study conclusions in other situations. To the extent that the case is wholly unique, however, replication will be impossible. Nevertheless, there may be some type of limited generalization, theorizing, or application that is possible on the basis of only a single case. The research design is thus most successful if it not only spurs many hypotheses, criticisms, and explanations of phenomena, but also provides such applications, especially predictive power in practical, environmental applications. One tests for the *reliability* of a research design by using a case-study protocol. A protocol is an organized list of tasks, procedures, and rules to be following in doing the case study. The protocol is specified, ahead of time, so that it can help insure that one takes account of all relevant variables and methods. In the spotted-owl study from the NAS report, for example, the protocol consisted of eight steps. One early step was to perform censuses (of the owl) on all national forest land. A subsequent step in the protocol was to determine habitat requirements for the owl. Still another step in the protocol was to perform a risk analysis of the demographic, generic, and geographical results of different management alternatives. The final step of the protocol was to monitor the various SOMAs, in order to determine whether those managing the owls were achieving their goals (Salwasser 1986, pp. 238–242). Other tests for the reliability of the research design require developing, amending, and continually improving a database against which the case study can be re-assessed. The final step in the spotted-owl protocol, for example, described just such an updating and revision of the spotted-owl plan and conclusions (Salwasser 1986, pp. 238–242). One also assesses the reliability of the research design, in part, by attempting to determine whether another researcher, evaluating the same case, would draw the same conclusions.

In addition to giving attention to research design, scientists using the method of case studies also need to take account of a second important factor: the characteristics of the investigator, since they affect the quality of the scientific work. The investigator performing the case study should be a person who, to the greatest extent possible, has a high tolerance for ambiguity; who is unbiased by preconceived notions; who has a firm grasp of the technical and epistemological issues being studied; who is adaptive and flexible; and who has an inquiring mind: that is, a person who is able to ask good questions and to see the situation in a variety of ways (see Yin 1984, pp. 55ff.; Merriam 1988, pp. 36ff.).

Besides the investigator, a third important factor affecting the quality of a case study is the evidence used. Evidence for case studies may come from at least six different sources: documents, archival records, interviews, direct observation, participant observation, and physical artifacts. Use of each of these six sources calls for different methodological procedures and techniques. (For a discussion of these six types of evidence and how they are employed, see Yin 1984, pp. 79–98; see also Merriam 1988, pp. 104ff.) In using each of these types of evidence, it is important for the scientist to engage in a comprehensive literature review; to use multiple sources of evidence; to create a data or evidentiary base; to report the findings of the case study; and to maintain a chain of evidence so that an impartial reader/observer is able to follow the reasoning, from the initial research questions, all the way through to the conclusions (see Merriam 1988, pp. 61ff.).

In examining, categorizing, combining, and evaluating all these different types of evidence used in the case study, the expert needs to employ a fourth component affecting the quality of the work: methods of analysis. In so doing, the scientist uses three general analytic strategies. The *first* such strategy is to develop descriptions of the case, and eventually a description that is capable of organizing the data and hypotheses around it. Formulating a description presupposes that one is able to develop categories in terms of which to recognize and collect the data. Developing categories, in turn, presupposes looking for regularities in the data (see Lincoln and Guba 1985; Merriam 1988, pp. 133ff.). A *second* evidential strategy is more theoretical. It consists of formulating hypotheses, patterns, or possible causal explanations for the data that are collected, typically through inductive methods (see Merriam 1988, pp. 13–17, 140ff.). Organizing inductive events chronologically is a common basis for time-series analysis, a form of generating patterns that is frequently useful for formulating hypotheses. Database-management programs can also be helpful in recognizing patterns and describing them. Often such descriptions help to generate possible chronological patterns, causal explanations, or hypotheses and vice versa. A *third* evidential strategy, informal testing, consists of comparing the empirically based patterns in the case study with the predictions generated by the hypotheses and causal explanations (see Merriam 1988, pp. 147ff.). Available statistical techniques are not likely to be relevant in using this third analytic strategy because, in a case study, none of the variables in the hypothesized pattern are likely to have a variance; each of them probably represents only a single data point (see Yin 1984, pp. 99–120; Merriam 1988, pp. 123ff., 163ff.).

After analyzing the evidence, the scientist can compose the case-study report. The main possible compositional forms of the report are chronological, theory-building, linear-analytic, or comparative. The chronological form consists of providing a case history in temporal order. Theory-building case studies provide an explanation of the case, usually in causal form. The linear-analytic form of composition is often followed in research reports, grant requests, and project reports. It consists of covering a sequence of topics, such as the problem being studied, methods used, findings from the data, and significance and applications of the conclusions. Comparative case-study reports assess alternative descriptions or explanations of the same case; this form requires one to repeat the same case study two or more times (see Yin 1984, pp. 126–135; Edelson 1988, pp. 278–308; Merriam 1988, pp. 185ff.).

The fifth and final component of the case-study method is to evaluate the case-study report and conclusions. Sometimes this can be done by checking internal validity, how well one's conclusions match reality. Frequently, one can also test reliability of case-study conclusions by attempting to replicate one's findings. Replication of a phenomenon is typically not possible, however, or one would not need to use the case-study method in the first place. Usually one assesses the scientific validity of a case study, in an informal way, by comparing the hypotheses and conclusions with alternative assumptions and explanatory accounts. One also evaluates the case study in terms of whether it is a significant example, not only from the point of view of validity and reliability, but also in terms of its practical, logical, methodological, and epistemological importance for science generally. Likewise, one assesses the case study in terms of standard explanatory values, such as completeness, coherence, consistency, heuristic power, predictive power, and so on. Often this final evaluation is best accomplished by procedures that call for outside evaluation by experts (see Merriam 1988, pp. 170ff.). In this outside evaluation, experts assess each of the five central factors affecting the quality of the case study: the research design; the characteristics of the investigator; the types of evidence accepted; the analysis of the evidence; and the evaluation of the case study.

5.4.3 Strengths of the method of case studies

Although the method of case studies typically employs many informal inferences that are difficult to evaluate, it has a number of strengths not shared by scientific methods that are clearer and more precise. James Byrant Conant, discussing the introduction of the method of case studies in the 1870s at Harvard Law School, by Dean Christopher Columbus Langdell, said that it was so innovative that "Langdell is to be placed among the great American inventors of the nineteenth-century." Conant claimed that Langdell's "uniquely American" contribution "was as revolutionary in its impact on the United States as, say, the McCormick reaper" (Evans 1981, p. xxiv).

As the natural-history knowledge gleaned from the vampire-bat study (see section 5.3) shows, one of the greatest assets of the method of case studies is that it meets many practical and scientific goals. (1) It enables ecologists to gain a measure of practical control over environmental problems, like pest management. Also (2) it allows us to make rough generalizations, for example, about a taxon's susceptibility to anticoagulants, even though exceptions to these generalizations cannot be treated in a systematic way. Such "weaker" general statements often suffice for perfectly sensible explanations (see Van Der Steen and Kamminga 1991). Finally (3) the method of case studies shows us how to use descriptions of a particular ecological case in order to study different, but partially similar, cases. These three assets of the method of case studies suggest that, even if community ecology cannot accomplish the *theoretical* task of discovering general theories and empirical laws that provide precise predictions in environmental applications, nevertheless ecology often can accomplish some important *practical* tasks: It can provide natural-history information, rough generalizations, lower-level theories, and a measure of needed control over our environment.

Apart from practical benefits, the method of case studies is also important because it is applicable to unique situations, to situations not amenable to statistical tests and to traditional hypothesis testing. It provides an organized framework for consideration of alternative models and explanatory accounts, for doing science in a situation in which exceptionless empirical laws typically are not evident or cannot be had. As Yin (1984, p. 19) puts it, case studies enable us to learn about phenomena when the relevant behavior cannot be manipulated. Indeed, in ecology, many ecosystems, habitats, and species are rare or poorly understood; as a result, very few situations admit of direct manipulation. (Some of the exceptions to this rule, for instance, are cases in which ecologists have withdrawn or added species to islands in such a way that they were able to perform controlled experiments; see Simberloff and Wilson 1969, for example.) Because "complexity is the dominant attribute of organic life" (Elsasser 1975, p. 205), however, use of case studies is often the only methodological option. Hence, the method of case studies has a special strength: its ability to deal with grossly imperfect evidence, even though controls, manipulation, and experimental tests typically are not possible. Case studies are also valuable for some of the same reasons that Kuhnian (Kuhn 1970, pp. 187–191) "exemplars" are important. They provide a locus for specific scientific values, as well as for concrete problem solutions. They show, by example, how the scientific "job" is to be done. Most significantly, exemplars and case studies both provide a way to see a problem as *like* other problems. If one sees the resemblance, as Kuhn (1970, p. 189) points out, then one grasps the analogy among different cases. As a result, one can attach symbols and explanations to nature in new ways.

Another benefit of the method of case studies is that, although it is often unable to provide information about regularities or to confirm hypotheses, it frequently enables us to see whether a phenomenon can be interpreted in the light of a certain model or assumptions (see Mowry 1985). More generally, the method of case studies offers a way to gather information and to formulate hypotheses. As the authors of the NAS study on applying ecological theory to environmental problems put it: "The clear and accessible presentation of the [case-study] plan . . . is of great value, because it focuses the debate and research needed for the achievement of its goals" (Orians et al. 1986, p. 247). Viewed in this light, the strength of the case-study method is its ability to deal with a full range of evidence in a systematic and organized way. Because of its systematic attention to a wide range of evidence, the method of case studies is often able to uncover or to illustrate crucial details sometimes missed by other, more formal, methods of science. Analysis of the case of Hertz's views on the nature of cathode rays, for example, illustrates the difference between conceptual and experimental error (see Hon 1987). It provides many suggestions for uncovering similar flaws in other areas of science. In short, the method of case studies often exhibits significant heuristic power.

5.4.4 Justifying the method of case studies

In attempting to justify the method of case studies – as one possible antidote for the limits of traditional scientific knowledge – we ought to explain why other responses (to the view that scientific claims reach beyond knowledge) do not work. One such response, the semantic conception of scientific theories, has been developed by philosophers of science representing different versions of this view (see, for example, Sneed 1971; van Fraassen 1980; Giere 1988; Suppe 1989; and others). According to the semantic conception, it makes sense to accept and use a scientific theory, but not to believe it. Belief makes no sense, on this account, because a scientific theory is not a set of claims that can be true or false but a complicated predicate that is true of some systems but not others. In other words, the goal of scientists who accept the semantic conception is to try to show that a system exhibiting some regularity may be treated as a system to which the complicated theoretical predicate applies (Glymour 1992). On this view, science is not so much the discovery of general propositions that are true but understanding how to embed various phenomena within systems of models.

Despite the importance of issues like the semantic conception of theories, we shall not address this conception here, because our concern is not primarily with meta-theoretical questions applicable to all science but with the actual practice of more applied sciences (like ecology) that are linked to environmental problemsolving. Also, discussion of the semantic conception itself would require a treatment so extensive that it would lead us too far from our fundamentally practical concerns about ecological methods and case studies.

A comprehensive justification of the method of case studies likewise would require us to defend a causal account of explanation, such as that given by someone like Salmon (1984, 1989), for example. We need to have an account, both of how causality operates and of how at least two independent avenues function, in causal explanation, for advancing our understanding of phenomena. Because this volume addresses the role of explanation in ecology, relative to environmental problemsolving, rather than the theoretical justification for some general account of causal explanation, we shall not defend any particular version of a causal account of explanation. Moreover, it is not clear that any fully developed, specific account of causality is yet available. Salmon (1989, p. 186), for example, notes that, despite all the ink spilled on the topic of causality, it remains a "hoary philosophical chestnut" on which "considerably more work is needed." Since we do not propose to crack this chestnut, we shall attempt to show merely that a causal account of explanation – focused on the singular claims and unique events of case studies – is prima-facie plausible. It is prima-facie plausible for four main reasons. *First*, even general causal laws require reference to singular claims, if they are to work. *Second*, even general causal laws exhibit an unreliability that cannot be removed by examining the probabilities in a randomized experiment. *Third*, there is no recipe for moving from singular claims to abstract regularities; the move makes sense only in the context of the unformalizable training of the scientist. *Fourth*, pragmatically speaking, many complex situations (like those in ecology) have no obvious other methods that appear applicable. We shall discuss these four lines of justification shortly, beginning with the fourth and last defense.

Several authors have used neo-Hegelian, phenomenological, and hermeneutic arguments (see Cronbach 1957, 1975, 1982, 1986; Phillips 1976; Bandura 1977, 1978, 1983; Kenny and Grotelueschen 1980) in attempting to defend the method of case studies. All of these defenses emphasize the importance of wholistic thought, qualitative methods, and interaction effects, rather than unchanging, exceptionless, descriptive generalizations. The more plausible justifications for the method, however, appear to focus on the four defenses noted in the previous paragraph. The *fourth*, or pragmatic, defense of the method is that it is more useful, appropriate, and workable than other methods – such as hypothesis deduction – when one is dealing with unique situations in which testing and experimental controls are difficult, if not impossible (see Merriam 1988, pp. 20–21). In other words, in many situations, there is no reasonable alternative to the method of case studies. The *third*, or Wittgensteinian–Kuhnian justification for the method of case studies is that it relies on the unformalizable training of scientists, on their seeing situations as like each other. Because it relies on exemplars, this type of knowledge cannot be reduced to mere verbal rules (see Kuhn 1970, pp. 191–204). Instead, it is embodied in the practices (the relevant actions and dispositions) of the scientific community. The philosopher Ludwig Wittgenstein emphasized that we learn about the meaning of words from the way they are used: practices reveal meanings. Analogously, it is arguable that there must be room, in scientific method, for the rationality of practice. There must be room, in scientific method, for a way of grasping a rule (in the verbal or non-verbal sense) that is exhibited in obeying the rule, rather than in being able to formulate it (see Baker 1986, p. 255). On this Wittgensteinian–

Kuhnian view, what typically justifies particular instances of the method of case studies are the practices of the scientific community. Moreover, because these practices involve an implicit reference to a community of persons (as Kripke 1982; Bloor 1983; Peacocke 1986; and Smith 1988 suggest), they are not purely subjective (see Newell 1986). The criterion for correct practices, for Wittgenstein, does not involve a testable hypothesis but whether the practices enable us "to go on" to "make sense" of further practices, to see likenesses among different cases (Wittgenstein 1973, pp. 47–54, 1979, pp. 61, 77–79; Eldridge 1987; Ackermann 1988, p. 131). On this criterion, if a particular analysis of a case enables us "to go on" or to "make sense" of further aspects of the case, then this analysis is likely acceptable.

Moreover, as we note in our second justification for the method of case studies, it is not flawed in having only singular claims, rough generalizations, and repeated practices, rather than exceptionless rules, to guide the practices in a particular case. As Kripke (1982) and Cartwright (1989a, b) point out, no rule can determine what to do in accord with it, because no rule for the application of a rule can "fix" what counts as accord. Therefore, every rule generates the same problem: how is it to be applied? Likewise, every law in science has some level of unreliability. If rules and laws cannot guide us in following them, then the practices and examples of well-trained scientists must do so. And if the practices and examples of experienced practitioners ultimately guide scientists in justifying and applying laws and rules, then it is reasonable to believe that practices can also guide scientists in helping to justify and apply the method of case studies (see Wittgenstein 1973; Baker and Hacker 1985, 1986; Baker 1986; Picardi 1988; Smith 1988). Admittedly, for Wittgenstein, practices are normative and not purely subjective, in that the existence of practices requires a "multiplicity of occasions" (Baker and Hacker 1985, p. 151), a normative regularity among actions that exemplify a technique. Because the method of case studies is typically applied to a unique phenomenon, rather than to a multiplicity of identical occasions, one might wonder how the use of the method is justified by the Wittgensteinian notion of practices. The answer is that unique events, even laws instantiated only once or without any instantiation, may be tested indirectly (see Olding 1978). Although the method of case studies is used to elucidate unique phenomena, scientists' informal inferences in describing, explaining, and hypothesizing about a unique phenomenon can be evaluated on the basis of past scientific practices of describing, explaining, and hypothesizing – past practices that are analogous to present ones. Also, as we discussed in section 5.2, even *unique* events may be explained, in principle, on the basis of common concepts or general laws, if one is able to supply appropriate initial conditions (see, for example, Fetzer 1975; Van Der Steen and Kamminga 1991).

Two additional defenses of the method of case studies are (1) that all laws require reference to singular claims, and (2) that all laws exhibit an irremediable unrealizability, as we noted in our first two justifications for the method of case studies as a causal method. Let us examine each of these defenses more closely. They both come down to the claim that the flaws infecting the method of case studies also infect other scientific methods and, hence, the method of case studies may be no less defensible than they. What does it mean to say that deductive and non-deductive methods, like the method of case studies, are similar in that both rely on singular claims and individual cases? Deduction addresses all the possible singular instances that support a particular principle, whereas case methods address only some of the instances, often one at a time. In other words, deduction addresses what is true of instances in general, whereas case methods address what is true of them, instance after instance. Moreover, Wisdom (1965; see Newell 1986, p. 110) argues that, because deductive justification of an inference relies on claims about all singular instances, in general, in order to draw a conclusion about a subset of singular instances, it is circular. Regardless of whether or not deductive methods are circular, however, one faces a fundamental problem in using either deductive or case methods: Both types of method may transmit truth, but both are incapable of initiating it. Hence all scientific methods exhibit unreliability. As Wisdom (1965; p. 6; see Newell 1986, p. 92) puts it: "My point is that this [deductive method] isn't the only sort of reflection, and that the other sorts [of methods] are not poor relations." But if the method of case studies is not merely a poor relation of deduction, and if all scientific methods have some of the same flaws, then the method of case studies may not be less justified than other methods. In other words, if persons like Wisdom are right about the similarities between deductive and non-deductive reasoning, and if persons like Cartwright (1989a, b) and Fetzer (1971, 1974a, b, 1975), for example, are right about the fact that all justification ultimately appeals to parallel cases and to singular claims, then the non-deductive character of the method of case studies does not necessarily render it less appropriate than other methods for doing science. And if not, then the various steps, techniques, and inferences of the method of case studies, while not purely deductive and conclusive, may be as grounded in scientific practices, in standard procedures and competencies that can be taught (see Baker and Hacker 1985, pp. 162–164; Smith 1988), as other scientific methods. Experienced users of all scientific methods, including the method of case studies, thus have "rules of thumb," practices, and heuristics "that make them excellent practitioners" (Smith 1988, p. 7).

Indeed, the practices that can be learned and mastered – the practices referred to in the third justification for the method of case studies – are essential to all forms of knowing because all knowing requires some appeal to tacit knowledge. Tacit knowledge is the inarticulate knowledge that we share with non-human animals and that is situated behind language (see Polanyi 1959, pp. 13, 26). Tacit knowing is required when we: discover novelty; reorganize experience; understand world and symbols; distinguish what is meant from what is said; and understand in a gestalt or wholistic way (Polanyi 1959, pp. 18–29). Tacit knowledge is also required when we value something; when we know reasons and not merely causes; when we understand subsidiary rather than focal points; when we grasp unique things; and when we make methodological value judgments in science, for example, "reagent x is the best one for the next test" (Polanyi 1959, pp. 38–93).

Although the method of case studies relies on tacit knowledge and on understanding gained through practice, it is important to point out that not only all knowing, but science generally, even hypothetico-deductive science, also relies (in part) on tacit knowledge and on scientific practice. Whenever one *applies* a generalization, law, or theory to a particular case, as Kripke (1982) realized, one must use tacit knowledge. Explicit knowledge typically does not tell us when we are justified in a particular application and, in principle, we cannot test our judgments of applicability. Rather, we must rely in part on knowledge gained through examples and practice – tacit knowledge – whenever we address the question of applicability. Hence, if there is a problem with the tacit knowledge that characterizes the method of case studies, there is likewise a problem with tacit knowledge, generally, in science (see Polanyi 1964). It is tacit knowledge that tells a scientist what needs to be explained (see Adelman 1974, p. 223), and what counts as a criterion for justification (see Gutting 1982, p. 323). As Wittgenstein pointed out in discussing the foundations of mathematics, even mathematical proofs proceed by means of analogy, by means of recognizing that one case is like another (Bloor 1983, p. 95). Indeed, all justification of scientific method, as in Goodman's defense of induction, relies on the plausibility of the ultimate premisses assumed by the "justifier." These ultimate premisses, in turn, often rely on intuition (see Gutting 1982, pp. 323–

326). Because no ultimate premises of scientific method can be established conclusively, all such methods employ tacit knowledge or intuition.

Admittedly, in contrast to other scientific methods, all of which employ tacit knowledge, the method of case studies bears an additional burden. This is the burden of being able, at best, only to show the rationality of a particular scientific conclusion, not to confirm it on the basis of repeated instances. According to some accounts of other methods of science, investigators are often able both to confirm conclusions and to show that they are rational (see Plantinga 1974, pp. 220–221). For the method of case studies to be defective, however, because it is able merely to show that its conclusions are rational, *something more* than an illustration of rationality must be possible in the situations in which the method of case studies is employed. Because it is not obvious that, in the situations in which it is used, there are alternative methods that are able to do more than the method of case studies, it is not obvious that using the method is inherently flawed. This is the fourth, or pragmatic, defense of the method of case studies. Moreover, in at least one respect, inductive and deductive "confirmation" of a conclusion, by means other than the method of case studies, is neither stronger nor more legitimate than an argument that dispenses with general premises and appeals directly to similarities and differences, as does the method of case studies. This is the point of our first defense of the method of case studies. Deduction is no better because, as Wisdom (1965), Cartwright (1989a, b; see also Kuhn 1970, 1977; Dilman 1973, pp. 115–120; Bambrough 1979, ch. 8; Newell 1986, pp. 88–94), Fetzer (1975, pp. 95–96), and others point out, all reasoning and justification, pushed to their limits, rely on parallel cases, on behavior being of a certain type. Inductive justification likewise presupposes the recognition of regularities, and this recognition presupposes the perception of similarities and differences. Therefore, the decision about whether certain cases are regular cannot be justified inductively. And if not, then in this one respect, induction is not a stronger method than case studies.

In summary, then, the method of case studies can be justified on the grounds that it is more appropriate (than other methods) for dealing with unique situations (the fourth defense). Also, science often depends on actions that are unbiased, rather than merely on propositions that are impersonal (the third defense). Likewise, the method of case studies can be justified if one realizes that there is no decision procedure in science for settling issues decisively; we do not have foolproof rules that enable us to avoid all disagreement (the second defense). Moreover, the method of case studies is not especially defective, as a scientific method, once one realizes that all explanation requires reference to singular claims (the first defense), that any demonstration generates an infinite regress of premisses that cannot terminate in a rule, and that all inferences in science require one to grasp similarities and differences among cases (see Newell 1986, pp. 95–97, 100, 105). Hence, for all four reasons, the method of case studies appears at least prima-facie defensible in science.

5.4.5 Shortcomings of the method of case studies

Given the brief outline of the characteristics of, and the justifications for, the case-study method, it is important to point out some of its weaknesses. One shortcoming of the method, often mentioned in the literature, is that, because analysis of examples via case studies follows no algorithms, it can easily be biased by the practitioner, or turn into indoctrination (Dalton 1979, p. 17; Callahan and Bok 1980, pp. 5–62; Hoering 1980; Guba and Lincoln 1981, p. 377; Gini 1985; Carson 1986, p. 37; Edelson 1988, pp. 239–243; Merriam 1988, pp. 33ff.). This problem of bias, in fact, is one of the main insights of Grunbaum's (1984, 1988) analysis of the problems besetting the case-study method as used in psychoanalysis. Although there is no failsafe way to avoid all bias in using the method of case studies, often researchers forget that bias can enter the conduct of all experiments (see, for example, Shrader-Frechette 1985a, pp. 68ff., 1991, ch. 4). Also, as Hull (1988, p. 22) recognized, science does not require that scientists be unbiased, but only "that different scientists have different biases." If they have different biases, then alternative conceptual analyses, accomplished by different scientists, will likely reveal these biases. Hence, bias is not the unique problem of the method of case studies, and it is not necessarily a serious problem. Bias does arise more easily in this method, however, because it employs primarily informal schemes of inference. Such inferences are more difficult and controversial to use than are formal or deductive methods.

To remedy or avoid possible bias in using the case-study method, it is important that the description, observation, evaluation, and practical reasoning employed in the method be wide-ranging and open (see Gini 1985, p. 352; Carson 1986, p. 37; Merriam 1988, pp. 87ff.). Also, so far as possible, ecologists using the method of case studies should attempt to confirm their results, in a partial way, by using independent data and other case studies (see Berkowitz et al. 1989, p. 195). In comparing the case-study results with those from other investigations, one might be able to avoid bias – or at least to make it explicit – by developing rules for assessing similarities among system components or among initial and boundary conditions. By developing explicit rules, it will be easier to specify the assumptions and methodological value judgments that are central to the case study. Another way to guard against bias is to use multiple methods and multiple sources of evidence (Berkowitz *et al.* 1989, pp. 196–197). By using a variety of evidence and methods, we can also attain an important objective of the case-study method: discovering new insights, because of the specifics of a case, rather than merely molding the case along the lines of one's existing assumptions. Because it has the potential for facilitating many diverse insights, the case-study method, if done appropriately, can contribute to both flexible and impartial scientific reasoning (de Vries 1986, p. 195). Such flexibility can be attained, however, only by a method not slavishly dependent upon algorithms or purely deductive inferences. For example, in case-study work on the gopher tortoise, ecologists were able to discover a number of insights – such as the directional positions of entrances to tortoise burrows – even though they had no algorithms or deductive methods to guide them (McCoy *et al.* 1993). The case-study method facilitated flexible use of natural-history information. Hence, although the case-study method, if misused, is susceptible to bias, the bias is possible only because of an asset: the flexibility of the method. Moreover, if bias always presented a serious difficulty for the method of case studies, then it would be puzzling why persons continue to employ it. Much social-science research is dependent upon the method of case studies, and its continued use suggests that, although it may be plagued with a greater tendency to reflect the researcher's bias, in certain situations there is no alternative to the method.

Another response to the case-study problem of bias is that the stereotype of the method is wrong. The method is not subjective, irrational, or biased merely because the method cannot be represented "by formal logico-mathematical procedures." Rather, rationality and objectivity need not be defined in so limited a way (see Elsasser 1975, p. 17). Yin (1984) makes exactly this point, and he argues that the method of case studies does not allow scientists to draw whatever conclusions they wish. Rather, because it is an *organized* means of obtaining information that can be scrutinized, and because it proceeds in a step-by-step fashion (problem definition, research design, data collection, data analysis, composition of results, and reporting them), it can be used in an objective way. Because case-study procedures, techniques, interpretations, uses, and conclusions are open to change on the basis of rational evaluation, the method of case studies is, in principle, objective and able to avoid bias (see Shrader-Frechette 1989b), in part by means of the critical evaluation of other scientists. For example, a number of philosophers of science and scientists have repeatedly been able to argue that a given case study does not illustrate what its practitioners claim, or that it does not fit the model imposed on it; others have argued that specific case studies were factually deficient, or were misrepresentations (see, for example, Beckman 1971; Adelman 1974). Such criticisms indicate that, because use of the method of case studies is open to analysis, therefore it is rational and objective, at least in the Wittgensteinian sense of being "public." It is public, and not private (or subjective), in two ways. (1) Experienced practitioners are often able to distinguish a better interpretation/application of the method from a worse one. (2) Following the method, and thinking that one is following it, are not the same thing (see Wittgenstein 1973, pp. 243ff.; Baker and Hacker 1985, pp. 150–185; Baker and Hacker 1986, pp. 330–333). Because they are not the same thing, it is possible to criticize particular instances of the method of case studies. Indeed, there are a number of criteria according to which one might argue that treatment of a particular case is subjective or irrational. For example, it might fall into inconsistency or dogmatism (Hoering 1980, pp. 132–133); or it might fail to take account of certain data or interpretations (see Beckman 1971; Adelman 1974); or it might make faulty inferences based, perhaps, on the fallacy of affirming the consequent or on the fallacy of assuming that two conjoint phenomena have a cause–effect relationship (see Edelson 1988, pp. 255–266, 319ff.).

Admittedly, of course, each of these criteria, in a given case study, must be interpreted in terms of background assumptions and methodological value judgments that themselves are never wholly immune from criticism. In such a value-laden context, the best guarantee of objectivity is repeated criticism by the scientific community, continual investigation of a range of different value judgments, alternative evidence, and a variety of background hypotheses. In other words, in arguing that the case-study method is not subjective in a damaging sense, it is important to repeat the Wittgensteinian insight that objectivity is tied to the practices of people, as well as to propositions. Beliefs, criteria, or rules do not alone secure objectivity for Wittgenstein; rather, "action is at the bottom of knowledge" (Newell 1986, p. 105). This insight is similar to Kuhn's (1977, pp. 309–313) point that ostention – acting or pointing – is the primary mode of learning. As

Wittgenstein puts it: "Giving ground comes to an end; but the end is not certain propositions striking us immediately as true, i.e., it is not a kind of *seeing* on our part; it is our *acting*" (Wittgenstein 1969, pp. 204; see also Newell 1986, p. 63). On this Wittgensteinian view of objectivity, we can explain certainty as a kind of *acting*, rather than merely as a kind of *seeing*. Of course, our more traditional accounts of objectivity are tied to seeing. On these traditional accounts, beliefs about the world must hold good independently of experiences or states of mind on which people rely for their assertions about the world. Objectivity, according to these accounts, is tied to impersonality, and it attaches to judgments. Typically, we do not attach praise or blame to *judgments* (about seeing) that fail to be objective in this sense (see Newell 1986, p. 16ff.).

The newer, Wittgensteinian account of objectivity is tied to *actions*, not to judgments – to behaving in a way that lacks bias, to behaving in a way that is impartial. Usually, we do attach praise or blame to *persons* who fail to be objective in this sense. Objectivity in this second, more recent sense seeks out human actions, not external particulars, as its guarantee. Responsibility for objectivity in this second sense lies with the person, not with some rule (see Newell 1986, pp. 23, 30). Moreover, if a judgment is thought to be objective in the first sense, then obviously a single counterinstance may be enough to discredit it and to render it subjective. Objectivity in the first, more traditional sense is not compatible with error. However, if a person is objective in the second, more recent sense and says "I know," then this claim does not entail "I cannot be mistaken" (Newell 1986, p. 82). Objectivity in this second sense, because it requires merely freedom from bias, is compatible with error. The point of distinguishing these two senses of objectivity is that the method of case studies, tied as it is to actions and practices, as well as to rules or propositions, is not an infallible method. Moreover, once we realize that objectivity is not necessarily tied to judgments and to infallibility, then it is possible to recognize that the method of case studies may be objective, at least in some instances.

A second problem with the method of case studies is that it provides little basis for scientific generalization (see Yin 1984, p. 21). Obviously, it is difficult to generalize on the basis of a single case. In the NAS spotted-owl case study, for example, generalizations about habitat requirements were different because the owls' needs varied from place to place. In California, each pair of spotted owls used 1,900 acres of old-growth forest. In Oregon, the per pair acreage was 2,264, and in Washington, 3,800 acres per pair (Wilcove 1990, p. 77; see also Thomas *et al.* 1990).

How could one generalize about the needs of spotted owls in all three places?

While concerns about the ability to generalize are well placed, it is important to point out that this apparent problem is mitigated by two considerations. *First*, if Cartwright (1989a), Fetzer (1971, 1974a, b, 1975), Humphreys (1989, 1991), and others are correct, then it may be possible to establish some singular causal claims without first establishing regularities and to do so reliably. *Second*, analogous difficulties with generalizations face all experiments, and hence the method of case studies is not unique in this respect. Let us discuss each of these points in more detail. Because it is problematic to generalize on the basis of a single experiment, scientific "facts" typically are based on a multiple set of experiments, a set that replicates the same phenomenon under different conditions. Hence, the single case study and the single experiment face at least one common problem: both can be generalizable to theoretical propositions but not to populations or to universes (see Cartwright 1989a, b). In other words, both the single experiment and the case study face the problem of induction. Neither of them represents a sample and the scientist's goal is not adequately accomplished merely by enumerating frequencies (see Fetzer 1971, 1974a, b, 1975, for example). Instead, the scientist must expand and generalize theories. Although the single case-study or experiment is not sufficient for scientific theorizing, multiple case studies or experiments, alone, are likewise not sufficient. Therefore, it is reasonable to obtain as much knowledge as possible from a single case study or experiment and then to replicate it whenever one is able to do so. Of course, there is no algorithm for theorizing within the method of case studies, but this problem is placed in perspective by realizing that there is no algorithm for scientific theorizing generally. Because it provides us with procedures for gaining case-specific information (e.g., natural-history information in ecology) and for criticizing it, however, the method of case studies often may provide a basis for scientific theorizing, as well as for practical environmental problemsolving. Indeed, the use of the method of case studies accomplished both these goals in the NAS analysis of the vampire bat. More generally, single cases and single sets of experiments, even in physics, are often the basis for scientific theorizing. In the case of parity non-conservation, for instance, Friedman and Telegdi presented their limited and preliminary data before it was replicated, simply because it was so important (Franklin 1986, p. 100). Similarly, in the Einstein–de Haas experiment – a "one-shot experiment" described by Cartwright (1989a, p. 349) – the singular claim, "orbitting electrons caused the magnetism in *this* iron bar," is itself sufficient to justify the move to the general law, "orbitting electrons cause magnetism." These examples suggest that often controversies are decided on the basis of a crucial set of experiments or even a "one-shot" experiment. Indeed, a single experiment, despite its associated value judgments, is sometimes adequate to settle an issue, as the question of CP (charge parity) violation shows (Franklin 1986, pp. 192ff.). Single cases and sets of experiments are important because, as Popper (1965, pp. 28ff., 251ff.) pointed out, mere replication often is not sufficient to corroborate a theory; rather, what is important is the severity of the tests. Hence, single, but severe, tests are often "convincing."

Admittedly, assessing a single test, experiment, or case is often difficult. As Yin (1984, p. 22) puts it, people know when they can play the piano or do differential equations; they can be tested easily for such skills. It is less easy to know when one is employing the method of case studies correctly. Only the best practitioners of a discipline are likely to be able to make this judgment. The same is often true for science generally, except perhaps, to a lesser degree, at the stage of confirmation of some hypotheses. Even physicists are often unable to assess a single experiment and are forced to rely on "unformalizable training" to do so (Cartwright 1989a, p. 354). Hence, it is not clear that use of case studies poses many difficulties that are, in principle, more problematic than those encountered generally within other scientific methods.

The method of case studies is also frequently criticized, for example, for circularity. Critics claim that it can evaluate only those interpretations that it already presupposes. However, any method of confirmation has this same difficulty: it can evaluate only hypotheses or interpretations that have already been discovered (see Hoering 1980, p. 135). Moreover, if the method of case studies is open to critical evaluation, then its conclusions are not merely begged. They can be amended or rejected after such an evaluation. Hence, to the degree that the method can use evaluation to avoid bias, it can also avoid circularity. At the root of criticisms of the method of case studies – that it cannot deliver empirical generalizations or that it is circular – is the allegation that it is not testable. If, by definition, a method applies only to one unique case, how can the findings of the method be tested?

Grunbaum (1984) and Edelson (1988, p. 265) both provide some insights as to how one might test the conclusions of a case study, either by using analogous data from other sources or by employing results from different case studies, in order to help confirm or eliminate hypotheses. Recognizing that direct replication of a case study is typically impossible, Edelson (1988, p. xxxiii) claims that "systematic replication across cases when crucial characteristics are varied one at a time" is a useful form of testing. Edelson also argues persuasively that, within the method of case studies, as well as within other scientific methods, strict testing is not as important as inference to the best explanation or causal story (Edelson 1988, p. 363). On his view, one justifies a case-study conclusion by pitting it against rival hypotheses (Edelson 1988, pp. 231–365). Using partial replication, the method of case studies presents an "argument" for the scientific credibility of an hypothesis, an "argument that a theoretical explanation of . . . regularities is better than rival explanations" (Edelson 1988, p. 120). On the Edelson scheme, partial replication and pitting hypotheses against each other are the key to testing a case study.

Although Grunbaum (1984; see Edelson 1988, pp. 233, 275, 276) claims that the data in an individual case, such as a psychoanalytic situation, cannot be used to *test* psychoanalytic propositions, he maintains that one can use experimental and epidemiological tests of the conclusions of a case study. For both Grunbaum (1984) and Edelson (1988, p. 275), the canons of eliminative induction are the methods to be used for testing the conclusions of a particular case study: one seeks confirming instances, and one excludes plausible alternative explanations. Using such canons, one can obtain intersubjective agreement about the tests and hence about the conclusions of a case study (see Meehl 1983).

Arguing that it is possible to test the conclusions of a case study, Edelson (1988, pp. 255–267; see Glymour 1980) gives three necessary conditions for claiming that an hypothesis has been tested, and that a case study supports it. These are (1) that the hypothesis can best explain the phenomena; (2) that the hypothesis runs the *risk* of being rejected; and (3) that the hypothesis is more credible than its rivals. We know that condition (2) has been met, says Edelson (1988, pp. 258–264), if we choose a case for study that is least likely to confirm the hypotheses in which we already have vested interests; if we choose a case for study in which supposed rare causes and effects co-occur, as they did in the spotted-owl case, rather than a case in which the cause occurs frequently; if the predictions made by the case study are improbable and precise; if the case study supports multiple independent deductions from the same hypothesis; and if a subset of independent hypotheses are supported by converging independently on the same outcome. Edelson terms these five conditions (for risky predictions), respectively, "the least likely cause argument"; the "rare cause argument"; the "probable outcome argument"; the "convergence argument"; and the "bootstrap argument." Supporting Edelson's views, other philosophers (see, for instance, Fetzer 1971, pp. 478–479) have given similar arguments for how one may "test" hypotheses in individual cases. Glymour (1980), for example, says that bootstrap arguments are capable of testing some hypotheses. Moreover, negative consequences would follow if one argued that it was impossible to test the conclusions of a case study. If case studies were relegated to the context of discovery, then this would discourage rigorous argument about the relationship among hypotheses and evidence in case studies. Hence, a practical reason for claiming that the conclusions of case studies can be tested, in some minimal sense, is that such a claim is necessary if rigorous argument about hypotheses and evidence is to be possible (Edelson 1988, p. 254).

Another important problem with the case-study method is that, because it follows no purely deductive scheme of inference, its practitioners often fall victim to fuzzy or uncritical thinking (see Hoering 1980, p. 135; Francoeur 1984, p. 146); to erroneous inductive inferences; or to the fallacy of false cause. Admittedly, problems of illicit inductive and causal inferences have plagued the use of case studies in many areas of science, in psychoanalysis, for example (see Grunbaum 1984, 1988). Also, community ecologists have been divided recently over the causal role of competition, versus random chance, in structuring biological communities. As a consequence of this division, different ecologists (using the same case study) often make controversial inductive and causal inferences regarding alleged competition data (see, for example, Simberloff 1976a; Simberloff and Abele 1976; Diamond and Case 1986a,b,c).

The solution to controversies over inferences in the case-study method is to subject our inductive and causal judgments to repeated criticism, reevaluation, and discussion and to seek independent evidence for them. In part, this can be accomplished by making it a point to seek alternative analyses of the same case (see Edelson 1988, pp. 237–251, 286ff., 319ff.), or to seek evaluations of a particular case study by persons having divergent scientific, epistemological, and personal presuppositions. If doctrinaire Freudians, for example, wished to guard against the fallacy of false cause, they would do well to read Grunbaum's (1984, 1988) criticisms of many of the central causal and inductive inferences of psychoanalysis. In evaluating cases drawn from evolutionary theory, for example, Sober (1987, p. 466) has discussed in detail which sorts of causal inferences are justified, and which are not, in discussing evidence of a species' shared genealogy. More recently, Sober (1988b) has discussed the problem of when to infer common ancestry among species, and he has issued some important caveats regarding the inferrability of a common cause. In general, much of the literature (like Sober's) that discusses defects in the "principle of the common cause," as defended by Reichenbach (1956) and Salmon (1984), as well as the literature that discusses problems with inductive inferences, is informative about how to avoid questionable inferences in assessing case studies. Those who discuss case studies, whether in science or elsewhere, must be careful neither to generalize on the basis of a small or non-representative sample, nor to confuse mere affinity or correlation with causality. Because most of the inferences employed in the case-study method are not formal, however, there is no alternative to continual vigilance, continual searches for alternative points of view, and continual criticism of one's insights and analyses.

A fourth problem with the case-study method is that most real-life scientific decisions are made in dynamic contexts, whereas the case study presents a static situation. "Every hour brings fresh information to the decision maker" (Donaldson 1990, p. 21). Hence, in the real world, a practicing ecologist making decisions must continually decide when to seek, or wait for, new information and when to make a decision. A single new piece of information could be sufficient to change the interpretation of the entire case study. One obvious remedy for the problem of the static character of the case study is to update information on the case continually and to examine the way that changed factual information impacts conclusions. By examining alternative epistemological and scientific positions and the consequences associated with them, one can determine how sensitive particular conclusions are to different methodological assumptions. Another suggestion would be to continually update the analysis of the particular case/example.

5.4.6 Conclusion

Later in the volume, we shall provide and evaluate our own case study, that of the Florida panther. This study will illustrate some of the benefits of the case-study method. It will also show how natural-history information can be useful, in order to provide an ecological foundation for environmental policy. We intend this example to provide yet another illustration of what ecology can do. As we have argued, and as the study of the Florida panther will reveal, practical and precise knowledge of particular taxa, coupled with low-level theories – rather than general ecological theory – are the keys to the ecological insights necessary to provide predictive power for preservation and environmental policy. This practical and precise knowledge of natural history, coupled with conceptual and methodological analysis, is a critical departure from the general mathematical models and the untestable principles of past ecological theorizing. This natural-history knowledge, joined to very low-level theories and to conceptual analysis in the method of case studies, is also more capable of being used in practical applications of contemporary ecology than is the formulation of null models. While an excellent, classical ideal for ecological method, null models fail to address the uniqueness, particularity, and historicity of many ecological phenomena. Hence, in addition to a top-down account of ecological explanation, we also need to emphasize a bottom-up approach, like that provided through case studies. Likewise, in addition to a logic of falsification, ecology needs a logic of case studies.

6 · Ecology and a new account of rationality

A DECADE AGO, Dan Simberloff bemoaned the fact that essentialism and determinism were still dominant, if not rampant, in ecology. He attributed their persistence to ecologists' physics envy and to their diffidence in the face of the "apparent sloppiness" of their discipline (Simberloff 1982, p. 83). If the arguments of the previous chapters are correct, then Simberloff's criticisms are well placed. Essentialism appears to be driving some conceptions of "stability" (chapters 2 and 3) and of "species" (chapter 5) that run counter to the theory of evolution. Indeed, because of their heuristic power, deterministic models have been used to undergird some hypotheses about proposed community structures (chapter 3; see Simberloff 1982, p. 85). Yet, as we have argued, such hypotheses often fly in the face of the apparent uniqueness and randomness of ecological situations. Part of the reason why scientists appear to have underestimated this uniqueness and randomness, we suggested (chapter 4), is that ecology is permeated by a misguided and naive positivism and by the belief that science can avoid value judgments (see, for example, Peters 1982; see also Fretwell 1975; Rosenzweig 1976; McIntosh 1982, pp. 27ff.). Our revisionist account of ecological method, as applied to conservation problems, is premised on the need to accept the shortcomings of positivistic, hypothetico-deductive science, even as we attempt to make ecology more rigorous, empirical, and testable. We believe that the uniqueness and randomness of ecological phenomena, as well as the lack of conceptual and theoretical clarity in the discipline, often suit it to a "bottom-up" rather than a "top-down" account of scientific explanation (see section 5.3 of the previous chapter). Insofar as ecology is applied to cases of practical problemsolving, we believe it is primarily a science of case studies and rough generalizations, rather than a science of general theory and exceptionless empirical laws.

149

6.1 Phenomenological, scientific, and ethical rationality in ecology

In this chapter and the next, we shall argue that, although ecology is primarily a science of case studies and rough generalizations, this is not a defect. As we explained in the previous chapter, the natural-history knowledge gleaned from case studies (like that of the vampire bat) meets many pragmatic and scientific goals. (1) It enables ecologists to gain a measure of practical control over environmental problems, like pest management. (2) It allows us to make rough generalizations, for example, about a taxon's susceptibility to anticoagulants, even though exceptions to these generalizations cannot be treated in a systematic way. (3) It shows us how to use descriptions of a particular ecological case in order to study different, but partially similar, cases. For example, natural-history knowledge of cave-dwelling bats suggested the importance of the grooming scenario in controlling vampire bats. Because the organisms groomed themselves immediately after returning to the cave, any substance (in this case, an anticoagulant lethal to bats) would be distributed throughout the population. Ecologists' knowledge of this natural-history fact about grooming has enabled them both to predict and to control the behavior of a variety of bats. Hence, although there is at least one *theoretical* task that community ecology may not be able to accomplish, namely, discovering exceptionless empirical laws that are always and everywhere true, at least it can accomplish the *practical* task of providing rough generalizations and a measure of needed control over our environment. Ecology, then, has no defect if it must sacrifice universality for utility and practicality, or if it must sacrifice generality for precision in knowledge.

If ecology shows itself to be, primarily, a practical and applied science of case studies, rather than a pure science of general theory, then this fact will have consequences for any account of scientific explanation and rationality in ecology. One consequence is that ecological rationality may not turn out to be the same as that in pure physics (if there is such a thing) or in pure anything. In doing pure science, experts typically have followed a notion of rationality that is epistemic or *scientific*. Epistemic or scientific rationality (as we shall explain in more detail in the next chapter) is based primarily on using scientific theory (whether in ecology or economics, for example) to assess the *probability* associated with various competing *hypotheses* and their consequences. Scientific rationality is a rationality of beliefs. When ecologists apply their theories in situations of practical, environmental problemsolving, however, we shall argue that they ought to follow not only epistemic or scientific rationality, but also *ethical* rationality. Ethical rationality (as we shall explain more fully in the next chapter) is based on using ethical theory and norms (about rights, duties, and ideals) to assess the *moral goodness or badness* associated with alternative *actions* and their consequences. Ethical rationality is a rationality of actions. For an ecologist, alternative actions might be recommending building nature reserves of one size and shape rather than another, or recommending using biological rather than chemical pest control in a given area. In this chapter and the next, we shall argue that what ecology can do is often limited by ecologists' views of scientific explanation and scientific rationality. We maintain that, provided ecologists understand the rationality appropriate to their discipline – rationality that is both scientific and ethical – including how to apply ecology in situations of uncertainty and potential statistical error, they can do much to provide a foundation for environmental policy. We shall argue that, if ecology appears to have failed environmental policy, it is only because it has been misapplied and because ecologists have misunderstood the character of explanations used in ecological problemsolving. In this chapter we argue for an important prima-facie principle: that ecological rationality, because of the predominantly practical and applied nature of the science, must be both ethical and scientific. According to the current, partially misguided, hypothetical-deductive scientific paradigm, however, "rationality" is purely scientific or epistemological and not also ethical. According to this paradigm, ethical and other values ought to be kept out of science. After arguing that there are prima-facie reasons for ecologists to follow an ethical, as well as a scientific, notion of rationality, we shall show that the ethical nature of ecological rationality makes ecology especially useful for environmental problemsolving.

Although we shall provide prima-facie arguments for an ethical, rather than a purely scientific or epistemic, notion of ecological rationality, it is important to point out that our analysis is premised on at least two important caveats. *First*, our defense of ethical rationality is a prima-facie defense, an argument that is presumed true, unless it is rebutted in a particular situation. In subsequent chapters, we shall discuss specific cases having the potential to rebut the prima-facie arguments given in this chapter. Hence, it is important to point out that this chapter will provide only prima-facie arguments for our position, whereas later chapters will assess objections to it. *Second*, although we shall defend an ethical (as well as a scientific) account of ecological rationality, we believe that it is important to point out that scientific rationality represented, at one time, an important advance in accounts of ecological explanations. Ecological studies based on epistemic or scientific rationality were an advance over most early ecological research, which employed purely phenomenological or corroborative rationality. Because of the heterogeneity of ecological entities and their interactions, and because of the organismic character of ecological phenomena generally, most early ecological research was phenomenological or corroborative. That is, as Strong (1982a, pp. 245ff.) points out, it focused on collection of data without ostensible hypotheses, or on interpretation of data (without rigorous testing) so as to corroborate positive hypotheses. Both the phenomenological and corroborative accounts of ecological rationality tended to develop deductive theory that treated an hypothesis as true or that unified circumstantial evidence which corroborated an hypothesis or theory (Strong 1982a, p. 247). Such a notion of rationality is problematic, however, because it is insufficiently critical and falsificationist. Also, if phenomenological or corroborative rationality is carried to an extreme, corroboration comes close to advocacy in science. Skeptical of approaches to ecological theory building that were insufficiently critical, Williams (1964), Simberloff (1970), and others attacked corroborative rationality and posed null hypotheses for several major questions of island biogeography. In part because of these criticisms, ecologists began to move away from a purely phenomenological or corroborative account of rationality and to move toward a scientific or epistemic view. This scientific account of rationality was aimed at hypothetical-deductive and Popperian testing of hypotheses and at explicit formulation of precise null models. With the move away from corroborative or phenomenological research and the emphasis on H-D falsification, ecology became more empirical and more rigorous.

The increased rigor of the scientific or epistemic account of ecological rationality, however, did not resolve all the difficulties with ecological method. As we have already argued (see chapter 3), null hypotheses have been difficult to formulate and typically controversial. Moreover, methodological value judgments and the absence of clear, unambiguous ecological concepts have hindered both hypothesis deduction and the formulation of null hypotheses in ecology. Also, as we shall argue in this chapter, the scientific account of ecological rationality often gives problematic advice in situations of factual or statistical uncertainty. In situations of uncertainty, ecologists following a scientific account of rationality typically minimize type-I (rather than type-II) statistical error. In subsequent paragraphs, we shall show that their doing so is often wrong and that, in situations of uncertainty, scientists ought to minimize type-II (rather than type-I) error, when both cannot be avoided. We shall argue that ecologists probably need to follow an ethical notion of rationality, rather than a purely scientific account.

6.2 Ecology and uncertainty

To begin our consideration of statistical error and rationality in ecology, recall the 1986–1988 deforestation/extinction controversy in the pages of the *ESA Bulletin*. We discussed this controversy in chapter 4 and pointed out that ecologists were divided on the issue of how to interpret ecological studies that could be used to justify destruction of the tropical environment. Scientists on both sides of the dispute invoked the notion of statistical errors of types I and II to defend their positions. Noss argued that, in situations of ecological uncertainty, the desirable and conservative course of action would be to risk type-I, rather than type-II, errors (Noss 1986, p. 278). Simberloff, however, argued that in a situation of uncertainty, "risking type-I rather than type-II error is not the most conservative course" (Simberloff 1987, p. 156). Since neither argument has been developed in detail, it will be instructive to investigate them and to see what the dispute reveals about the nature of uncertainty, rationality, and explanation in ecology. We shall argue that, in a situation of uncertainty, there are prima-facie grounds for siding with Noss. That is, in a situation of uncertainty, when both types of error cannot be avoided, there are prima-facie grounds for risking type-I (over type-II) error. Hence, in cases of uncertainty, ecologists ought to adopt an ethical (rather than a purely scientific) account of ecological rationality.

To understand how avoiding certain types of statistical errors can help provide prima-facie guidelines for actions under uncertainty, it might help to consider some of the examples of scientific, technological, and environmental uncertainty that currently plague policymakers. Whether one is attempting to halt contamination from Chernobyl or Bhopal, to contain an Alaskan oil spill, or to prevent extinction of the Florida panther, the main problem is the same. One must act quickly, because of the high stakes, despite the absence of needed scientific theory and empirical information. Consider the case of scientists who must assess the consequences of developing a liquefied natural gas (LNG) facility. Given a volatile but uncertain situation, with many vested interests and policy consequences, what are the ethical constraints on how scientists ought to interpret the results of their studies to the public, to developers–industry, and to environmentalists? If the scientists overemphasize the LNG risk, in a situation of uncertainty, the community and industry could suffer serious economic losses because of their desire to avoid development of a LNG facility. If they underemphasize the risk, in a situation of uncertainty, the community could suffer serious environmental and health losses in the event of a LNG accident that could kill hundreds of persons. How should the scientists decide? The best studies, produced in West Germany, the Netherlands, the UK and the USA, disagree. Expert estimates of risks to persons living near LNG terminals vary by a factor of 100 million (Otway and Peltu 1985, p. 12)! Much of the expert disagreement regarding uncertain environmental consequences, like LNG risks, is caused either by new technologies or by the empirical underdetermination of the scientific information with which we must work. In the first case, experience with new technologies, like nuclear fission and LNG, is so limited that the frequency of low-probability, high-consequence accidents is uncertain (Shrader-Frechette 1983, pp. 82–85). For example, before the Browns Ferry nuclear accident occurred, government experts said that it had the same probability as that a large meteor would strike the earth. Assessors likewise called the Chernobyl accident "highly improbable" before it happened (Raloff and Silberner 1986, p. 292). This illustrates that it is difficult to assess the likelihood and the environmental impacts of a new technology (see Shrader-Frechette 1993).

Empirically underdetermined ecological information likewise militates against assessing the probability and the scope of certain environmental consequences. Because there are no general, quantitative laws and only a few rough generalizations governing species extinctions and the design of nature reserves, for example, ecologists like Noss, Simberloff, and Kangas are dependent upon situation-specific, species-specific empirical studies in order to determine how to achieve preservation. But such empirical data are in as short supply as are frequency studies for low-probability, high-consequence environmental impacts. Because of this empirical underdetermination and uncertainty, scientists are forced to make methodological value judgments (see chapter 4) in order to provide requested input to policymakers. In such situations, one value judgment (that scientists must make) concerns which type of error is more preferable, type-I or type-II, given a situation of uncertainty in which both kinds of error are not avoidable.

6.3 Type-I and type-II statistical errors

Statisticians tell us that when a decision is made about an hypothesis, at least two different types of error may occur. Errors of type-I occur when one rejects a true null hypothesis; errors of type-II occur when one fails to reject a false null hypothesis (see, for example, Lindgren 1968, p. 278). A null hypothesis is a claim of no effect. One null hypothesis, for example, is that "Drug x has no detectable beneficial value." Statistical procedure dictates that we make assumptions about the size of each of these types of error that can be tolerated, and on this basis we choose a testing pattern for our hypothesis. The concept of *significance*, for example, is often defined in terms of a type-I risk of error of either 0.01 or 0.05, where there is not more than a 1 in 100 or a 5 in 100 chance of committing the error of rejecting a true hypothesis. Determining significance, however, is not a sufficient basis for answering an important question. Which is the more serious error, type-I or type-II? An analogous issue arises in law. Is a more serious error to acquit a guilty person or to convict an innocent person? In assessing environmental impacts, in a situation of uncertainty where both types of error cannot be avoided, ought one to minimize type-I error (rejecting a true null hypothesis)? Churchman says that when we minimize type-I error, we minimize the error of rejecting a harmless development. He calls this the "Producer Risk." Or ought one to minimize type-II error (not rejecting a false null hypothesis)? Churchman says that when we minimize type-II error, we minimize the error of accepting a harmful development. He calls this the "Consumer Risk" (see Churchman 1947; see Axinn 1966).

In the case of the endangered spotted owl, for example, Churchman's "Producer Risk" and "Consumer Risk" might be better labeled, respectively, "developer risk" and "public risk." This is because those who produce the risk to the owl are most likely to be land *developers*, whereas those who are most likely to be "consumers" of the benefits of owl preservation are members of the *public*. In this revised terminology, minimizing developer risk amounts to minimizing the chance of type-I error, the chance of rejecting the null hypothesis (because significance is set at a high level). One null hypothesis might be, for example, that protection by setting aside *x* amount of old-growth forest will not prevent the extinction of the owl. Minimizing the chance of rejecting this hypothesis means increasing the chance of accepting it. And to the degree that this null hypothesis is accepted, to that same extent will there be no argument for setting aside old-growth forest. If there is no other argument for protecting such forests, then presumably the land that would have been used for the owls can be developed. Such use of the land would presumably benefit developers and reduce their risk, all things being equal, although it would increase the risk to the public as a whole, since the public at large probably has a greater interest in conservation rather than development. (The objection that the public has a greater interest in development, not conservation, will be treated later, in chapter 7). Hence, it is prima-facie true that minimizing developer risk (in Churchman's sense) would increase public risk. An analogous argument can show that it is prima-facie true that minimizing public risk would increase developer risk. For example, minimizing public risk would increase the chance that we shall set aside some old-growth forests. Presumably such protection would benefit the public at large, as opposed to the developers. Statistically, however, although minimizing the probability of type-I error would increase the probability of type-II error, minimizing the probability of type-II error would not increase the probability of type-I error. Moreover, formulating the null hypothesis differently could result in changing the bearer of the risk from the public to the developer. The formulation is based on Churchman's associating type-I error with producer or developer risk and type-II error with consumer or public risk (see Churchman 1947; see Axinn 1966).

How does one decide whether to run the (developer) risk of rejecting a true null hypothesis, for example, that protection by setting aside x amount of old-growth forest will not prevent the extinction of the endangered spotted owl? Or ought one to run the (public) risk of not rejecting an allegedly false null hypothesis, for example, that protection by setting aside x amount of old-growth forest will not prevent the extinction of the owl? To decrease developer risk might hurt the public, and to decrease public risk might hurt the developers, as was already illustrated in the previous paragraph (Churchman 1947; see Axinn 1966). In subsequent pages, we shall argue that, contrary to current practice, ecologists have a prima-facie obligation (see the discussion in section 6.1) to minimize public risk in cases of uncertainty that involve potentially grave threats to welfare. In subsequent chapters, we shall evaluate objections to this claim about our prima-facie obligation.

6.4 Current practice: Assessors minimize developer or type-I risk

Environmental impact assessors (as opposed to ecologists) typically make the value judgment that type-II (over type-I) errors are preferable. They support an *epistemic* or *scientific* concept of rationality under uncertainty. That is, following Churchman's account of type-I and type-II errors, assessors tend to prefer not to reject the null; they prefer the risk of not rejecting a dangerous development to the risk of rejecting a harmless development. Consumers and the public generally, however, tend to support an *ethical* concept of rationality under uncertainty. They tend to reject the null and to prefer type-I (over type-II) errors when both cannot be prevented. That is, on Churchman's account, the public tends to prefer the risk of rejecting a harmless development to the error of not rejecting a dangerous development (see Churchman 1947; see Axinn 1966). After examining some of the reasons why assessors tend to minimize developer risk, we shall argue that, in cases involving public welfare, we can make a stronger prima-facie case for minimizing public risk (when both kinds of risk cannot be avoided) and hence for supporting ethical, rather than merely scientific, rationality under uncertainty.

Assessors' preferences for type-II errors and for minimizing type-I or developer risks might arise, in part, because they appear more consistent with scientific practice. Scientific rationality has traditionally emphasized minimizing type-I errors. Hypothesis-testing in science operates on the basis of limiting false positives (assertions of effects where none exists), or limiting rejections of a true null hypothesis. In order to minimize type-I errors, scientists design studies to guard against the influence of all possible confounding variables, and they demand replication of study results before accepting them as supporting a particular hypothesis. They apply tests of statistical significance which reject results whose probability of being due to chance, whose p value, is greater than, for example, 5 percent. Moreover, it is difficult to see how the scientific enterprise could function without such rigorous reluctance to accept positive results. "The scientist usually attaches a greater loss to accepting a falsehood than to failing to acknowledge a truth. As a result, there is a certain conservatism or inertia in the scientific enterprise, often rationalized as the healthy skepticism characteristic of the scientific temper" (Kaplan 1964, p. 253; see also Connor and Simberloff 1986; Shrader-Frechette and McCoy 1992). The preference for type-II errors, for public risks, is also consistent with the standards of proof required in criminal cases, as opposed to cases in torts. Our law requires the jury in a criminal case to be sure beyond a reasonable doubt that a defendant is guilty, before deciding against him. Standards of proof in criminal cases thus also reveal a preference for type-II error, a preference for not rejecting the null hypothesis or innocence, a preference for the risk of acquitting a guilty person. However, our law requires the jury in a case in torts to believe no more than that it is more probable than not that the defendant is guilty; standards of proof in civil cases thus apparently reveal no preference for either type-I or type-II error. If standards of proof in cases of developer (or type-I) risks ought to be analogous to those in criminal cases, since both involve grave harms, then this analogy provides a good reason for minimizing developer, rather than public, risk and for supporting purely scientific rationality. (As later sections of this chapter will argue, however, standards of proof in assessing environmental impacts are analogous neither to hypothesis-testing in pure science nor to determination of guilt in criminal cases.)

Preferences for scientific or epistemic rationality, for type-II error or public risk, likewise might arise in part from the fact that many impact assessments (e.g., US Nuclear Regulatory Commission 1975) are done by those who are closely associated with the development being evaluated and who are therefore sympathetic to it and to those who implement it. Such assessors typically underestimate environmental risks (Cooke 1982), at least in part because it is difficult to identify all such hazards, and because unidentified risks are typically assumed to be zero. Preferences for minimizing developer risk, in a situation of ecological uncertainty where both kinds of risk cannot be avoided, also likely arise as a consequence of the fact that experts almost always use widely accepted Bayesian decision rules based on expected utility and subjective probabilities. Typically, Bayesians maximize *average* expected utility. The maximin decision rule, however, requires one to choose the option whose worst outcome is better than the worst outcome of all the other options (Harsanyi 1975, p. 594). Using a Bayesian decision rule (especially when those sympathetic to development provide the subjective probabilities) almost always generates a choice in favor of a low probability, but potentially catastrophic, technology or irreversible environmental impact (like species extinction), whereas using a maximin decision rule likely produces a verdict against an uncertain (but catastrophic or irreversible) environmental impact (Cooke 1982, pp. 341–342). In other words, different norms for rational decisionmaking under uncertainty produce conflicting evaluations about the acceptability of the environmental impact. Contrary to most assessors, we shall argue that there are prima-facie grounds for minimizing public, rather than developer, risk – for minimizing type-II error in cases of uncertainty – and hence for supporting ethical as well as scientific rationality in ecology.

6.5 The prima-facie case for minimizing public risk

Arguing that there are prima-facie grounds (see section 6.1) for reducing public risk amounts to showing that the burden of proof (regarding risk acceptability) should be placed on the person wishing to reduce developer, rather than public, risk when both cannot be avoided. If this argument is correct then, in the absence of evidence to the contrary, one has grounds for assuming that public risk ought to be minimized, and that the ecologist ought to err on the side of preservation or conservation.

There are a number of reasons for holding that assessors' and ecologists' prima-facie duty is to minimize type-II errors, viz., (in Churchman's terms) to minimize the risk of not rejecting a dangerous development/environmental action, or to minimize public risk. Most of these arguments focus on minimizing the risk faced by the public, as the *kind* of risk most deserving of reduction. The remaining arguments focus on the public as the *locus* of decisionmaking regarding environmental risk, since it is typically laypersons who argue for reducing public risk. (In addition to these prima-facie arguments, a great many other considerations could be introduced regarding minimizing public (type-II), rather than developer (type-I) risk, although there is neither time nor space to sketch them here. Some of these considerations (see Shrader-Frechette 1991, ch. 8), for example, reiterate the famous debate between Rawls (1971, pp. 152ff.) and Harsanyi (1975) over choosing a maximin, rather than a Bayesian, expected-utility decision rule.) Examining these main prima-facie arguments, as well as the important objections to them, will provide a number of insights about prima-facie principles that are applicable to cases of ecological decisionmaking under uncertainty.

6.5.1 Rights to protection, risk–benefit symmetry, and public needs

Minimizing the chance, in a situation of uncertainty, of not rejecting false null hypotheses – viz., minimizing judgments that a harmful environmental impact is harmless – is prima-facie reasonable on ethical grounds. Most political theorists, regardless of their persuasion, would probably agree that it is prima-facie more important to protect the public from serious harm (e.g., loss of species, nuclear accidents) than to enhance welfare (e.g., by permitting land development, by providing electrical power on demand). This is in part because the right to protection against those who cause harm is more basic than rights to welfare. It is more important, in society, to prevent acts that cause serious harm than to promote acts that enhance welfare. As part of the Hippocratic oath puts it: "First, do no harm." But this raises at least two questions. (1) What if persons do not accept the fact that loss of a species, subspecies, or a unique habitat is a harm against which they ought to be protected? This objection raises the question of the importance of environmental education. We shall address it later. (2) Why is protecting society against loss of a species, subspecies, or a unique habitat a case of protection against harm, rather than a case of enhancing welfare?

The answer to question (2) involves many considerations, not all of which can be treated here. One important factor is that a species, subspecies, or a unique habitat contributes to diversity, and presumably this is at least an aesthetic benefit to humans. Species, subspecies, and unique habitats also enhance human welfare on instrumental and utilitarian grounds, because of their medicinal and economic importance, or because they contribute to human health, food, industry, or shelter. Moreover, even for species, subspecies, or habitats with no known economic benefits, medicinal or otherwise, future scientific discoveries leave room for the possibility that they may be useful at a later date. Also, apart from economic considerations, species and habitats have both inherent worth and a variety of intrinsic and instrumental values for humans (see Taylor 1986). Because species, subspecies, and habitats contribute to well-being in all these ways, causing their extinction or disappearance, while sometimes ethically defensible, is nevertheless an act that, on prima-facie grounds, is harmful to our well-being. To cause extinction or disappearance of a species, subspecies, or habitat is also questionable because it is to destroy something that already exists. Presumably if one brought a new species or subspecies to some area or introduced a new habitat, a case could be made, under some circumstances, that the act constituted an enhancement of welfare. But if one causes a species or subspecies to go extinct or a habitat to disappear, then one has destroyed something that already exists. As a consequence, humans can no longer enjoy the species, subspecies, or habitat. One has reduced welfare, and one has failed to protect against loss of a good (the species, subspecies, or the habitat). If one fails to allow economic development in a given area, however, one is not reducing welfare. One is not taking away something, like a species or subspecies, that already exists there. Hence, to permit economic development is more a case of enhancing welfare, rather than a case of protecting against harm. And if so, then all things being equal, it is more important (on prima-facie grounds) to protect the public from (type-II errors) not rejecting a seriously harmful environmental impact than to protect it from (type-I errors) rejecting a harmless impact. This is at least in part because protecting from serious harm seems to be a necessary condition for enjoying other freedoms (see, for example, Lichtenberg 1981; Shue 1981). Later, in subsequent chapters, we shall consider objections to this prima-facie conclusion.

Bentham (1962a, p. 301), in discussing an important part of liberalism, argued that the sole object of government ought to be the greatest happiness of the greatest possible number of the community, and that happiness consists in maximum enjoyment and minimum suffering. However, he cautioned, much as Nozick (and others who argue for only minimal ethical obligations) might, that "the care of providing for his enjoyments ought to be left almost entirely to each individual; the principal function of government being to protect him from sufferings." In other words, Bentham, among others, established protection from serious harm as more basic than providing/enhancing welfare. If he is right, then it is more important to the ecologist to protect from harm (via preservation/conservation) than to enhance welfare. Admittedly, it is difficult to draw the line between what avoids harm and what enhances welfare. Nevertheless, just as there is a basic distinction between negative rights (such as the right not to be murdered) and welfare rights (such as the right to medical care; see, for example, Becker 1984, p. 76), so also there is a basic distinction between protective laws (e.g., prohibiting infringements on already existing species, subspecies, or habitats) and welfare laws (e.g., providing some economic good). Moral philosophers continue to honor distinctions similar to this one. Indeed, they distinguish not only between protective laws and welfare-enhancing laws, but also between closely related concepts, such as killing vs. letting die, and between acts of commission and acts of omission (see, for example, Bentham 1962b, p. 36; Feinberg 1973, pp. 29, 59; Rachels 1980, p. 38; Gewirth 1982, p. 228; Shrader-Frechette 1985b, pp. 77–78). But if so, then there seems to be greater prima-facie grounds for minimizing type-II errors or public risks, since these appear to prohibit positive harm, to protect rather than to enhance welfare, and to govern commissions rather than omissions.

Another prima-facie reason for minimizing public risk is that those who develop land, not the public in general, receive the bulk of benefits from the development. Moreover, even in a socialist country, development would benefit only a subset of the public (present persons), rather than the public at large (present and future persons). Because developers typically receive most of the benefits of their projects, they ought to bear most of the risks and costs. For one large set of persons (the public) to carry most of the risks of an environmental impact (land development), while a small subset (developers) receives most of the benefits, is unfair. Moreover, as one considers the public interest over subsequent generations, it becomes even more obvious that the present and future public bears most of the costs of development, whereas a small subset of present persons (developers) receives most of the benefits. Such a situation is asymmetrical, in an ethical sense, since those who bear the costs ought to receive the benefits. Such a situation also amounts to a gerrymandering of the concepts of justice and property (see Hoffman and Fisher 1984, pp. 211–220).

Of course, it might be objected that ecologists have a duty, for the good of the *economy* (which allegedly maximizes overall welfare) to minimize developer, rather than public, risk. (Harsanyi (1975) uses this argument.) To defend this point, however, the objector would have to establish two main points. He would have to show (1) that minimizing developer risk contributes to overall welfare more than minimizing public risk. Later, in this and the next chapter, we shall argue that (1) is false. The objector also would have to show (2) that his position does not amount to violating a basic ethical rule. This ethical rule prohibits the use of some persons (the public) as a means to the ends of other persons (developers), or as a means to the end of economic welfare. As such, this rule (prohibiting the use of persons as a means to an end) is presupposed both by most moral philosophers and by tort law and by the legal guarantees of the Fifth and Fourteenth Amendments to the US *Constitution* (see, for example, Kant 1964, pp. 95–98; Gewirth 1982, p. 226; Shrader-Frechette 1983, pp. 33–35, 1985b, pp. 71–72). It should be difficult to defend the claim (2) that minimizing developer risk does not violate this ethical rule. Such a defense would be implausible, because it would require justifying violation of persons' rights to bodily security and to equal protection (from developer-induced adverse impacts). If some persons may be treated as means to the ends of other persons, then those in the former group obviously have no claims to either sort of right. Rather, they are victims of discrimination practiced in the name of economic efficiency. If persons could be discriminated against, however, whenever it was economically expedient to do so, then the concept of rights would have no meaning. Since persons do have rights to bodily security and to equal protection, however, there must be an ethical rule against using persons as a means to the ends of others. But if there is such a rule, then maximizing economic welfare cannot justify a preference for type-II error or for public risk (see Frankena 1962, pp. 10, 14; Lichtenberg 1981; Shue 1981). And if not, then economic considerations do not necessarily support development over conservation/preservation.

Of course, someone might object that many development projects do maximize overall welfare while avoiding using persons as means to the ends of other persons. Obviously, some development is good, and much of it is unavoidable. For example, in a socialist society, someone might claim, development is especially likely to maximize welfare and to avoid violating this ethical rule. The difficulty with the socialist defense of development over conservation, however, is that maximizing the welfare of all *present* persons does not guarantee that one is maximizing the welfare of all *present and future* persons. Hence, even in a socialist society, one could be using future persons as means to the ends of present persons. If one is to defend minimizing developer (as opposed to public) risk, then one bears the burden of proof (1) that minimizing developer risk contributes to overall welfare (present and future) more than minimizing public risk. As we mentioned several paragraphs earlier, we shall argue in this and the next chapter that (1) is false. Our subsequent argument is neither socialist nor capitalist. Rather, it has to do with both equity and ecology: Ecological decision-making ought to take account of all persons, not just those with the most capital, not just members of present generations, and not just those who are well informed about environmental issues and their own welfare. (Later, in chapter 7, we also shall argue that conservation is economically beneficial. In chapter 9, we shall argue that consideration of the greater good outweighs economic efficiency in making public policy).

There are also prima-facie grounds for limiting public, rather than developer, risk because the public typically needs more risk protection than do developers. The people need more protection because they usually have fewer financial resources than developers. They also have greater needs because they usually are privy to less information about how to deal with societal/environmental hazards created by industry and by developers, and because they are often faced with bureaucratic denials of public danger or threats to their interests. Laypersons' vulnerability in this regard is well established in a number of cases of environmental risk. For example, when the toxic polybrominated biphenyl (PBB) was accidentally used in cattle feed in Michigan, it was the most widespread, least reported, chemical disaster ever to happen in the western world. There was strong evidence of contamination in September 1973, but detailed articles on the problem did not appear, even in the local papers, for two more years. Larger newspapers, like the *Detroit Free Press* and the *Detroit News*, did not examine the crisis until four years after it was evident. The reason for ignoring the problem for so long was that the local bureaucrats denied the claims made by the farmers. Typically, what happened was that a reporter would interview the owner of a contaminated farm, who would tell him about the massive problems of contamination. Next, the reporter would check with the Michigan Farm Bureau and the Michigan Department of Agriculture which would tell him that the PBB contamination was under control, and that the farmer's allegations were unfounded and exaggerated. Because of all this bureaucratic denial, PBB led to the deaths of tens of thousands of farm animals and to the contamination of nine million persons who ate tainted meat (Peltu 1985, p. 132).

The case of mercury poisoning in Japan likewise is a good example of typical failures to protect against public risk because of bureaucratic denials, industry indifference, and the isolation of the afflicted. In Japan, the dangers of mercury poisoning were identified in 1940, deaths were reported in 1948, and Minimata poisoning occurred in 1953. Only in the 1960s, however, did public awareness of the problem cause officials to take action against mercury contamination. Because of denial, indifference, and similar instances of whistle-swallowing (rather than whistle-blowing) in cases such as asbestos, biotechnology, and chemical dumps, there is a strong possibility that new public risks will be ignored. Hence, there is reason to believe that the public, rather than industry and developers, has a greater need for protection (Peltu 1985, pp. 132–136). And if so, then ecologists have a prima-facie obligation, in situations of uncertainty involving grave threats to welfare, to err on the side of preservation/conservation, rather than development. And if ecologists have such a duty, then ecological rationality is also ethical, rather than merely epistemic or scientific.

6.5.2 Rights to compensation and to consent

Yet another reason for minimizing public risk, especially in cases of uncertainty, is that the public ought to be accorded rights to protection against developers' or industrialists' decisions that could impose incompensable damages. These rights arise out of the consideration that everyone has an obligation to compensate those whom he harms. Apart from damage to the earth, minimizing type-I error can cause uncompensated harms to persons who have an interest in environmental welfare and in maintaining species/subspecies or habitat diversity. To the degree that environmental benefits, like biodiversity and clean air, are part of the "commons," then to that same degree do we all have rights to them. As Aldo Leopold put it, in his introduction to *A Sand County Almanac*: "the chance to find a pasqueflower is a right as inalienable as free speech" (1949, vii). To the degree that we all have similar natural claims, to that same extent ought we to minimize public risk, risk to this "commons." But if so, then those who impose or increase public risk have a duty either to minimize the risk, or to protect persons from it, or to compensate the public for its imposition. To see why this duty follows, consider the three basic forms of protection against damages caused by others.

The problem of protecting the public against the extended effects of development/industrial decisions typically addresses three general kinds of protection, namely, *prevention, transferral* of loss, and *retention* of the risk. When the public protects itself against losses due to the decisions of others by maintaining enough assets to sustain damages caused by those decisions, it protects itself by *retention* of the risk. In the case of losing a species or subspecies, however, it is obvious that the public cannot retain enough assets to prevent or to counter this harm. When the public uses mechanisms like insurance and legal liability to *transfer* some of the risk/loss, it is protecting itself against harms resulting from other persons' (industry's or developers') decisions by transferring some of the loss to someone else, namely, the insurer or the liable party. The practical advantage of risk transfer over retention is that it does not require one to retain as many assets, idle and unproductive, as a way of guarding against damages. The moral advantage is that, if the harm itself is caused by another legal/moral "person," an industry or developer, then that person is liable, not the individual whose interests are harmed. And if the person causing the damage is liable, then there are practical grounds for using this moral responsibility as a basis for making the developer, producer, or his insurer financially responsible to those whose interests are hurt. Obviously insurance can help repair some damages (e.g., financial losses caused by a leaking toxic waste facility), even though it cannot repair the damage caused by irreversible environmental impacts such as species or subspecies extinction. Where environmental damage can be alleviated, insurance is probably a better vehicle for risk transfer than is liability, since the transaction costs involved in being awarded benefits are probably less (Denenberg *et al.* 1964).

Prevention, of course, is the most thorough way for members of recipient populations to protect themselves against damages resulting from the decisions of others. As is already evident, neither retention nor transfer of certain environmental risks is feasible when the harms are irreversible and cannot be adequately compensated. Thus, by eliminating/preventing the sources of the environmental risk, the potential victim has more to gain, practically speaking, than by using insurance and retention as means of protection. This is because prevention does not tie up any of the potential victim's assets. The moral grounds for preventing environmental impacts are that, in cases where those responsible/liable cannot redress or compensate the harms done to others by their faulty decisions, the risks should be eliminated. Causing a subspecies or species to become extinct or a particular type of habitat to be destroyed is not like causing a car to be wrecked. The car is replaceable and compensable; the species or subspecies is not, and the habitat is not. And if not, then the risks to the public because of threats like extinction should be minimized. In other words, if all persons have rights to have harm done to them redressed/compensated, and if those who make faulty industrial/developmental decisions cannot make good on the injury to persons' interests or welfare that they have caused, then they ought not be allowed to put the interests of others in jeopardy. They ought not place themselves in a position where they have responsibility for societal or development decisions. To do so, when they cannot meet claims against them, is to deny in-principle rights of victims to compensation or redress of damages.

If we consider Judith Jarvis Thomson's notion of "incompensable harms," harms so serious that no amount of money could possibly compensate the victims, then it appears that death and extinction, at least, are obviously "incompensable harms." They are incompensable because there is no way to compensate a dead person or to reverse an irreversible change like extinction. As Thomson puts it, speaking of another case, "however fair and efficient the judicial system may be, . . . [those] who cause incompensable harms by their negligence cannot square accounts with their victims" (Thomson 1986, p. 158). This means that anyone who imposes a significant risk (e.g., death) on another, without his free, informed consent, is imposing an *incompensable*, and therefore morally unjustifiable, harm. But if imposition of incompensable risks might be justified in cases in which potential victims give free, informed consent, then this suggests another reason for minimizing public risk, as opposed to producer/developer risk: The public is less likely than the developer/producer to have given full, informed consent to the imposition of an environmental or technological risk. Yet, there ought to be no imposition of risk without the free, informed consent of those who must bear it. This dictum holds true in medical experimentation, and it could easily be shown to have an analogue in managing environmental risks imposed by humans (Shrader-Frechette 1985b, pp. 107ff.).

The public is less likely to have given free, informed consent to an environmental risk because producers/developers are often privy to scientific or technical information that they do not share with the public. Patents, profits, and competition with other businessmen often keep them from providing information about risk to the public. For example, universities often do not provide information (and indeed frequently suppress it) about campus crime to students and prospective students. The public as a whole is also less likely than industrialists or developers to give free, informed consent to a dangerous environmental impact, both because the public often has less scientific and technical expertise than risk imposers, and because professionals frequently behave in a paternalistic way toward the public. Since governments or vested interests sometimes suppress information about scientific and environmental risks, this further jeopardizes the public's right to free, informed consent. Moreover, as we shall argue later, there is evidence that most of those bearing high levels of public risk have not given free, informed consent. For all these reasons, it is probable that members of the public are less likely to give free, informed consent to uncompensated and incompensable risks than are developers/producers. Hence there are prima-facie grounds for minimizing public risk, rather than developer/producer risk, in situations of uncertainty, and for erring on the side of preservation/conservation, rather than development. But if so, then there are prima-facie grounds for arguing that ecological rationality, in cases of uncertainty posing grave threats, ought to be ethical as well as scientific.

6.5.3 Minimizing public risks by giving the public decisionmaking power

There are also strong economic grounds for minimizing public risk whenever this minimization is consistent with consumer preferences. It makes sense to let members of the public decide the fate of proposed land developments (and therefore to minimize public risk, if they wish), because consumer sovereignty is not justified merely by reference to the alleged unseen hand controlling economic events, but by democratic process or "procedural rationality." (For analyses of collective strategies whereby the public might exercise its sovereignty, see Shrader-Frechette 1985a, pp. 286–312. For discussion of procedural rationality, see Bartlett 1986, pp. 223ff.) This justification is a revered one: "no taxation without representation" (Schelling 1984, pp. 145–146). Welfare economics establishes the convenience and efficiency of consumer sovereignty, and citizens themselves, as Schelling (1984, pp. 145–146) notes, have safeguarded it by means of "arms, martyrdom, boycott, or some principles held to be self-evident. . . . [It] includes the inalienable right of the consumer to make his own mistakes." Minimizing public risk, in the name of public self-determination, is also consistent with most ethical theories about situations in which paternalism is/is not justified. And if so, then developers ought not behave paternalistically toward the public, in alleging that impositions of environmental risk are in the interests of society. But if not, then the public itself needs to have the liberty to decide about the legitimacy of risk imposed on it. To exercise such liberty, the public needs information about the total risks of conservation and development.

In his classic discussion of liberty, in 1859, Mill (1986) makes it clear that it is acceptable to override individual decisionmaking only to protect others or to keep someone from selling himself into slavery. Any other justification for a limitation on individual freedom, claims Mill, would amount to a dangerous infringement on individual autonomy. If Mill is correct, then there are no paternalistic grounds for overriding societal hesitancies about accepting a particular environmental impact. In other words, paternalism appears acceptable only to protect from slavery the person whose judgment is overridden or to protect others from being harmed by the person whose judgment is overridden. And if so, then there are no prima-facie grounds for using paternalism to justify decisions that threaten environmental welfare, especially if the public chooses to protect it. Admittedly, the public may make bad choices, but this defect is not grounds for denying persons' rights to self-determination. Rather, it suggests that we have a duty to educate the public about authentic environmental risks. We shall discuss this point later in more detail.

Minimizing public risk also appears desirable because doing so might be less likely to lead to social disruption and political unrest than minimizing developer risk. Although defending this point is not the goal of this chapter, it appears that there are pragmatic and political, as well as ethical and economic, grounds for following society's preferences to minimize public risk. The willingness of indigenous peoples to die rather than to have their lands developed, and the readiness of numerous persons to engage in civil disobedience – to protect the environment – illustrate the fact that management of environmental welfare cannot even be begun without cooperation between developers and the public. Moreover, political control is no substitute for this cooperation. Both developers and the public must agree to do without some things and to accept substitutes for others. They must vote sensibly, act reasonably, and engage in much give-and-take over planning and environmental standards. They must obey the law, and they must use the legal system sensibly. If they do not, then the plans of any developer could be crippled. In other words, "even if the experts were much better judges of risk than laypeople, giving experts an exclusive franchise for . . . [environmental] management would mean substituting short-term efficiency for the long-term effort needed to create an informed citizenry" (Slovic *et al.* 1982, p. 488).

6.6 Give priority to the public

The consequentialist analysis in this chapter argues that there are prima-facie reasons for giving priority, in situations of uncertainty, to public welfare and public decisionmaking. It argues that ecologists ought to employ both ethical and scientific rationality in such cases and that they ought to give priority, in cases of uncertainty, to conservation/preservation, rather than to development. In emphasizing the prima-facie priority of third-party obligations, we are emphasizing the primacy of public, democratic control of conservation decisions. Our conclusion reemphasizes a point that Jefferson made: the only safe locus of power in a democracy is the people. Minimizing public risk or type-II error, in a situation of uncertainty when the public demands more environmental welfare, is one way to locate power with the people. It is also one way to make policymaking both more democratic and more sensitive to the ethical dimensions of environmental impacts. By arguing that ecologists in a situation of uncertainty have a prima-facie obligation to minimize type-II (rather than type-I) errors, we are arguing that ecological rationality ought to encompass ethical analysis of *actions*, as well as epistemic or scientific consideration of *hypotheses*. In other words, in a situation of uncertainty where the public faces catastrophic or irreversible consequences as a result of ecologists' decisions, we ought to employ ethical rationality.

7 · Objections to ethical rationality in ecology

JOHN STUART MILL, in his 1859 classic *On Liberty* (Mill 1986, pp. 60–61), argued that the surest way of getting to the truth was to examine all the important objections that could be brought against each candidate opinion. He believed that dogmatism, orthodoxy, and ideology are the enemies of science and philosophy, precisely because their proponents fail to consider objections to their positions. Gordon Allport (1950, p. 59) made a similar point in a more psychological way; he said that commitments were "mature" only if they were open-ended and able to take account of objections to them. In this chapter, we examine the most important objections likely to be brought against our claim that, in situations of ecological uncertainty with potentially grave consequences, where avoiding both types of error is impossible, ecologists have a prima-facie ethical obligation to minimize type-II statistical error, or public risk. In other words, we argue that ecologists ought to follow ethical as well as scientific rationality, in part because our duties to the public and to preservation are primary. Therefore, ecological decisionmaking under uncertainty ought to reflect this fact. Ecological rationality, we explain, is not the same as that in much of science, because ecological decisions often have consequences that affect our duties to others, our own rights, and ethical ideals. Because they often affect welfare, both ethical and epistemological considerations need to be taken into account. Hence, we argue that ecology typically requires (what we defined in the last chapter as) "ethical rationality." Against these conclusions, some scholars are likely to object on a variety of grounds.

Even if they are correct, the arguments for minimizing public and environmental risks, and for following ethical rationality, raise at least two questions. (1) When is someone imposing an incompensable risk or harm on others without their free, informed consent? And (2) how can one speak of incompensable damage done to the *environment* (e.g., species, subspecies, or habitats) as comparable to harms done to *persons*, since the law protects the latter much more than the former? Another formulation of this second objection is as follows. Since the law doesn't always recognize that persons' interests are hurt when the environment is harmed, except in cases of damaging persons' property, how can one speak of minimizing environmental risk, on the grounds that it threatens persons' interests? Let us examine the first question first. Later we shall address a variety of objections brought against the prima-facie arguments discussed in previous chapters.

7.1 What is incompensable harm?

When is someone imposing an incompensable harm on others without their free, informed consent? Although the boundary cases would be difficult to decide, incompensable harms appear to be those either that cause human death (because one cannot compensate a dead person) or that result in irreversible environmental damage (because one cannot compensate for serious damages when the harm and its effects are neither completely reversible nor capable of being assented to, especially by future persons affected by them). Insofar as potentially catastrophic technologies like nuclear power place a significant risk of death on humans, and insofar as they impose perpetual, irreversible radiation damage on the environment (damage that is neither completely reversible nor capable of full mitigation), such technologies appear to be paradigm examples of those that impose incompensable harm. For example, the US government admits both that a nuclear accident could kill 150,000 persons, and that the core-melt probability, for all existing and planned US commercial reactors, is 1 in 4 during their 30-year lifetimes (Shrader-Frechette 1983, pp. 85ff.). Moreover, US citizens are prohibited by law (the Price–Anderson Act) from obtaining full compensation from the negligent utility, in the event that there is a commercial nuclear catastrophe (Shrader-Frechette 1991, 1993). Hence, despite obvious problems with other energy technologies, there are strong grounds for believing that the nuclear risk is a public risk that is uncompensated and perhaps incompensable.

Other cases of incompensable harm seem to arise most often in connection with catastrophic, irreversible impacts that are incapable of full mitigation and whose magnitude is uncertain, for example, deforestation causing possible species extinction. Precisely because such impacts are catastrophic, irreversible, and incapable of full mitigation, they have the potential for causing incompensable harm. Therefore, one might argue that the risks they impose are unjustifiable. This is all the more true if the probability of harm is uncertain, because the persons causing the risk are in principle unable to know how grave a danger they are imposing. And if there is uncertainty about the quantity and nature of the harm, then it also would be difficult (if not impossible) to prove that imposing such a risk would lead to greater good for all. This is because, in a situation of uncertainty, one would have to employ a (fallacious) "argument from ignorance" to defend the risk imposition. And if so, then the risk imposition is likely indefensible.

7.2 Why is environmental damage harm to humans?

But the notion of "greater good for all" brings us to the question of how one can speak of incompensable harms and damage done to the *environment* (e.g., non-human species and subspecies or habitats), as opposed to harms done to *persons*, since the law protects the latter but not always the former. Why is environmental damage a public risk? And why are humans said to have rights to the environmental commons? Both of these questions are important if we wish to explain, to the public at large, the benefits of environmental preservation. Many members of the public do not share a biocentric outlook, and hence it is important to reveal the anthropocentric, as well as the biocentric, basis for our arguments.

It is evident that much law throughout the world (including rights to life, liberty, due process, equal protection, and informed consent) protects humans against environmental threats to their bodily security, for example, because of toxic waste. The case for protection against largely environmental harms (that pose no immediate physical danger to humans), such as species extinction, is much harder to make. It is more difficult to show that largely environmental threats, as opposed to serious, physical threats to human welfare, ought to be avoided. Despite this difficulty, however, there are a number of reasons for arguing that threats to environmental welfare are also important public risks that ought to be avoided. For one thing, humans, like other organisms on the planet, are dependent on the earth for life and health. This means that whatever threatens the environmental welfare of the planet ultimately threatens human well-being. Over the long term, human and environmental well-being are inseparable. Human and environmental welfare are intimately connected and interdependent. Human life-support systems ultimately depend on non-humans.

Threats to environmental well-being (to species, habitats, or ecosystems, for example) are also threats to public welfare because the environment is a great commons, as we suggested earlier. Later, we shall examine objections to this prima-facie thesis (that threats to environmental welfare are also threats to humans). Prior to this examination of counterarguments, however, we can say that we subscribe to a principle that is prima-facie true: The principle is that, when the commons is damaged, through air and water pollution or species extinction, then the natural rights of all persons, present and future, to this commons are jeopardized (see Hardin 1968, pp. 1243–1248; Callahan 1971, 1973, 1974; Shrader-Frechette 1981, pp. 239–269). One reason for our failure to recognize these natural rights to the environmental commons is that our political and ethical traditions have been misinterpreted. Although Locke, one of the main architects of these traditions, has typically been hailed as the defender of unlimited capitalistic appropriation of property (see Strauss 1953; Macpherson 1962), careful reading of his views actually lends support to restriction of property rights, especially in natural resources like land (Caldwell and Shrader-Frechette 1993, ch. 4). This careful reading reveals that there are at least four reasons for arguing that, although he may not have intended it, Locke provides a foundation for limiting individual property rights to natural resources like land, so as to make them subservient to the common good. One reason is that Locke makes property subject to the requirements of what he calls the "original community" and "the law of nature." In the original community of humanity, all property was held in common; Locke even points out that God gave the earth to humans in common (Locke 1960, II, 25–26). Moreover, Locke says that the fundamental "law of nature" is "the preservation of Mankind" (Locke 1960, II, 135). This law "bounds" property, he says, so that it must be used for the good of all (Locke 1960, II, 31).

The main justification for believing that Locke provides a basis for the claim that property rights ought to be circumscribed by considerations of the common good is his famous "Proviso." In the Proviso, Locke argued that we had a natural right to whatever we could use (without waste) from the environmental commons, provided that there was "as much and as good" left for all other persons (Locke 1967, p. 306). That is, Locke believed that our rights to land, for example, were circumscribed by the rights of other persons to equal opportunity to obtain land. Another reason why there may be no Lockean support for full property rights in land, much as developers appear to claim, is that the value of land, for Locke, is not derived completely from labor (Locke 1960, II, 40). No humans labored to create natural resources like land, and hence no humans ought to have complete control over, or property rights in, land. Much control over land must rest with the community, acting as trustee for all persons to whom land and resources have been given in common. Finally, because all property, including land, is subject to Locke's productivity criterion, it is subject to community control. Locke argued that, because there is an obligation in natural law to help preserve humankind, there must also be an obligation to use resources "to the best advantage of life and convenience" (Locke 1960, II, 25). In other words, Locke's claims appear to require that we use land so as to insure long-term human survival and welfare; hence he explicitly provides a reason to prohibit short-term, economic interests such as those exhibited by some land developers.

Because of these four Lockean restrictions on property, especially property in natural resources like land, there is prima-facie support, in Locke, for preserving habitats and non-human species. If Locke is correct – and both tradition and intuition are on his side – then no development of land or resources can be justified unless "as much and as good" (or at least some compensation or something equivalent in value) is left for others and unless the common good of all persons is served. To the degree that serious, irreversible damage is done to the part of the commons that is appropriated or destroyed (e.g., in human-induced species, subspecies, or habitat extinction), and to the degree that full mitigation of the serious harm is not possible, then it is difficult to argue that "as much and as good" are left for other persons. Hence both Locke and the equal-opportunity doctrine provide a rationale for why any serious environmental harm is ultimately harm to persons. Because much property law is grounded in Lockean notions (Post 1986), if Locke's views can be used to support restrictions on property rights in natural resources like land, then there is a strong basis for saying that both our traditions and institutions support restrictions on individual property rights in land.

The fact that the US has passed the 1973 Endangered Species Act, and that states like Florida have passed the 1977 Endangered and Threatened Species Act, also indicates that humans believe that environmental harms constitute human harms (US Congress 1973b, c; see also Sagoff 1980; Norton 1986, 1987; Varner 1987). The federal act prohibits only federal projects that would destroy the habitat of an endangered species or subspecies, and it was amended in 1978 to allow exemption of certain activities that serve the best interests of a region or of the nation. Nevertheless, it establishes a prima-facie connection between environmental and human welfare as well as a prima-facie obligation to protect endangered species and subspecies, and therefore the public, against dangerous developments that threaten their interests. Moreover, apart from whether the law was passed because of an erroneous belief in the diversity–stability thesis (see the earlier discussion in chapter 4), it remains a law and hence evidence of public support for environmental preservation.

7.3 Is conservation economically beneficial?

At this point, developers might object that the public wants the benefits associated with land development and environmental risks. Hence, developers might claim that those arguing for reducing public or environmental risk must bear the charge of behaving paternalistically toward those who do not want environmental damage minimized. In other words, the objection is that the public often wants (and benefits from) development rather than conservation; hence they want (what we call) "public risk." The objection is that damaging environmental impacts are not necessarily public risks, and that development and its associated impacts may produce a net benefit for the public.

Admittedly, the objection is correct in at least one sense: Sometimes the environmental costs of an action, for example, smallpox eradication, are so minimal that they are offset by benefits to humans. The smallpox case is an extreme, and therefore easy, case because smallpox interacted with no organisms except humans. The question in general, however, is how great the human benefits must be to offset seriously harmful environmental impacts and associated development – for example, building the Aswan Dam, or causing massive extinctions. This is a difficult question because representing hypothesized public or environmental interests is not necessarily representing all the interests of various persons in society. Hence, both environmentalists and developers could claim to be representing the public interest (see Bayles 1981, p. 117). Who actually speaks for the public? There are a number of reasons for believing that environmentalists, not developers, more accurately and more often represent the public. One reason is that, if a law or policy involves no violation of the basic rights of any persons, and if it benefits the public as a whole, then one ought to follow it, rather than those laws and policies that benefit only a subset of the public, for example, developers. Once one realizes that conservation/ preservation benefits all persons, *present and future*, whereas development of an area benefits primarily present developers and those present persons who benefit from development, it appears that a greater number of persons benefits from conservation. Each year, for example, Americans spend more than \$14 billion (\$14 \times 10^9) on nonconsumptive wildlife-related recreation (Duda 1987, p. 108). If the figures for consumptive, wildlife-related recreation were included, the numbers would be many times higher. They illustrate that conservation appears desirable, even on purely economic grounds (see Vining 1990).

While it is true that the current economic benefits of development, at least for some persons, may be greater than the current environmental benefits of preservation, at least for some persons, it is not clear that this makes development morally preferable. It is not necessarily morally preferable because no one has a *moral right*, as such, to develop a particular area. Although a developer may have a *legal right* to certain land, by virtue of purchasing it, he has no moral or legal right to develop it any way he wishes, for at least two reasons. For one thing, there are legal limits imposed by police power and by takings (see Harr and Liebman 1977, pp. 969–979) and by the fact that exclusionary property rights would be incompatible, as Posner points out (see Haar and Liebman 1977, p. 113). There also are moral limits imposed on property rights by the fact that property is only a weak, and not a strong, right in Dworkin's (1977) sense. Weak rights are those whose exercise is contingent on whether they serve the common good; they can be overridden when the common good demands it. Strong rights are those that can never be overridden, for any reason. Among legal and philosophical scholars, there is virtual unanimity that property is not a strong right (see Dworkin 1977, pp. 267–279).

Development also is not prima-facie preferable to preservation because, as we argued earlier, all persons have moral rights to equal opportunity to obtain/use environmental resources such as land. Because of these rights, the burden of proof is on developers to show that their appropriation of land leaves "as much and as good" for others, according to the Lockean criterion. The burden of proof is on the developer – as it would be on anyone who is a potential threat to the environment – to show that, even if a majority of persons appears to prefer actions that threaten the commons, these represent *authentic preferences*, that is, authentic indicators of welfare. For example, even if a majority of present persons appears to prefer destruction of the old-growth forests that are the habitat of the endangered spotted owl, the burden of proof is on them to show that their preferences are authentic indicators of welfare, for both the present and the future. Since using land as a conservation corridor or as a reserve, by definition, leaves it available for the use/enjoyment of all (including future) persons, conservation appears better able than development to leave "as much and as good" for others. If so, it is prima-facie arguable that preservation (as opposed to development) is more in the public interest, and that preservation is an authentic indicator of welfare.

Preservation also appears preferable to development in the light of the fact that there is substantial social-scientific and philosophical evidence that those bearing high levels of public or environmental risk have not given free, informed consent to imposition of the risks (Emmett 1978, pp. 367–374; Egerton 1981, pp. 43–45; Shrader-Frechette 1985b, pp. 97–122). This is obviously true for future persons who will bear the environmental impacts/risks of present generations, but it is also correct for many present persons. Economists have long recognized that risk imposition represents a diminution in welfare for those on whom it is imposed (Starr 1976, p. 16). Since developers impose some risks on the public, along with possible benefits, developers ought to bear the burden of proof in justifying the imposition, particularly since citizens typically have not given free, informed consent to the imposition. In the absence of such a proof, it is not clear that development, with resultant public risk, is more beneficial than is conservation or preservation. Likewise, development is not, in general, more beneficial to the public than preservation because, in at least some cases, technologies/developments with questionable environmental impacts also have at least the potential to "set back" the economy and to reduce overall public welfare. Nuclear technology, for example, has "set back" the economy in the sense that it could not have survived without protection from normal market mechanisms. This protection from the market has, in turn, reduced general welfare because it has allowed the industry to impose an uncompensated risk on the public. If there were no government-guaranteed liability limit for catastrophic accidents involving commercial nuclear fission, then no major US atomic interests would ever have gone into generation of electricity. Even the major pro-nuclear lobby, the Atomic Industrial Forum (AIF) admits this (Shrader-Frechette 1983, ch. 1; 1991). The upshot is that, although nuclear utilities have been relieved of the burden of competing in an open market, including the liability market, they nevertheless have the potential to cripple the economy with a dangerous accident that could (on the government's own estimates) destroy an area the size of Pennsylvania. Regardless of one's position on commercial nuclear power, it is clear that, because of the liability limit, the developer or producer risk is minimized, while the public risk from nuclear power is maximized, a maximization that could easily contribute to economic harm (Shrader-Frechette 1983, ch. 4; 1993).

Hazardous technologies could also "set back" the economy and general welfare in the sense that many of the most dangerous industries (in terms of high public risk and risk aversion) are also among the most capital intensive. Because they are so capital intensive, they threaten the flow of available money for other societal projects and hence jeopardize the economic well-being of society (see, for example, Lovins and Price 1975). Even land development could "set back" the economy and public welfare. Because species extinctions and damage to habitats are not priced on any market but instead are externalities, they are typically ignored in benefit–cost studies. Ignoring such social costs means that policy actions (in which environment-related externalities figure prominently) are based on skewed benefit–cost analyses. Because such analyses reflect only part of the problem, part of the liabilities, they misrepresent welfare and economic measures of it. As a result, policymaking based on such misleading economic analyses has the potential to "set back" the economy, at least in the sense that it might encourage uneconomical decisionmaking (Shrader-Frechette 1985a, especially pp. 133–134). Environment-related externalities, for example, have clearly "set back" the economy in the case of oil spills. Apart from court actions and customer boycotts, the public and economic effects of spills are typically not costed on any market. Indeed, there are liability limits protecting those responsible for oil spills. Only to the degree that company expenditures for oil cleanup are transferred to the public – through higher prices – are such externalities actually costed in part on a market (US Congress 1976, pp. 16, 51–56). This means that, just as the losses associated with habitat damage and species extinction are not exhibited on economic ledgers, so also the losses associated with oil spills do not appear. Costing both sorts of harm as zero, as is typically done, means that policy decisions regarding environmental impacts could be radically uneconomical, at least in the sense that they fail to address authentic losses of welfare. Hence, even on economic grounds, environmental preservation may be preferable to development.

Likewise, although there are numerous methodological problems with existing benefit–cost schemes of evaluating environmental impacts (see Shrader-Frechette 1985a, pp. 121–151), strong arguments can be made that "reasonable environmental measures reduce more environmental damages than they cost" (Wicke 1990, p. 52; see Vining 1990). For every dollar spent to clean up the air, for example, we receive from \$3 to \$15 in avoided environmental damage (Wicke 1990, p. 52). Moreover, whenever we do not act so as to preserve air, water, species, and habitats, our failures cause economic losses. Annual environmental damage in western countries is typically 6 percent of the GNP. In the former West Germany this was DM 103 billion (DM 103×10^9) per year (Wicke 1990, p. 41). At a minimum, environmental destruction should be costed as the amount of money necessary to correct the harm or make the environment whole again. Many economists (Westman 1977; Eden 1990b; McNeeley *et al.* 1990; Potier 1990), for example, explain how the tasks that non-human organisms and habitats perform for society can be quantified and evaluated. Habitats provide a direct harvest of marketable products, for example, fish, minerals, medicines, as well as genetic resources of valuable species for potential use in areas such as agriculture. They also provide quantifiable benefits in terms of pest control, pollination, recreation, aesthetic enjoyment, and study. They provide watershed protection, regulate climate, and keep options open for the future (McNeeley *et al.* 1990, pp. 12, 19; see also Pearsall 1984). Most importantly, habitats generate benefits by virtue of the interdependence of their species and their organic and inorganic individuals. Various interdependencies among species, individuals, and populations result in photosynthesis; breaking down and absorbing pollutants; cycling nutrients; binding and producing soil; degrading organic waste; controlling radiation, climate, and gases in the air; and fixing solar energy.

Preservation also provides even more easily measured benefits of a largely economic nature. For example, the resale dollars lost on US homes near polluted rivers and lakes is $5 billion ($$5 \times 10^9$$) annually; in the former West Germany the annual figure was DM 1 billion (DM 10^9) (Wicke 1990, p. 47). Likewise, the National Wildlife Federation discovered after a recent study, for example, that a mere $200 investment in backyard habitat management can increase real-estate values anywhere from 3 to 10 percent (Duda 1987, p. 108). Their study suggests that, because persons value nature, they are willing to pay more for real estate that is environmentally managed. And if so, then destructive development of a habitat can cause both environmental and economic damage that is costly both to the property owner and to the public. When a habitat becomes unhealthy, society incurs numerous costs, for example, providing waste-water-treatment facilities, once wetlands are destroyed. In fact, one group of researchers calculated the cost of artificially duplicating natural waste-water-treatment facilities and fisheries by other means at $205 thousand per hectare, and this figure does not take into account the value of the site for sulfate reduction, carbon-dioxide fixation, oxygen release, and waterfowl support. Another ecologist obtained a minimum annual value of $1.8 million for a Georgian river–swamp–forest habitat that "performed" ecological services such as groundwater storage, soil binding, water purification, and streamside fertilization (Westman 1977, p. 961; see also McNeeley *et al.* 1990, pp. 27–28). Other persons have calculated that wetlands, for example, perform functions worth between $50 and $80 thousand per acre per year (Sobetzer 1979, p. 214; for economic methods for assigning value to natural resources, see Krutilla and Fisher 1975; Pearce 1976; Sinden and Worrell 1979; Cooper 1981; Fisher 1981; Hufschmidt *et al.* 1983; Brown and Goldstein 1984; Peterson and Randall 1984; Prescott-Allen 1986; Johansson 1987; Barrett 1988).

Apart from the economic value of functions performed by various habitats, an additional reason for preservation is that damage to them is quite costly, as is the expense of repairing them. Neither of these amounts is included in the value of a potential development site, and repair costs for ecological damage can run quite high. For example, because of the pollution of wetlands and water bodies, the National Commission on Water Quality estimated, more than a decade ago, that the cost of treating point sources and storm water by current technology would be $594 billion ($594 × 10^9$). Yet, presumably this amount is only a fraction of that needed for cleaning up already existing problems in US surface waters, as specified in the 1972 Federal Water Pollution Control Act. Moreover, the figure has likely risen in the last ten years, both because of increases in pollution and inflation, and because the annual federal expenditures on waste-water facilities are less than needed. Even in 1977 they were only about $5 billion ($5 × 10^9$) per year, not the $594 billion ($594 × 10^9$) needed (Westman 1977, p. 961). In the former West Germany, the *annual increase* in the cost of drinking water, because of pollution, was DM 6 billion (DM $6 × 10^9$) (Wicke 1990, p. 37), and the figures are even worse for the US.

Some ecologists, studying absorption of air pollution by soil and vegetation, have calculated that there is a net loss of pollution absorption of 440 kilograms of carbon monoxide per hectare per year for every hectare of San Bernadino Freeway built through pasturelands. Yet this figure represents only the partial costs of the loss of pasture. Air-pollution damage alone, for example, from the San Bernadino Freeway has been estimated at $27 million per year, although admittedly some alternatives to the freeway might be just as costly. This damage occurs in part because of the freeway's interfering with plants' ability to absorb other pollutants, bind the soil, and control radiation (Westman 1977, p. 962; see Wicke 1990, p. 52). In practice, of course, all the damages to habitats cannot be repaired. We can't repair species extinction or loss of a unique habitat, for example. Nor can we fully repair many of the effects of groundwater pollution or of contamination by long-lived toxics; likewise we cannot repair already existing damage to global climate. We do not have the technology to accomplish such things and, in many cases (such as extinction), the technology is not even possible. Nor is it always desirable; it is not obvious that preventing smallpox extinction, for example, is as important as preventing extinction of other species. Nevertheless, humans are causing extinction of species at an unprecedented rate. For example, humans caused the extinction of 90 percent of the mammalian genera of the Mediterranean after the development of agriculture (McNeeley et al. 1990, p. 20), and these species cannot be replaced. Although utilitarian reasons are not the only basis for arguing against species extinction, it is important to point out that most of our medicines come from the wild, and over 98 percent of the US agricultural produce is derived from non-native or wild species (McNeeley et al. 1990, p. 57; see also Eden 1990b, pp. 171–186).

One of the main reasons why many damages to habitats and species cannot be repaired is that, although some of them can be recognized and quantified, many of them cannot. Some of the damages result from the interconnectedness of complex ecological systems, damages that are not reducible merely to losses of individual processes. Nevertheless, it is useful to attempt to quantify and assess the value of nature's services because there is such a large gap between present undervaluing of environmental goods and the valuing that ought to be done, even on economic grounds, if a complete accounting is required. Although economic analyses are inadequate, in important ways, to the full task of environmental evaluation, nevertheless it is important to point out that, even on economic grounds, we are undervaluing the environment (see Johansson 1987; Barrett 1988; McNeeley et al. 1990, pp. 26ff.; Vining 1990). Once these full values are recognized, then it does not appear reasonable to argue that, even on economic grounds, development is more beneficial – over the long term – than environmental preservation (Wicke 1990, p. 52).

But what makes development often seem beneficial? Because land development is typically viewed as a good, without any market-based costs being placed on the harmful environmental impacts that it causes, a given development could be uneconomical but seen as desirable. Roads (highways) and canals are typically seen as economical, for example, yet when one tallies all the costs and benefits (excluding ecological benefits and costs and psychological–social benefits and costs), the market-based costs are typically twice as great as the benefits (Wicke 1990, p. 52). This is because the opportunity costs of development are usually ignored, and development is controlled by the idiosyncracies of how an individual might wish to exercise property rights. Some of the opportunity costs of developing certain tracts of land are that it can never again sustain the same aesthetic worth. It can never again contain the same species, habitats, and ecosystems. These opportunities are foreclosed forever. The economic effects of such foreclosures, together with their effects on future generations, are rarely calculated in typical instances of making either economic policy or individual decisions about property. Because of this failure, and because environmental goods are typically "free goods," it could well be that a given development is uneconomical over the long term, but economical (if at all) only in a shortsighted sense, over the short term (see Eden 1990b; McNeeley et al. 1990; Potier 1990; Wicke 1990). The case for development being uneconomical is especially strong for subsidized road-building, logging, mining, and grazing on public lands. Often such activities appear economical only because one ignores the opportunity costs, the unmarketed services, and the value of the flexibility in decisionmaking preserved by foregoing development (see Irland 1976, pp. 28–29, for example). Each year in Florida, for example, timber sold from national forests amounts to about 95 million board feet, and timber cut totals approximately 122 million board feet, for which the state receives approximately $5 million. Although the $5 million is counted as a benefit of logging, no dollars are calculated for the opportunity costs of logging, costs that include, for example, destruction of part of the habitat for 38 threatened, endangered, and sensitive plant species and 61 threatened, endangered, and sensitive animal species living on national forest land in the state. Likewise, for instance, no dollars are calculated for opportunity costs of logging that include threats to watershed protection. National forests in Florida produce nearly 2 million acre feet of water annually for surface and groundwater systems, and logging threatens not only this water production but also the purity of 36,000 acres of lakes and four of the state's largest rivers (Forest Service Southern Region 1990). Were the value of all these ecological services of forests calculated, as well as the opportunity costs of logging and the costs of government subsidies to the logging industry (through road-building to remove timber, for example), then preservation could likely be justified as more economical than logging.

In other words, insistence on the operation of an authentically free market (free from regulations, free from liability limits to minimize developer or producer risk, free from government subsidies, and free to reflect the costs of all actions, even those not traded on a market, like a species extinction) might be very risky to loggers and other producers/ developers. If markets were truly free, and if, following the presuppositions of neoclassical economics, all actions (including environment-related ones) were costed close to their real value, then it is arguable that development could be shown to be quite uneconomical. It often only appears economical because developers do not "pay their way" in terms of liabilities, subsidies, externalities, and providing needed services in the developed areas (see Wicke 1990, p. 52). One recent Florida study showed, for example, that 1,000 new residents, attracted by developers, would include 270 new families, 200 school children, 19 blind persons, 68 aged persons, 11 juvenile delinquents, 16 alcoholics, and 30 mentally retarded persons, all of whom would require special government services (Healy 1979, p. 10). If all these services were actually costed, then development could well be a net loss, not a gain, in actual economic terms. This is why one author was able to show, for example, that the taxpayers of Lexington, Massachusetts, could save money if they would buy up 2,000 acres of vacant land. The cost of schools, fire and police protection, sewage treatment, drainage, and welfare costs for new residents on the 2,000 acres would add up to far more than the annual cost, $75,000 per year, to retire a $1 million acquisition bond (Little 1979, pp. 83–98; see Potier 1990; Wicke 1990). The conclusion to be drawn from such considerations is not that we ought never develop lands but that, often, development is a net loss, even on economic terms.

If they are consistent proponents of the free market, producers/ developers will have to pay the social costs of their development projects, without liability limits and without externalities costed as zero. If they "pay their way," then it might be difficult to argue that development represents a net benefit for all humans, especially since development requires an increase in taxpayer-funded services (see Healy 1979, p. 10). Moreover, proponents of maximizing public or environmental risk and minimizing developer risk are often inconsistent; developers and industrialists often wish to interfere with the market, so as to protect themselves (e.g., through liability limits), but they complain when environmental regulation interferes with the same market, in order to protect the public. Given this inconsistency, it is unclear why a serious irreversible, incompensable risk (like species or subspecies extinction) should be borne by those who did not cause the loss, the public, rather than primarily by those who are responsible for it, namely developers (see Cooke 1982, pp. 345–347).

Another problem with the objection that minimizing public or environmental risks might not maximize welfare, especially economic welfare, is that it appears to sanction using humans as means to the end of economic development. Such means/ends arguments are always morally questionable. For example, the same means/end presuppositions that are central to this objection also dominate several lines of reasoning that many persons take to be erroneous. For instance: (1) "We can't abolish slavery, because this would destroy the economy of the South." Or (2) "we can't pass the Equal Rights Amendment (ERA), because women won't stay home and take care of their children, and this would hurt the family." In (1) slavery is assumed justifiable because it is a means to the end of promoting the southern economy. In (2) opposition to the ERA is assumed justifiable because it is a means to the end of achieving childcare. What is peculiar about these means/end arguments is that they all pit important values, like family and economic well-being, *against* moral values, like citizen welfare or abolishing racism and sexism. The arguments are troubling because they force us to choose between two goods, and because they suggest that one can use unethical means to achieve an ethical end, provided that the end is important.

Judith Jarvis Thomson's response to arguments like (1) and (2) is simple. They force us to choose between risking our life, or destroying a species or rainforest, versus starving. "It is morally indecent that anyone in a moderately well-off society should be faced with such a choice" (Thomson 1986, p. 172), a choice between environmental welfare and economic well-being, or between women's autonomy and family welfare. Arguments like (1) and (2), arguments about environmental degradation, slavery, and women's rights, all err because they propose using humans – whether citizens at risk from environmental degradation, or blacks who are victims of slavery, or women who are disadvantaged by sexism – as *means* to some economic or social *end*. Yet, if Kant was correct, as most moralists maintain, humans ought never be used as means to some end of other persons, especially not if all humans have equal rights and equal dignity (Kant 1964, pp. 95–98; see also Rawls 1971, pp. 179–183). As we shall argue in more detail in chapter 9, humans (indeed, all living beings having inherent worth) ought not be used as mere means to some social or economic end. They are ends in themselves, and they each deserve equal consideration of their interests. Hence, as we shall explain in chapter 9, considerations of the "greater good" always trump considerations of economic efficiency.

It is true that we do often have to weigh the interests of one group in society over those of another, and we do often discriminate against some persons and in favor of others. Yet the only grounds justifying discrimination, the failure to treat one person as equal to another, as Frankena has pointed out, is that the discrimination will work to the advantage of everyone, including those discriminated against. Any other attempt to justify discrimination fails because it would amount to sanctioning the use of some humans as means to the ends of other persons (Frankena 1962; see, for example, Kant 1964, pp. 95–98; Gewirth 1982, p. 226; Shrader-Frechette 1983, pp. 33–35, 1985b, pp. 71–72). We can apply this insight about justified discrimination to the case of uncertain environmental impacts, as well as to type-I and type-II statistical errors. A necessary condition for discriminating against the public generally – especially citizens who prefer preservation and strict environmental standards – would be to prove that rejecting such standards, in a given case, would work to the advantage of everyone. In other words, the burden of proof is on the producer or developer – indeed anyone – attempting to put the public at risk. Hence the prima-facie desirable position, in a situation of uncertainty, is to minimize public risk or type-II error, for all the reasons already stated.

7.4 If preservationists are wrong, they lose credibility

Another objection to minimizing type-II error (public or environmental risk) owes much of its formulation to Simberloff and Cox (1987) and to Simberloff *et al.* (1992). Their reasoning appears to be as follows: Suppose ecologists choose to interpret their studies so as to minimize public risk or type-II error; if so, then they will be choosing to minimize the chance that a potentially false null hypothesis will not be rejected. One such hypothesis, for example, is that creating conservation corridors will not delay extinction of the Florida panther for at least 20 years (see Ballou *et al.* 1989, p. 2; US Fish and Wildlife Service, 1987). But if we minimize the chance that this particular null hypothesis will not be rejected, then we increase the chance that it will be rejected. Rejecting this hypothesis, however, means that it is more likely that conservation corridors will be created. But if conservation corridors are created, and if they do not delay panther extinction for at least 20 years, then the ecologists who argued for the corridors will lose credibility. One could argue against corridors on the grounds that their effectiveness is uncertain, and therefore that they represent a potential loss of time and money that could better be spent on other conservation projects. Also, one could argue that panther survival is more dependent on "minimum viable populations and minimum critical sizes of ecosystems" (Simberloff 1987, p. 156). Moreover, one could also argue that, if ecologists lose credibility by supporting corridors (while ignoring other factors such as minimum viable populations), they may lose the ability to affect future ecology-related policy actions.

In other words, Simberloff's objection to minimizing type-II error is that, although losing a species (or subspecies) is worse than losing credibility, "the two are not unconnected" (Simberloff 1987, p. 157). And if not, then his argument is that erring on the side of preservation, and causing a loss of scientific credibility, is not necessarily preferable to erring on the side of development and causing loss of a species. This is because loss of credibility could also cause loss of species in the future, by jeopardizing our ability to affect preservation policy (Simberloff 1987, pp. 156–157). This is an excellent objection, at least in part because it recognizes the importance of science in undergirding environmental policy, and because it seems to admit that a loss of species (or subspecies) is more important than a loss of credibility. If the objection were based on factually correct presuppositions, it would be a compelling reason, in a situation of uncertainty, to minimize type-I error (or developer risk) and to maximize scientific credibility. But how correct are its factual presuppositions?

Simberloff appears to believe that loss of scientific credibility could cause future loss of species, because policymakers might not listen to scientists. He writes (1987, p. 157):

> scientific credibility . . . is not nearly as important as loss of species, but the two are not unconnected . . . South American government officials need unassailable scientific information to resist powerful constituents favoring development. When an economist can easily dissect the shaky underpinnings of early estimates of tropical extinction rates . . . , one can only wonder whether scientists' influence on decisionmakers will suffer.

At least in the South American case that he was discussing, the main presupposition of Simberloff's objection is that loss of scientific credibility could cause loss of future species because policymakers might not listen to scientists whom they viewed as not credible. Obviously, Simberloff is correct to infer that, in at least some cases, loss of scientists' credibility has affected, and could continue to affect, the conservation causes they espouse. Much evidence, however, suggests that perhaps we ought to take the risk of ecologists' being wrong because scientists' loss of credibility, by virtue of their making mistakes, does not always lead to serious consequences. For example, disproving the alleged scientific foundations of the Endangered Species Act did not cause the act to be repealed. The main scientific underpinning for this act was the traditional version of the diversity–stability thesis (see chapter 2), as both a number of authors and the congressional debate reveal (see, for example, Commoner 1971, p. 38; US Congress 1973a, p. 25668; Myers 1983). Within a decade after the act was passed, however, the diversity–stability hypothesis was questioned by many ecologists, as we discussed in chapter 4. The loss of credibility of the diversity–stability hypothesis, however, did not cause Congress to reject the Endangered Species Act. Nor did a majority of the public demand rejection on scientific grounds. This counterexample suggests that the consequences of being wrong are not always disastrous. Neither loss of credibility, nor the loss of the ability to influence environmental policy unavoidably occur because of scientists' making a mistake.

It also seems questionable to assume, on the basis of Simberloff's remarks, that ecologists' being wrong (about conditions for species preservation) will cause a general loss of credibility of all ecologists. Although Simberloff is correct to emphasize loss of credibility and its consequences, his factual presupposition ignores the fact that scientists on the side of development also have often been wrong on technical matters. Moreover, for "preservationist scientists" to lose credibility, it might be necessary for their errors to be seen as more serious than the mistakes of the "pro-development scientists." In other words, possible loss of credibility is not merely a function of one's errors, as Simberloff appears to presuppose, but also (1) a function of the severity of one's errors, relative to those of others and (2) a function of the political climate in which those errors occur. Error, alone, is not a sufficient condition for loss of credibility, and it may not even be a necessary condition.

Assessing errors made on the "pro-development" side puts Simberloff's worries about credibility into perspective. Consider the egregious error made by Cal Tech founder and Nobel Prize winner, Robert Millikan (1930, pp. 119–130). He was wrong in calling belief in nuclear power a "myth" less than a decade before the existence of fission energy was proved. Yet Millikan did not lose credibility after he was disproved. Likewise, if the work of Kahneman, Tversky, and others is correct, then experts are chronically in error, even in their own fields of expertise, when they reason probabilistically. In employing necessary heuristic strategies to render their problems malleable, they fall victim to the same errors as laypersons, for example, the representativeness bias (Kahneman and Tversky 1982a, b). But if so, then expert errors are nothing new. If making serious errors were a sufficient condition for loss of scientific credibility, few scientists would be credible. For example, consider the case of scientists' assessing failure rates of subsystem components in commercial nuclear reactors in the most comprehensive assessment of such risks ever accomplished, the US Rasmussen Report, WASH 1400 (US Nuclear Regulatory Commission 1975). This is the best risk assessment ever performed, according to the scientific community. It examined subsystem failures that included loss-of-coolant accidents, auxiliary feedwater-system failures, high-pressure injection failures, long-term core-cooling failures, and automatic-depressurization-system failures for both pressurized and boiling-water reactors. When Dutch researchers compared failure frequencies from operating experience to the WASH 1400 calculations for failure rates for seven key reactor subsystems, they discovered some startling facts. Amazingly, *all* the failure-frequency values from operating experience fell *outside* the 90-percent confidence bands in the WASH 1400 study. However, there is only a subjective probability of 10 percent that the true values should fall outside these bands. Moreover, a majority of the values fell above the upper confidence band, suggesting that the WASH 1400 calculations, the product of 30 experts working together, are too low (Cooke 1986; see Shrader-Frechette 1991). If the Dutch studies are correct, then the allegedly best risk assessment (the Rasmussen Report, WASH 1400) ever accomplished contains a flagrant overconfidence bias. This means that the most complete study of nuclear safety has lost credibility; the US Nuclear Regulatory Commission has partially withdrawn its support from it. Despite this loss of credibility, however, the US has not closed its nuclear plants, just as it did not repeal the Endangered Species Act after the diversity–stability thesis was abandoned.

Moreover, the failure of US scientists and engineers in the Rasmussen Report is not atypical. Scientists were wrong when they said that irradiating enlarged tonsils was harmless. They were wrong when they said that X-raying feet, to determine shoe size, was safe. They were wrong when they said that the *Titanic* would not sink. They were wrong when they said that irradiating women's breasts, to alleviate mastitis, was harmless. They were wrong when they said that the Tacoma Narrows bridge would not collapse. And they were wrong when they said that witnessing A-bomb tests at close range, in the western US and in the Pacific, was harmless (see Korchmar 1978). Likewise, geologists were proved wrong, by six orders of magnitude, ten years after they calculated that hazardous waste at Maxey Flats, Kentucky, would not migrate offsite (see Meyer 1975). Despite this geological error, the government did not stop employing scientists to assess site potential for hazardous-waste facilities. When allegedly reliable assessments – of the environmental risk associated with the LNG facility in Oxnard, California – differed by three orders of magnitude (Kunreuther *et al.* 1987, p. 261), the Oxnard City Council did not shut down the facility. And when government assessments of the risk of a serious accident at Three Mile Island (TMI) differed by two orders of magnitude (Rasmussen 1981), the US Nuclear Regulatory Commission did not close TMI. It took an accident, not loss of scientific credibility, to do that. Likewise, when 500,000 US GIs were exposed to injurious levels of radiation (levels called "safe" by government scientists) during the "Smokey" weapons tests in the US in the 1950s (see Korchmar 1978), the scientists did not lose credibility. Even though many servicemen died of testing-induced leukemia, the US Atomic Energy Commission and the US Nuclear Regulatory Commission continued to seek the advice and support of the very scientists who had misled them in the weapons-testing debacle. All these examples suggest that scientists' *being wrong* may be less important in the credibility issue than being on the "wrong" side, that is, the side with the least political and economic power. Unfortunately, scientists offering environmental advice are often on the wrong (political) side, the side having less economic power. When they are wrong, they often lose credibility. Vested interests, however, not the scientists' errors, appear to be the more important cause of the loss of credibility.

Even if being wrong were a sufficient condition for a scientist to lose credibility, however, it is not clear that this credibility loss would be likely to jeopardize the chances of most or all scientists to influence public policy, as Simberloff appears to suggest. Rather, the loss of credibility, if it occurred at all, would likely accrue only to some of the errant scientists. For example, when the Dutch researchers discovered the inconsistencies between expert calculations of nuclear-reactor component failures and the frequency rates for the same failures obtained through operating experience, they did not discredit all experts. Rather, they argued that each expert ought to be calibrated, on the basis of his past correct calculations. In other words, the Dutch researchers proposed that each expert's opinion be weighted positively or negatively on the basis of past frequencies confirming or disconfirming his calculations (Cooke 1986). Admittedly, however, because it is a new discipline, ecology is often not able to supply evidence to confirm or falsify the conclusions of its researchers. Indeed, ecology is frequently unable to provide precise predictions, let alone confirm or falsify them, in part for some of the reasons discussed earlier in chapters 2 and 3. Hence, in ecology, calibration might not be useful at present, and it might not protect ecologists' credibility.

Another problem with the presupposition (that ecologists ought to take environmental, or type-II, risks in order to avoid loss of credibility) is that it ignores the importance of scientists' intentions. Loss of credibility might be more positively correlated with deliberate intent to deceive, rather than with error alone. If so, and if scientists' apparent intentions play a role in the way we evaluate their errors, then there is reason to believe that ecologists might not need to fear their professional mistakes to the degree that Simberloff suggests. Admittedly, however, because of ecology's conceptual and theoretical problems (discussed in earlier chapters), ecologists might be especially vulnerable to loss of credibility. Hence, Simberloff's main point is a correct one: in the face of uncertainty, ecologists ought to be conservative in their conclusions, analyses, and interpretations. This is undoubtedly true. But what counts as being conservative?

7.5 Minimizing type-I errors is more conservative

In one policy-related debate over conservation biology, Simberloff stated quite clearly: "Risking type-I rather than type-II error is not the most conservative course" (Simberloff 1987, p. 156). Presumably, the most conservative course, in a situation of uncertainty, would be the course least prone to error, all else being equal. One reason why Simberloff appears to believe that risking type-II error (when both types of error cannot be avoided) is more conservative, at least in the nature-reserve case, is that risking type-II error amounts to risking not rejecting a false null hypothesis, for example, that conservation corridors will not delay the extinction of the Florida panther for at least 20 years.

Apparently, Simberloff believes that not rejecting the null hypothesis is conservative, even in conservation cases like that of trying to save the Florida panther, because building corridors may not represent an efficient use of conservation dollars, and because there are many unresolved biological questions surrounding conservation corridors. Some of these unresolved questions include the "necessary dispersal corridor widths," the ways to prevent spread of contagious diseases through the corridors, whether corridors are needed to offset problems of inbreeding depression, and the minimum viable panther populations and minimum critical sizes of ecosystems (Simberloff 1987, p. 156; Simberloff and Cox 1987, pp. 68–69; see Grumbine 1990). Because of all these economic and biological problems, Simberloff concludes that "it is not automatic that large and connected reserves insure the fewest extinctions" (Simberloff 1987, p. 156). Hence, a conservative course, for Simberloff, appears to be to avoid positing an effect (the importance of corridors in delaying panther extinction for at least 20 years), in a situation of uncertainty, and to avoid a type-I error, rejecting the null hypothesis.

As we explained earlier, there are both scientific and legal precedents for Simberloff's allegedly conservative course of risking type-II (environmental or public) errors and for minimizing type-I (developer or industry) errors, that is, for limiting false positives. Indeed, if the arguments presented earlier are correct, then scientists in general appear to prefer to minimize type-I errors, in a situation of uncertainty, as does Simberloff. Hence, there seems to be little question that Simberloff is correct in affirming that scientific or epistemic rationality is conservative and hence supports being scientifically cautious, viz., avoiding positing an effect. Scientific rationality, in a situation of uncertainty, requires that the burden of proof be on the person positing the effect and risking type-I error.

7.6 Scientific rationality and ethical rationality

The important question, however, may not be the nature of *scientific* rationality, and whether it is associated with minimizing type-I error in a situation of uncertainty, but rather, whether scientific rationality is the most appropriate basis for decisionmaking in conservation cases, like that of the nature reserve discussed by Simberloff. If it is not, then Simberloff may be giving the right answer to the question about scientific rationality, but he may be asking the wrong question. There are a number of reasons (to be explored in a moment) for believing that the most appropriate question, in a situation of uncertainty, is not whether minimizing type-I or type-II error is more rational, from a scientific point of view. Rather, the most appropriate question may be whether scientific rationality provides the best model for environmental decisionmaking, as exemplified by cases like those involving species or subspecies loss, deforestation and nature reserves.

In its broadest sense, scientific or epistemic rationality is based on using scientific theory (whether in ecology or in economics, for example) to assess hypotheses and their consequences. Scientific rationality, as we mentioned in section 7.1, is primarily a rationality of *belief*. It assesses both the various degrees of *probability* that are associated with competing hypotheses, and the practical, economic, and scientific *consequences* following from acceptance of alternative hypotheses. Hence, on this view, scientific rationality focuses on both epistemic and practical considerations. In its *narrowest* sense, scientific rationality focuses only on epistemic considerations, since the utility associated with a hypothesis can have no bearing on whether the hypothesis is true. In its *broadest* sense, the sense that Simberloff and others appear to presuppose, scientific rationality often encompasses the use of some type of *decision theory* to assess the various degrees of *expected utility* (probability times outcome utility), the various costs and benefits that are associated with competing hypotheses (see, for example, Harsanyi 1975, 1977, 1986). However, ethical rationality, as we mentioned in section 7.1, uses *ethical theory* to assess the moral goodness or badness of alternative actions. It is primarily a rationality of *action*.

In a situation in which a scientific decision has important consequences, but the data are uncertain, scientific rationality in its fullest sense might dictate deciding in favor of an hypothesis with slightly lower probability, but whose expected utility, benefits over costs, were significantly greater than that of another hypothesis. In a similar situation, ethical rationality might dictate deciding in favor of an hypothesis that would lead to the greatest ethical good. For example, suppose one were attempting to determine whether it was more rational to claim that a leak of a corrosive chemical at a factory could be controlled within two hours, versus the claim that the leak could not be controlled within two hours. Suppose the former hypothesis appeared to have a slightly higher probability than the latter, but the latter had a significantly higher outcome utility than the former. The utility of the latter hypothesis might be higher, since accepting it would result in taking actions to prevent loss of company property and consequent manufacturing "down time." In such a situation, considerations of scientific rationality might dictate accepting the hypothesis that the leak could not be controlled. In such a case, "accepting" this hypothesis would not mean "taking to be true," since the utility associated with a potential state of affairs can have no bearing on whether or not that state of affairs is actual. Hence, "accepting" this hypothesis means "being prepared to act as if it were true." In this case, accepting the leak hypothesis would not be merely a matter of the probability of a particular occurrence, but also a question of the associated costs and benefits of accepting a given hypothesis. The judgment would be a matter of scientific rationality, in its fullest sense.

Suppose, however, one were faced with a slightly different case. Suppose one were attempting to determine whether it was more rational to claim that a leak of a slightly toxic, but non-corrosive, substance at a factory could be controlled within two hours, versus the claim that the leak could not be controlled within two hours. Suppose also that the leaking substance, while slightly toxic, would cause some acute, but no life-threatening or permanent, effects if it escaped. Likewise, suppose the hypothesis that the leak could be controlled appeared to have a slightly higher probability than the hypothesis that it could not be controlled. Suppose, too, that the former hypothesis had a much higher utility, because accepting the latter hypothesis would result in notification of authorities, possible evacuation, and massive negative publicity, even if the leak were stopped. Hence, scientific rationality might dictate our choosing the former hypothesis, because of its higher utility.

Judgments of utility associated with scientific rationality do take account of costs and benefits and economic consequences, however, although they do not address the ethical issues associated with choosing a particular hypothesis. Ethical rationality, in the case of the toxic leak, might require one to choose the hypothesis that took account of citizens' rights to know, rather than the hypothesis that was associated with the higher utility. In other words, even if the utility were lower, even if the probable damage were minimal, and even if current regulations did not require notification, one might be obliged ethically to recognize the rights of persons likely to be affected by the slightly toxic substance. Making decisions on the basis of ethical rationality thus may be more important, in some cases of science, than making decisions on the basis of scientific rationality. If others have the right to be protected against the adverse effects of toxic leaks, however slight, and if judging that a leak can be controlled decreases the probability that persons will be evacuated and hence protected, then it is rational (from an ethical point of view) to guarantee their protection (see Shrader-Frechette 1991, chs. 7–8). In other words, in any case in which one's judgment about a hypothesis affects the interests of, and duties to, other persons, what is rational is not merely a matter of scientific rationality. What is rational is also a matter of moral and legal obligation, fairness, consent, voluntariness, and so on. That is, when one moves from *"pure"* science to *applied science* affecting policy, what is rational moves from epistemological considerations to both ethical and epistemological concerns. Likewise, when one moves from considerations of *utility* to those of *ethics*, one moves from scientific rationality to ethical rationality.

Returning to conservation cases, like the one discussed by Simberloff, Kangas, and Noss, a crucial question is whether, given a situation
of uncertainty, scientific rationality is more appropriate, on prima-facie
grounds, for decisionmaking. Because the questions about whether
conservation corridors will help protect the panther, for example, and
whether certain land ought to be preserved, have social and policy
consequences affecting the interests of many people, the questions do
not appear to be either a matter of "pure science" or a matter of utility –
a matter merely for scientific rationality. Instead, the social and policy
consequences/interests dictate that one needs to assess (1) the outcome
utilities, (2) the probabilities that the corridors will or will not delay
extinction, and (3) the probabilities that preservation will or will not
enhance the common good – and meet ethical obligations – more than
will development.

Following the model of scientific, versus ethical, rationality, it is
arguable that the prima-facie rule of scientific rationality dictates
minimizing type-I errors and not rejecting the null hypothesis in a
situation of uncertainty. That is, given the problems of *scientific theory*
associated with rejecting the null hypothesis, for example, in the
Florida-panther case (e.g., necessary dispersal corridor widths, ways to
prevent spread of contagious diseases through the corridors, and so on),
it is easy to see why the *probability* that the null hypothesis ought to be
rejected is likely low, just as Simberloff surmises. But if the probability
is low – that the null ought to be rejected – then the *truth* of the null
hypothesis is more likely, and therefore there are prima-facie grounds
for minimizing type-I error. It is also arguable, however, that in
situations of uncertainty, ethical rationality dictates a prima-facie rule
of minimizing type-II errors and rejecting the null hypothesis in cases
like that of the Florida panther. If loss of a species is more important
than loss of credibility (as Simberloff 1987, p. 157, suggests), and if
preservation of a species or subspecies enhances ethical obligations and
the common good more than does development, as we argued earlier,
then what follows? Ethical rationality might dictate minimizing type-II
errors and rejecting the null hypothesis in cases of uncertainty in which
ecology is used to make environmental decisions. In other words, the
ethical consequences associated with loss of a species, subspecies, or
habitat could be so great that, even if the probability (for example) that
conservation corridors would delay Florida-panther extinction for at
least 20 years is low, it might still be rational (in an ethical sense) to
attempt to avoid species or subspecies extinction. In other words,
ethical norms might be better served if one minimized type-II errors

and rejected the null hypothesis, in conservation cases involving uncertainty, than if one minimized type-I errors. In any case, we believe that the prima-facie correct position, in a situation of uncertainty involving policy, where both types of errors cannot be avoided, is to minimize type-II errors. In the next two chapters we shall evaluate objections to our prima-facie position, objections that are specific to the case of possible Florida-panther extinction.

One could also argue, using decision theory, that in situations of probabilistic uncertainty and potentially catastrophic or irreversible consequences, there are prima-facie grounds for following the maximin decision rule (see Rawls 1971, pp. 75–83, 1974). In other words, whenever potential losses are especially great, there might be prima-facie grounds for behaving in a very conservative way and for following the maximin rule, rather than the Bayesian rule, according to which we maximize expected utility. Given such a situation, the maximin decisionmaker deemphasizes the rationality of belief, for example, belief in alleged probabilities, and emphasizes the rationality of action, avoiding extremely undesirable consequences. Because the maximin rule enjoins one to avoid accepting the hypothesis leading to the worst policy consequences, in situations of uncertainty it dictates minimizing type-II errors and rejecting the null hypothesis. In cases of extinction, presumably the prima-facie worst policy consequence would be losing species or subspecies, for example, and presumably this consequence could follow from acts or omissions such as failure to establish conservation corridors. In the next two chapters, we shall evaluate objections to our prima-facie arguments, especially as they are relevant to the Florida panther and the construction of corridors.

For ecological cases of uncertainty, like those discussed by Kangas, Noss, and Simberloff, following the maximin rule amounts to minimizing type-II errors or public risk. Moreover, it is common knowledge among decision theorists and moral philosophers that following the maximin decision rule is often the action that is most conservative with respect to ethics. This is because it avoids the most ethically reprehensible, or worst, risks. That is, in cases of ethical rationality, the most conservative course of action is frequently to ignore uncertain probabilities and instead to focus on the ethical quality of outcomes or consequences. Hence, it is arguable that, if ethical rationality (rather than *scientific* rationality) is relevant to conservation cases like that of deforestation and reserve design, then we ought not focus on low probabilities or utility alone. It might be misguided to focus on the allegedly low probability of saving a particular species, for example, as the sole grounds for risking species extinction (see Simberloff 1987; Simberloff and Cox 1987, pp. 68–69). If the situation is one in which we ought to use ethical rationality, and especially maximin decision rules, then the ethical quality of an act's consequences may be far more important than probabilities and utilities. Hence, the conservative course of action in such a case would be to minimize type-II error. The most conservative course of action, in a case of scientific rationality and uncertainty, however, is to minimize type-I error. This means that Simberloff's claim ("that risking type-I rather than type-II error is not the most conservative course") is correct only if one ought to use merely scientific rationality rather than also ethical rationality, in conservation decisionmaking under uncertainty (see Simberloff 1987, p. 156). From the prima-facie arguments already given, it is clear that the panther case (and any environmental situation like it) ought to involve considerations of ethical rationality. It is not one appropriate merely for decisionmaking in terms of scientific rationality. Unlike Noss, Simberloff and others appear to make no explicit appeal to ethical norms. In this, we believe they are wrong.

If these arguments have been correct, then in the Simberloff–Kangas–Noss debate (Kangas 1986, 1987; Noss 1986, 1988; Simberloff 1987; Simberloff and Cox 1987), Simberloff is indeed correct, in the sense that epistemic or scientific rationality supports minimizing developer risk (errors of type I) in a situation of probabilistic uncertainty. More importantly, Noss is correct, in the sense that ethical rationality supports minimizing loss of species. Hence, according to ethical rationality, since the burden of proof is on the person whose actions present the greatest threat to ethical norms and to the common good, one ought to minimize public risk, that is, errors of type II. One reason why ethical rationality is so important in conservation cases is that it recognizes that, where welfare, ethics, and vested interests are concerned, one ought to have a predisposition in favor of the vulnerable parties (the public, the environment), at the expense of the powerful parties (developers). This amounts to a prima-facie predisposition in favor of minimizing public risk and errors of type II. Although he may not intend to do so, Simberloff appears to overemphasize the importance of epistemic or scientific rationality and to underemphasize the significance of ethical rationality. He seems to *overemphasize epistemological errors* resulting in bad science, and to *underemphasize ethical errors* resulting in bad policy and bad applications of science. Because it is often used as a practical and applied science, ecology requires both concepts of rationality. For a variety of prima-facie reasons, we have also argued that ethical rationality is likely to be more important in serving public and environmental interests. In the next two chapters, we shall examine arguments against our prima-facie case. There, we shall argue that both ecological information, via case studies – and the ethical rationality appropriate to ecology – serve environmental decisionmaking.

8 · A case study: The Florida panther

THE FLORIDA PANTHER is a natural symbol of Florida, in much the same way that the bald eagle is a natural symbol of the United States. Yet, only approximately 40 members of the endangered subspecies remain, largely in the swampy, southern parts of Florida. An important question faced by many ecologists, both within and outside the state, is whether it is possible to save the Florida panther in the wild. In this chapter, we shall attempt to create a version of this question that can be evaluated scientifically and then answer it.

One might argue that the Florida panther is not an especially good subject for a case study. Ecology probably cannot do much for it, because it is too close to extinction. Perhaps the manatee or black bear might provide a better example from Florida. We maintain, however, that the case-study approach is applicable to any phenomenon, irrespective of differences of opinion regarding the importance of the phenomenon being investigated. Moreover, the mood surrounding Florida-panther preservation is emotionally charged, and the subject is of great interest to the public. Both of these conditions beg for the rational, cautious approach offered by the case-study method. In any event, our goal here is primarily to illustrate what ecology can do, particularly in a case that is of public, as well as scientific, interest. Although ecology has neither general theories nor exceptionless empirical laws capable of providing precise predictions for environmental decisionmaking, it can help provide answers to particular questions of conservation. As this chapter illustrates, applied ecology is not primarily a hypothetical-deductive science. Nor does it have close analogies, as a discipline, to physics. Instead, it is mainly a science of case studies, a science in which rough generalizations aid us in practical problem-solving. We shall investigate the case of the Florida panther in order to see how and why this is so. First, we examine in detail the biological and ecological characteristics of this subspecies. Next we trace the evaluative and scientific dilemmas facing ecologists as a result of the empirical and conceptual uncertainties in the case. Finally, we explain our research design of the Florida-panther study, including the questions to be evaluated; the hypotheses to be examined; the types of evidence to be used; the logic linking the data and the hypotheses; and the criteria for interpreting the findings. After presenting our conclusion regarding the possibility of preserving the Florida panther in the wild, we close by evaluating the validity, reliability, explanatory fertility, heuristic power, and completeness of our conclusions, relative to alternative accounts.

8.1 Background

Felis concolor (cougar, mountain lion, puma, and many other common names), has 15 recognized subspecies in North America, one of which is the Florida panther, *F. concolor coryi* (Hall 1981). The most recent taxonomic review of the species (Goldman 1946) describes the Florida panther as "a medium-sized, dark subspecies, with pelage short and rather stiff." Its long limbs, small feet, and rich ferruginous color (Bangs 1898) are distinctive. Three external characters that are often observed on Florida panthers are not found in combination on other subspecies of *F. concolor* (Belden 1987): a right-angle crook at the terminal end of the tail, a whorl of hair resembling a "cowlick" in the middle of the back, and irregular white flecking on the head, nape, and shoulders (see Goldman 1946). Hence, from at least one point of view, the Florida panther is unique (we shall explore the question of the "uniqueness" of subspecies later).

Felis concolor once ranged widely throughout North America, but now the species' range is fragmented (Hall 1981; Dixon 1982). Substantial populations remain only in parts of western North America. Some of these populations are contracting, some are expanding, while others have remained unchanged for a significant time (see Dixon 1982). *F. concolor coryi* formerly ranged throughout much of the southeastern United States, from eastern Texas to South Carolina (Hall 1981), but now almost surely occurs only in remote areas of southern Florida. The largest collections of individuals of the Florida panther seem to be at Big Cypress (estimated to be about 18 individuals), at Raccoon Point (estimated to be between 2 and 6 individuals), and in the Everglades (estimated to be between 4 and 6 individuals) (Ballou *et al.* 1989). The total number of individuals remaining in the wild probably is less than 40 (Ballou *et al.* 1989). The Florida panther and one other subspecies, *F. c. costaricensis* (found only in southern Central America and probably Colombia), are listed (as endangered) by the US Fish and Wildlife Service (1986).

The Florida panther, like many other large, warm-blooded predators, occupies a precarious ecological position (see Colinvaux 1978). Because the Florida panther is a relatively large mammal, its energy demand is high. Because it is an active predator, its energy expenditure in searching for, capturing, and handling prey also is high. These two facts taken together mean that the Florida panther must use prey items with high energy content, high enough to offset the energy expended to acquire them. The panther primarily exploits the white-tailed deer (*Odocoileus virginianus*), the largest ungulate in its range, and the feral pig (*Sus scrofa*) (see Dixon 1982; Maehr *et al.* 1990). High energy demand and expenditures also mean that populations of the Florida panther may be affected very strongly by even transient shortages of readily available preferred prey items. It is likewise true that the per capita reproductive output of the Florida panther is low, between two and three young per female biennially (Ballou *et al.* 1989). High energy demand and low reproductive output suggest that population sizes of the Florida panther have never been absolutely high, even before extensive human settlement of its natural range (maybe 1400 individuals in Florida (Cristoffer and Eisenberg 1985)). All of these aspects of the life history of the Florida panther have predisposed it to the decline in distribution and abundance that it has undergone since the arrival of European settlers (see US Fish and Wildlife Service 1987). Because the Florida panther is a predator, settlers viewed it as a competitor, and most populations were eliminated even before 1900. Those populations that were not eliminated have survived because of their remoteness from humans; eventually, survivors remained only in southern Florida.

Reduction of high-quality prey populations for the Florida panther, as a result of human activities, exacerbated the direct hunting pressure on the subspecies. McBride (1985) estimated that adult Florida panthers ordinarily need to consume one deer or similar-sized prey item per week, and that pregnant females need to consume two such prey items. From these numbers, it is easy to see that a wild population of about 50 individuals (see Ballou *et al.* 1989) would require a very large and accessible prey population. Populations of large prey items, however, have become increasingly rare in the southeastern United States since European settlement. In fact, in southern Florida, where the few remaining individuals of the Florida panther survive, poor habitat quality seems to have promoted chronically low densities of deer, relative to many other parts of the panther's presettlement range (US Fish and Wildlife Service 1987).

The most severe current threats to the survival of the Florida panther are small population sizes and increased human presence (US Fish and

Wildlife Service 1987). Small population sizes increase both the vulnerability of any organism to extinction caused by adverse environmental change and the chance of depressed genetic viability. Researchers have claimed that populations of large cats (O'Brien *et al*. 1985; Wildt *et al*. 1987) and other large carnivores (Laikre and Ryman 1991; Wayne *et al*. 1991) have suffered such depressed genetic viability, probably as a result of severe reduction of population sizes sometime in the past (a so-called "genetic bottleneck"). The Florida panther itself displays a higher percentage of abnormal sperm than other subspecies of *Felis concolor* examined (Roelke *et al*. 1985). This abnormality may have resulted from too much inbreeding.

Expansion of human activities such as agriculture, industry, water management, and housing likewise has reduced and fragmented the lands available to the Florida panther in the southern part of the state. The lands that have not been developed often are accessible to off-road vehicles. Such vehicles reduce the suitability of the habitat for the subspecies in various ways, including scaring away prey items or destroying concealing vegetation. Fragmentation of their habitat has forced panthers to cross inhospitable terrain and thus to expose themselves to additional risks. In particular, deaths of individuals on roads now account for much of the known mortality of the Florida panther. Between 1980 and 1986, for example, ten individuals are known to have died after being struck by vehicles (US Fish and Wildlife Service 1987).

We shall now outline and attempt to resolve some of the problems facing ecologists interested in preserving the Florida panther. We shall use the case-study method, as discussed in chapter 5. Recall that the approach includes an examination of: (1) the questions to be investigated, (2) the hypotheses, (3) the types of evidence, (4) the analysis of evidence, (5) the criteria for interpreting findings, (6) the conclusions, and (7) the evaluation.

8.2 The questions to be investigated

Ecologists and policymakers interested in preserving the Florida panther face at least two problems. First, they must decide *why* preservation of this subspecies should be attempted, in preference to preservation of other subspecies and species. Second, if they judge such preservation to be justified, they must decide *how* preservation of the panther should be undertaken. The first of the two problems probably is the more difficult to address, in part because it involves more policy issues and value judgments. Even if we resolve this problem and make the value judgment that attempting to prevent extinction of particular taxa can be justified, however, we shall still face the other problem: How should ecologists undertake specific preservation efforts for the Florida panther? Of course, ecologists should not worry about *how* to undertake preservation efforts, if preservation is in practice impossible. Thus, the second problem hinges on answering a carefully formulated version of the question that we presented at the beginning of this chapter: Is it scientifically possible to specify the conditions that will guarantee the survival of the Florida panther in the wild for approximately 20 years (the estimated mean time to extinction (Ballou *et al.* 1989))? To answer this question, ecologists must establish a set of criteria by which the potential scientific success of preservation efforts may be determined and then apply these criteria to the case of the Florida panther.

8.3 The hypotheses

Two working hypotheses appear to be central to the ecological question we have posed:

H1: We understand the biology of the Florida panther well enough, at present, to predict the minimum viable population size (MVPS) that is capable of sustaining it in the wild, at least for 20 years.

H2: We can manipulate the environment of the Florida panther, at present, in order to maintain MVPS. That is, we can, at present, place MVPS in the context of the metapopulation (see Ballou *et al.* 1989).

We use the term "MVPS" to mean a population size that sets the probability of population extinction, because of genetic, demographic and/or environmental variation, at an acceptable level. An acceptable probability of population extinction must be decided upon in advance, in part by specifying length of time over which persistence is desired. We use the term "metapopulation" to mean a population that is not a single, homogeneous unit, but rather a system of subpopulations, each of which is connected to at least one other subpopulation by movements of individuals. It is important to point out that the fate of individual subpopulations, within a metapopulation, need not be the fate of the entire metapopulation. Some subpopulations may prosper while others fail, and the distribution of prosperous and failed subpopulations may change in space and time. As a consequence, the MVPS of a metapopulation (consisting of a system of subpopulations) need not be the same as the MVPS of a single homogeneous population of the same taxon, all else being equal. One reason for this difference in the two MVPSs is that the relative isolation of subpopulations is likely to enhance the ability of the metapopulation to withstand stochastic environmental variation − provided that the variation is at least partially independent among subpopulations and that colonization reestablishes the subpopulations that do go extinct (Goodman 1987b).

8.4 Types of evidence

In order to evaluate H1 and H2 in the panther case, we need to assess both the major inferences whose justification is necessary or sufficient for affirming H1 or H2 and to investigate the quality of the evidence for these inferences. The evidence and the inferences form the logic linking the hypotheses with the data. Although numerous inferences are relevant to H1 and H2, at least three of them are necessary conditions for confirming H1 and H2. These are:

IN1: We can distinguish, at present, the Florida panther from all other organisms.
IN2: We possess, at present, the demographic, genetic, and environmental data necessary to predict the MVPS for the Florida panther.
IN3: We possess, at present, the population and environmental data necessary to predict the range expansions and habitat modifications that will promote metapopulation dynamics and maintain the MVPS for the Florida panther.

The evidence relevant to inferences IN1–IN3 comes from documents in the scientific literature and government publications. These documents, in turn, are based on observation, controlled experimentation, and speculation based on comparisons with related cases in the literature. Some of the documents we employ directly address the Florida panther, while others relate only indirectly and are based on analogous cases. We use documents of the second kind to address some of the larger theoretical questions underlying the three inferences about Florida-panther preservation.

We examined more than 180 documents relevant to the biology of the Florida panther. We discovered these documents by employing several potential sources of information. We conducted a computer search of four databases that we thought might contain useful literature: BIOSIS, SCISEARCH, LIFE SCIENCES COLLECTION, and ZOOLOGICAL RECORD. In order to find information, we also used two of the most recent and comprehensive status and planning documents on the Florida panther (US Fish and Wildlife Service 1987; Ballou *et al.* 1989) and two of the most recent scientific publications on its genetics and ecology (Maehr 1990; O'Brien et al. 1990). Finally, we used our own knowledge of the literature to locate documents addressing larger theoretical questions about preservation. References to the documents we located independently are in the next section.

Of the more than 180 relevant documents that we examined, we judged about 52 percent to relate directly to the Florida panther, and about 48 percent to relate only indirectly. Most of the documents that we judged to be related indirectly addressed reintroduction of organisms into the wild; genetics of small populations, especially of large cats and other carnivores; models of MVPS; metapopulation dynamics; the ecology of large carnivores; and species concepts. We placed the documents that we judged to be related directly (to the case of the Florida panther) into 12 categories of content. We selected these categories to make our evaluation of the literature easier; we do not claim either that they are the least ambiguous or the best categories possible or that they are mutually exclusive and exhaustive. They do, however, provide one way of organizing the panther research according to major themes. The 12 categories (and the percentages of documents in the categories) are (1) geographical distribution (23.8%); (2) natural history (19.8%); (3) population biology (12.9%); (4) status or well-being (12.9%); (5) systematics (5.9%); (6) diseases (5.0%); (7) preservation plans (5.0%); (8) propagation and reintroduction (4.0%); (9) metapopulation dynamics (3.0%); (10) study methods (3.0%); (11) genetics (2.0%); and (12) MVPS (2.0%).

If our set of documents is representative of the entire literature on the Florida panther, and we believe it is, then less than 25 percent of all documents focus on population biology, propagation and reintroduction, metapopulation dynamics, genetics, and MVPS. Yet, information about these topics forms the core of plans to preserve the Florida panther. Ballou et al (1989), for example, present a recent population viability analysis of the Florida panther and recommendations for ensuring its long-term survival. They list the goals and premises of their analysis, they review the status of the present Florida-panther population, and they predict the consequences (for the panther population) of current and planned interventions in management of the wild population (such interventions include treatment of injured individuals, vaccination in the wild, local expansion of habitat, and reduction of adult mortality). Ballou et al. (1989) also identify the need for captive and multiple wild populations (a metapopulation) and list recommended actions both for the establishment of a captive population and for the enhancement of existing subpopulations. Most of the recommended actions for establishing a captive population are aimed at promoting genetic diversity and increasing the survival of young individuals. The recommended actions for enhancing existing subpopulations involve introductions or reintroductions of individuals from the captive-breeding program and the reestablishment of natural corridors. Finally, Ballou *et al.* (1989, p. 4) list 13 research priorities to address the "immediate problems important to the management of the Florida panther . . . that are amenable to resolution by current research methodologies if supported." These priorities include studies of the genetics, reproductive biology, and ecology of the panther, as well as upgrading the population viability analysis based upon new information.

The recently published recovery plan for the Florida panther (US Fish and Wildlife Service 1987) also outlines a series of research priorities. These priorities or "tasks" are more than 50 in number and are aimed at achieving "three viable, self-sustaining populations within the historic range of the animal" (p. 14). The 50 tasks are grouped into three broad categories: (2) to "identify, protect, and enhance existing Florida panthers rangewise and protect and manage habitats" (pp. 14–18); (2) to "establish positive public opinion support for the management of Florida panther" (pp. 18–19); and (3) to "reintroduce Florida panthers into areas of suitable habitat" (pp. 19–20). Like the priorities established by Ballou *et al.* (1989), these 50 tasks focus on areas of study, particularly population biology and ecology, that are not particularly well represented in the literature

8.5 Analysis of evidence for the first inference

What does the evidence tell us regarding the first inference necessary for evaluating the two hypotheses, H1 and H2, about the scientific basis for the success of panther-preservation efforts? Recall that this inference is IN1: "We can distinguish, at present, the Florida panther from all other organisms." In order to predict or maintain a MVPS for the Florida panther, we need to be able to justify IN1. Can we do so?

The entire species *Felis concolor* is not notably at risk of extinction, but certain subspecies, such as *F. c. coryi*, are. Therefore, we must be able to distinguish the Florida panther from all of its related subspecies in some non-arbitrary way. This seemingly simple task actually is a difficult one. As we mentioned earlier (in chapter 5), there is not a single species concept but, in fact, at least four of them. And, if "species" is not well defined, then certainly the subspecies is even more difficult to circumscribe. To understand why, we must examine how biologists think about species and subspecies.

The four species concepts are the genetic, or biological, species concept (BSC), the evolutionary species concept (ESC), the phylogenetic species concept (PSC), and the ecological species concept (ECSC). The controversy among advocates of the various concepts has been a bitter one (e.g., Cracraft 1987; Ghiselin 1987; Mayr 1987; de Queiroz and Donoghue 1988; Frost and Hillis 1990). Advocates of the BSC typically view species as ". . . groups of interbreeding natural populations that are reproductively isolated from other such populations" (Mayr 1969, p. 26). Proponents of the ESC usually view a species as "a single lineage of ancestral–descendant populations which maintains its identity from other such lineages and which has its own evolutionary tendencies and historical fate" (Wiley 1978, p. 18). Advocates of the PSC typically view species as "the smallest diagnosable cluster of individual organisms within which there is a parental pattern of ancestry and descent" (Cracraft 1983, pp. 169–170). Proponents of the ECSC maintain that a species "is a lineage (or a closely-related set of lineages) which occupies an adaptive zone minimally different from that of any other lineage in its range and which evolves separately from all lineages outside its range" (Van Valen 1976, pp. 223–224; see Rosenberg 1985, pp. 198–200). The specific definitions we have chosen for these four concepts probably do not represent the views of every biologist, but they serve to illustrate some of the most important differences among the concepts. Moreover, as we noted earlier, there are conceptual and empirical difficulties with employing each of the four concepts.

How do the various species concepts accommodate subspecies? The BSC, ESC, and ECSC appear not to preclude the recognition of subspecies, although the criteria used may not be the same as those used to identify species. Under the BSC, for example, subspecies may be recognized by ". . . internal geographic character integrity coupled with juxtapositional reproductive compatibility" (Smith 1990, p. 123). The PSC, on the other hand, is not consistent with recognizing subspecies, because subspecies do not exist if taxa are defined as diagnosable groups or organisms, and species are defined as the smallest such units (see Rosen 1979). Even though subspecies are legitimate units under the BSC, ESC, and ECSC, they are somewhat more arbitrary and conventional units than are species themselves. Subspecies are invented by taxonomists mostly to encompass a suite of external characters (e.g., the crook in the tail of the Florida panther) that they deem distinct enough to warrant recognition. Coincidentally, members of a subspecies share a unique geographic range or habitat, and a unique natural history, relative to other conspecifics (see O'Brien and Mayr 1991).

An important question, then, is: Can the mere phenotypic distinction of an isolated subspecies suffice to separate it from other members of the species? If we were to answer "yes," then we would need to defend our position against at least two criticisms. The first is that we have made our distinction at an arbitrary level of organization. Why not, one might suggest, treat each individual within a species as a "subspecies," because each individual is phenotypically distinct and, in many senses, isolated from other individuals? The second criticism is that we have made our subspecies distinction at an arbitrary point in time and space. Subspecies, one might argue, can be extremely transient, and they can even disappear or appear as the result of very modest environmental changes. Despite such criticisms, a growing number of systematists suggests that – given a rigorous application of many of the species concepts to practical taxonomy – phenotypic distinctions can suffice to separate subspecies from other members of a species (e.g., Frost and Hillis 1990; Collins 1991). Furthermore, they suggest that the phenotypically distinct, isolated entities classically named as "subspecies" often might better be considered as species.

Regardless of the precise position one takes on the distinguishability of subspecies, we suggest that if the characters used to recognize subspecies are to have genuine validity and not mere utility in making a distinction, then such characters need to have a genetic basis. Following this line of reasoning, we conclude that if a subspecies cannot be demonstrated to have a genetic makeup that somehow distinguishes it from other subspecies, then the first inference, IN1 (we can, at present, distinguish the Florida panther from all other organisms), may not be justified. Recent comprehensive molecular genetic analyses (O'Brien et al. 1990) indicate that some individuals previously thought to be purebred Florida panthers actually are descended primarily from individuals recently introduced into Florida from South or Central America. Other individuals living in The Big Cypress Swamp, however, appear to be descended solely from the ancestors of the Florida panther (O'Brien et al. 1990). Put simply, then, if there are such purebred descendants, and if we adopt the viewpoint that a genetic basis is needed to discriminate subspecies, then the Florida panther is a recognizable subspecies, and the first inference is justified. If there are no such purebred descendants, however, then the Florida panther is not a recognizable subspecies. And if not, then it is not possible to distinguish it from other, non-endangered, subspecies. Furthermore, if it is not a recognizable subspecies, then one inference, IN1, necessary for confirming our hypotheses, is likely either not justified or questionable. At present, questions about both the genetic "purity" of the subspecies and about its relevance to our judgments regarding IN1, remain open.

One reason that the relevance of the panther's genetic purity is not clear is that even a hybrid Florida panther might be distinguishable from all other organisms, as required by IN1. One might argue that hybridization among subspecies could preserve some portion of the genome that was unique to the Florida panther and, therefore, that hybridization is defensible on genetic grounds (O'Brien et al. 1990). In fact, one might also argue that the Florida panther is better off, genetically, as a result of ancestral hybridization than it would have been without it (O'Brien and Mayr 1991), although the consequences of hybridization, termed "outbreeding depression," can be just as damaging as inbreeding depression (see Vrijenhoek 1989; Woodruff 1989). Similarly, one might maintain that questions of hybridization are irrelevant for subspecies, like the Florida panther, because subspecies ". . . retain the potential to freely interbreed as part of ongoing natural processes" (O'Brien and Mayr 1991, p. 1188).

Because hybridization reduces the genetic differences among subspecies that have accumulated over time, it might also reduce our ability to distinguish the Florida panther from other subspecies. Hence, practical questions of subspecies identification and preservation lead naturally to questions about precisely what levels of hybridization can be allowed without obscuring the original distinctions among subspecies. Some persons might respond (1) that any hybridization at all taints the "uniqueness" of the subspecies, while other persons might claim (2) that no subspecies is totally unique in the first place and, therefore, that hybridization need not affect "uniqueness" greatly. Neither view rests on very firm footing. The whole matter of hybridization causes the epistemological problem of distinguishing one subspecies, such as the Florida panther, from another to become even more a matter of subjective analysis than it is in the purebred case. Moreover, neither proponents of (1) nor proponents of (2) appear to gain any advantage, regarding panther survival, from their respective positions, so the argument seems moot: Those who take position (1) cannot claim with certainty that, with only purebred individuals, it will be more difficult to preserve the subspecies, because its members are smaller in numbers.

Proponents of (1) cannot make this claim with certainty principally because Ballou *et al.* (1989) have shown that, at least for numbers of Florida panthers less than 80, conclusions about the probability of extinction based on demographic considerations are not particularly sensitive to number of individuals. Such conclusions are sensitive, however, to age at first reproduction. Because of the findings of Ballou *et al.* (1989), similar reasoning (about the controlling effect of age at first reproduction) can show that counting the hybrids as Florida panthers, as proponents of (2) might do, probably would not decrease their probability of extinction.

What is our conclusion about inference IN1, about our ability to distinguish the Florida panther from other subspecies of *Felis concolor*? We are not convinced that we can do so in some non-arbitrary way, unless we rely on molecular genetic analyses (see O'Brien *et al.* 1990). However, even if such a distinction were not possible, it would not mean that ecologists should not be interested in an isolated population like that of the Florida panther, on the grounds that it was not genetically distinct. The population nevertheless could possess tremendous scientific and heuristic value, for example. Nor would the impossibility of such a distinction mean that conservationists should not be interested in the panther. The subspecies obviously possesses aesthetic, cultural, educational, symbolic, and other similar values. The impossibility of such a distinction would mean, however, that it might be difficult to defend one's decision to treat the Florida panther as a unique subspecies.

8.6 Analysis of evidence for the second inference

What about the other inferences whose justification is necessary for confirming our hypotheses about the scientific basis for believing in the success of panther-preservation efforts? Let us consider the evidence relevant to the second inference, IN2: that we possess, at present, the demographic, genetic, and environmental data necessary to predict the MVPS for the Florida panther in the wild. As we shall argue in detail, the justification for this inference is likewise questionable.

The process of calculating any MVPS is a difficult one. Woodruff (1989) has said that defining a MVPS is the "most pervasive" problem underlying species-management practices. This difficulty may account for the fact that MVPSs have been determined for very few species (Atkinson 1989). If it is true, however, that MVPS ". . . calculations routinely guide species-management in captivity" (Western 1989), then we must conclude that it is much more difficult to calculate MVPS for species in the wild. Why is the process more difficult? One reason is that it requires full sight of some set of objectives. That is, one must establish a tolerable probability of extinction and time frame for persistence as targets. If the probability of extinction is set too low, or the time frame too long, the resulting MVPS could be unattainable. Of course, to set probability of extinction and time frame reasonably, the ecologist needs sound information about genetic, demographic, and environmental variation (see Gilpin 1991; Hanski and Gilpin 1991; Hansson 1991; Harrison 1991; Sjogren 1991).

Another reason that calculating MVPS is difficult is that estimates for it derived primarily from one set of factors could be different from those derived primarily from another set of considerations. For example, if ecologists thought it important for the future well-being of the Florida panther to preserve some type and percentage of genetic variation over time, then estimates of the MVPS might well be different than if ecologists ignored genetic variation. Their calculations of the MVPS also would be commensurately more complex and require additional information, such as effective population size, if ecologists were to attempt to preserve some type and percentage of genetic variation. (Effective population size is that number of individuals which theoretically would demonstrate the amount of genetic drift observed, if there were random breeding (see Emlen 1973).) Effective population size is maximized when all parental individuals have an equal probability of being the parents of any progeny individual. Effective population size almost always is smaller, often much smaller, than population size determined from counts of individuals. Therefore, the MVPS almost always would be larger if researchers employed effective population size, rather than counted population size. Ballou et al. (1989) suggest that effective population size for the Florida panther is about 25–50 percent of the adult population. At present, no practical method allows calculation of an estimate for the MVPS that simultaneously incorporates genetics, demographics, and environmental variation, although most certainly they interact.

A third reason that the process of determining MVPS is difficult is that the models available for assessing risk of extinction in relation to population size are still in the formative stages (see Goodman 1987b; Woodruff 1989). Hence, because of their extremely limited scope, they can provide only ranges, sometimes very broad ones, of population sizes that can buffer the population from stochastic variation. Furthermore, the implementation, even of refined models, would seem to require a better understanding of community dynamics than we now possess (Soulé 1989; see also chapters 2 and 3).

In spite of the difficulties in calculating the MVPS, Ballou *et al.* (1989) did so for the Florida panther. They set the parameters of their model at values derived from observations of the demographies of existing populations. They then used stochastic simulation to model population extinction, starting with a specified number of males and females of each pre-reproductive age class and a specified number of males and females of breeding age. For example, if age at first reproduction, adult mortality, litter size, and initial population size are set optimistically – at two years, 25 percent, three, and 60 (30 adults, 30 juveniles), respectively – and carrying capacity is set realistically – at 45 – Ballou *et al.* (1989) estimate the probability of extinction in 100 years at 0.22 (mean time to extinction = 58 years). Ballou *et al.* (1989) found that populations of initial size 80 (40 adults, 40 juveniles) persist only an average of four years longer than do populations of initial size 45 (30 adults, 15 juveniles), and that increasing the population carrying capacity from 30 to 80 prolongs population-persistence times only by about one year. They found that age at first reproduction was far more important in increasing persistence times.

Although their analysis of the demographic data indicates that changes in population sizes (for populations of fewer than 80 individuals) have relatively little effect on persistence times of the Florida panther, Ballou *et al.* (1989, p. 39) note that "genetically, . . . smaller population sizes would lose variability more rapidly." Even for the most optimistic ("best case") demographic scenario that Ballou *et al.* (1989) describe (age at first reproduction = two years, adult mortality = 25 percent, litter size = three, carrying capacity = 80), however, the population retains only between 50 and 70 percent of its current level of heterozygosity after 100 years. This loss of heterozygosity could result in depressed survival and/or reproduction, as we discussed earlier, although admittedly, the relationship between heterozygosity and survival and/or reproduction in the wild is not understood precisely (Vrijenhoek 1989). Hence it is not clear whether the Ballou *et al.* (1989) estimates of MVPS are realistic.

Another difficulty with their MVPS estimates for the Florida panther is their ignoring environmental variation. Ballou *et al.* (1989, p.38) note that "consideration of environmental variation might lead to greater extinction probabilities . . ." than those calculated purely from "best case" demographic data. Yet, detailed ecological data concerning the effects of environmental variation on the Florida panther are the data that seem to be least available. Detailed ecological data intended to address highly specific questions are not easy to obtain. Consider, for example, the four tasks listed in the panther recovery plan (US Fish and

Wildlife Service 1987) that are aimed at determining "population levels and habitat requirements for known inhabited areas" (B111, p. 14: (1) ". . . conduct studies in Everglades National Park . . . using radio-telemetry and . . . consider the need for additional studies in south Florida . . . ," (2) ". . . conduct radio-tracking studies in Fakahatchee Strand State Preserve . . . and Big Cypress National Preserve . . . ," (3) ". . . expand studies to private lands north of S.R. 84 (Alligator Alley) in cooperation with landowners," and (4) ". . . conduct population surveys to monitor panther activity in Florida Panther National Wildlife Refuge . . ."). Unfortunately, the small number of panther observations (of movements, food habits, predator–prey relationships, energetics, reproduction, mortality, and so on) that can be made on approximately 40 individuals inhibits the timely collection of vital information. Hence, it seems obvious that tasks which rely on knowledge of population levels and habitat requirements for known inhabited areas – in order to predict them for uninhabited areas (B311, p. 19, for example: "Develop priority list of potential reintroduction sites") – will be completed even less expeditiously than the four tasks listed above.

Because of the lack of relevant data on the potential effects of environmental variation on the Florida panther, we do not know whether or not a realistic estimate of the MVPS for a population in the wild has been derived. Without relevant environmental data, we cannot guarantee the correctness of any estimate of MVPS. Therefore, we cannot guarantee the correctness of the estimate provided by Ballou *et al.* (1989). Hence, at present, we are uncertain regarding our ability to predict the MVPS, for the Florida panther. In fact, because of the lack of ecological data in general and the small number of remaining individuals, it may be that a realistic estimate cannot be derived at all. And if not, then the second inference, IN2, necessary for confirming our two hypotheses, is not justified. We hasten to point out, however, that even were sound data available to indicate that environmental variation did not seriously reduce the probability of survival from present estimates, this fact would not help us. The prognosis for the panther is so bleak from consideration of demographic data alone (mean time to extinction is 58 years under an "optimistically realistic" demographic scenario (Ballou *et al.* 1989), that the whole matter of environmental variation may not be significant.

However, given the probability of extinction calculated by Ballou *et al.* (1989) under this scenario – 0.22 probability of extinction in 100 years – it is clear that the Florida panther may still be able to survive in the wild. After all, previous predictions about "doomed" species have been proved wrong. Miller *et al.* (1929), for example, listed nine species of birds that experts called "beyond saving." More than 60 years later, none of the species has in fact gone extinct, although the ivory-billed woodpecker is now restricted to Cuba, and the California condor is extinct in the wild. The flamingo, golden plover, Hudsonian godwit, buff-breasted sandpiper, and upland plover (sandpiper) all recovered once over-exploitation ceased, although the latter species still suffers from loss of habitat. The recovery of the other two species, the whooping crane and the trumpeter swan, are testimonials to the results that can be achieved by the aggressive application of basic biological information. Population sizes of both species continued to decline, as Miller *et al.* (1929) thought they would, reaching their lowest numbers in the 1940s. After that time, greater knowledge about the two species, apparently coupled with increasing motivation to do something to save them, allowed the development of well-conceived management plans. These plans have brought the total numbers of individuals of both species into the 100s. Granted, these are small numbers, but they reflect a far better situation than that 50, or even 20, years ago. Other dramatic examples of recovery from very small population sizes include the Père David deer and the Przewalski horse (see Woodruff 1989; but, also see Simberloff 1986c). Environmental conditions, technology, and attitudes change: even apparently doomed organisms sometimes can be saved from the black hole of extinction. Hence, extinction of the Florida panther may be a matter of *uncertainty*, not a foregone conclusion, even if we cannot predict the MVPS, as inference IN2 states.

8.7 Analysis of evidence for the third inference

A third major inference whose justification is necessary for confirming H1 and H2 (our ability to predict and to maintain a MVPS for the panther) is IN3: We possess, at present, the population and environmental data necessary to predict the range expansions and habitat modifications (for the Florida panther) that will promote metapopulation dynamics and maintain the MVPS. To evaluate the evidence for inference IN3, we first consider the scope of the task of establishing and maintaining the MVPS for the Florida panther in the wild.

Assuming that inference IN2 (regarding predicting the MVPS for the panther) were justified, then perhaps the largest remaining questions – necessary to determine the feasibility of panther preservation – concern habitat in the wild. What, precisely, are the ecological circumstances that support Florida panthers (we shall call these circumstances "panther habitat")? How much land is needed to ensure enough panther habitat to support MVPS? Is that much land available? The answers to these questions require more detailed ecological knowledge about the Florida panther than one might suspect. This is because panther habitat entails much more than just certain kinds and amounts of undeveloped land. It entails, among other things, the circumstances to maximize effective population size, to facilitate natural social behaviors, and to minimize the adverse effects of extrinsic forces (see Simberloff 1986c; Western 1989). The ranges of the remaining wild individuals encompass widely varying prey densities and levels of disturbance, as well as a variety of other factors that might also be important in defining panther habitat. The entirety of a particular range, for example, is not likely to be equally suitable for the Florida panther. Some parts of a range are likely to have low prey densities and/ or to cover areas of inherently poor soil conditions. Under such circumstances, the panthers' physical condition and reproduction may suffer (Maehr 1990). This means that what we have called "panther habitat" is likely to comprise only a portion of any range, and the portion is likely to vary among ranges. To determine precisely what part of a particular range is panther habitat, one must therefore know a great deal about the interrelationships between the Florida panther and its environment. Although numerous valuable data on these interrelationships have been gathered by radio-tracking and other techniques, we think it is fair to say that precision in specifying the suitability of particular pieces of land for the Florida panther is lacking. And, it is not surprising that precision is lacking. In the case of a severely endangered taxon, like the Florida panther, the "value" of each individual prevents much experimentation and acquisition of new information to aid in determining precisely what constitutes suitable habitat for released individuals.

The importance of the questions we have posed about panther habitat is illustrated easily by consideration of captive propagation and reintroduction into the wild. The need for these two strategies is prominent among the suggestions that have been made to aid the recovery of the Florida panther. Indeed, it appears that any effort to preserve the Florida panther is doomed without due consideration of captive propagation and reintroduction (see, for example, Ballou *et al.* 1989). Yet, even if the appropriate technologies exist to raise healthy, fertile panthers in captivity, there is no guarantee that these panthers can help maintain an MVPS in the wild. High costs, logistical difficulties, and the shortage of habitat often make reintroduction infeasible

(Kleiman 1989). In a populous location, like Florida, shortage of habitat could be expected to be an especially pressing difficulty.

Shortage of panther habitat could be manifested in at least two ways. First of all, road closures, hunting restrictions, and other similar measures most certainly will be part of attempts to promote panther recovery in the wild. Such strategies are likely to generate conflicts with inconvenienced humans, and these persons may choose convenience over panther preservation. In such a case, shortage of habitat may result from resolution of conflicts in favor of human convenience. Shortage of habitat also may result from shortcomings in our knowledge of the Florida panther. Because ecologists cannot determine precisely what portion of a range consists of habitat suitable to maintain an MVPS for the Florida panther (for example, what portion supports appropriate prey density or is too close to human activity), cataloging remaining pieces of land that might support the organism is not a very profitable undertaking. Unsuitable habitat could be catalogued and ultimately acquired, only to prove of little value to panthers.

Without much information on suitable habitat for the Florida panther, it still may be possible to estimate the amount of land necessary to support a MVPS from what is known about the distribution of the subspecies and its relatives. We must caution, however, that such estimates are valid only if a similar, although unknown, portion of all land is assumed to be comprised of suitable panther habitat. Data from subspecies of *Felis concolor* residing in western North America (data from Central American subspecies might be more relevant, but they are not readily available) indicate that home range may vary between 194 and 575 km^2 for males, and between 104 and 268 km^2 for females, depending on season and method of estimating home range (see Dixon 1982). Data from *F. c. coryi* in Florida indicate that home ranges are, on average, about 666 km^2 for males and 192 km^2 for females (see US Fish and Wildlife Service 1987). If we take 500 km^2 (123,550 acres) as an estimate of home range size for an individual Florida panther and assume that ranges tend to overlap somewhat, the estimate compares favorably with the published density estimate of about one individual per 50,000 acres (see Harris and Gallagher 1989). We judged (from maps) the current distribution of the Florida panther to cover some 1,710,000 acres, while Maehr (1990) estimated (from telemetry data) it to cover 2,176,000 acres. If we use these two area estimates, and take the number of individuals as 40 (see above), then the density of individuals is one per 42,750 acres for the first area estimate and one per 54,400 acres for the second area estimate. These figures again compare favorably with the published density estimate of about one individual per 50,000 acres. Using all three density estimates, and assuming that a viable population must consist of at least 50 individuals (see above), we can calculate a potential range of area requirements of the smallest viable population. The range is from (50 individuals × 42,750 acres/individual =) 2,137,500 acres to (50 individuals × 54,400 acres/individual =) 2,720,000 acres.

The area requirement for a minimum viable population of the Florida panther can be estimated in other ways, most of which yield even larger figures. R. F. Noss (unpublished report to The Fund for Animals), for example, derived estimates of 6.9–13.8 million acres (and rounded these estimates upwards to 10–15 million acres, to provide a margin of safety). His estimates were derived by assuming (1) the sex-ratio is near 1:1; (2) the population consists of 50–100 males, to yield an effective population size of 50; and (3) the average male home range is 558 km² (137,600 acres). Furthermore, he suggests that ten such units should comprise a metapopulation, and that additional lands will be needed for buffer zones and corridors.

Public lands in south Florida contained within known or potential panther range encompass 3,597,020 acres (Maehr 1990). However, two considerations suggest that this figure is deceptively large and, therefore, that existing public lands may be inadequate to preserve the Florida panther. The first problem, which we have discussed previously, is that not all of the acreage can support panthers, and exactly how much can support them is undetermined (Maehr 1990). The second problem is that not all of the acreage is contiguous (Maehr 1990). Likewise, if a second viable population were to be established in northern Florida, for instance, then all of the potential locations for the population would be individually much smaller than necessary. For example, Osceola National Forest is only about 160,000 acres in size. If it were considered part of an interconnected complex of wildlands serving as potential locations for introductions of the Florida panther, then public lands in north Florida (available for this purpose) would rise to some 1.2 million acres, according to US Fish and Wildlife Service estimates. These 1.2 million acres, however, would still be almost 1 million acres short of those needed for the smallest MVPS. Hence possible places for undertaking preservation of the Florida panther are limited (see Maehr 1990). A key component of any plan to preserve the Florida panther in the wild would be expanding the amount of available habitat. Because public lands do not appear sufficient, expansion would require land acquisitions, easements, and minor restoration of linkages (by road closures). R. F. Noss (pers. comm.) estimates that if such expansion devices were successful, then some 10 million acres would be potentially available for reintroduction in the Osceola National Forest–Okefenokee National Wildlife Refuge complex of northern Florida and southern Georgia.

Even if enough land were available to support a metapopulation, however, inference IN3 would still be problematic because placing MVPS of the Florida panther into the metapopulation framework (see Ballou *et al.* 1989) remains an extremely vexing task. (Recall that by "metapopulation," we mean a population that is not a single, homogeneous unit, but rather a system of subpopulations, each of which is connected to at least one other subpopulation by movements of individuals. Recall further that the MVPS of a metapopulation need not be the same as the MVPS of a single homogeneous population of the same taxon, all else being equal.) One particularly troublesome aspect of the task of placing the MVPS of the Florida panther into the metapopulation framework seems to be ensuring a rate of exchange of individuals among subpopulations that will accomplish the goals of the preservation effort. Some persons have suggested that so-called "corridors" should be provided to allow individuals to move among subpopulations. Because of the potential importance of corridors to a metapopulation framework, we shall explore the movement of individual panthers among subpopulations and, in particular, the controversy over the role of corridors in enhancing panther movements among subpopulations.

Harris and Gallagher (1989; see also Noss and Harris 1986; Noss 1987b) represent one side of the corridors controversy. They tout the benefits of corridors in general, noting that they are a normal part of the landscape. Observing that many of the public lands in southern Florida are too small individually to support viable populations of the Florida panther, they suggest that these tracts could be linked by corridors to create a viable metapopulation of panthers. Likewise, they suggest that Osceola National Forest in northern Florida and Okefenokee National Wildlife Refuge, mostly in southern Georgia, could be linked by corridors to accommodate a viable metapopulation of reintroduced, captive-bred individuals. Such suggestions for corridor systems for the Florida panther are similar to others offered previously (see Simberloff and Cox 1987).

Simberloff and Cox (1987; see also Simberloff *et al.* 1992) represent the other side of the corridors controversy. While they agree that increasing the population size and the range of the Florida panther probably is essential to its persistence, they are not convinced that corridors are important tools for achieving those ends. One of their concerns is that, while advocates of corridors implicitly assume that the Florida panther will use corridors, no evidence is available to demonstrate that they are likely to do so. If corridors are long and narrow, individuals simply may choose not to run the gauntlet between subpopulations. Another worry is that corridors may facilitate disease transmission among subpopulations, thus producing a simultaneous outbreak over the metapopulation. Yet another concern is that extant levels of genetic variability may not be preserved as well by more-or-less free interbreeding among individuals as by isolation of subpopulations, coupled with selective interbreeding. Perhaps their greatest concern is the cost-effectiveness of corridors, especially relative to other conservation efforts in Florida.

The basis of the controversy over the role that corridors play in a metapopulation framework is easily summed up by reiterating two observations about the metapopulation: (1) isolation of subpopulations may increase time to extinction of the metapopulation by buffering it against stochastic environmental variation, and (2) isolation of subpopulations may decrease time to extinction of the metapopulation by restricting interchange of individuals among subpopulations. Clearly these two observations mean that there is some "optimal" subdivision of a metapopulation such that it will maximize persistence time of the metapopulation (see Hanski 1989). Furthermore, the observations suggest that while corridors may benefit the metapopulation by reducing isolation, they also may harm it by increasing the chance that stochastic environmental variation will be correlated among subpopulations. Therefore, the controversy seems to rest on whether one chooses to emphasize potential benefit or potential harm to the metapopulation or to take some middle ground. The choice typically must be made without very much of the ecological information that would allow designation of an "optimal" subdivision of the metapopulation. Lack of information seems to be the key to the whole dispute.

While corridors are indeed a normal part of the landscape, as Harris and Gallagher (1989) suggest, the fact is that, as far as the Florida panther is concerned, the landscape is no longer "normal." The important question then becomes: Can even the best corridor system, created or set aside by humans as part of a metapopulation framework, mimic one that occurred naturally? The clear answer at this point is: We don't know. Even if we did know, however, the question itself may be irrelevant in relation to preservation of the panther because, as Ballou *et al.* (1989, p. 10) note, ". . . as wild populations become fragmented, natural migration for recolonization may become impossible." Instead, animals may need to be moved around by humans to offset the adverse effects caused by the smallness of individual subpopulations.

In sum, it does not appear that we possess enough information about the ecology of the Florida panther to estimate its habitat requirements with much certainty. Distributional data can provide an estimate of the land necessary to support a population of 50 individuals (either counted or effective population size), but we do not know how much suitable habitat is contained within the current range of the panther. Furthermore, without corridors, the amount of contiguous, available land is much less than the amount probably needed to support even one population although, admittedly, the precise habitat needs of the panther are uncertain. Because of the real and potential fragmentation of panther habitat, a wild population certainly will be comprised of a group of semi-isolated subpopulations – a metapopulation. These subpopulations will need to be connected, but the prospect of doing so with "natural" corridors is uncertain. It appears that humans may need to move individual panthers about, and perhaps even rotate them from a captive "metapopulation" (in zoos and small reserves) to a wild metapopulation, and back again. Clearly, the chance of establishing a self-sustaining wild metapopulation is uncertain. And, if so, then the third inference, IN3, necessary to confirm our two hypotheses (about the success of the Florida panther preservation) is also uncertain.

8.8 Criteria for interpreting findings

If our analyses in the last three sections have been correct, then we appear not to possess the scientific data and inferences essential to confirming the likely success of panther preservation. Let us examine more closely, however, the criteria for interpreting our three inferences and the data relevant to them. Four of the criteria that figure prominently in interpreting the findings of our case study are internal consistency, external consistency, explanatory fertility, and predictive power. *Internal consistency* requires our various inferences and interpretations of evidence in the Florida-panther case to be unified and consistent with each other. *External consistency* requires the various inferences and interpretations of evidence in the Florida-panther case to be consistent with relevant analyses and interpretations in other analogous cases involving preservation of a taxon. *Explanatory fertility* requires us to assess the degree to which our inferences and interpretations have accounted for all the major scientific problems associated with panther preservation, as well as the degree to which our account might be able to yield further insights about how to explain remaining panther-preservation problems in the future. *Predictive power* requires us to assess the degree to which our two hypotheses can survive risky testing and, indeed, to test them ourselves, in order to determine how reliable they are.

In using these four criteria for interpreting our findings, we shall focus on our two hypotheses. These are H1: "We understand the biology of the Florida panther well enough, at present, to predict the MVPS that is capable of sustaining it in the wild, at least for 20 years," and H2: "We can manipulate the environment of the Florida panther, at present, in order to maintain the MVPS." According to our analysis, we have interpreted both hypotheses as uncertain. Our judgments about the uncertainty of these two hypotheses have followed as a consequence of our failure to justify three important inferences that are necessary for confirming the hypotheses. These inferences concern identification of the Florida panther; demographic, genetic, and environmental data necessary to predict the MVPS; and population and environmental data required to promote metapopulation dynamics and maintain the MVPS for the panther.

How well do our judgments – about the likely uncertainty of the two panther hypotheses – fare according to the four criteria of evaluation? Essentially, we must ask whether on grounds of internal consistency, external consistency, explanatory fertility, and predictive power, it is more reasonable to conclude that the hypotheses are true, or false, or indeterminate (uncertain).

The indeterminacy of the first hypothesis, H1, is consistent with, and follows from, the lack of relevant data on the potential effects of environmental variation on the Florida panther. Obviously, however, the question to be addressed here, if we are considering the internal consistency of our judgment of indeterminacy, is the degree to which it is compatible with the predictions of Ballou *et al.* (1989) regarding probability of extinction of the Florida panther. The need for compatibility between our judgments and those of Ballou *et al.* (1989) derives from the fact that both sets of judgments come from independently constructed case studies of the Florida panther. Did Ballou *et al.* (1989) believe that the lack of relevant data on the potential effects of environmental variation on the Florida panther precluded predicting a realistic MVPS? How is it consistent for us to claim that an hypothesis (about the ability to predict the MVPS for the Florida panther in the wild) is indeterminate, when Ballou *et al.* (1989) appear to have used some predicted MVPS in order to arrive at their probabilities of extinction? Is our position consistent with that of Ballou *et al.* (1989), and are both (Ballou *et al.*'s (1989) and ours) sets of conclusions regarding the MVPS for the panther internally consistent with the allegations (1) that there is a lack of relevant data on the potential effects of environmental variation on the panther, and (2) that this lack precludes predicting the MVPS for the panther?

We submit that the two case studies, Ballou *et al.*'s (1989) and ours, do reach internally consistent conclusions. The key to recognizing their consistency may be found in the demands made by each case study of an estimate of MVPS. Ballou *et al.* (1989) used the best *demographic* data available to calculate a range of extinction probabilities for the Florida panther and the best *genetic* data available to calculate the potential loss of heterozygosity. Their calculations admirably illustrate the severe plight of the Florida panther, even if we employ extraordinary measures to relieve some of the current sources of mortality and to enhance reproductive output. The material that Ballou *et al.* (1989) did not consider – indeed, could not consider – was *environmental* infor-mation, namely, the effect that placement of a population in the wild, with the concomitant chance of environmental variation or even catastrophe, might have on estimates of the MVPS. It is precisely this information that we demanded be included in estimates of the MVPS. In essence, then, Ballou *et al.* (1989) demanded of the existing data exactly what they had to offer, namely demographic and genetic information, while we demanded of them more than they had to offer, namely, environmental information. Hence our respective conclusions are internally consistent.

Our judgment that we are uncertain about the second hypothesis, H2, regarding our ability to maintain the MVPS through environmental manipulation, is likewise internally consistent with, and follows from, the fact that we do not have the ecological information necessary to identify Florida-panther habitat. Therefore, we do not have the knowledge (1) to choose potential locations for population expansions or reintroductions wisely; (2) to designate an "optimal" subdivision of the metapopulation; or (3) to predict the likely success of corridors. Our position is thus internally consistent because it maintains that infor-mation is inadequate either to confirm or falsify the claim that we can promote metapopulation dynamics. Moreover, although our position on corridors differs from that of Harris and Gallagher (1989), it is internally consistent with the evidence on which Harris and Gallagher (1989) base their view. They presuppose the truth of the second hypothesis, they support corridors, and hence they believe they can promote metapopulation dynamics and maintain the MVPS by means of corridors. Although we are skeptical about using corridors to promote metapopulation dynamics, our position of skepticism is nevertheless consistent with the same evidence about the panther that is used by Harris and Gallagher (1989).

We suggest that the difference in position between Harris and Gallagher (1989) and us stems from the different demands that each view makes on the strength of evidence necessary to ascribe "worth" to environmental manipulations, in this case to the creation and/or maintenance of corridors. We note that the difference comes about despite the fact that both sides most certainly would agree that for a wide-ranging animal such as the Florida panther, an appropriate land-conservation strategy would need to incorporate large blocks of habitat. One position, taken by Harris and Gallagher (1989), seems to be that judgments about "worth" are a function of several observations, key among them being: (1) that corridors appear to have been part of the landscape prior to disturbance by humans; (2) that the importance of corridors to populations is suggested by (island biogeographic and metapopulation) theory; (3) that the importance of corridors to populations is validated, at least indirectly, by studies of the effects of isolation on island populations; (4) that the importance of corridors to populations is validated, in the case of the Florida panther, by their documented use of at least one corridor (see Maehr 1990); (5) that the importance of corridors is logically appealing; and (6) that the importance of corridors can be "sold to" the public and its representatives. Our position (see also Simberloff and Cox 1987) is less generous in ascribing "worth" to corridors. Because our position demands direct evidence that corridors will work to help preserve the Florida panther, we agree with half of the observations listed above, (1), (5), and (6), but not with the other half. Yet, it is observations (2), (3), and (4) that specifically address the "worth" of corridors in terms of ecology. Because we have pointed out problems (chapter 3) with the application of island-biogeographic theory, we are uncertain about observations (2) and (3). Regarding observation (4), we suggest that records of one or a few instances of "corridor" use do not establish, *de facto*, the importance of corridors as a management tool. In fact, the number of such recorded instances, for any taxa at all, is quite small (Simberloff *et al.* 1992). Moreover, the exceedingly nebulous conception of exactly what constitutes a corridor clouds the value of even these few instances in suggesting the importance of corridors (Simberloff *et al.* 1992). For instance, if one were to observe a panther using a highway underpass of several meters in length, does such an observation suggest that "corridors," in general, are important? What if one were to observe a panther using a power line cut of several tens of meters in length, or a riparian strand several hundreds of meters in length? We also recognize that corridors could have adverse effects on the Florida panther – for example, by helping to spread disease – and that, despite the fact that panthers may have employed particular strips of land as "corridors," ecologists do not have the first clue as to how to design corridor systems that are likely to be used as they intend them to be used. For all these reasons, we believe that our position is internally consistent with all the evidence (although not with the value judgments) on which Harris and Gallagher (1989) base their view.

As well as being internally consistent with the available evidence, our judgments that both hypotheses are uncertain or indeterminate also appear to be more internally consistent with the available evidence about the panther than would be a judgment that the hypotheses are true, or that they are false. The judgment of uncertainty is superior, with respect to internal consistency, because there is evidence, in the Florida-panther case, neither of successful predictions of the MVPS in the wild nor of successful promotions of metapopulation dynamics. Hence, neither hypothesis can be known to be true. Their truth value is not obviously false, however, because it might happen that, in the future, our current estimates of the MVPS, for example, turn out to be true. Whether we can predict (H1) or maintain (H2), the MVPS cannot be decided at present. Hence, at present, our position appears internally consistent with the available evidence.

How well does our analysis of the Florida-panther case fare when we assess it on the basis of the second criterion, external consistency? Are our judgments about the uncertainty of the two hypotheses consistent with similar conclusions that other scientists have drawn in analogous preservation/extinction cases? To answer these questions, we must digress briefly to examine the philosophical underpinnings of related case studies dealing with the preservation of taxa.

Most preservation-related case studies, like that of Ballou *et al.* (1989) regarding the Florida panther, are "recovery plans" (the term is used here in an unofficial sense) for specific taxa. In turn, most of these recovery plans are sponsored by the federal government. Therefore, they adopt the philosophy of the federal government concerning recovery: "The primary goal of the Endangered Species Program is to conserve animal and plant species and, if possible, restore them to healthy populations so that they are no longer in danger of extinction"

(US Fish and Wildlife Service 1981, p. 8). An important, but apparently overlooked, component of this philosophy is the phrase "if possible." This phrase could be interpreted to mean that a particular restoration technique should be employed if any chance at all exists that it will work. We believe this is the viewpoint adopted in most preservation-related case studies. We discuss two such cases in detail below. The use of language like "if possible" suggests that if a preservation technique has theoretical, or empirical, or even logical backing, then it should be tried. Because many such techniques may suggest themselves in a particular case, and it is usually impractical for ecologists to try them all, some method must be employed to choose among preservation techniques. The method often employed is expert consensus. Using the so-called "Delphi Approach," a group of scientists and/or policymakers typically chooses particular techniques designed to foster preservation of taxa in cases where it is possible.

The phrase, "if possible," however, could also be interpreted to mean that a particular restoration technique should be employed only if the chance of success has been demonstrated to be acceptably high in the case at hand. We know of no preservation-related case studies that appear to adopt this viewpoint. The authors of most case studies recognize, nevertheless, the obvious value of achieving some acceptable chance of success, and they almost always are quick to point out that the data necessary to assure success simply are not available. Moreover, the public (or, at least, its representatives) might prefer preservation-related case studies to use this more demanding interpretation of the phrase "if possible" (see our subsequent discussion). Regardless of the relevant preferences, because there is still a chance of saving the Florida panther, despite our uncertainties and our limited knowledge, we maintain that we should not close off this possibility. We also believe that our position is externally consistent with the informed conclusions of the authors of other case studies.

Because we have taken on the extremely unusual role of both creator and critic of our case study of the Florida panther, we cannot expect our conclusions to be completely externally consistent with those of all other relevant case studies, given our misgivings about the typical way in which preservation studies are done. Those who adopt the first viewpoint (a particular restoration technique should be employed if any possibility at all exists that it will work) clearly would be much more likely to conclude, from our analyses of the evidence for inferences IN1–IN3, that hypotheses H1 and H2 are true or, at least, uncertain, than those who adopt the second viewpoint (a particular restoration technique should be employed only if the possibility of success has been demonstrated to be acceptably high in the case at hand). Proponents of the second position would be more likely to conclude that the two hypotheses are false. Let us look at the comments of the creators and critics of two other case studies, in order to show how this difference in viewpoints is manifested, and that our position, the first, appears to be a superior way of interpreting the criterion of external consistency.

The case studies we shall examine are those of (1) three taxa of Hawaiian waterbirds (Walker *et al.* 1977, and subsequent comments on the report that were solicited by the sponsors, the US Fish and Wildlife Service) and (2) the northern spotted owl (Thomas *et al.* 1990; US Congress 1990, which is a transcript of Senate testimony on the report of the Interagency Scientific Committee; and Gutierrez and Carey 1985, which is a compendium of biological information on the northern spotted owl). The case study of Hawaiian waterbirds (Walker *et al.* 1977) is a recovery plan for Hawaiian subspecies of the relatively widespread black-necked stilt, American coot, and common gallinule (common moorhen). Walker *et al.* (1977) estimated that there were fewer than 3,000 individuals of each taxon at the time they constructed their plan. They suggested that the primary reason for the documented historical decline of the three taxa, as with most taxa, was loss of habitat. They admitted (p. 3), however, that "such loss has not been quantified but is obvious and significant." To forestall further decline of the three taxa, it was necessary to prevent additional loss of habitat, that is, to prevent loss of the individual wetlands that supported the remaining birds. One objective of their recovery plan, therefore, was (p. 11) ". . . to provide and maintain populations of at least 2,000 [total individuals of each taxon] in, at a minimum, the habitats [individual wetlands] . . . existing in 1976. . . ."

Walker *et al.* (1977, p. 13) decided that ". . . the plan's objective to provide and maintain self-sustaining minimum populations . . . appears biologically feasible . . ." However, they recognized the failure of their plan to provide some level of assurance that it would actually meet the intended objectives of saving the waterbirds. They said (pp. 13–14): "It is believed that through implementation of all aspects of the plan, the Hawaiian stilt, coot and gallinule can be restored and will remain as viable members of Hawaii's avifauna. But until the precise ecological needs of each species are determined through study and action programs devised to meet those needs, no assurance can be given that they will ever be other than threatened or endangered." Because of this admission that data on the birds were lacking, Walker *et al.* (1977) anticipated that their case study of Hawaiian waterbirds indeed would be criticized for lack of knowledge of "precise ecological needs." A letter from the State of Hawaii, Department of Land and Natural Resources (dated November 30, 1977), for example, commented ". . . that the minimum population levels [2,000 total birds of each species] . . . were determined arbitrarily" and that ". . . classification of habitats . . . is not based on a firm foundation of data." The Department of Land and Natural Resources, probably with an eye toward cooperating in the implementation of the recovery plan, decided that more specific information than Walker *et al.* (1977) could give was needed in this case.

One might argue that it was not possible, given the theoretical and empirical states of ecology in the mid 1970s, to be as precise in determining the MVPS for each waterbird and the chance of success in a particular case, as one might want. Such an argument leads one to wonder whether ecologists now can be more precise. In some ways, they can. For instance, ecologists can now attach some level of significance to their estimates of MVPS and thus forestall criticism that their numbers are arbitrary. The body of relevant, low-level theory and empirical data regarding conservation strategies has grown, and this information now allows ecologists, at the very least, to eliminate many problematic strategies from consideration. But, as ecology becomes more sophisticated, so too does the criticism of it. Hence, instead of attacking, for example, the estimates of the MVPS, critics may now attack the assumptions used to derive the estimates. Regardless of the line of attack, however, the MVPS numbers continue to be uncertain. They can be neither confirmed nor falsified at present. Hence, the uncertainty in the Hawaiian waterbirds' case appears externally consistent with our conclusions about uncertainty in the panther case. In this light, let us examine a more modern case study, that of the northern spotted owl, to see what it tells us about our panther conclusions.

The Interagency Scientific Committee to Address the Conservation of the Northern Spotted Owl (Thomas *et al.* 1990; we shall henceforth refer to this committee as the "Interagency Committee") recommended protecting a system of blocks of habitat (HCAs = Habitat Conservation Areas) in California, Oregon, and Washington. Based on models of population persistence and empirical studies of bird populations, the HCAs within the system contained a minimum of 20 pairs of owls, whenever possible. As well, based on radio-tracking of juveniles to determine dispersal distances, the HCAs within the system were, at most, 12 miles (19.3 km) apart, boundary to boundary. The Interagency Committee decided that corridors of forest between HCAs were unnecessary, provided that there were suitable forest lands outside the HCAs. ("Suitable forest lands" means 50 percent of the forest lands maintained in stands of timber with an average d.b.h. (= diameter at breast height) of 11 inches (28 cm) or greater and at least 40 percent canopy closure.) The Interagency Committee also recommended that logging and other silvicultural activities cease within the HCAs.

Before we examine the particular criticisms leveled at these recommendations regarding the owls, let us look at some of the assumptions underpinning them. The volume edited by Gutierrez and Carey (1985) provides a diverse and thorough compendium of knowledge on the ecology and management of the northern spotted owl (see also Dawson *et al.* 1987). Two of the contributions to the volume are particularly relevant to our comparison among case studies, because they address MVPS (Barrowclough and Coats 1985) and metapopulation dynamics (Shaffer 1985). How precise do these authors judge their analyses to be in suggesting a possibility that particular management techniques will work for the northern spotted owl? Barrowclough and Coats (1985, p. 81) say:

> We must limit our analyses to the genetical effects of the SOMP (Spotted Owl Management Plan) under realistic "best case" conditions.

Likewise, Shaffer (1985, pp. 97–98) says:

> This issue [land-use planning for the conservation of viable populations] is complicated by the lack of a scientific consensus on standards for what constitutes such a population and by the inescapable reality that we are being asked to project the dynamics of a system without being given the time to examine it empirically or experimentally. I see no solution . . . except . . . to stimulate theory to provide guidance and general hypotheses that may be tested in the context of the management programs which will be implemented without complete knowledge.

In neither instance is there an indication that these results will, or are even intended to, provide precise estimates of the chance of success in preserving the owls. Clearly, the door is open to critics who demand such precise estimates.

For particular criticisms leveled at the recommendations of the Interagency Committee, we turn to the transcript of Senate testimony

(US Congress 1990) on the report of the Interagency Committee (Thomas *et al.* 1990). Two quotations will serve to illustrate the general tone of the proceedings. The first is from Senator Wallop (p. 7):

> The decision-making process used by the . . . committee is embarrassing to anyone calling himself a scientist . . . I . . . find it incredible that the committee could try to justify as science the process of pure guesswork they call the "Delphi Approach," which is just a fancy term for a group of people sitting around a table guessing at the best solution to a problem which has no scientific answer . . . This report gives a whole new meaning to the computer phrase "garbage in, garbage out."

The second quotation is from Senator McClure (p. 17):

> The . . . committee report is really a sophisticated use of the "Delphi Technique" of convening experts to render conclusions in areas where the data are not adequate to base these conclusions on experimental results. . . . The science is not clear. . . . In short, I believe the report is not credible . . . If current trends continue, I predict that our National Forest will be completely operated and managed by unelected court officials and questionable "reports."

During the Congressional hearings on the spotted owl, the Senators asked of representatives of the Interagency Committee many pithy questions. Here is a selection:

> 'Would you please explain why your committee first decided how large the HCA's should be, and then began looking for empirical evidence to support your decision?' (p. 229)

> 'Am I correct that the field of 'conservation biology,' on which your conservation strategy is based, is a brand new scientific field which only came into existence during the 1980's and is recognized, even by its defenders, to be in its infancy?' (p. 258)

> 'Am I . . . correct that there is no standard textbook in the field of conservation biology and that no classes in the subject had ever been offered in universities until the past three or four years?' (p. 259)

> 'Do you know of any 'conservation strategy' for wildlife species, based on principles of conservation biology, which has ever been tested in the real world?' (p. 260)

'Do you agree that the field of conservation biology has not yet been fully accepted as an area of scientific endeavor equal in rigor to the hard sciences such as physics and chemistry?' (p. 260)

'Do you agree that there is inherently a lower degree of scientific certainty to findings in the field of wildlife biology than in the hard sciences?' (p. 262)

'Do you have any ways of calculating how likely it is that your conclusions about the current and future prospects of the Spotted Owl are correct?' (p. 263)

'What is the scientific method used to verify whether the distance between HCA's called for in the plan is in fact required for protection of the Spotted Owl? Is it reasonable that the distance between HCA's is an issue where reasonable, responsible persons could easily reach different decisions through the use of judgment?' (p. 296)

'Habitat conservation areas are recommended to be large enough to hold 20 pairs of owls. This recommendation is based on studies of birds on islands off the British coast and the coast of California. Are there differences between birds living on islands and birds living in the forests of the Pacific Northwest?' (p. 308)

'. . . you draw a number of conclusions. Lacking sufficient scientific data, how do you arrive at these conclusions? Please provide supporting data.' (p. 382)

In the face of such questions, how were the representatives of the Interagency Committee able to defend their recommendations regarding the owl? As these questions illustrate, the assumptions, theories, and methods that the Interagency Committee employed came under severe attack. Let us use direct quotations from the Interagency Committee (in fact, its chair, Dr. Jack Ward Thomas) to show the defense it employed. When asked to summarize the report, Dr. Thomas said (p. 30):

'It (the conservation strategy) was based on five [sic] principles. That blocks of habitat that contain multiple pairs (of owls) are better than smaller. Those blocks closer together are better than blocks further [sic] apart. Contiguous habitats within the blocks is [sic] better than fragmented habitat. Habitat blocks connected by good habitat are better than those that are not so connected.'

Recall that these principles were inspired by island-biogeographic theory (see chapter 2). Concerning the Interagency Committee's recommendation that HCAs each contain 20 pairs of owls, Dr. Thomas said (pp. 97–98):

'We came with a hypothesis, given all the mapping that we had done as to what was possible . . . [namely,] would 20 pair areas be satisfactory in terms of the habitat conservation strategy. [sic] We then tested that with empirical data. . . . There were . . . five studies, essentially from various places around the world that involved islands, and how long would the population persist on that island [sic] . . . the basic theory for birds of that size seemed relatively consistent in the empirical data that we could find . . . then, we went to a considerable modeling exercise.'

To sum up the whole procedure, Dr. Thomas said (p. 99):

'There were two tests. One was the empirical evidence from island biogeography and actual studies of birds of the appropriate size, and the next was the mathematical modeling.'

When asked about how likely it was that the Interagency Committee's conclusions were correct, Dr. Thomas replied (pp. 263–264):

'A satisfactory model to compute an exact persistence likelihood for the Spotted Owl does not exist. However, it is possible to compare different owl management scenarios and rank them in terms of how likely they are to contribute to the species' long-term viability. . . . Management of biological systems is uncertain by nature.'

In the same vein, he said (pp. 271–272):

'Small populations tend to 'wink out' (go extinct) relatively quickly. We know of no exceptions to this pattern, so we believe it is the same for Spotted Owls. The Spotted Owl management plans now in place . . . provide relatively isolated patches of suitable habitat . . . for small clusters of owl pairs or for single pairs . . . We have proposed a strategy that we think is likely to succeed to replace one that was likely to fail.'

Further, he affirmed (p. 296):

'Our entire conservation strategy is basically a hypothesis that only time, monitoring, and further research can confirm or deny . . . it is our opinion (however) that if this same question were addressed by other teams of scientists with the same or greater level of collective knowledge about general animal ecology, wildlife biology, the vital role of dispersal in population dynamics, and, most importantly, Spotted Owl biology and population dynamics, they would settle on a guideline near that proposed in our strategy.'

Our skeptical judgments regarding the ability of ecologists, at present, to predict and maintain the MVPS of the Florida panther may not seem to be externally consistent with the confident judgments made by ecologists who examined the case of preserving the spotted owls. They admitted modelling uncertainties, for example, but nevertheless concluded that their strategy was "likely to succeed." We admitted comparable uncertainties, however, but concluded that we were also uncertain about the ultimate success of panther preservation. In other words, our uncertainty about the two panther hypotheses may seem inappropriate because we have adopted a viewpoint about interpretation and use of scientific evidence nearer that typically held by critics of conservation strategies. Ecologists studying the owl, however, have adopted a viewpoint about evidence that is typically held by advocates of conservation strategies. We suggest, however, that judging the two hypotheses, H1 and H2, to be uncertain, rather than true or false, makes more sense on the criterion of external consistency. It makes more sense because we know of no analogous cases in which crucial biological information was missing, as in the Florida-panther case, but in which ecologists actually were able to predict and maintain some MVPS successfully. In fact, we know of no analogous cases in which some crucial biological information was *not* missing. We also suggest that judging that these two hypotheses are uncertain, rather than false, makes more sense on the criterion of external consistency, because the hypotheses have not been falsified at present. As we noted earlier, we shall have to "wait and see" if the hypotheses turn out to be false. In the face of subjective judgments about hybridization or missing data that are essential to the task, one does not claim that hypotheses regarding the task are either true or false. Rather, one claims that confirmation or falsification cannot be accomplished without the information and, hence, that the inferences are uncertain. Therefore, despite the differences between our conclusions and those of ecologists studying the owl, we believe that our conclusions are *externally consistent* with the actual evidence used in the spotted-owl case.

Our judgments about the uncertainty of the two panther hypotheses likewise meet the criterion of explanatory fertility because they encourage us to develop further lines of experimentation and theory regarding the Florida panther. Because our conclusions are skeptical about our current predictive abilities regarding the Florida panther, they encourage us to obtain the data that we do not have, perhaps by following the 13 research priorities of Ballou *et al.* (1989, p. 4) or by achieving the more than 50 research "tasks" of the recovery plan for the Florida panther (US Fish and Wildlife Service 1987). Our conclusions also exhibit considerable explanatory fertility because they are based on at least three important inferences, IN1–IN3, necessary to predicting and maintaining the MVPS. With a clear vision of what we do not know regarding IN1–IN3, we have a fertile program for the lines that future panther research ought to take. Admittedly, however, if we were to judge that the two hypotheses were false, this stance would likewise probably encourage further research into MVPS and metapopulation dynamics for the taxon. Hence, both judgments of uncertainty and of falsity regarding the hypotheses would likely yield explanatory fertility. If we judged the hypotheses true, however, there might be a tendency, for example, to create and/or maintain corridors on the supposition that our theory and data relevant to the Florida-panther case were adequate. This supposition might not encourage the further development of theory and data in the Florida-panther case, since ecologists might be likely to believe that they had found the answers to their problems with MVPS and metapopulation dynamics.

How well do our judgments about the uncertainty of the two panther hypotheses meet the criterion of predictive power? Could the judgments survive risky testing? They have already undergone a sort of testing, because scientists in fact have not predicted a MVPS for the Florida panther in the wild that we can confirm, at present, as successful. Likewise, scientists in fact have not promoted Florida-panther metapopulation dynamics that we can confirm, at present, as successful. To the degree that current conjectures and actions of ecologists regarding the Florida panther constitute a sort of test of our ability to predict and maintain MVPS, then to that degree the test has failed to confirm the hypotheses. The jury is still out. However, there is no way either to confirm or falsify our current capabilities or inabilities regarding MVPS prediction or maintenance, short of waiting, over the long term, to see whether any of the predicted MVPS and metapopulation promotions turn out to be successful. These capabilities or inabilities ultimately will be either confirmed or falsified by the future preservation or extinction of the panther in the wild. At present, however, the criterion of predictive power has vindicated no position regarding our ability to predict and maintain MVPS. Hence, at present, according to the criterion of predictive power, we are uncertain regarding our ability to predict and maintain MVPS.

8.9 Conclusions regarding H1 and H2

Where have the four criteria (internal consistency, external consistency, explanatory fertility, predictive power) brought us regarding our interpretation of the two panther hypotheses? Our judgment that the two hypotheses are uncertain appears to be supported both by the criterion of internal consistency and by the criterion of external consistency. Support based on the latter criterion, however, is strong only if analogous preservation cases have been subjected to serious criticism and have survived the analysis. Providing such criticism has been one goal of our discussion of these other, relevant case studies of the waterbirds and the owl. As such, the studies illustrate both an "advocacy" portion (contributed by the case-study creators, usually ecologists or conservationists), and a "criticism" portion (usually contributed by representatives of those who disagree with the position taken by the creators). As our analysis illustrates, a good case study must take account of relevant objections to the case-study conclusions, especially objections based on external consistency.

With respect to explanatory power, our judgment of the uncertainty of the two panther hypotheses is not clearly superior to judging the hypotheses true or false, because our uncertainty regarding our ability to predict and maintain a MVPS cannot help us explain anything, although it may be consistent with the uncertain or deteriorating status of the Florida panther. Regarding the fourth criterion, predictive power, the jury is still out. It is undetermined whether the hypotheses are true, false, or uncertain. Their status will be determined by whether the predictions of current ecologists are borne out by subsequent events. If we assume that each of the four criteria for evaluating the evidence (internal consistency and so on) in the Florida-panther case are to be given equal weight, then the preponderance of evidence appears to be on the side of our judgment that it is uncertain whether we can predict, at present, an MVPS for the Florida panther that is capable of sustaining it in the wild, at least for 20 years (H1), or that we can manipulate the environment, at present, in order to maintain panther MVPS in the wild, at least for 20 years (H2). But if the preponderance of evidence is that the two hypotheses are uncertain, then two conclusions follow:

C1: We cannot guarantee, at present, that we understand the biology of the Florida panther well enough to predict the MVPS in the wild.

C2: We cannot guarantee, at present, that we can manipulate the environment of the Florida panther in order to maintain the MVPS in the wild.

Given these two conclusions, we have a rough, and unsurprising, answer to the question posed earlier in the chapter: Is it possible to save the Florida panther in the wild? The answer to our question is "yes and no." Yes, preservation is, in principle, possible. No, in practice, we cannot guarantee that our efforts will be successful. Our analysis has shown that at least three main inferences (IN1–IN3) necessary to affirm the truth of our hypotheses H1 and H2 are questionable. Because of our uncertainty regarding these essential inferences and because, on the basis of at least two of the four evaluative criteria, the hypotheses appear uncertain, our two conclusions above appear reasonable. Hence, if predicting the MVPS is essential to saving the Florida panther in the wild, and if manipulating the environment so as to maintain the MVPS is likewise essential to saving the taxon in the wild, and if the success of neither can be guaranteed at present, then we must conclude that it is uncertain, at present, whether we can save the Florida panther in the wild for at least 20 years.

Of course, we have not addressed the possibility either that the Florida panther could be saved in the wild sometime in the future or that it could be saved in partial or complete captivity. Our conclusions, however, do put the burden of proof on persons who argue that the extinction of the Florida panther is a foregone conclusion. Moreover, if our prima-facie argument in chapter 6 – about avoiding type-II errors in cases of uncertainty – is correct, then our uncertain conclusions do not jeopardize conservation efforts. Indeed, they support them.

8.10 Evaluation of our conclusion

How well will our unappealing conclusion – that it is uncertain, at present, whether we shall be able to save the Florida panther in the wild for at least 20 years – stand up to criticism? As we mentioned in the previous section, one of the best ways of evaluating a case-study conclusion is to analyze the objections likely to be made to it and therefore to determine if the objections can be answered in a reasonable manner. This raises an obvious question. What are the main objections to our case-study conclusion, namely, that it is uncertain, at present, whether the Florida panther can be saved in the wild for at least 20 years? Scientists, conservationists, and proponents of corridors might raise at least four objections to our conclusion. One objection is (1) that we have criticized potentially important environmental manipulations, corridors, in particular, even though there is no evidence that they will not work. Another objection is (2) that admitting the uncertainty of panther preservation might lead to a self-fulfilling prophecy of extinction and might guarantee that the Florida panther will not be saved in the wild, since persons do not know whether preservation efforts are likely to be successful. A related objection is (3) that admitting the uncertainty regarding panther preservation guarantees that the Florida panther will not be saved in the wild, since persons are likely to direct efforts toward "savable" taxa. Still another objection is (4) that admitting the uncertainty of panther preservation will demoralize preservationists. This demoralization could guarantee that the Florida panther will not be saved at all, and it could diminish public interest in conservation effort in general.

Of the four objections to our panther conclusion, (1) is based on an epistemic assessment of the scientific merits of our conclusions, whereas (2), (3), and (4) are based on a utility assessment of the normative strengths of our conclusions. Since this chapter deals only with the method of case studies as a method of science practiced by scientists, rather than with the policy considerations that are within the purview of all citizens, we shall respond to question (1) here. Later, in the next chapter, we shall address the policy issues raised by objections (2), (3), and (4).

How compelling is objection (1)? Is it true, in concluding that we are uncertain whether the Florida panther can be saved in the wild, at least for 20 years, that we have criticized corridors without testing them, without first trying to see if they will work? In response to this objection, first of all, we admit that we have indeed criticized corridors without testing them. The hidden suggestion in this objection is that we were somehow wrong to do so. It seems to us, however, that whether or not a particular preservation technique is employed depends at least on two considerations. The first consideration, which we have already addressed, is the "worth" of the technique. From this consideration the objection arises: advocates of corridors ascribe more "worth" to them than we do. They are certain that the logical, theoretical, and empirical arguments in favor of corridors are relevant to the case of the Florida panther, whereas we are not convinced. We would prefer to see the potential value of corridors (for management of the panther) tested in some rigorous manner, even though we admit that such a test would be an extremely difficult undertaking (see Nicholls and Margules 1991; Simberloff *et al*. 1992).

The second consideration – relevant to employment of a preservation technique – we already have addressed in part. This is the potential cost of the technique. Advocates of corridors typically either ignore attendant costs or minimize their importance. One reason that advocates would not emphasize attendant costs of corridors is that they have become convinced in advance that potential corridor benefits outweigh potential risks. Other persons, however, take a more conservative position on the balance between potential benefits and risks. They maintain that attendant costs, as we have also indicated, can be substantial (see Simberloff and Cox 1987; Simberloff *et al*. 1992). Beyond direct costs, like risk of disease transmission and increased predation, they maintain that there is an enormous potential indirect cost, damage to the conservation effort itself, if the corridors failed. In the case of the Florida panther, we think that damage could accrue even as a result of testing the value of corridors, in part because funds used for testing could be used to save other habitats and species.

We are also concerned, in the case of the Florida panther, that testing the value of corridors could seriously diminish our capacity to try other techniques – and, perhaps, even to preserve other taxa if corridors fail. Because the number of panthers is so low, a reliable test of corridors, one that encompassed enough observations to determine their value unequivocally, would need to involve the creation of virtually an entire corridor system. Furthermore, this extensive corridor system would need to be monitored for long periods of time. The investment in testing the importance of corridors to the Florida panther, particularly in terms of time, would be so great that other conservation efforts would be likely to suffer. Perhaps this "all-your-eggs-in-one-basket" strategy would be justified if the success of corridors were guaranteed, but no reasonable person would say that success is guaranteed. Hence, we agree in principle with testing corridors, but only if doing so does not jeopardize or preclude other equally important conservation efforts or other attempts at panther preservation. (In the next chapter, we shall say more about the opportunity costs of conservation schemes.) As we shall argue later, our concerns appear to hold, even if one took a view of corridors closer to that held by many advocates. This view is that a corridor system would not need to be created but is already in place and, therefore, that the existing "natural" corridors need only to be maintained and that the partially degraded corridors need only to be relieved from the spectre of further degradation.

An additional answer to the objection, that we have criticized corridors without testing them, involves the specification that the Florida panther be preserved in the wild. Suppose that corridors indeed were proved to be effective in promoting interchange of individuals among subpopulations, that interchange were demonstrated to be a good thing, and that a useful corridor system were in place. Given all of these suppositions, we (see also Simberloff and Cox 1987; Simberloff *et al.* 1992) maintain that the corridor system might need to be managed, if it were relatively long and narrow, to prevent disturbance to dispersing individuals, to prevent the vegetation from becoming overgrown and impassable, and so on. The number of persons needed to manage a corridor system would likely be at least as great as the number needed to move individuals "artificially" from one isolated subpopulation to another. We think that a heavy investment in personnel strains the meaning of "preservation in the wild." On the other hand, the corridor system might not need to be managed so strictly if it consisted of relatively large blocks of habitat. We likewise believe that such a system strains the meaning of "corridor." Hence, use of corridors is likely to generate criticisms either that they require extensive personnel, or that they presuppose a stipulative definition of "corridor," or both.

8.11 Epilogue: Has the method of case studies helped us?

An obvious response to our analysis of the Florida-panther case is that the method of case studies – including our work on the Florida panther – is nothing new. Indeed, it might appear to some to be nothing more than exploratory data analysis (EDA). In this final section of the chapter, we shall argue that the method of case studies goes well beyond EDA.

EDA has gained prominence, in part, because it often enables us to accomplish things we are unable to do in mathematical statistics. Mathematical statistics is based on the process of inferring or generalizing from small samples. Such inferences, however, sometimes hold little relevance for those who are trying to analyze features of the natural world, particularly when experimentation is not available as a method. As one writer put it (Marsh 1988, p. xviii):

> What is the point of having very elaborate rules of proof, governing what evidence is required before conclusions can be drawn about a population, if we have no developed techniques for discovering the evidence in the first place?

Another author formulated the same idea in a slightly different way (Tukey 1977, p. v):

> It is important to understand what you can do before you learn to measure how well you seem to have done it.

He continues (p. vii):

> The best way to understand what can be done is no longer – if it ever was – to ask what things could, in the current state of our skill techniques, be confirmed (positively or negatively). Even more understanding is lost if we consider each thing we can do to data only in terms of some set of very restrictive assumptions under which that thing is best possible – assumptions we know we cannot check in practice.

As these excerpts reveal, the techniques of exploratory data analysis (EDA) are based on a different philosophy from the deductive logic of the inferential approach (see chapter 5). Instead of testing the data, to see if they can be proclaimed "significant," researchers attempt to discover hypotheses hidden in the data. They "torture . . . them until they confess" (see Good 1983), and then they wait for a response – for hypotheses to emerge – before proceeding. In this sense, EDA seems very near to retroductive science, because description, classification, summary, and conjecture are necessary to both (Tukey 1977; Good 1983; Marsh 1988).

Because data are expensive, natural scientists cannot afford to restrict their attention to those hypotheses which they thought of before they collected data (Marsh 1988). The techniques of EDA provide a way of exploring the data to force attention on any patterns that might be present. In non-experimental research, when many variables may be operating simultaneously, these techniques can prove especially valuable, for example, in the pattern-matching stage of the method of case studies. Likewise, EDA techniques are important for discovering causal relations. As Marsh (1988, p. 237) notes:

> Causal inferences are constructions built upon a foundation of assumptions, and cannot be more valid than the assumptions. If this induces a feeling of unease in you such that you start routinely checking the concrete around the foundations of inferences drawn from natural science data, so much the better. Your job, however, is to mend any plausible cracks you observe – to do a better survey, measuring and controlling important new variables – not to walk away from the edifice declaring it to

be a hazard. Remember how poor lay reasoning about causation is: not to even try to collect the data required to test a hypothesis about the relationship between smoking and lung cancer, for instance, would be to leave the doors open only to those who jump to conclusions on the basis of a sample of one.

Obviously, there are good reasons for using exploratory data analysis. While EDA is a part of what we do in the method of case studies, the method goes beyond EDA. For one thing, the method of case studies is applicable to phenomena that may not admit even of the causal inferences characteristic of EDA. In the method of case studies, we may need to use retroductive or other informal inferences. The method of case studies also is different from EDA in that it is not merely a halfway house (like EDA) on the scientific road to classical, controlled experimentation or statistical testing. Rather, the method of case studies often forces us to remain at the level of quasi-experimentation, because of the uniqueness of phenomena being investigated (see chapter 5). Moreover, it provides us with a step-by-step consideration of alternative points of view, an organized framework short of statistical/experimental testing, for evaluating our conclusions and inferences. In forcing us to focus on *criteria* for our inferences, for the worth of data, for our interpretations of data, and for the types of evidence that we use in evaluating hypotheses, the method of case studies is philosophical and epistemological, and not merely statistical.

9 · Policy aspects of the Florida-panther case

E. O. WILSON (1988, p. 13) noted recently that the current rate of loss of species is between 1,000 and 10,000 times greater than it was before human intervention. If our conclusions in the case study in the previous chapter are correct, then although development pressures have threatened the Florida panther, it is not clear whether it is scientifically possible to specify the conditions that will guarantee the survival of the subspecies for at least 20 years. Hence, despite our efforts, the taxon could be yet another example of the losses chronicled by Wilson.

Because ecology is, in large part, an applied science, it is important not to end our investigation of the Florida panther with the scientific analysis in the last chapter. Like all applied scientists, ecologists need to give some thought to the possible policy consequences of their scientific conclusions. We have just argued, in the previous chapter, that it is uncertain whether it is scientifically possible to specify the conditions that will guarantee the survival of the Florida panther, in the wild, into the next century. Despite our scientific uncertainty, however, does it make sense – on ethical and policy grounds – to try to save the panther? This is the question we shall address in this chapter. We ask the question, not because panther preservation has high ecological priority but because it has strong popular support and because it can provide insights into using the method of case studies. Moreover, if there are ethical grounds for trying to save the panther, despite the odds, what specific philosophical arguments might support our attempt? Note that we raise the issue of saving the Florida panther in terms of its being self-sustaining on public lands. Presumably, public lands (e.g., national forests) provide the best chance of maintaining the panther in its traditional habitats, since privately owned areas are very fragmented. Otherwise the answer to our question, of whether we ought to try to save the subspecies, could be quite different. Perhaps sophisticated biotechnological means could save the Florida panther in

240

a highly managed situation, like a zoo (see Kleiman 1989, p. 152). Our concern here is not with intensively managed situations.

In addressing this ethical and policy question, we shall provide a taxonomy of epistemological, ethical, cultural, scientific, and aesthetic considerations. Our account suggests how an ecologist, facing a situation of ethical rationality, might make a decision about whether we ought to try to save the panther, despite the apparent odds. This analysis, however, is not meant to suggest that preservation of the Florida panther is one of the most important ecological or environmental issues facing scientists. It is merely an example. Also, this analysis is not meant so much to provide closure on the questions we have raised as it is to illustrate how ecologists might begin to draw rough ethical and policy generalizations on the basis of a case study. It offers merely a useful framework within which we might begin to think about the scientific and ethical rationality appropriate to ecology and to conservation/environmental policy. Just as the principles articulated in the National Environmental Policy Act do not tell us how to evaluate the ethical and policy aspects of every environmental effect, nevertheless they do provide us with a list of criteria (e.g., consideration of the distributive equity of impacts) that help us make sound judgments regarding environmental actions. Likewise, our epistemological and ethical considerations are neither mutually exclusive nor exhaustive. Our arguments will not tell us how to evaluate the ethical and policy aspects of every ecological conflict (like that surrounding the panther), but they will give us a list of rough generalizations, a set of criteria that might help us make better judgments regarding conflicts in similar ecological cases.

9.1 Policy analysis ought not rely only on experts

Indeed, if Bryan Norton's (1987, pp. 243–257) excellent analysis is correct (and we believe that, in the main, it is), then valuing species or habitats is not merely a scientific matter to be decided by experts, but also a socioeconomic, ethical, aesthetic, political, and cultural matter to be decided by the people. This is part of our point in arguing earlier for using an ethical, as well as a scientific, account of rationality in ecology. If this new account of ecological rationality is plausible, then one of the first ethical difficulties we shall face in attempting to assess species and habitats is that often many societal values regarding the environment are skewed, misinformed, or inconsistent. This problem cannot be corrected by expert judgments alone; it also requires us to engage in epistemological, ethical, and other analyses and to re-educate the public regarding the results of our analyses. In the absence of analysis, it is impossible to provide a taxonomy of principles that are sufficient, operationally, to make ethical and policy decisions about habitats and species.

From an ethical point of view, the considerations we provide in this chapter's analysis are of two kinds: *biocentric* or *ecocentric* (ecology-centered) and *anthropocentric* (human-centered). Admittedly, not all ethical or policy arguments, for example, Kant's, are either ecocentric or anthropocentric. Since many of these other arguments require one to make metaphysical presuppositions that we do not have time to address here, we shall not consider them. (For a discussion of anthropocentrism and non-anthropocentrism, see Norton 1987, pp. 135–150.) Most traditional ethics, however, fall into the anthropocentric category, and one goal of this chapter is to suggest a more inclusive point of view, one that is based on both an ecocentric and an anthropocentric (Rolston 1986, especially chs. 5–6; Taylor 1986; Norton 1987, pp. 9–13) foundation for environmental policy.

9.2 First-order and second-order principles

From an epistemological point of view, the considerations about panther policy that we provide are based either on *first-order* (*prima-facie*) or on *second-order* arguments regarding panther preservation. First-order or prima-facie principles (see Rawls 1971, pp. 340–341) are those that ought to be obeyed, in the absence of rebutting considerations. First-order principles are principles that provide reasons to do something, unless other factors outweigh them. Because they provide reasons (in the absence of rebutting arguments) to do something, they place the burden of proof on the person who does not accept them in a particular case. Obviously, there are prima-facie principles, for example, that we ought to treat persons equally, or that we ought to conserve natural resources such as habitats, species, and ecosystems. No one will disagree with such principles; they are like truisms about patriotism, motherhood, or apple pie. Most persons agree with them because they appear intuitively true, and because they ought to be followed, except in a few, specific cases when other principles override them. They are rough generalizations. First-order principles, however, are not sufficient for practical decisionmaking, unless there is no conflict among them. Yet, the absence of such conflict is rare. First-order or prima-facie principles only provide guidance at a very general level. The real test of an ecological decision or conservation policy is whether it can provide second-order principles, rules, or values for how to adjudicate conflicting claims among prima-facie or first-order principles.

Many ecologists and environmentalists fail to provide policy norms, not because they say something erroneous, but because they fail to distinguish these two levels of practical analysis and provide only prima-facie or first-order principles. Holmes Rolston (1986, pp. 197–198), for example, in his environmental ethics, provides imperatives like "keep remaining public wildlands off the market" and "increase options." He does not always spell out what to do, at the level of second-order principles, when such first-order principles conflict. Despite his excellent discussion, he also does not clearly distinguish these two different types of principles used at different stages of ethical analysis.

First-order principles, like those of Rolston and others, are correct as far as they go, but they don't go far enough. They are of little help in courtroom controversy, or when alternative conservation strategies are competing, or when human interests are pitted against environmental welfare. Moreover, if moral philosophers and applied scientists have no arguable second-order principles, then the outcome of their analyses could be arbitrary or subjective. This is the point often made by philosophers like Rawls, who employs second-order principles, against utilitarian philosophers like Harsanyi, many of whom have no such principles. Hence, in order both to avoid arbitrariness or relativism and to provide criteria for adjudicating environmental controversies, we need both first-order and second-order ethical principles. Even then, however, because ecology is a science of case studies (see chapter 8), we may not always be able to adjudicate controversies, but only to learn more about them through our evaluations. In particular, our analyses may need not merely to develop second-order principles to use when our first-order principles conflict. We may also have to develop third-order principles that we can employ when our second-order principles are at odds, and fourth-order principles to use when our third-order principles conflict, and so on. Because our analysis in this volume is a first step at using case studies to evaluate second-order ethical principles, it is, of course, not complete. To the degree that it begins evaluation of ecological problems in terms of ethical rationality, however, we hope that our investigation provides a partial framework for later analyses of third- and higher-order ethical principles.

9.3 First-order principles: Ecocentric and anthropocentric

Bearing in mind the distinctions between first-order and second-order ethical principles and between (biocentric or) ecocentric and anthropocentric ethical norms, how might one approach the controversial issue of whether ecologists ought to try, despite the scientific uncertainty involved, to help the Florida panther become self-sustaining on public lands? The first step would be to list all of the most relevant first-order or prima-facie principles, and then to see where conflicts arise. The next step would be to analyze the conflicts, in an attempt to arrive at second-order principles applicable to our particular case study. On our account, the main *ecocentric*, first-order principle applicable to this case is that, because all living beings have inherent worth (Taylor 1986), the Florida panther has inherent worth, and therefore we ought to try to preserve the subspecies. Simply because living beings exist, they have inherent worth, in themselves, because each individual has a good of its own, continued existence, completely independent of (anthropocentric) human needs, welfare, or knowledge (see Regan 1983; Taylor 1986, pp. 71ff.).

Apart from the ecocentric, prima-facie principle about the inherent worth of all living beings, all of the remaining prima-facie principles (to which we subscribe) are anthropocentric in one of two senses. They are either epistemologically anthropocentric or substantively anthropocentric. Principles are *epistemologically anthropocentric*, for us, if they are based on an assertion that something has a given value. Assertions that something has value are epistemologically anthropocentric because only humans are able to make value judgments. Nevertheless, if the value itself is not dependent upon human knowing or willing (that is, if humans don't create this value), then assertions about the value are not substantively anthropocentric. They are merely epistemologically anthropocentric. Although the values (like scientific knowledge) that they posit are important, independent of human recognition of them as values, only humans can make the judgment that they are values. Some important prima-facie principles that are epistemologically anthropocentric include the claims that the Florida panther has intrinsic value because of its importance to science, to aesthetics, to life support, to culture, to ecotourism, and so on. The Florida panther has scientific, instrumental, and aesthetic value, for example, in part because of its rarity and uniqueness. Of course, humans do not create intrinsic values (like scientific value). Nevertheless, because only humans can recognize intrinsic values, they are epistemologically anthropocentric. Other epistemologically anthropocentric principles posit moral values. They include the claim, for example, that because humans owe other humans reparation for destroying species and subspecies, therefore they ought to work to preserve species and subspecies. Another epistemologically anthropocentric principle based on moral value is that humans have duties to future generations not to cause species or subspecies to become extinct.

Principles that are *epistemologically anthropocentric* are essential to environmental policy and ecological decisionmaking because they are based on value judgments that only humans can make. Also, as we explained earlier in chapter 2, there is no clear, unambiguous way – no purely ecocentric way – to define scientific concepts like ecological balance, stability, or equilibrium. Hence, humans must make epistemic and methodological value judgments before they can understand or apply any of these concepts. As Kenneth Boulding (1991, p. 6) put it, biological systems have no mayor or president. And because "nature" cannot direct us in environmental decisionmaking, we humans must do it ourselves, often through making epistemologically anthropocentric value judgments.

Ethical principles are *substantively anthropocentric*, for us, not only in the sense that humans alone can make value judgments, but also in the sense that the value at issue in the argument is dependent both on human knowing, caring, or willing and on its serving human goals or needs. Typically, values that serve human goals are instrumental values; they are substantively anthropocentric. Arguments based on substantively anthropocentric principles include the claims that preserving habitats, species, or subspecies is important because nature has the power to transform our lives in beneficial or therapeutic ways, or because it has the power to benefit us economically. Other substantively anthropocentric principles include the claims that we ought to preserve subspecies like the Florida panther because we humans are interdependent with nature, or because nature has recreational or cultural value. Most substantively anthropocentric arguments are closely related to what Norton (1987) calls "strong anthropocentrism." They base value judgments about nature on its ability to fulfil human demands.

We shall not provide detailed analyses of prima-facie or first-order principles, either ecocentric or anthropocentric, for at least three reasons. (1) Much of what we could say is given elsewhere (e.g., sec Taylor 1986). (2) Used alone, the first-order arguments resolve no controversies. (3) First-order principles are trumped by second-order principles or rules. Given these three considerations, it is reasonable to focus our analysis, in the panther study, only on the few first-order or prima-facie principles that are most relevant to the case and, instead, to spend most of our time assessing the second-order principles that are able to adjudicate conflicts among first-order principles.

What prima-facie principles are most relevant to the question of whether, despite the odds, we ought to try to save the Florida panther in the wild? As already mentioned, perhaps the most important prima-facie principle is (1) that the panther has inherent worth, intrinsic value, instrumental value, and so on, and therefore we ought to try to save the subspecies. One of the most important prima-facie principles likely to conflict with this one, about the value of the panther, is the prima-facie principle (2) that human beings have legal and moral rights to bodily security, equal protection, and property, including property that may be panther habitat. But if humans have rights, do panthers also have rights?

Although there is neither time nor space for a complete discussion of the question of panther "rights" here, the dominant philosophical position – with only a few exceptions, such as Regan (1983) – on the question is that the panther does not have moral rights. According to this position (see Feinberg 1974), only beings that have aims, wants, or desires can have moral rights, because only such beings have *interests*, and having interests is a necessary condition for having moral rights. To ascribe moral rights to a being without interests, on this view, is to use the term "moral right" in a metaphorical way. Hence, according to the classical historical, political, and philosophical position, use of the term "moral right" is restricted, because moral rights typically trump all other considerations. Hence, not everyone can have moral rights, or there would be no trump, no way to adjudicate conflicts among beings, not all of whom are said to have moral rights. Moreover, because the concept of a "moral right" arose only recently as a response to attempts at human oppression, the term has typically been used in a very precise and narrow sense. Legal rights have been employed, however, in a somewhat wider sense, often because utility or consensus has provided a foundation for ascribing legal rights to some entity. Municipalities, ships, and corporations have legal rights, for example, and it is arguable that we ought to extend legal rights to entities such as land, trees, and panthers (see Stone 1974; Caldwell and Shrader-Frechette 1993). Extending legal rights to certain entities simply gives them legal standing in court, such as the right to sue for damages. The good of society and the environment thus may dictate that we extend *legal rights* to entities such as panthers. Insofar as moral rights historically have been invoked only under very precise conditions (such as those discussed earlier), we do not believe that it makes sense to attribute *moral rights* to panthers. Admittedly, however, attributing legal rights to them may be both reasonable and desirable.

Although it might be reasonable to challenge the dominant historical, political, legal, and philosophical usage of "moral right," we shall not do so here, both because some others have already done so (see

Regan 1983, for example), and because one need not ascribe moral rights to plants, animals, habitats, and ecosystems, in order to preserve them. Rather, if one possesses an accurate understanding of human (moral) rights, it will become obvious – as we shall argue shortly – that humans have no prima-facie (moral or legal) rights to destroy or harm members of the non-human world.

In the case of whether we ought to try to preserve the Florida panther, the two prima-facie or first-order ethical principles likely to be in conflict are (1) that one ought to preserve the panther, because of its inherent worth, intrinsic and instrumental value, and so on, and (2) that humans have property rights, including rights to panther habitat. In other words, in order to determine whether we ought to try to save the Florida panther, despite the odds, we need to develop a number of second-order ethical principles that will enable us to adjudicate conflicts between principles like (1) and (2), between panther preservation and human interests, including public preferences, economic efficiency, and so on. In subsequent pages of this chapter, we shall develop a number of second-order ethical principles that will help us adjudicate conflicts between those who wish to save the panther and those who oppose it or who believe that it is impossible. On the basis of these second-order principles, we shall be able to offer a reasonable case for attempting to preserve the Florida panther, despite the odds.

9.4 Greatest-good considerations outweigh economic efficiency

One of the greatest ares of controversy over whether we ought to attempt to save the Florida panther is between those who follow prima-facie or first-order principles of optimizing economic efficiency in decisionmaking, and those who follow principles of maximizing the overall welfare of society. In the course of a detailed analysis, we shall argue for the principle that greater-good considerations outweigh economic efficiency, and hence that this second-order principle ought to be followed in deciding whether to attempt panther preservation. Our analysis is built, in part, on some of the considerations we raised in chapter 7. Two of the most important of these considerations are that humans ought not to be used merely as means to some social or economic end, and that conservation and preservation are often economically beneficial (see section 7.3; see also Orians *et al.* 1990).

Those who pursue economic efficiency, as a first-order principle, might not be opposed to attempting preservation of the panther, any more than they are opposed to other environmental or human goods.

However, they might argue that economic priorities outweigh a particular conservation goal. They might agree that the Florida panther has intrinsic value and inherent worth, scientific value, life-support value, aesthetic value, and so on. Nevertheless, they might argue that the most economical thing to do with the Florida panther habitat is to develop it and to allow the subspecies to go extinct. (We use the term "Florida panther habitat" to mean the habitat that, according to our best information, is suitable for the taxon. Note that, following our discussion in the previous chapter, there are some uncertainties regarding what is actually "Florida panther habitat.") Indeed, the forces for development in Florida are quite powerful. From 1980 to 1990, Florida population increased by 28.5 percent, and this trend is likely to continue into the foreseeable future (Duda 1987, pp. i, 13). Developers likely reason that allowing the Florida panther to become extinct would ultimately increase the welfare of Floridians more than would attempting to preserve its habitat, because development of the habitat could provide land for homes and for farms. On their view, economic efficiency provides a criterion for adjudicating conflicts among first-order or prima-facie ethical principles; they believe that economic efficiency requires that we do not use our best resources and abilities in trying to save the Florida panther.

Moreover, even if one argues that all species and subspecies ought to be preserved, it is important to note that there are at least 52 rare, threatened, and endangered subspecies of amphibians, reptiles, birds, and mammals in Florida (Wood 1991). Of all these subspecies at risk, the Florida panther would be the most costly to attempt to save. This is because the land area needed to do so is enormous (and therefore the money required to purchase private land and convert it to public land is also substantial; see chapter 8). Saving any one of the 32 other mammal subspecies on the Florida rare, endangered, or threatened list would be much easier/cheaper than saving the Florida panther. This is because it is, in general, more difficult to save large carnivores (like the panther) than either small carnivores or herbivores or omnivores. Black bears, for example, have a quite varied diet; as a consequence, each of them has only one-third the area requirements of a Florida panther. The panther, however, is a big-bodied carnivore, one that must feed largely on deer and pigs (in order to avoid expending more energy to capture food than it gains from the food). Hence, the panther is more difficult to feed (at least in Florida where there are fewer prey) and thus more difficult to save in the wild than are other subspecies and species at risk. This suggests that, all things being equal, it may be more important to save those species or subspecies that can be saved most cheaply first. Perhaps species or subspecies that are more expensive to save, all things being equal, probably ought to be saved last; this could be in part because, for the same funds, one could save many more species. Hence, trying to save these other species appears more economically efficient than trying to save the Florida panther.

Admittedly, however, it may be important to try to save the Florida panther because of its role as an "umbrella" taxon. An umbrella taxon is one that can be shown to be responsible for the continued existence of other taxa. For example, a taxon that digs burrows which serve as the sole habitat for other taxa could be considered an umbrella taxon. Umbrella taxa, therefore, might be thought to possess ecological "worth" because they forestall the extinction of other taxa. In one sense, large vertebrate taxa, like the Florida panther, can be thought of as "umbrella" taxa. Because large vertebrates in general require large amounts of space (see McNab 1963), preservation of such taxa requires conservation of large areas of suitable habitat. Smaller taxa of vertebrates, as well as many taxa of invertebrates and plants, could be saved as a consequence of preservation of large vertebrate taxa. Hence, because of its role as an umbrella taxon, it may be economically efficient to try to save the Florida panther.

Given the cost of attempting to save the Florida panther and the agricultural and real-estate value of the panther habitat, however, it is likely that short-term (20 to 30 years) economic efficiency argues for development of the land, rather than for attempts at preservation. But this raises the question of whether short-term economic efficiency, with its consequent value to humans, ought to be the deciding factor in dealing with the panther. Although it is obviously important, surely short-term economic efficiency ought not be the deciding factor in this case, because there are a number of considerations that outweigh it, some of which we already mentioned in chapter 7. For one thing, long-term economic efficiency would benefit more persons than would short-term. This is because short-term efficiencies usually yield the greatest benefits only to developers and not to society (including future persons) as a whole. Second, preservation of the Florida panther and its habitat may lead to long-term economic efficiencies, because of the value of recreational, aesthetic, scientific, and cultural benefits. In the last ten years, for example, economists have made great strides in quantifying the value of threatened and endangered species (see, for example, Gregory et al. 1989, pp. 400ff.; see also Brown 1990; Dasgupta 1990; Goldstein 1990; Hanemann 1990; Harvell 1990; Johnson 1990;

Noll 1990; Orians *et al.* 1990; Strang 1990). Moreover, although there are extensive government subsidies to users of public lands (grazers, miners, loggers), and although at least some of the subsidies are clearly not in the public interest (Irland 1976, pp. 28–29), nevertheless preservation (rather than development) of public lands generates significant revenues. In Florida, for example, recreation-user fees for national forests generate approximately half a million dollars annually (Forest Service Southern Region 1990). Often such benefits of long-term preservation and conservation are not quantified, thus skewing environmental analyses toward the costs of preservation (see Gregory *et al.* 1989, p. 400). When preservation benefits are included (see chapter 7), however, preservation can often be shown to be beneficial (see Orians *et al.* 1990). Also, preservation promotes "ecotourism." The existence of zoos, nature reserves, and botanical gardens, for example, testifies to the fact that persons are willing to spend money to support ecological values (see Duda 1987, pp. iii, 100–101; Vining 1990). These expenditures, in turn, may be necessary conditions for increasing our sensitivity to the preservation values that are economically efficient over the long term.

Preservation of the Florida panther and its habitat (rather than habitat development) – assuming preservation is possible – also would likely provide more benefits, because it would do so for a greater number of persons and for a longer period of time. The welfare of all persons, present and future, who can enjoy the panther, might outweigh the present economic benefits to those interested in development of the panther habitat, and for at least three additional reasons, as we argued in chapter 7. First, no one has a moral or legal right to develop land. Second, conservation and preservation are often economically beneficial. Third, development of the Florida panther habitat is not necessary to prevent a loss of human life or security. Given no moral right to develop land and no necessity to develop land as a potential means of saving human lives, there appears to be no prima-facie argument against preservation of the panther. And if not, then we may be bound to follow the duty to recognize the inherent worth and intrinsic value of the subspecies by attempting to avoid extinction of the Florida panther.

Moreover, it appears that many societies recognize that long-term preferences and welfare are served by preservation. For example, the US and the state of Florida have passed endangered species acts. Given that both the state and federal acts enjoin us to protect the rare, threatened, or endangered species and subspecies, it is clear that preservation of the Florida panther could arguably take priority over economic efficiency. And if so, then proponents of economic efficiency may not be able to provide a second-order argument for allowing inaction in a situation in which the Florida panther might become extinct. To allow inaction in such a situation, it would probably be necessary for developers and other interested parties to show that alternative uses of the panther habitat were essential either to recognizing the strong rights (see chapter 7) of some persons, or necessary to serving the greatest good of the greatest number of persons, present and future. Presumably, developers might be able to demonstrate both of these latter claims (1) if there were a better use of conservation dollars, all things considered, than to spend them on a "flagship" taxon (highly visible species/subspecies whose well-being is taken as indicative of that of other taxa) such as the panther; (2) if there were no more available land to be developed; (3) if the current land had been used as efficiently as possible; and (4) if current use of the panther habitat were necessary to avert some great harm such as human starvation. Although there is clearly less land available than in the past, obviously the Florida situation is not one of starvation, as might be the case in some developing nations. Also, current Florida land has not been used as efficiently as possible for human needs, present and future. Hence, because saving the panther does not appear to threaten strong human rights, the burden of proof appears to be on the person who argues against attempts at preservation.

Admittedly, because the panther habitat is ubiquitous, and because most persons do not perceive it as glamorous or unusual, compared to other habitats, developers might argue that it presents one of the least objectionable areas for future Florida development. To sustain this argument, however, the developers would have to show that current land was already being used as efficiently as possible, as discussed above in (1)–(4). Another obstacle to development is the fact that, because of the shortage of fresh water in Florida, it is arguable that much development may need to stop. Recognizing the problems brought by development, the Florida Environmental Land and Water Management Act of 1972 provides for designation of "Areas of Critical State Concern" that have a significant effect upon resources or the environment. The act also requires regional planning councils to review impact proposals and to provide for oversight of these functions by the Department of Community Affairs. Under the State Comprehensive Plan and Growth Management Act, regional and local governments must prepare growth-management plans and insure protection of natural resources (Fernald 1989, pp. 46ff.). If development must stop in areas where critical resources like water are threatened, then development may not take precedence over the Florida-panther habitat.

All these considerations suggest that, although economic efficiency is an important first-order criterion, it does not obviously mandate development of the panther habitat. Economic development, in this situation, may be outweighed by greater-good considerations. Moreover, following the arguments already given in chapter 7, long-term economic goals, rather than short-term ones, are likely to be served by panther preservation rather than by development. Hence, at least one second-order principle supports attempts at panther preservation. This principle is that preservation typically provides a greater contribution to the common good than does development.

9.5 Conservation decisions ought to be made by the public, not only economists and ecologists

First-order principles posit the inherent worth and intrinsic value of all species, subspecies, and habitats. But if there are limited conservation dollars, then not everything can be preserved. What does a second-order analysis reveal about whether we ought to try to preserve the panther, given other conservation priorities? Moreover, should conservation priorities be set by experts alone, by economic efficiency, by lay values, or by some other means?

One group of ecologists appears to have argued for the second position, claiming that funding conservation corridors (for panther preservation) may not be a rational thing to do since it would take monies away from other conservation efforts. As Simberloff and Cox put it: "the cost of this proposed corridor system may detract from other valuable conservation and management efforts in Florida . . . the matter of whether the same money and effort [as would be spent on panther preservation and establishing conservation corridors] might be spent better in other ways deserves more consideration" (Simberloff and Cox 1987, p. 69). However, it is not clear that such a response, on Simberloff and Cox's part, will work. In arguing that money and effort spent on conservation corridors and panther preservation might be better spent otherwise, they appear to presuppose that *rational* policy choices are *economically efficient* choices, getting the most conservation for the fewest dollars, or at least the same dollars. Sometimes other ecologists also appear to use economic efficiency as a criterion for deciding which species to save (see, for example, Brown 1990, p. 207; Oldfield in Strang 1990). While we are sympathetic to such a definition of rational policy choice, and while we believe that expert opinion is often on the side of economic efficiency, it is not clear that ethical rationality, especially in a democracy, always vindicates the arguments of ecologists like Simberloff and Cox. We shall argue in subsequent pages that reasonable, consistent persons do not always save the "cheapest," or the most, species/habitats first, because they need to consider other factors such as diversity, rarity, and feasibility. Earlier in this chapter, we showed that, although economic efficiency might dictate panther preservation, as opposed to development of panther habitats, nevertheless we also argued that economic efficiency, alone, is not necessarily the best criterion for how to make preservation decisions. In addition, it is not clear that, on grounds of economic efficiency, "other valuable conservation and management efforts in Florida" (Simberloff and Cox 1987, p. 69) are more important than trying to save the panther, because often the various strategies competing for conservation dollars are not comparable.

Indeed, even welfare economists realize that decision strategies are rarely comparable. Hence, for example, they almost never argue for maximizing economic efficiency in the area of risk assessment, and for a related reason: the various ways of reducing risks, across economic opportunities, are non-comparable solely on the basis of an economic criterion. They realize that sound policy is a matter of more than economic interests. In cases when they do argue for maximizing economic efficiency, however, they do not face the problem of the conservationist. This is because, in such cases, they spend dollars so as to save the greatest number of human lives for the least amount of dollars, and they save the "cheapest" lives first (Shrader-Frechette 1985b, pp. 55–64). Ecologists, however, could not realistically argue for spending dollars solely to protect the greatest numbers of species, subspecies, or habitats, because they would need to consider other factors such as rarity and feasibility (see, for example, Soulé and Kohm 1989). Moreover, there is no common denominator among species and habitats, as there is among human beings. Conservationists who used the criterion of economic efficiency to choose conservation strategies would be comparing apples and oranges. They would not be doing what the welfare economist does, for whom all human lives are counted the same.

Even if it were possible to apply notions of economic efficiency to conservation biology, another problem with the Simberloff–Cox argument is that using the economic-efficiency criterion, alone, would require one to make a number of questionable value judgments.

Admittedly, it makes sense to spend limited conservation dollars wisely. If one uses only economic efficiency as a criterion, however, one runs into problems. Because there are no common denominators among the costs, risks, and benefits of various conservation programs, decisionmakers would have to make numerous evaluative assumptions in order to *define* various parameters as a basis for economic comparison among alternative conservation programs. They would have to define biological importance as worth more or less, economically, for example, than aesthetic interest, popular demand, anthropocentric needs, and so on. In other words, since species and habitats are not traded on markets in the same way that commodities are, their market price would not be a measure of their value, and hence not a measure of authentic preservation priorities. This means that ecologists would have to define some parameters as economically more important than others, if one were to follow Simberloff's and Cox's criterion of economic efficiency. Moreover, decisions about which conservation program to fund might be different, depending on which criterion/parameter were used. Our point is not that any conservation decision can be justified – it cannot. Rather, our point is that one ought to avoid unacknowledged value judgments in using criteria such as economic efficiency.

Another problem with defining rational policy in terms of economic efficiency, alone, is that rational persons often decide not to maximize economic efficiency, at least in certain cases, but to maximize another variable, like pleasure. Many persons who decide to reside in a large city with a high cost of living, such as Washington, DC, New York, or San Francisco, do not maximize economic efficiency. Eating gourmet foods is also likely not economically efficient; few of the finer things in life are economically efficient. Moreover, persons repeatedly choose to maximize temporal, rather than economic efficiency, each time they fly in a plane rather than ride on a bus, or each time they drive a car rather than walk. Numerous ordinary activities, like having children, can hardly be said to be justified on grounds of economic efficiency. But if so, then at times, a number of parameters are more important, even to rational persons, than is economic efficiency. Therefore, one ought not use economic efficiency alone. The insufficiency of the economic-efficiency criterion, when used alone, illustrates very well what Shackle calls "the problem of the single maximand" (Shackle 1972, p. 82). There is no single parameter according to which two different things – including conservation programs – may be ranked. This is because problems of resource allocation require multivariate solutions, taking many variables into account, rather than maximizing only the cost or effort factor. As Shackle put it: society has no "weighing machine for the value of two actions" (Shackle 1972, p. 82).

Admittedly, Simberloff and Cox are correct in their analysis, in focusing on the importance of using conservation dollars wisely, on opportunity costs, and on the fact that conservation dollars spent on one program cannot be used for another. Nevertheless, they appear to ignore the fact that, even in choosing conservation programs, society must promote many different values, in addition to economic efficiency, and that there is no unilateral way to adjudicate controversies among these different values, in part because they are matters of social choice (see Soulé and Kohm 1989). In forgetting these other values, ecologists who assign too great an importance to economic efficiency appear to be subscribing to a positivistic, hypothetico-deductive (H-D) concept of rationality that ignores the multiplicity of value judgments discussed earlier in chapter 4. Also, following our discussion of ethical rationality in chapters 6 and 7, we believe that ecologists (who use economic efficiency as the sole criterion for conservation priorities) may be misled by employing only a concept of scientific rationality. Instead, what we also need in the panther case is ethical rationality, a rationality that takes account of rights, duties, and the common good, relative to a particular ecological choice. Only if the ethical and factual consequences were the same, in two competing conservation cases, might it then make sense to use the criterion of economic efficiency to decide between them. This is because, as we have already argued, economic efficiency is not alone a desirable criterion for all policy decisions. And if not, then it makes sense to use this criterion only when all other relevant decision variables and values are the same.

In order for ethical consequences to be the same, in two different conservation proposals, it appears that the two competing programs would need to have the same constituency receiving *benefits* from the program and the same constituency paying the *costs* of the program. They would also need to share a quite narrow purpose and value, and to address the same sorts of hazards having the same types of effects. If the competing programs had all these similarities, then it appears likely that there would be common denominators (like economic efficiency) on the basis of which to make a decision about which program to fund. If they did not have these common denominators, then policymakers and ecologists would be forced to do analysis of competing facts, values, ethics, outcomes, and utilities. This is not an algorithmic process, but one done on a case-by-case basis. In the absence of such a case-by-case analysis, ecologists are faced squarely with the (economists') problem of the single maximand (Shrader-Frechette 1985b, pp. 80–83). There is no algorithm that enables us to maximize two variables. And if not, then conceptual and empirical analysis of an individual case is the only option, not a leap to a criterion like economic efficiency.

This observation, about certain common denominators being necessary in order to use a criterion like economic efficiency, is analogous to another observation, one widely accepted among moral philosophers. Just as unequal treatment tends to be less justifiable, in a given situation, to the degree that all persons are equal in all relevant respects, so also unequal treatment of different species, habitats, populations, and individuals appears to be less justifiable to the degree that the constituencies, goals, risks, benefits, and consequences of the conservation programs are similar. Consistent with the principle that equal beings in similar situations ought to be treated equally, this observation (about constituencies, and so on) specifies relevant respects in which conservation situations might be similar or dissimilar. As such, this observation reveals the *factual* conditions under which discrimination among conservation policies is likely to be justified and rational. In other words, to the degree that species, subspecies, and habitats are different, to that extent ought they to be treated differently. And if they ought to be treated differently, then economic efficiency ought not be used as a common denominator to rank them in terms of their preservation value (see Shrader-Frechette 1985b, pp. 55–96). Preservation decisions can be made, of course, on the basis of factual and ethical analyses, but not merely on the grounds of a simple economic algorithm.

Even if several conservation programs shared the same goal – minimizing loss of species, subspecies, or habitats – a goal that the 1986–1988 Simberloff, Kangas, Noss debate (over tropical deforestation) seems to presuppose (see Simberloff 1987, p. 156; see chapter 4 in this volume), this would not guarantee that funding decisions regarding conservation were easy. They would not be easy, in part, because the constituencies involved could be different (e.g., birdwatchers as opposed to scuba divers). Each group might be interested in preserving different species or habitats, because of their different human interests. Moreover, even though one program might save more species, a rational person could place a high value on saving a particular species in a program that saved fewer species overall. For example, it is well known that the public supports high-visibility programs designed to save "charismatic megavertebrates" (Soulé 1986a; see also Gregory *et al.*

1989) – furry, cuddly, or variously appealing mammals – rather than other kinds of organisms (see Duda 1987, pp. ix, 110–111). The public is much more interested in animals than in plants, and much more interested in pandas and panthers than in snail darters and red-cockaded woodpeckers. Therefore, it may be politically impossible to gain public support for the conservation actions that allegedly achieve the greatest amount of good from a scientific or economic point of view, or that save the greatest number of species or habitats. And if so, then one cannot merely use economic efficiency to make preservation decisions, because public preferences may not be based merely on economic efficiency. Obviously, if public preferences are skewed, as we mentioned in earlier chapters, the solution is not to take decisionmaking power from the people. Rather, as Thomas Jefferson argued, the solution is to educate the people, so that they can make wise choices. Without public support for scientifically grounded conservation choices, the best decisions cannot be sustained politically. Hence, it is important for experts to educate the public. Indeed, there is some evidence that federal agencies sometimes realize the importance of ethical rationality and taking account of public preferences and welfare. For example, when time and money are short, the US General Accounting Office (GAO) found that the US Fish and Wildlife Service (FWS) "generally ignored most species highest on the priority [threatened] list, concentrating instead on those with high 'public appeal' or facing imminent recovery" (Raloff 1989, p. 79). In 1986, for instance, the FWS "directed 25 percent of all recovery funds not congressionally earmarked for specific species to just four animals – the American peregrine falcon, southern sea otter, gray wolf, and Aleutian Canada goose. None of these is listed as endangered . . . or is even highly threatened throughout most of its range" (Raloff 1989, p. 79). This suggests that there are strong pragmatic, political, and ethical grounds for using glamour taxa, like the Florida panther, as a springboard for other conservation and conservation-education efforts. It also suggests that economic efficiency in species preservation is not necessarily measured in obvious ways or by expert opinions about what is best or cheapest to save.

9.6 Saving species does not always supersede saving subspecies

Another controversial issue in the panther case concerns the conflict between the first-order or prima-facie principle that species have inherent worth, intrinsic value, and so on, versus the prima-facie principle that subspecies also have all these values and worth. If one cannot save all species and subspecies then how does one resolve the conflict between two first-order principles? How does one decide whether to try to save species or subspecies, or sometimes a species and sometimes a subspecies? One potential second-order principle is that ecologists and policymakers always ought to save species before subspecies. Someone might argue for the principle on the grounds that, all things being equal, science is helped more by the preservation of endangered or threatened species than by the preservation of endangered or threatened subspecies, like the Florida panther. In other words, the objection is that, if we subscribe to the biological species concept, then we have an obligation to preserve taxa that are biologically distinct, that are reproductively isolated, as species are. On this view, taxa are reproductively isolated in that they can produce viable offspring only with members of their same biological species.

On the reproductive-isolation criterion, subspecies need not be preserved, all things being equal, according to the objector, because they are not biologically distinct and reproductively isolated. Although they are defined by taxonomists to encompass certain external characteristics (like the Florida panther's right-angle crook at the end of the tail, the whorl of hair in the middle of the back, irregular white flecking in the coat, and the tawny color), members of the Florida subspecies are not distinct biological entities, if one uses the reproductive-isolation criterion. Hence, according to this objector, the focus of conservation efforts ought to be on species – since they are reproductively and therefore biologically unique – and not on subspecies. Because subspecies are not biologically unique, the objection is that great scientific value would not arise from preserving them, as it would from preserving species.

One reason why biologists are reluctant to claim that subspecies are biologically unique is that the criteria (e.g., color) for distinguishing one subspecies from another are quite arbitrary. However, such criteria are difficult, epistemologically, to defend, and it is quite problematic on empirical/operational grounds ever to claim that a distinct subspecies exists. As a consequence, it is difficult to argue that there are objective grounds for ascribing scientific worth to a particular threatened subspecies, if the species is not at risk. This is because there is no way to specify, biologically, the boundary conditions on the genetic differences exhibited by different subspecies. Arguing for a subspecies' uniqueness, on empirical grounds, and for the duty to preserve a particular subspecies, is arguing on a classical "slippery slope." A related argument against directing special conservation effort toward

Table 9.1. *The numbers of species, subspecies, and populations of non-aquatic vertebrates in Florida listed as endangered and potentially endangered (Wood 1991)*

	Amphibians/reptiles	Birds	Mammals
Species	16	24	8
Subspecies	11	18	5
Only one in Florida	5	4	3
More than one in Florida	6	14	2
Populations	4	1	1

subspecies is that such effort is, in a sense, antithetical to evolution (see John Eisenberg in Ballou *et al.* 1989, p. 10, Minutes). The effort holds the subspecies static, so that the genetic constitution of the species is not able to change and, therefore, the species is not able to evolve. (Evolution is defined here as change in gene frequencies. According to this definition, evolution can include both the origination and extinction of subspecies.) On this view, holding the subspecies static amounts to blocking its evolutionary pathway.

In response to such arguments based on the biological concept of "species," however, ecologists can claim that the notion of species is just as problematic as that of subspecies, for many of the reasons briefly sketched earlier in chapters 5 and 8. For example, conservationists might question the relevance and importance of the "reproductive-isolation" criterion, on the grounds that biologists do not test reproductive isolation, but instead use secondary characteristics and geographic distribution to distinguish species and subspecies. Hence, to the degree that use of the reproductive criterion is absent or replaced, and therefore somewhat subjective, to the same extent is the distinction between the importance of subspecies, relative to species, likewise questionable. If species are no more clearly defined than subspecies, then both concepts rely on operational, practical considerations in deciding when something is a species or subspecies or not. And if so, then there is no clear biological criterion that justifies preserving species before subspecies, when both cannot be saved. Hence, there might be as much reason to save subspecies as species.

The arguments against directing special conservation efforts toward subspecies also reflect a position that differs from the one taken by most agencies that formulate conservation laws. By law in Florida, for instance, protection can be offered to species, subspecies, or even populations (see Wood 1991 and Table 9.1). The question of whether or not special conservation effort should be directed toward subspecies (or populations) clearly is a very difficult one to answer. It probably cannot be answered solely from an ecological perspective. Nevertheless, there are two reasons why ecologists, at least, are likely to select risk of extinction as their principal criterion for attempting to preserve one taxon, rather than another, and hence why they might argue for preserving a subspecies, if it were more at risk of extinction. The first reason is that ecologists, by the nature of their work, are concerned with biodiversity and with the role of organisms in ecosystems. More than those outside the discipline, ecologists are likely to understand the significance of loss of taxa. The second reason is that, once a taxon is extinct, any other "worth" that it may have possessed, in increasing scientific knowledge for example, is lost. Any loss of taxa, therefore, could also directly affect the ecologists' profession, and perhaps even their own research.

How can risk of extinction be compared among taxa? If ecologists possess certain information about the life history of a taxon (demography, spatial distribution, mating system), they can estimate time to extinction if no action is taken to lower the risk. (We discussed this estimation technique more fully in chapter 8; see Ballou *et al.* 1989, in relation to the Florida panther.) Times to extinction, therefore, could be employed as a way to rank risks of extinction of taxa. An important limitation on this method, of course, is availability of information necessary to calculate times to extinction for all taxa. Usually, even the most rudimentary information is available only for those taxa already judged to be at risk. Rarity and associated genetic problems could form the basis for criteria by which risk of extinction may be determined (see Ballou *et al.* 1989, in relation to the Florida panther). Rarity of taxa, however, may be of different kinds. Rare organisms may be limited in geographical distribution, and/or they may be restricted to few habitats, and/or they may have small population sizes everywhere they occur (see Rabinowitz *et al.* 1986). Using these criteria to determine whether particular taxa are rare is a difficult and highly subjective process. The outcome of the determination may not please even other persons familiar with the taxa (see McCoy and Mushinsky 1992). In addition, characteristics of organisms other than geographical distribution, habitat specificity, and population sizes, may contribute to rarity. For example, large-bodied and/or carnivorous taxa tend, even under the best of circumstances, to have smaller population sizes than small-bodied and/or herbivorous taxa, and thus are at greater risk of extinction (see Burke and Humphrey 1987; Harris and Gallagher 1989).

Lists of species and subspecies designated by government organizations as "endangered," "threatened," "rare," "of special concern," etc., may be thought to be a practical way to identify taxa at risk of extinction, and therefore a way to decide about saving particular species rather than subspecies and vice versa. However, government organizations do not use rational and comparative analysis of all taxa to make decisions to include or exclude particular taxa from their lists. Rather, they add particular taxa by the process of advocacy and then sometimes remove them in the same way. Because of the manner in which taxa gain placement on such lists, many considerations other than rarity come into play, even considerations that many ecologists might view as whimsical, such as conspicuousness and public opinion (see McCoy and Mushinsky 1992). Despite these features of government lists, we think that, in lieu of anything better, they can help to identify which taxa we ought to save.

In addition to emphasizing the fact that subspecies may be at risk of extinction, conservationists (who favor saving subspecies) also can argue that, because different subspecies are *genetically unique*, they ought to be preserved. On this criterion, there are prima-facie aesthetic or scientific grounds for preserving virtually everything. And indeed the only point to be established here is that the Florida panther has prima-facie, intrinsic scientific value. Another prima-facie argument for trying to preserve the subspecies, apart from whether it has the same importance as a species, is that, if human activities have isolated a subspecies, then it is arguable that humans have a prima-facie obligation (through reparation) to preserve it. Of course, those who agree with this prima-facie or first-order obligation might nevertheless disagree that there is a second-order obligation to preserve the Florida panther subspecies. One of their premises is likely to be that the separation of the Florida panther from other members of the species was artificial, that is, caused by human interference in the panther habitat. On these grounds, it is arguable that trying to keep the subspecies from going extinct is equally artificial, and hence that there is no obligation to attempt to do so.

In response to the artificiality argument, a conservationist can make at least three claims for the scientific value of a subspecies and for the duty to preserve it and its associated intrinsic value. *First*, the artificial separation of the Florida panther was induced by humans, and therefore humans ought to bear responsibility for the subspecies that has been separated. *Second*, if humans are absolved from responsibility for the preservation of "artificial" subspecies which humans' actions have caused to be artificially isolated, then in the future, humans could artificially isolate other individuals, cause their subspecies to become extinct, and then claim to have no responsibility for doing so. Without fear of recrimination, humans could justify their extinction of a subspecies. This is because, if the artificiality of the isolation of a subspecies is grounds for absolving humans of responsibility for the subspecies, then humans could shed such responsibilities whenever they wanted by acts that cause artificial isolation. This means that "artificiality" arguments for not saving the Florida-panther subspecies, and instead for saving species, could contribute to further threats against populations. *Third*, although it is reasonable to allow a subspecies with a small number of individuals to die off or go extinct "naturally," and although it is reasonable to allow nature to take its course, the case of the Florida panther is not one of natural extinction, both because the rate at which the subspecies is moving toward extinction appears to be quite high, and because the threat has been almost entirely caused by humans.

In summary, a strong argument for Florida-panther preservation, in the name of science (or recreation, aesthetics, and other intrinsic values), is that it is quite vulnerable to disappearance, in large part because of local rarity and the human threat. The rarity argument is underscored by the human role in causing the rarity and hence the threat to scientific knowledge. These considerations of evolution, rarity, and ethical responsibility suggest both that species ought not necessarily be preserved before subspecies, and that, in the case of the Florida panther, there is likely no second-order principle that justifies attempting to save species before subspecies.

9.7 Saving habitats does not always supersede saving species

Likewise, there may be no second-order principle that justifies either saving habitats before species or subspecies, or saving habitats before developing an area (see Gregory *et al.* 1989, p. 403). In the latter case, for example, obviously ecologists ought not claim that all habitats everywhere ought to be preserved because, if they were, then there would be no land left for future development and for an expanding human population. Moreover, even if one were to argue that all development ought to be stopped, and that existing areas ought to be redeveloped and replanned for better use, it is arguable that it is impossible to stop all future development everywhere. If areas were able to support a greater population then it is arguable that they could be developed; if areas were unable to support their existing human population, then it is arguable either that they ought to be replanned or that development ought to cease.

Because habitats differ in their carrying capacity, and because some populations of plants and animals are increasing, it is likely impossible to conserve all habitats, species, and subspecies. And if so, then we must discover what considerations argue for preservation of the panther habitat, given limited areas available for preservation and finite amounts of conservation dollars. In other words, confronted with the practical realities of possible panther preservation – including competing economic, social, and political priorities – what second-order principles might be relevant to our decision (see Soulé and Kohm 1989)? What principles might help us adjudicate controversies when there are conflicts, for example, between duties to preserve habitats and those to preserve species or subspecies (see Soulé and Kohm 1989)? We believe that there is no universal rule that one ought to preserve habitats before species or subspecies. This is, in part, because preservation is not merely a question that can be decided on the basis of scientific rationality. And if not, then arguing for a policy alternative to panther preservation requires arguing that public preferences and financial resources can be marshalled to support a realistic alternative. It is not clear that they can.

Aesthetic and human-interest preferences of the public sometimes are at odds with ecosystemic or scientific criteria for the best conservation program. Laypersons often prefer to save large animals, for example, the American eagle, rather than whole habitats necessary for saving many species (see, for example, Fisher and Myers 1986, pp. 12–15; Franklin 1987, pp. 74–76). In other words, laypersons are often able to recognize great intrinsic value only in large mammals like the Florida panther and other "glamour species" (Duda 1987, pp. ix, 110–111). In fact, public recognition of the value of the Florida panther may occur, in part, because it is unique to Florida. It is a sacred animal of the Florida Seminole Indian tribes, and it has a rich symbolic value because of its place in our culture. Because of the cultural, historical, and symbolic value of glamour species like the panther, persons may require less education and biological understanding to appreciate the panther's intrinsic value and inherent worth than that of rare and unique places like the Florida scrub habitat. Indeed, this is why so much of the effort of groups like the World Wildlife Fund is targeted at mammals, because persons have already learned to recognize their value (Fuller 1990, p. 1).

If persons prefer to save glamour species rather than habitats then, apart from whether taxpayers have the right to exercise their (perhaps) idiosyncratic preferences for preservation, their opinions either need to be re-educated or to be taken into account. Apart from who is right in the continuing debate over the place of expert opinion in environmental policy, it may be realistically possible only to save certain species and certain habitats – and not necessarily the ones ecologists most want to save. To the degree that ecologists argue against programs for panther preservation on the grounds that other programs are more desirable, from a scientific point of view, to that same extent ought they to be able to argue that the alternative programs are politically realistic, and stand as good a chance of public support as the panther program. It is not clear that Simberloff and Cox have made these pragmatic and realistic political arguments (1987, pp. 68–69). And if not, then at best, they have shown that it is theoretically desirable to spend funds on alternative conservation programs, not on panther preservation. Arguments about theoretical desirability, however, are not sufficient to establish ethical/policy directives. Moral philosophers know that *ought* implies *can*. Before one is morally obliged to do something – for example, pursue programs that are alternatives to saving the panther – it must be possible to pursue those programs. If it is possible, then we have met one necessary condition for a moral imperative to pursue those programs. If it is not possible, if there is no *can*, then there is no *ought*. And if not, then we may be morally bound only to fight the most winnable conservation battles, rather than the most (scientifically) defensible ones.

This point about being forced to fight the most winnable, rather than the most scientifically defensible, conservation battles is illustrated well by the current controversy in the conservation community between those who emphasize preserving individual species, versus those who focus on preserving habitats or ecosystems (see, for example, Fisher and Myers 1986, pp. 12–15; Franklin 1987, pp. 74–76). In a recent article in *Endangered Species Update*, for example, Bryan Norton criticizes the "triage formulation" of the problem of conservation priorities. According to this formulation, "efforts toward species preservation are best concentrated in the third category," species that are endangered but capable of being saved, rather than species that are either not endangered or not capable of being saved (Norton 1988, p. 1). Norton's rationale for criticizing triage conservation is that "the goal of protecting biological diversity should not be reduced to the goal of protecting remnant populations of threatened species." He opposes this reduction because it relegates species merely to the role of commodities, repositories for sets of genes. Biological diversity, for Norton, is a broader concept than genetic diversity because the former includes the populations and associations in which species exist, as well as the aesthetic and cultural values dependent upon varied landscapes (Norton 1988, p. 1). Norton also argues for protecting habitats, rather than merely endangered species, because the former is necessary for the latter. Large, spectacular species that are designated for protection exist at the top of food chains, dependent on those below them (Norton 1988, p. 4). Of course, Norton is correct on this point, that protecting habitats is necessary for protecting species. His analysis also shows why protection of the two cannot be separated, as some of his remarks suggest. Habitat protection is needed in order to protect species, and species protection, especially protection of "glamour species," may be needed as a public incentive for protecting habitats.

Another reason that Norton wants to preserve natural habitats or biological diversity, rather than merely genetic diversity, is that attempting to accomplish the latter is self-defeating. Working at saving endangered species, he claims, "leads to insoluble problems"; it "will result only in a continual scramble to save individual species." He says that the habitat-protection approach, however, "has a reasonable chance of success . . . by keeping healthy populations from undergoing decline" (Norton 1988, pp. 1, 3). In other words, Norton claims that we should recognize the broader forces that bring species to the endangered stage. Once we adopt the holistic approach of halting habitat destruction, he maintains that we shall not have to devote so much individual attention to the scramble to protect particular species.

Although Norton is correct in arguing that focusing on mere preservation of species leads to an insoluble problem, a continual scramble to save species, it is not clear that habitat preservation would avoid this scramble, and for several reasons. One reason is that, given population pressures, it is not realistic to believe that all habitats can be saved. And if not, then not all species (for which a habitat is necessary) can be saved. Hence, the "continual scramble" of which Norton spoke is probably unavoidable. Admittedly, of course, triage thinking probably intensifies the scramble, because triage thinking is so short-sighted. The continual scramble is also unavoidable because species are continually coming into existence and going out of existence. Extinction has always occurred, and would continue to occur, even in a world with no humans. And if so, then habitat preservation would not stop extinction, but only possibly slow it down. Of course, Norton is correct that more species would probably be saved by habitat preservation than by focusing on preserving a single species. However, it is not clear that saving many species is always better than saving a single species. Nor is it always clear that saving one species is better than saving another, since all species have inherent worth. A value judgment is required to determine which is preferable, from scientific, aesthetic, cultural, and ethical grounds. And if so, then there is no obvious algorithm according to which saving more species is always better than saving less, particularly if those in the latter category have special importance to humans, or according to which saving one species is always better than saving another.

The criterion problem does not occur only when one is attempting to decide which or how many species to save. It also occurs at the level of saving habitats. It occurs because not all habitats can be saved, and because value judgments must be made as to which ones ought to be preserved. This means that, just as Norton charged that a "continual scramble" regarding which species to save would occur if we focused only on species preservation, a similar problem faces his own conservation alternative. Given that not all habitats can be saved, a "continual scramble" occurs regarding which habitats to save. This means that, although Norton has provided good grounds for holistic, ecosystemic preservation, he has not addressed the fundamental criteria problem troubling conservationists. What his approach does is transfer this problem from the level of which *species* to protect to the level of which *habitat* to protect. All the same issues of choosing conservation criteria and adjudicating conflicts between economic and ecological values still exist.

Norton's fourth argument for protecting habitats, rather than merely endangered species, is that it makes more biological sense. He argues that "more species will be saved by efforts directed at habitat protection than by efforts to identify, list, and develop recovery programs for each individual endangered species" (Norton 1988, p. 4). Something like this argument is probably what Simberloff (see section 9.5) had in mind when he argued that panther protection does not represent the best use of conservation dollars; from a biological point of view, he argued that other preservationist goals were more important and a better way to spend funds. Norton and Simberloff are obviously correct in saying that we ought to protect as much habitat in as large preserves as possible. Despite their reasonable arguments for, or sympathies toward, habitat preservation, nevertheless they seem to fail to address a number of practical conservation problems. As a result, it is not clear that either Norton or Simberloff has provided reliable grounds for the second-order claim that habitat preservation ought to be pursued rather than species or subspecies preservation, or vice versa. From an ecological point of view, habitat preservation is obviously a better *scientific choice* than mere species preservation. However, this fact does not mean that habitat preservation is a better *policy choice* or a better choice in terms of ethical rationality. Moreover, conservation must be multifaceted, because it must address diverse goals of diverse constituencies (see Soulé and Kohm 1989). If public preferences are not aligned with good ecological thinking, the public needs to be educated so that its aesthetic and anthropocentric preferences for preserving large mammals take account of the importance of habitat preservation. Until persons are thus educated, however, conservation dollars are held hostage to existing preferences. Thus, although they are correct, in one sense Norton and Simberloff "speak to the converted": to those who already know how to make conservation judgments from an ecological or scientific perspective. Yet, even many conservation groups do not construct their arguments from such a perspective.

But if an important policy problem is how to deal with the "unconverted" persons who make preservation decisions quite differently from the experts, then pursuing the "triage strategy" of conservation may be a necessary evil, until we can accomplish better conservation education. Stephen Jay Gould (1990) speaks of the "political reality" of using attractive "umbrella" or "indicator" species as surrogates for a larger ecological entity that we wish to save (see Duda 1987, p. iii). If he is correct, and we believe that he is, then it may be necessary to do what it is politically possible to do. And it may be more possible to obtain funds for trying to save individual species than for saving habitats, especially when all conservation arguments must compete against powerful economic forces pushing for development of an area. This means that conservationists who pursue species preservation may not be viewing species as commodities, as gene pools (as Norton suggests), but as objects of a political-conservation strategy that is more feasible than habitat preservation. In other words, ecologists and policymakers who follow a strategy of species, rather than habitat, preservation may be following public preferences, values, and welfare. They may be following a model of ethical rationality in applying ecology (see chapters 6 and 7), rather than a model of scientific rationality that dictates decisions be made from only a biological perspective.

9.8 Repairing injustice takes precedence over property rights

Another second-order controversy concerning whether one ought to try to save the Florida panther is between those who follow first-order principles of reparation and those who follow first-order principles of property rights. Proponents of the first principle claim that we humans are responsible for panther preservation now because our activities in the past have caused the subspecies to become endangered. Proponents of the property principle claim that those who own land have the right to develop it, because human interests take precedence over panther preservation. How does one adjudicate the conflict between first-order principles of reparation and property rights? We shall consider arguments on both sides, showing that it is reasonable to follow the second-order principle that reparation takes precedence.

Humans have viewed the panther as a competitor because it is a predator. As a result, most panther populations were eliminated even before 1900. In fact, the Florida panther has probably only survived for so long because of its remoteness from human settlements. All this suggests that, if the Florida panther has inherent worth and intrinsic value, as we already argued, then we humans have a prima-facie or first-order duty to repair some of the damage that our inattention to these values has brought. Admittedly, in some cases, perhaps humans had no realistic choice but to develop and use the Florida panther habitat as we have. Nevertheless, once we admit that the subspecies embodies several types of values – including an ecocentric inherent worth – that its members are not worthless, and that we have a prima-facie obligation to recognize both ecocentric and anthropocentric values, then it follows that we owe some compensation, some reparation, to all beings whose interests have been harmed by our actions. This means that, because we have destroyed or developed much of the panther habitat and threatened the subspecies and its associated intrinsic values, we have an obligation (to all those who enjoyed those values) to prevent their further destruction.

This prima-facie obligation arises straightforwardly out of justice. If persons A have an interest in the Florida panther, because of one or more of its intrinsic values, and if persons B destroy part of the subspecies' habitat, making its continuance and realization of those values more difficult to obtain for persons A, then persons B have an obligation either to repair the damage, or to compensate those whose interests were threatened, or to do as much as possible to prevent further harm in the future. In other words, there are purely anthropo-centric reasons for arguing that humans ought not be allowed to harm the interests of other persons. Even if such damage is justifiable (e.g., developing Florida panther habitat to meet important human needs) then, at a *minimum*, we humans have an anthropocentric obligation in justice to see that those whose interests have been harmed (by destruction of areas necessary for panther survival) are not jeopardized further. Moreover, to the degree that we have duties to respect the inherent worth and intrinsic value of non-humans hurt by our actions, then we also have an ecocentric or biocentric obligation to them. (We shall not address further the issue of whether humans have duties with respect to non-humans, and for two reasons. *First*, although we believe there are such duties, there are numerous excellent works regarding our obligations and duties with respect to non-humans. *Second*, the focus of this book is not our duties regarding non-humans but our duties in a situation of ecological uncertainty.) The fact that the Florida panther is locally rare, and that humans pose a great threat to it, as we argued earlier, provides the factual basis for claiming that some sort of reparation or compensation is due those who benefit from the intrinsic value and inherent worth of the subspecies. Similarly, because humans have destroyed many individuals in the subspecies, they have duties to avoid future destruction, or at least to avoid it so far as possible. In other words, proponents of reparation claim that humans have an ethical responsibility, through justice, to prevent the destruction or extinction of those habitats or species that have been placed in danger because of human activity.

Those who believe that, in the panther case, property rights take precedence over reparation to humans — whose interests have been harmed by panther depletion — are likely to counter with several questions. One question is why humans ought to repair damage done as a consequence of human-induced species or subspecies extinction, since humans are merely causing what other biological forces cause: extinction. The response to this question is that humans, on the whole, are not merely doing what also occurs independent of human agency. The *rate* of human-induced species extinction is much faster than what typically occurs where there is no human activity. In fact, some scientists believe that humans will cause half of all existing species to become extinct by the year 2000 (Sawyer 1989, p. 4). Species naturally exhibit turnover, and speciation and extinction have progressed at various rates through time. The ethical problem with human activities is that they have accelerated extinctions for which humans (unlike members of other species) are accountable. Hence, persons have reduced biodiversity and harmed welfare (see Wilson 1988; Colwell 1989, pp. 4–5).

Other questions confront the reparation-versus-property-rights argument. At what biological level does the reparation obligation occur (species or subspecies, for example)? What biological entities does it cover (vertebrates or invertebrates)? For example, do humans have the duty to repair damage done as a result of causing some insect species to go extinct? The answer here is that the degree of reparation owed to humans is proportional to the degree to which their interests were harmed by damaging species or habitats. Likewise, the degree of reparation owed to non-human beings is proportional to the degree to which the harm to them was avoidable. These answers, however, raise at least three conceptual problems. *First*, one obviously cannot repair or compensate for damage to an individual Florida panther by attempting to preserve other individuals of the same species. If the first animal is dead, it is not compensated by saving the second. This is the same sort of argument that arises in cases of compensation for racism. If person C was a victim of a racist murder, then it is not possible to compensate him for the racism, if he is dead (see Goldman 1977, p. 322; Nagel 1981, p. 7). Even though humans cannot compensate beings who are destroyed, however, if humans have duties to respect nature and not to jeopardize the inherent worth of any organism, then humans who fail in their duties in this area nevertheless have an obligation to do whatever they can to stop destruction of such organisms in the future. They have this obligation, not because they have duties to dead beings but because, as Boxill puts it, the damage done was so great that no one was unaffected by it. Hence, just as all black persons have been hurt by racism, to some degree (Boxill 1984, pp. 184–185), therefore, we owe all black persons some debt of compensation. Similarly, to the degree that all human interests have been hurt by nearly extinguishing the Florida panther, therefore we owe all humans a debt in reparation. Such obligations do not in fact compensate those that were destroyed, but they recognize the fact that endangering the Florida panther, for example, puts the destroyer in the debt of many persons in the biosphere. The destroyer has jeopardized the particular scientific, cultural, and other values represented and embodied in the Florida panther. Hence, the appropriate compensation (preserving the Florida panther in the future), while not benefiting all those who have been harmed because of the destroyed habitat or the dead organisms, could repair some of the debt to some of the persons whose interests were adversely affected.

One difficulty, of course, with arguing for panther preservation is that not all persons affected by the welfare of the Florida panther believe that every individual panther ought to be preserved. Nor do they believe that killing a member of the threatened subspecies is an act for which reparation is owed. The Seminole Indians, for example, hold the Florida panther as a sacred symbol, important to their cultural and ritual life. As part of their ritual, they have killed members of the subspecies. Their argument, presented during prosecution for the killing of one of the animals, is that, because the panther is sacred to them and important to their cultural life, they are not bound to obey laws that prohibit panther killing. Moreover, it is arguable that white persons, not the Seminoles, have caused the panther to be threatened. Were it not for white persons' actions, it is arguable that the panther would not be threatened, and hence that the Seminoles could continue to kill a few of them as part of their tribal rituals. Hence, goes the argument, it is clear, for example, neither that Seminoles ought to avoid killing any panthers, nor that they owe reparation if and when they do.

Even if the Seminoles have not caused the panther to go extinct, and even if their tribal cultural values – including ritual killing – are as important as panther preservation, it is not obvious that it is acceptable for Seminoles to continue to kill Florida panthers. The killing would be acceptable, presumably, (1) only if it were absolutely essential to Seminole tradition, life, and culture; (2) only if no one (other than Seminoles) had an interest in the panther, and (3) only if such traditions were obviously more important than protecting threatened species. Given the myriad ways in which Seminole traditions may have been modified in contemporary times, it may be problematic to claim that the panther killing, at present, is essential to such traditions. The ethical acceptability of panther killing, whether caused by a careless motorist or by a Seminole Chief, is in part a function of the relative number of panthers existing at a given time. Moreover, despite the value of diverse cultural traditions, like those of the Seminoles, it does not appear justifiable to claim that a small set of persons (the present-day Florida Seminoles or careless motorists) can risk preempting the rights of a much larger set of persons to enjoy the Florida panther. If the goods of the earth are a commons that all may enjoy, then no group has the right to destroy part of that commons without the consent of other persons. Presumably that consent cannot be obtained, in the case of the panther, because our laws protect it, and presumably our laws are justified on the basis of implicit consent.

Of course, white persons are members of the main group that have threatened the panther. They have thus placed themselves in the debt of all others who wish to enjoy the environmental commons, including the Florida panther. If white persons, without recrimination, have reduced the Florida panther to near extinction, does it make sense to prevent the Seminoles from doing what others have done, to a worse degree, before them? Given the interests of all persons in enjoying the environmental commons, part of which includes the Florida panther, it is not clear that Seminoles have a right to violate this commons, just because others have done so. Otherwise, there would be little sense in which we all had a right to the commons. What the white persons' near extinction of the panther does suggest is that, because the extinction has threatened continuation of certain Seminole rituals or traditions, therefore we owe the Indians a debt of reparation or compensation. In other words, while it is not obvious that the Seminoles ought to be able to destroy a common good, like the panther, it does appear that they deserve to be compensated for the way in which others have destroyed it. They deserve to be compensated because the near extinction of the panther has threatened Seminole life and rituals in a heightened way. Those who have caused this cultural loss somehow need to compensate for damage to the Seminoles, although compensation ought not take the form of allowing panther killings that jeopardize the interests of still other persons. Hence, the Seminole case presents no important obstacle to our reparation argument.

A second conceptual problem with the claim – that those who have been destroying the Florida panther habitat and endangering the subspecies, have duties to compensate or repair for this damage – is that this argument seems to contradict ordinary notions of property rights. Provided that those who owned the developed/destroyed panther habitat had property rights to it, and provided that their development did not disobey any laws, then it is arguable that they have no responsibility to compensate anyone because they endangered the subspecies. While this argument is quite reasonable and traditional, it ignores the fact that property rights have never been absolute. Indeed, as our earlier discussion of Locke and Dworkin made clear, persons have rights to use property only in ways that do not harm the common good or jeopardize the interests of other persons. Yet another conceptual problem with the claim – that we humans who have threatened habitats or taxa have an obligation not to let rare or threatened organisms remain at risk – is that this argument seems to presuppose that species and subspecies, rather than individuals, are moral subjects to whom we have duties. Hampshire (1972, pp. 3–4) and Feinberg (1974, p. 56), for example, have both argued that we do not have prima-facie duties to species (or subspecies) as such, independent of the individuals that comprise them; rather, they argue that we have duties to future human beings. Hampshire and Feinberg are correct, in that duties must be to individuals, not to taxonomic units having no existence. It makes no sense to have a duty to a being that does not exist at least potentially. Hampshire and Feinberg provide an incomplete analysis if they ignore the fact that many non-human beings, like plants and animals, have a good of their own, continuation of their lives, independent of human recognition. Because they are alive, they are worthy of human respect and they have inherent value (see Taylor 1986).

But as we already argued, if members of endangered species and subspecies are worthy of respect and are moral subjects to which we owe prima-facie respect, then we do have duties to them. Although individual, non-human organisms and groups of such organisms do not have moral rights (see the earlier discussion in this chapter; see also Feinberg 1974), humans do have duties to them, apart from whether human beings are interested in these duties or not. Since humans have the ability to interfere or not with the good – continuation of life – of organisms, and because the organisms exist, independent of human assistance, therefore persons have prima-facie obligations not to interfere with them. Moreover, once one accepts the biocentric claim that all living beings have inherent worth, then it is arguable that we have no prima-facie right to interfere with organisms that have such inherent worth. (For discussion of duties regarding species preservation, see Norton 1987, pp. 1–24, 46–72, 169–242.)

In the case of the Florida panther, our duties to try to preserve it are based in part on protecting the common good/interest. The common good is harmed by individuals who, in the name of full control over their property, have damaged panther habitat. As we argued earlier in chapter 7, no society has ever sanctioned absolute property rights to land, because land is part of the commons and hence subject to the constraints of serving the common good (see Soper 1983, pp. 113–129). Therefore, there are no prima-facie grounds for arguing that property rights supersede the common good, the interests of those concerned, for example, with preservation. But if the common good takes primacy over property rights, then we humans have a duty to compensate for, and to repair, whatever damage to the common good has been caused by our exercise of property rights. And if we have duties to repair our damage to the commons, then this suggests that we ought not place present or future persons in situations in which our harming the commons harms them. If we harm them by preempting their choices regarding biodiversity and enjoyment of various species and subspecies, then we owe them compensation inasmuch as we have preempted their receiving all the benefits of preservation. We owe them due process of law (see Abramovitz 1989). Therefore, because species and subspecies extinctions and habitat destruction preclude exercise of equal opportunity to the benefits of preservation, and because they preclude due-process rights in the present, and especially in the future, it is arguable that human-induced extinctions ought to be avoided. They ought to be avoided, in particular, because the extinctions and their consequent threats to welfare are irreversible. The damage induced by extinction can never be compensated fully, because it is irreversible. Therefore, those who lose the opportunity to enjoy the Florida panther in the future also lose their due-process rights to be compensated fully for the loss.

In terms of maximizing anthropocentric benefits, however, persons interested in panther preservation would have to argue about more than the existence of due-process rights. They would also have to show that protecting the Florida panther habitat was a higher ethical priority than developing it, and that due-process rights superseded welfare rights or property rights to develop the land. This argument could probably best be made by claiming that present persons have no right to preempt the choices of future persons, since everyone has rights to equal opportunity. Therefore, regardless of how much benefit would accrue to present persons if they preempted the rights of future persons to enjoy the commons, equity would prevent their justifying this preemption. And presumably allowing the Florida panther to become extinct would preempt future choices. Allowing the Florida panther to go extinct now would be to foreclose the option of enjoying the subspecies in the future. It would be to limit the opportunities to which our descendants have access, opportunities like enjoying and stewarding our common ecological birthright, our common ecological heritage of biodiversity. The message is simple: no taxation without representation. No loss of the Florida panther without representation of the interests of all persons – even future persons – concerned about the subspecies. In the panther case, one relevant second-order principle is that compensation and reparation for previous wrongs take priority over property rights to develop panther habitat. They take priority because reparation is a duty owed through justice, whereas property rights are defined so as to serve the common good, and justice typically takes precedence over serving the common good.

9.9 One has an obligation to do only what is possible

So far, all our analyses have argued for second-order principles that recommend panther preservation, in the ecological and policy case facing scientists. In this section, we shall examine another second-order argument based on the fact that one has an obligation to do only what it is possible to do. Moral philosophers have long recognized that one is not morally or ethically bound to do what it is not possible to do. "Ought implies can." One ought to be required to do only what it is possible to do. Hence, an important consideration relevant to adjudicating controversies over preservation of the Florida panther is whether it is possible to save the subspecies (in the wild). There are at least two senses in which it might be impossible to save the Florida panther. It might be in-practice impossible, or it might be in-principle impossible. Things that are in-practice impossible are possible, but practical considerations prevent their occurrence. Things that are in-principle impossible are prevented from occurring, either because their happening would violate some law of logic, or because their occurrence is prohibited by existing scientific law.

Preservation of the Florida panther appears to be both in-principle possible (although uncertain) and in-practice possible (although highly unlikely). It is in-practice possible because no facts prevent it, even though, practically speaking, the state appears unwilling to set aside the vast tracts of land that appear necessary to try to save the subspecies in the wild. As we discussed earlier in chapter 8, the home range requirement for an individual panther is about 30,000 to 50,000 acres; for a minimum viable population of about 50 individuals, therefore, the area requirement is at least 1,512,500 acres and may be as high as 2,500,000 acres. Even the largest proposed panther preserve (in Osceola National Forest) is only one-fifteenth the size of the smallest necessary range. Under perhaps the best of circumstances, in which Osceola National Forest is part of an interconnected complex of wildlands, these lands would total about 1.2 million acres. However, even this total remains short of panther area requirements. The large area requirement for the Florida panther (two and a half million acres) represents approximately 10 percent of all Florida land. Even though the acreage suitable for the panther may be ubiquitous in the state (panther habitat is essentially wherever there are deer or pigs), it may be unrealistic to suppose that Florida would allocate 10 percent of its total land simply to try to save one subspecies. This allocation may be unrealistic because it would require most of the remaining areas of Florida to be closed to development. Even if such closure were desirable, it is not likely to occur. Nevertheless, as we argued earlier, unless far larger tracts of land (than that in Osceola National Forest, for example) are dedicated to the panther, or unless corridors are instituted and are effective, then scientific data on the panther's range requirements make clear that, although preservation is in-principle and in-practice possible, it is not highly probable that we can save the subspecies in the wild (Ballou *et al.* 1989, p. 2). Part of the improbability (regarding appropriating more land) can be removed, but whether it will be done is questionable, given development pressures in the state. The improbability could also be negated by use of corridors, provided they prove effective. However, this question of effectiveness is also uncertain.

Very likely it is in-principle possible to save the Florida panther (in the wild) into the next century because we do not know enough to determine that preservation is, in principle, impossible. Regardless of whether conservation corridors would work (see chapter 8 and the early sections of this chapter), there still may be a way for the taxon to survive. Admittedly, the subspecies has so few members (less than 40, as we noted earlier) that inbreeding depression may have weakened its potential for long-term survival. Indeed, because of the small size of the Florida-panther population, and because of uncertainties surrounding the minimum viable population size (MVPS), the best experts give the Florida panther an 85 percent chance of becoming extinct during the next 25 years (Ballou *et al.* 1989, p.2). Hence, regardless of the practical steps that might be taken (providing more conservation monies; buying more land), there may be no way to overcome the in-principle difficulty of inbreeding depression and the small population size. Nevertheless, the probability of extinction is not 100 percent. Because it is not, the Florida panther appears still to have a chance. And if so, then it is neither in-practice nor in-principle impossible for the taxon to survive in the wild into the next century. Because its survival is uncertain and because, in similar situations of uncertainty, we have an obligation to minimize type-II (rather than type-I) error, we have a duty to attempt to preserve the panther.

If our reasoning is correct, then we may ultimately disagree with one of Simberloff's conclusions (about the prima-facie desirability of using certain efforts to try to save the panther). Likewise, Simberloff appears to suggest that there are a number of second-order principles that argue against trying to save the panther. These include the claims that we ought not try to save the panther, because doing so could cause scientists to lose credibility; that it would not minimize type-I statistical errors; and that it may not be an efficient use of conservation dollars. Because we believe that the panther is both in-principle and in-practice possible to save, even though it is improbable, we believe that we have both a prima-facie and a second-order ethical obligation to try to do so. We have disagreed with all three of Simberloff's arguments, as sole grounds for environmental policymaking, primarily because they appear to reflect decisionmaking based only on scientific rationality, rather than on both scientific and ethical rationality (see chapters 6 and 7).

Admittedly, our conclusion leads to a very disturbing consequence: the problems facing the Florida panther were in large part created by humans, and humans have an obligation to try to save the subspecies, yet it is not certain that it is scientifically possible to specify the conditions that will guarantee the survival of the Florida panther in the wild. How can we be obligated to do something, even though we are not certain that our efforts will be successful? At least part of the answer is that it cannot be ethically acceptable to absolve persons from moral responsibility for situations − like the panther's being endangered − that they have created. If not, then there appears to be a moral responsibility, through reparation or compensation, to attempt to save the subspecies and perhaps to perform other conservation/preservation acts, such as working to save other threatened habitats, species, and subspecies in Florida. This notion that we have a debt of reparation or compensation, because of what persons have done to the Florida panther, seems plausible in part because loss of the subspecies has and will hurt the human and biotic community in Florida, and hurt it in a variety of scientific, cultural, symbolic, aesthetic, and economic ways. Hence, those responsible for the loss owe something to the community in return.

The obligation to compensate the community for the damage done to the Florida panther is analogous to the duty imposed on many offenders when judges sentence them to community service. Admittedly such "community service" may not save the panther, but it does deal with some of the compensation, and hence with some of the relevant moral, responsibilities raised by the issue of panther preservation. Bryan Norton anticipated our conclusion, in part, in arguing against "triage thinking" in preservation. He said that we must stop trying to save almost-extinct species, since this is a costly and a losing battle. Instead, he emphasized saving whole habitats. Our consideration of the Florida panther shows that, although Norton has some insights about almost-extinct species, he may be wrong about habitat preservation always being preferable to species preservation. Habitats and species, in the individual case studies, do not admit of easy rules like: "save habitats before species." Only analysis of cases, not pursuing exceptionless rules, ought to guide our choices. Both ecological science and environmental policy, as the panther issue reveals, may require us to look more at statistics and search less for deterministic laws, to spend more time with case studies and less effort with mathematical models, and to let practice, rather than theory alone, be our guide. More importantly, ecological science and environmental policy, as we have argued, may require us to move beyond purely scientific rationality and into ethical rationality, into a real recognition of ecological interdependence, not only among all living beings, but also among science and our deepest values.

10 · Conclusions

TWO CALIFORNIA ECOLOGISTS, Robinson and Quinn (1988), have studied an experimentally fragmented California grassland. They noted that there is debate over how subdivision of a habitat will affect extinction, and then they concluded that extinction, immigration, and species turnover are "relatively independent of the degree of habitat subdivision" (pp. 71–82). Another ecologist, Dennis Murphy of Stanford University, questioned the scale and methodology of the Robinson and Quinn undertaking and found both of them lacking. He also criticized the consequences likely to follow from the results of the controversial 1988 study: "their conclusions are what every land developer and every timber industry representative wants to hear — chopping up natural habitats does not really put species at risk" (Murphy 1989, p. 83).

If applied ecology is, in fact, tied to case studies, to natural history, and to rough generalizations rather than to exceptionless empirical laws and a deterministic general theory (see Shrader-Frechette 1986; Shrader-Frechette and McCoy 1990), then scenarios like the one involving Robinson, Quinn, and Murphy are likely to occur repeatedly. Indeed, every application of ecology, in a controversial situation involving environmental welfare, could be one in which battles over conservation principles will have to be fought anew in different places and at different times. Applications of ecological science, in other words, will parallel the problems of decentralized democratic decision-making. Wholly decentralized decisionmaking, however, could be both inefficient and unjust. For example, without national laws like the 1964 US Civil Rights Act, virtually every town and state in every country would be forced to pass some sort of regulations of its own to deal with various local problems of racism. Without a protective national law, towns or cities often would make no such efforts, or the efforts would be half-hearted, or they would fail to deal with important social problems related to race. As a consequence, local government often would not protect the rights of blacks and other minorities. Indeed, before the passage of the 1964 US Act, this is exactly what happened in the US. As an economist would say, without the help of a federal law, the transaction costs involved in curbing discrimination, in thousands of different situations, would be typically so high that they would preclude effective action against racism.

Analogously, without predictive, general, ecological theory that is applicable to environmental problems, and without exceptionless empirical laws, virtually every town and state in every region of the world will be forced to deal, on its own, with various local problems of environmental policy. Without powerful, general ecological theory and law – that provides precise predictions applicable to conservation decisions – often persons will make no efforts, or the efforts will be half hearted, or they will fail to address adequately conservation and other environmental problems. As a result, and probably because of powerful vested interests pushing for development, environmental deterioration will occur, just as Murphy warned in the California grassland case. The transaction costs (education, public mobilization, lobbying, and so on) involved in local decisionmaking regarding environmental policy will be so high that, in most cases, they will preclude effective and ecologically sound decisions.

If the analogy between federal laws and racism – and ecological laws and environmental deterioration – holds, then our account of the rationality characteristic of much ecological science appears to lead to a number of problems in the practical world of decisionmaking. In a nutshell, these problems arise because, in a science without deterministic, exceptionless empirical laws, it may appear that ecology is insufficiently predictive to be useful in environmental problemsolving. In this chapter, we shall argue that, given the account of value-laden ecological science that we have defended in this volume, ecology is useful, in part because it frequently is able to distinguish phenomena that are prohibited from those that are permitted. Even though our case-study account of ecological rationality might appear to render the claims of ecology purely conventional, our analysis does not do so. We shall argue that, and in what sense, ecology is objective, even though it appears to have no general theory and no exceptionless, deterministic, empirical laws that are able to provide precise predictions often needed for environmental decisionmaking. Moreover, we shall show that, even if ecology did have general theory and exceptionless empirical laws usable in such applications, its methodological value judgments would remain. They would persist because scientists, including ecologists, need to employ instrumental and categorical value judgments whenever they evaluate theory or data and whenever they apply exceptionless empirical laws – or even rough generalizations – to a particular situation. In such applications, ecologists must decide when the law or rough generalization accurately characterizes the situation, and when it is so idealized that it does not. Because ecologists must continually determine when the empirical fit of a law or generalization is close enough, they can never avoid methodological value judgments. Despite these judgments, we shall provide some suggestions for dealing with the problem of idealized theories, laws, and rough generalizations in ecology.

10.1 Why ecology is objective

As we argued in earlier chapters, many scientists accept the positivistic, H-D method because they believe that it is the best (if not the only) way to attain objectivity. We showed, however, that the positivistic, H-D account – despite its value as a scientific goal or ideal – has problems with respect to: (1) the imprecise status of ecological concepts, laws, and theories; (2) the difficulties associated with creating uncontroversial null models; and (3) the presence of unavoidable methodological value judgments in all science, especially in an applied science like ecology. The positivistic, H-D account of explanation in ecology erroneously presupposes a value-free account of objectivity. Value-free observation or data, however, do not alone provide the only objective reason for accepting one hypothesis rather than another. As we argued in chapter 4, there are other good reasons for accepting a scientific hypothesis, theory, or value judgment (see Skolimowski 1974, pp. 214ff.; Longino 1990, pp. 177–181) – reasons that make the acceptance objective. One good reason, as we illustrated in our case study (chapter 8), is that the hypothesis provides more explanatory power and is more consistent with the (value-laden) empirical data than are other hypotheses, despite repeated attempts to falsify it (see Hempel 1965, pp. 55–56, 1983, p. 91; Sellars 1967, p. 410; Cornman 1980, pp. 8–9, 15, 26, 67–88, 93). Another objective reason for accepting an hypothesis, theory, or value judgment is that it has successfully survived intelligent debate and criticism by the scientific community (Popper 1950, pp. 403–406, 1965, p. 56). In chapter 8 we provided a brief example of such debate over hypotheses.

Both these reasons for hypothesis or theory acceptance presuppose that empirical confirmability is not the only test of objectivity, either in science or anywhere else. This is because (as we argued in chapter 4) even confirmability is laced with unavoidable methodological value judgments. Rather, we often claim that a judgment is "objective," even in science, if it is not obviously biased or subjective, if it has survived intelligent debate and criticism, and if it appears to have more explanatory power and (internal and external) consistency than alternative judgments. Objectivity, in this sense, is not tied to value-free empirical confirmability, as the positivists and H-D proponents thought. Instead, our notion of objectivity is tied to the practices and procedures (intelligent criticism) of the scientific community, as well as to the practices and procedures of the method of case studies. It is also tied to avoiding *bias* values. It is tied to giving an even-handed representation of the situation. Presumably, one could be blamed for failing to be objective, in the sense of not being even-handed, if one were biased in a particular methodological value judgment – for example, by deliberately excluding or misrepresenting some of one's data. Since we do often blame persons for not being objective, in the sense of not being even-handed, it is clear that one can be more or less blameworthy, and hence more or less objective in this sense. Although there is no sufficient condition for guaranteeing objectivity, perhaps the best way to attain objectivity in this sense is to check the predictive and explanatory power of our hypotheses (even though our accounts are value laden) and to subject them to the procedures of repeated review, criticism, and amendment by the scientific community.

It appears reasonable to define objectivity in this procedural sense, in terms of predictive and explanatory power, and in terms of surviving the criticism of the scientific community, in part because such criticisms need not be wholly subjective. If ecologists criticize the objectivity of methodological value judgments about stability or alleged community structures, for example, then they are not merely speaking autobiographically. They are talking about the characteristics of external events that can be known by other persons. Admittedly, different persons may make different value judgments or interpretations of those events, but the events are external, not private and internal. Hence, reasoning and debate about ecological interpretations can be more or less objective, just as we argued earlier when we discussed the method of case studies. Moreover, even the methodological value judgments about such ecological events are a function of training, education, experience, and intelligence. The judgments are more or less objective, often because of factors such as field experience. And if so, then ecology does not always require empirical confirmation in order to guarantee the objectivity of an hypothesis. It requires only that the hypothesis be free from intentional bias; that it be reformulable on the basis of good reasons, new evidence, or better interpretations; that it be able to provide explanatory power superior to that of its competitors; and that it be able to survive sustained criticism, debate, and amendment by diverse segments of the scientific community. In other words, an hypothesis can be objective and have significant heuristic value, even if it is not ready to be subjected to rigorous testing.

Another reason for believing that our account of objectivity in ecology may be correct is that reasonable persons make value judgments and accept hypotheses when their evidence and their explanatory frameworks require them. Reasonable persons do not refrain from value judgments or theoretical commitments until they have allegedly value-free empirical confirmations of all their beliefs or judgments. Only if ecologists or other reasonable persons were engaged in a search for objectivity that came close to avoiding all error would it seem reasonable to complain about well-supported methodological value judgments or hypotheses (see Scriven 1982). Since even the most predictive sciences have never claimed such an unrealistic notion of objectivity (as infallibility), it does not seem reasonable to demand more of ecology. If we demand more than good reasons, more than explanatory power, in every instance, in order to defend the objectivity of hypotheses and theories, then we shall be forgetting the case-study, social, ethical, and decision-theoretic nature of ecological applications. Admittedly, no one has yet provided a wholly satisfactory account of "explanatory power." And, admittedly, ecology has not yet enjoyed extensive predictive successes. Nevertheless, our examination of cases such as the vampire bat, the spotted owl, and the Florida panther suggest that explanatory and predictive power ought not be rejected as ecological ideals, even though there are numerous ecological controversies over explanatory and predictive power. Many persons appear to believe that the existence of disagreements in a particular area of science constitutes evidence for its subjectivity. Great differences in scientific practice and belief, however, are compatible with objectivity. Disagreements do not mean either that there are no rough generalizations in ecology, for example, or that one generalization is as good as another, or that ecology can never provide explanatory and predictive power. Indeed, there must be some rational level of agreement, even among scientists who disagree, or else they would not make logical contact with each other. They must have some scientific assumptions, methodological values, or hypotheses on which they agree, or their controversies would be meaningless and incoherent. Hence, the disagreement itself provides some evidence for their agreement (at least in some areas), and therefore for the rationality of some of the views that they share.

Because objectivity in ecology – according to the account that we have been defending – relies in part on an hypothesis' ability to withstand criticism by the scientific community, objectivity is tied to practices more than rules. Especially in a predominantly applied science like ecology, this should be no surprise. Ecological objectivity is often tied to practices because, insofar as much of it is built on case studies and natural history, it requires that objectivity and rationality, in their final stages, be based on an appeal to particular cases as being similar to other cases believed to be correct. Our account of rationality and objectivity in ecology does not appeal to specific, value-free rules, applicable to all situations – although the general, value-laden norm of seeking to establish the predictive and explanatory power of an hypothesis is always applicable. Rather, our account relies on the ability of the trained and experienced ecologist to see one case as like another that is believed to be correct.

Moreover, something like our "practice" or "case" notion of rationality and objectivity, according to which theories are approximately true (see Longino 1990, pp. 17–29, 36–37, 59–61, 74), must hold for at least part of all science. Our account of rationality and objectivity must hold at the level of justifying the most foundational laws or principles of all sciences. All sciences, at their most ultimate level, must be built on practices or cases, for at least three reasons. *First*, all scientists who follow exceptionless rules or laws must ultimately avoid an infinite regress when justifying their judgments. Scientists cannot use a law to justify another law, in an infinite regress, because every law is built on concepts, assumptions, and interpretations which themselves must be justified. Hence no law, alone, can stop the regress. *Second*, judgments about rules or laws cannot rely on rules or laws. The justificatory rules would themselves need to be justified. *Third*, rules and laws, alone, cannot take account of all cases in ecology. They cannot take account of all cases because each case fails to fit an idealized law or rule in one way or another. (We shall discuss this third point in more detail in the next section.) For all these reasons, every ecological judgment – and every scientific judgment at some ultimate point – requires an appeal to cases, to practice, and to an account of objectivity that does not rely on confirmation alone (see Newell 1986; Shrader-Frechette 1989b, 1991, chs. 3, 12). Instead, this account relies on concrete problem solutions, just as Kuhn (1970; see Hull 1988, p. 112) recognized.

10.2 Idealization, rough generalizations, and particular cases

If ecology is objective and rational in the sense just outlined, then what criteria do ecologists use to apply rough generalizations to specific cases? How ought they to deal with the problem of idealization in ecology? Idealized laws or regularities are unavoidable in all science for at least two reasons. One reason is that all phenomena to be explained in science must be simplified if they are to be dealt with in a manageable way. The other reason is that, because they must be applicable to many different situations, all laws or rough generalizations must be general and, hence, descriptively false in particular situations. For example, Coulomb's law states that, around any point charge, a spherically symmetric electromagnetic field is produced by the charge. But, of course, not every point charge produces a spherically symmetric electromagnetic field; if there is a dense source of mass–energy near the point charge, then the metric of space–time is changed in that vicinity (Joseph 1980, p. 776; Shrader-Frechette 1989a, pp. 342ff.). To some extent, the presence of idealized laws, like Coulomb's, and rough generalizations is a problem for the H-D account of scientific method, because the idealizations falsify the real world, a world that is not as regular and uniform as the idealizations dictate (Shrader-Frechette 1989a, pp. 329–330). Because it is not, practicing scientists must make methodological value judgments about "how uniform is uniform enough" each time they apply some law or rough generalization. Their applications undercut the H-D claim to a science free of methodological – especially categorical – value judgments. Thus, even if one begins to recognize the limitations of the H-D account, as we have begun to do in this volume, idealized laws and rough generalizations will nevertheless present a problem for ecologists. They must still answer the question: when is a generalization, to be used in an applied situation, too idealized to be useful? When is a rough generalization, like the relationship between species number and reserve area, too idealized to be reliable (see Connor and McCoy 1979; Shrader-Frechette 1990a, b)?

One criterion that suggests itself, because of the observational difficulties in ecology, is that if one uses a rough generalization, like the species–area relationship, one ought to be able to correct for the factors that have been omitted or oversimplified. As Cartwright puts it, "If the idealization is to be of use, when the time comes to apply it to a real system we had better know how to add back the contributions of the factors that have been left out" (1983, p. 111). If the idealizations can be made realistic in a sense requisite for H-D falsification or confirmation, then this "adding back" will be dictated by fundamental, deterministic empirical laws. If there are no fundamental, deterministic empirical laws (as we believe is currently the case in ecology), then the "adding back" ought to be dictated by natural-history or phenomenological factors. If the "adding back" cannot be accomplished, even in the latter sense, then use of the idealized law likely adds little to our understanding because it cannot realistically be compared to, or checked by, what happens in the real world. The idealization is likely arbitrary. In the case of the species–area relationship, for example, the generalization may be too idealized because the "adding back" cannot be accomplished. Even when ecologists do "add back" factors like distance and latitude, the empirical fit between the species–area relationship and reality is poor (Connor and McCoy 1979; see also Dunn and Loehle 1988; Barkman 1989; Lomolino 1990).

In ecology, there are many problems with using idealized, rough generalizations for which there is no phenomenological basis for a precise correction factor. For example, how would one devise a phenomenological correction factor for a description of a situation whose boundaries (e.g., the limits of the community) could not be known precisely, especially if the phenomena being described within the situation were not uniform in all relevant respects, and if sampling were unable to reveal minor heterogeneities? In such a situation, virtually all that one could do would be to engage in *ad hoc* manipulations of the parameters in one's rough generalizations. Hence, one criterion for ideal (acceptable) idealizations in applied sciences, like ecology, might be that one ought to be able to employ at least a quantitative correction factor, one that is not *ad hoc*, in order to "add back" aspects of the phenomena disregarded by the idealization. It is not enough to know, for example, that specific rough generalizations do not work in certain situations. Rather, one needs to be able to take account of these deviations, so as to know how to add them back into the equation expressing the rough generalization. To be able to add them back, of course, presupposes that one has some measure of the distance between reality and the idealization. If one does, then one might be able, as Wimsatt (1987) explains, to use false models to generate better ones (see chapter 2). Obviously, in ecology, often one does not know the distance between reality and the idealization. Otherwise ecologists would not so often resort to modeling, rather than hypothesis-testing, in an attempt to understand community and population phenomena (see Brown 1981, pp. 881–882). Of course, use of an idealized, rough generalization might be more acceptable, from an epistemological point of view, if the error implicit in its application were somehow circumscribed, even if it were incapable of quantification. If the error was known to be in a particular direction, one might be able to fix an upper bound on it. For instance, one might accept application of an idealized, rough generalization about the species–area relationship, if one could know that use of the idealization always caused one to err on the side of conservation or safety, for example, always caused one to err such that one overestimated the number of species likely to be harmed by a particular action. In an applied science like ecology, use of this "directional" criterion for idealized, rough generalizations supports our earlier remarks about ecology's having both a scientific, including decision-theoretic, and ethical account of rationality. Using only idealizations that provided an idea of their "direction" of error would enable ecologists to perform a worst-case analysis. For all the reasons discussed earlier in chapters 6 and 7 – consent, compensation, equal protection – it is clear that, if ethical rationality is appropriate to ecology, then this notion of rationality would require ethical conservatism, and hence consideration of a worst-case analysis of situations likely to have important practical, real-world consequences (see Brown 1981, pp. 881–882; Shrader-Frechette 1991b, ch. 8; 1993).

10.3 New directions for ecology

If the conditions for using idealized, rough generalizations in ecological case studies require an ethical, as well as a scientific, rationality, then this suggests that applied ecology, as primarily a science of case studies, provides practical help in real-work decisionmaking in at least two senses. *First*, ecology can give us natural-history information, rough generalizations, and precise knowledge of particular situations, all of which enable us to exercise control over environmental phenomena (see Kingsland 1985, pp. 206ff., especially p. 208). *Second*, our account of explanation in ecology, especially applied ecology, provides additional ways to think about scientific problems. It enables us to use conceptual and methodological analysis to delineate the prohibited from the possible, and it helps us to constrain the candidate regularities in ecology (see Cooper 1990, pp. 167–169). *Third*, the philosophy of scientific method underlying the application of ecology to environmental problems, a philosophy tied to both scientific and ethical rationality, provides a basis for using ecology in many practical situations because it is a conservative rationality. It is conservative in that it puts the burden of proof (as chapters 6, 7, and 9 argued) on the ecologist who wishes to posit no detrimental effects from human manipulation of the environment. It puts the burden of proof on the ecologist who does not want to reject the null hypothesis.

In a sense, our arguments – for a science of ecology based on practical knowledge of taxa rather than on general theory, for a science of ecology based on case studies, practices, and natural-history information, and for a rationality that is both ethical and scientific – represent a mean between the non-testable, "soft" corroboration of early ecological studies and the optimistic null models of the most recent work. The early studies often expected too little of ecological method; the later emphasis on testability sometimes expects too much of it. Our path is between the two (see Abele *et al.* 1984, pp. vii–x; Wiens 1984, pp. 456ff.; Mayr 1988, p. 19; Cooper 1990). If our reasoning is correct, then both good ecology, as well as good epistemological and ethical reasoning about ecological method, provide help for environmental decisionmaking. As Clements (cited in McIntosh 1985, p. 303) put it, when he quoted General Smuts:

> Ecology must have its way; ecological methods and outlook must find a place in human government. . . . Ecology is for mankind.

References

Abbott, I., and P. R. Grant. 1976. "Non-Equilibrium Bird Faunas on Islands." *American Naturalist* 110: 507–528.

Abele, L. G., D. S. Simberloff, D. R. Strong, and A. B. Thistle. 1984. "Preface." In D. R. Strong, *et al.* (eds.), pp. vii–x.

Abrahamson, W. G., T. G. Whitman, and P. W. Price. 1989. "Fads in Ecology." *BioScience* 39: 321–325.

Abramovitz, J. N. 1989. *A Survey of US-Based Efforts to Research and Conserve Biological Diversity in Developing Countries.* World Resources Institute, New York.

Achinstein, P. 1971. *Law and Explanation.* Clarendon Press, Oxford.

Ackermann, R. 1988. *Wittgenstein's City.* University of Massachusetts Press, Amherst.

Adelman, H. 1974. "Rational Explanation Reconsidered: Case Studies and the Hempel–Dray Model." *History and Theory* 13, No. 3 (October): 208–224.

Akerman, N. (ed.). 1990. *Maintaining a Satisfactory Environment.* Westview Press, San Francisco.

Allee, W. C., O. Park, A. E. Emerson, T. Park, and K. P. Schmidt. 1949. *Principles of Animal Ecology.* W. B. Saunders, Philadelphia, PA.

Allport, G. W. 1950. *The Individual and His Religion.* Macmillan, New York.

Alyanak, L. 1989. "WWF Launches Biodiversity Campaign." *The New World* 8 (January–March): 1.

Andrewartha, H. G., and L. C. Birth. 1954. *The Distribution and Abundance of Animals.* University of Chicago Press, Chicago.

Andrews, R. (ed.). 1979. *Land in America.* Lexington Books, Lexington, MA.

Ashley, H., R. Rudman, and C. Whipple (eds.). 1976. *Energy and the Environment.* Pergamon, New York.

Atkinson, I. 1989. "Introduced Animals and Extinctions." In *Conservation for the Twenty-First Century*, D. Western and M. C. Pearl (eds.). Oxford University Press, New York, pp. 54–75.

Ayala, F., and T. Dobzhansky (eds.). 1974. *Studies in the Philosophy of Biology.* University of California Press, Berkeley.

Axinn, S. 1966. "The Fallacy of the Single Risk." *Philosophy of Science* 33: 154–162.

Baker, G. 1986. "Following Wittgenstein." In J. Canfield (ed.), pp. 223–263.

Baker, G., and P. Hacker. 1985. *Wittgenstein.* Blackwell, Oxford.

Baker, G., and P. Hacker. 1986. "On Misunderstanding Wittgenstein." In J. Canfield (ed.), pp. 321–364.

Ballou, J. D., T. J. Foose, R. C. Lacy, and U. S. Seal. 1989. *Florida Panther Population Viability Analysis.* Unpublished report.

Bambrough, J. R. 1979. *Moral Scepticism and Moral Knowledge.* Routledge and Kegan Paul, London.

Bandura, A. 1977. *Social Learning Theory.* Prentice-Hall, Englewood Cliffs, NJ.

Bandura, A. 1978. "The Self System in Reciprocal Determinism." *American Psychologist* 33: 356.

Bandura, A. 1983. 'Temporal Dynamics and Decomposition of Reciprocal Determinism.'' *Psychological Review* **90**, No. 2.

Bangs, O. 1898. ''The Land Mammals of Peninsular Florida and the Coast Region of Georgia.'' *Proceedings of the Boston Society of Natural History* **23**: 157–235.

Barkman, J. J. 1989. ''A Critical Evaluation of Minimum Area Concepts.'' *Vegetatio* **85**: 89–104.

Barnthouse, L. W., *et al.* 1984. ''Population Biology in the Courtroom: The Hudson River Controversy.'' *Bioscience* **34**, No. 1 (January): 17–18.

Barrett, S. 1988. ''Economic Guidelines for the Conservation of Biological Diversity.'' Paper presented at Workshop on Economics, IUCN General Assembly, Costa Rica.

Barrowclough, G. P., and S. L. Coats. 1985. ''The Demography and Population Genetics of Owls, with Special Reference to the Conservation of the Spotted Owl (*Strix occidentalis*).'' In R. J. Gutierrez and A. B. Carey (eds.), pp. 74–85.

Bartlett, R. 1986. ''Ecological Rationality: Reason and Environmental Policy.'' *Environmental Ethics* **8**, No. 12: 221–240.

Bayles, M. 1981. *Professional Ethics*. Wadsworth, Belmont, CA.

Becker, L. C. 1984. ''Rights.'' In L. C. Becker and K. Kipnis (eds.), pp. 70–78.

Becker, L. C., and K. Kipnis (eds.). 1984. *Property*. Prentice-Hall, Englewood Cliffs, NJ.

Beckman, T. A. 1971. ''On the Use of Historical Examples in Agassi's 'Sensationalism'.'' *Studies in History and the Philosophy of Science* **1**, No. 4: 293–296.

Begon, M., J. Harper, and C. Townsend. 1986. *Ecology: Individuals, Populations, and Communities*. Sinauer, Sunderland, MA.

Belden, R. C. 1987. ''Florida Panther Recovery Plan Implementation – A 1983 Progress Report.'' In S. D. Miller and D. D. Everett (eds.), pp. 159–172.

Bell, S. S., E. D. McCoy, and H. R. Mushinsky (eds.). 1991. *Habitat Structure: The Physical Arrangement of Objects in Space*. Chapman and Hall, London.

Bentham, J. 1962a. ''Principles of the Civil Code.'' In J. Bowring (ed.), pp. 297–364.

Bentham, J. 1962b. ''Principles of Morals and Legislation.'' In J. Bowring (ed.), pp. 1–154.

Berkowitz, A. R., J. Kolsds, R. H. Peters, and S. T. Pickett. 1989. ''How Far in Space and Time Can the Results from a Single Long-Term Study Be Extrapolated?'' In G. E. Likens (ed.), pp. 192–198.

Bernstein, C., and B. Woodward. 1974. *All the President's Men*. Simon and Schuster, New York.

Berryman, A. A. 1987. ''Equilibrium or Nonequilibrium: Is That the Question?'' *Bulletin of the Ecological Society of America* **68**: 500–502.

Blackstone, W. T. (ed.). 1974. *Philosophy and Environmental Crisis*. University of Georgia Press, Athens, GA.

Blondel, J. 1987. ''From Biogeography to Life History Theory: A Multithematic Approach Illustrated by the Biogeography of Vertebrates.'' *Journal of Biogeography* **14**: 405–422.

Bloor, D. 1983. *Wittgenstein*. Columbia University Press, New York.

Blouin, M., and E. Connor. 1985. ''Is There a Best Shape for Nature Reserves?'' *Biological Conservation* **32**: 277–288.

Boecklen, W. J., and N. J. Gotelli. 1984. ''Island Biogeographic Theory and Conservation Practice: Species–Area or Specious–Area Relationships?'' *Biological Conservation* **29**: 63–80.

Boecklen, W. J., and D. Simberloff. 1987. ''Area-Based Extinction Models in Conservation.'' In D. Elliot (ed.), pp. 247–276.

Boughey, A. S. (ed.). 1969. *Contemporary Readings in Ecology*. Dickenson, Belmont, CA.

Boulding, K. E. 1991. ''Environmental Ethics and the Earth's Economic System.'' In C. Poli and P. Timmerman (eds.), pp. 247–260.

Bowring, J. (ed.). 1962. *The Works of Jeremy Bentham*, Vol. 1. Russell and Russell, New York.

Boxill, B. R. 1984. *Blacks and Social Justice*. Rowman and Allenheld, Totowa, NJ.

Brandon, R. 1990. *Adaptation and Environment*. Princeton University Press, Princeton, NJ.

Brandt, R. (ed.). 1962. *Social Justice*. Prentice-Hall, Englewood Cliffs, NJ.

Braun-Blanquet, J., and E. Furrer. 1913. "Remarques sur l'etude des groupements de plantes." *Bulletin de la Société Languedociennede Géographie* 36: 20–41.

Brewer, R. 1979. *Principles of Ecology.* W. B. Saunders, Philadelphia, PA.

Brewer, R. 1988. *The Science of Ecology.* Saunders College Publications, Philadelphia, PA.

Brown, G. M., Jr. 1990. "Valuation of Genetic Resources." In G. H. Orians, *et al.* (eds.), pp. 203–228.

Brown, G. M., Jr., and J. H. Goldstein. 1984. "A Model for Valuing Endangered Species." *Journal of Environmental Economics and Management* 11: 303–309.

Brown, H. I. 1977. *Perception, Theory and Commitment.* University of Chicago Press, Chicago.

Brown, J. H. 1981. "Two Decades of Homage to Santa Rosalia: Toward a General Theory of Diversity." *American Zoologist* 21: 877–888.

Brown, J. H., and A. Kodric-Brown. 1977. "Turnover Rates in Insular Biogeography: Effect of Immigration on Extinction." *Ecology* 58: 445–449.

Brown, J. H., and M. V. Lomolino. 1989. "Independent Discovery of the Equilibrium Theory of Island Biogeography." *Ecology* 70: 1954–1957.

Brown, P., and H. Shue (eds.). 1981. *Boundaries: National Autonomy and Its Limits.* Rowman and Littlefield, Totowa, NJ.

Burke, R. L., and S. R. Humphrey. 1987. "Rarity as a Criterion for Endangerment in Florida's Fauna." *Oryx* 21: 97–102.

Burkhardt, D., and W. Ittelson (eds.). 1978. *Environmental Assessment of Socioeconomic Systems.* Plenum, New York.

Butts, R., and J. Hintikka (eds.). 1977. *Foundational Problems in the Special Sciences,* Vol. 10. Reidel, Boston.

Cain, S. A. 1947. "Characteristics of Natural Areas and Factors in their Development." *Ecological Monographs* 17: 187–200.

Caldwell, L. K., and K. S. Shrader-Frechette. 1993. *Policy for Land: Ethics and Law.* Rowman and Littlefield, Savage, MD.

Callahan, D. 1971. "What Obligations Do We Have to Future Generations?" *American Ecclesiastical Review* 164, No. 4: 265–268.

Callahan, D. 1973. *The Tyranny of Survival.* Macmillan, New York.

Callahan, D. 1974. "Doing Well by Doing Good: Garrett Hardin's 'Lifeboat Ethic'." *The Hastings Center Report* 4: 1–4.

Callahan, D., and S. Bok. 1980. *The Teachings of Ethics in Higher Education.* The Hastings Center, New York.

Callicott, J. B. 1989. *In Defense of the Land Ethic.* SUNY, Albany.

Campbell, D. T. 1969. "Reforms as Experiments." *American Psychologist* 24 (April): 409–429.

Campbell, D. T. 1975. "Degrees of Freedom and the Case Study." *Comparative Political Studies* 8 (July): 178–193.

Campbell, D. T. 1984. "Forward." In R. K. Yin (ed.), pp. 7–8.

Canfield, J. (ed.). 1986. *The Philosophy of Wittgenstein.* Garland, New York.

Carpenter, J. R. 1939. "The Biome." *American Midland Naturalist* 21: 75–91.

Carson, R. A. 1986. "Case Method." *Journal of Medical Ethics* 12: 36–37.

Cartwright, N. 1983. *How the Laws of Physics Lie.* Clarendon Press, Oxford.

Cartwright, N. 1989a. "Capacities and Abstractions." In P. Kitcher and W. C. Salmon (eds.), pp. 349–356.

Cartwright, N. 1989b. *Nature's Capacities and Their Measurement.* Oxford University Press, Oxford.

Caswell, H. 1976. "Community Structure; A Neutral Model Analysis." *Ecological Monographs* 46: 327–354.

Caughley, G. 1970. "Eruption of Ungulate Populations, with Emphasis on Himalayan Thar in New Zealand." *Ecology* 51: 53–72.

Chapman, J. A., and G. A. Feldhamer (eds.). 1982. *Wild Mammals of North America: Biology, Management, and Economics.* Johns Hopkins University Press, Baltimore, MD.

Chase, A. 1986. *Playing God in Yellowstone.* Atlantic Monthly Press, New York.

Chase, R. A. 1989. "U.S. Forests." *Forum for Applied Research and Public Policy* 4, No. 2 (Summer): 54–56.

Chesson, P. L., and T. J. Case. 1986. "Nonequilibrium Community Theories: Chance, Variability, History, and Coexistence." In J. Diamond and T. J. Case (eds.), pp. 229–239.

Christensen, N. L. 1989. "Wilderness and Natural Disturbance." *Forum for Applied Research and Public Policy* 4, No. 2 (Summer): 46–49.

Christensen, N. L., *et al.* 1989. "Interpreting the Yellowstone Fires of 1988." *BioScience* 39, No. 10 (November): 678–685.

Churchman, C. W. 1947. *Theory of Experimental Inference*. Macmillan, New York.

Clements, F. E. 1905, (1977). *Research Methods in Ecology*. University Publishing Company, Lincoln, NB (reprinted 1977, Arno Press, New York).

Clements, F. E. 1928, (1963). *Plant Succession and Indicators*. Hafner Publishing Company, New York (reprinted 1963, Arno Press, New York).

Clements, F. E. 1936. "Nature and Structure of the Climax." *Journal of Ecology* 24: 252–284.

Clements, F. E., and V. E. Shelford. 1939. *Bio-Ecology*. John Wiley and Sons, New York.

Cody, M. L. 1989. "Discussion: Structure and Assembly of Communities." In J. Roughgarden, *et al.* (eds.), pp. 227–241.

Cody, M. L., and J. M. Diamond (eds.). 1975. *Ecology and Evolution of Communities*. Harvard University Press, Cambridge, MA.

Cohen, J. E. 1978. *Food Webs and Nich Space*. Princeton Monograph in Population Biology. Princeton University Press, Princeton, NJ.

Cohen, R., and L. Laudan, (eds.). 1983. *Physics, Philosophy, and Psychoanalysis*. Reidel, Dordrecht.

Colinvaux, P. 1973. *Introduction to Ecology*. John Wiley and Sons, New York.

Colinvaux, P. A. 1978. *Why Big Fierce Animals are Rare: An Ecologist's Perspective*. Princeton University Press, Princeton, NJ.

Colinvaux, P. A. 1986. *Ecology*. John Wiley and Sons, New York.

Collier, B. D., G. W. Cox, A. W. Johnson, and P. C. Miller. 1973. *Dynamic Ecology*. Prentice-Hall, Englewood Cliffs, NJ.

Collins, J. T. 1991. "A New Taxonomic Arrangement for Some North American Amphibians and Reptiles." *Herpetological Review* 22: 42–43.

Colwell, R. K. 1989. "Natural and Unnatural History: Biological Diversity and Genetic Engineering." In W. R. Shea and B. Sitter (eds.), pp. 1–40.

Commoner, B. 1971. *The Closing Circle*. Knopf, New York.

Connell, J. H. 1978. "Diversity in Tropical Rain Forests and Coral Reefs." *Science* 199: 1302–1310.

Connell, J. H., and W. P. Sousa. 1983. "On the Evidence Needed to Judge Ecological Stability or Persistence." *American Naturalist* 121: 789–824.

Connor, E. F., and E. D. McCoy. 1979. "The Statistics and Biology of the Species–Area Relationship." *American Naturalist* 113: 791–833.

Connor, E. F., and D. Simberloff. 1978. "Species Number and Compositional Similarity of the Galapagos Flora and Avifauna." *Ecological Monographs* 48: 219–248.

Connor, E. F., and D. Simberloff. 1984. "Neutral Models of Species' Co-Occurrence Patterns." In D. R. Strong, *et al.* (eds.), pp. 316–331.

Connor, E. F., and D. Simberloff. 1986. "Competition, Scientific Method, and Null Models in Ecology." *American Scientist* 74: 155–162.

Cook, T. D., and D. T. Campbell. 1979. *Quasi-Experimentation: Design and Analysis Issues for Field Settings*. Rand McNally, Chicago.

Cooke, R. M. 1982. "Risk Assessment and Rational Decision Theory." *Dialectica* 36, No. 4: 330–351.

Cooke, R. M. 1986. "Problems with Empirical Bayes." *Risk Analysis* 6, No. 3: 269–272.

Cooper, A. 1982. "Why Doesn't Anyone Listen to Ecologists – and What Can ESA Do About It?" *Bulletin on the Ecological Society of America* 63: 348.

Cooper, C. 1981. *Economic Evaluation and the Environment*. Hodder and Stoughton, London.

Cooper, G. 1990. "The Explanatory Tools of Theoretical Population Biology." In A. Fine, *et al.* (eds.), Vol. 1, pp. 165–178.

Cornman, J. W. 1980. *Skepticism, Justification, and Explanation.* Reidel, Boston.

Cowles, H. C. 1901. "The Physiographic Ecology of Chicago and Vicinity; A Study of the Origin, Development, and Classification of Plant Societies." *Botanical Gazette* 31: 73–108, 145–182.

Cracraft, J. 1983. "Species Concepts and Speciation Analysis." In R. F. Johnson (ed.), pp. 159–187.

Cracraft, J. 1987. "Species Concepts and the Ontology of Evolution." *Biological Philosophy* 2: 329–346.

Crawley, M. J. 1987. "What Makes a Community Invasible?" *Symposium of the British Ecological Society* 26: 429–453.

Cristoffer, C., and J. Eisenberg. 1985. *On the Captive Breeding and Reintroduction of the Florida Panther in Suitable Habitats.* Unpublished report.

Cronbach, L. J. 1957. "The Two Disciplines of Scientific Psychology." *The American Psychologist* 12: 671–684.

Cronbach, L. J. 1975. "Beyond the Two Disciplines of Scientific Psychology." *The American Psychologist* 30: 116–127.

Cronbach, L. J. 1982. "Prudent Aspirations for Social Inquiry." In *The Social Sciences, their Nature and Uses,* W. H. Kruskal (ed.). University of Chicago Press, Chicago.

Cronbach, L. J. 1986. "Social Theory by and for Earthlings." In *Metatheory in Social Science,* D. Fiske and R. Shweder (eds.). University of Chicago Press, Chicago.

Curtis, J. T. 1959. *The Vegetation of Wisconsin.* University of Wisconsin Press, Madison, WI.

Curtis, J. T., and R. P. McIntosh. 1951. "An Upland Forest Continuum in the Prairie-Forest Border Region of Wisconsin." *Ecology* 32: 476–496.

Dalton, E. 1979. "The Case as Artifact." *Man and Medicine* 4, No. 1: 15–17.

Dasgupta, P. 1990. "Commentary." In G. H. Orians, *et al.* (eds.), pp. 229–232.

Davis, M. B. 1986. "Climatic Instability, Time Lags and Community Disequilibrium." In J. Diamond and T. J. Case (eds.), pp. 269–284.

Dawson, W. R., J. D. Ligon, J. R. Murphy, J. P. Myers, D. Simberloff, and J. Verner. 1987. "Report of the Scientific Advisory Panel on the Spotted Owl." *The Condor* 89: 205–229.

Dayton, P. K. 1979. "Ecology: A Science and a Religion." In R. J. Livingston (ed.), pp. 3–18.

De Angelis, D. L. 1975. "Stability and Connectance in Food Web Models." *Ecology* 56: 238–243.

Denenberg, H., *et al.* 1964. *Risk Insurance.* Prentice-Hall, Englewood Cliffs, NJ.

de Queiroz, K., and D. M. Donoghue. 1988. "Phylogenetic Systematics and the Species Problem." *Cladistics* 4: 317–338.

de Vries, p. 1986. "The Discovery of Excellence." *Journal of Business Ethics* 5: 193–201.

Diamond, J. 1971. "Comparison of Faunal Equilibrium Turnover Rates on a Tropical Island and a Temperate Island." *Proceedings of the National Academy of Sciences* 68: 2742–2745.

Diamond, J. 1975. "The Island Dilemma: Lessons of Modern Biogeographic Studies for the Design of Natural Reserves." *Biological Conservation* 7: 129–145.

Diamond, J. 1976. (Letter to the editor). *Science* 193: 1027–1029.

Diamond, J., and T. J. Case (eds.). 1986a. *Community Ecology.* Harper and Row, New York.

Diamond, J., and T. J. Case. 1986b. "Preface." In J. Diamond and T. J. Case (eds.), pp. ix–xi.

Diamond, J., and T. J. Case. 1986c. "Overview: Introductions, Extinctions, Exterminations, and Invasions." In J. Diamond and T. J. Case (eds.), pp. 65–79.

Diamond, J., and R. M. May. 1976. "Island Biogeography and the Design of Natural Reserves." In R. M. May (ed.), pp. 228–252.

Dice, L. R. 1952. *Natural Communities.* University of Michigan Press, Ann Arbor, MI.

Dilman, I. 1973. *Induction and Deduction.* Blackwell, Oxford.

Dixon, K. R. 1982. "Mountain Lion (*Felix concolor*)." In *Wild Mammals of North America: Biology, Management, and Economics,* J. A. Chapman and G. A. Feldhamer (eds.). Johns Hopkins University Press, Baltimore, MD, pp. 711–727.

Donaldson, T. 1990. "The Case Method." In T. Donaldson and A. R. Gini (eds.), pp. 13–23.

Donaldson, T., and A. R. Gini (eds.). 1990. *Case Studies in Business Ethics*. Prentice-Hall, Englewood Cliffs, NJ.

Drake, J. A. 1988. "Biological Invasions into Nature Reserves." *Trends in Ecology and Evolution* 3: 186–187.

Duda, M. April 1987. *Floridians and Wildlife*. Game and Freshwater Fish Commission, Nongame Wildlife Program, Technical Report No. 2., Tallahassee, FL.

Dunn, C. P., and C. Loehle. 1988. "Species–Area Parameter Estimation: Testing the Null Model of Lack of Relationship." *Journal of Biogeography* 15: 721–728.

Dworkin, R. 1977. *Taking Rights Seriously*. Harvard University Press, Cambridge, MA.

Earman, J. 1978. "The Universality of Laws." *Philosophy of Science* 45: 173–181.

East, R., and G. R. Williams. 1984. "Island Biogeography and the Conservation of New Zealand's Indigenous Forest-Dwelling Avifauna." *New Zealand Journal of Ecology* 7: 27–35.

Edelson, M. 1988. *Psychoanalysis*. University of Chicago Press, Chicago.

Eden, E. 1990a. "Wecology Guides Young Environmentalists." *Focus* 12, No. 2 (Spring): 2.

Eden, M. J. 1990b. *Ecology and Land Management in Amazonia*. Belhanen Press, New York.

Egerton, F. N. 1973. "Changing Concepts in the Balance of Nature." *Quarterly Review of Biology* 48: 322–350.

Egerton, J. 1981. "Appalachia's Absentee Landlords." *The Progressive* 45, No. 6 (June): 43–45.

Ehrlich, P. R., and L. C. Birch. 1967. "The 'Balance of Nature' and 'Population Control'." *American Naturalist* 101: 97–107. (Reprinted in W. E. Hazen (ed.), pp. 395–405.)

Ehrlich, P. R., and J. Roughgarden. 1987. *The Science of Ecology*. Macmillan, New York.

Einstein, A., and L. Infeld. 1947. *The Evolution of Physics*. Cambridge University Press, Cambridge.

Eldredge, N. 1985. *Unfinished Synthesis, Biological Hierarchies and Modern Evolutionary Thought*. Oxford University Press, Oxford.

Eldridge, R. 1987. "Hypotheses, Criterial Claims, and Perspicuous Representations: Wittgenstein's 'Remarks on Frazer's *The Golden Bough*'." *Philosophical Investigations* 10 No. 3 (July): 226–245.

Elfring, C. 1989. "Yellowstone: Fire Storm Over Fire Management." *BioScience* 39, No. 10 (November): 667–672.

Elliot, D. (ed.). 1987. *Dynamics of Extinction*. John Wiley and Sons, New York.

Elsasser, W. M. 1975. *The Chief Abstractions of Biology*. Elsevier, New York.

Elster, J. (ed.). 1986. *Rational Choice*. New York University Press, New York.

Elton, C. 1930. *Animal Ecology and Evolution*. Oxford University Press, New York.

Elton, C. 1958. *The Ecology of Invasions by Animals and Plants*. Methuen, London.

Emden, H. F. van, and G. F. Williams. 1974. "Insect Stability and Diversity in Agro-Ecosystems." *Annual Review of Entomology* 19: 455–475.

Emerson, A. E. 1954. "Dynamic Homeostasis: A Unifying Principle in Organic, Social, and Ethical Evolution." *Scientific Monthly* 78, No. 2: 67–85.

Emerson, R. W. 1910. "The Uses of Natural History." *Journals* 3: 208.

Emlen, J. M. 1973. *Ecology: An Introductory Approach*. Addison-Wesley, Reading, MA.

Emmett, B. A. 1978. "The Distribution of Environmental Quality." In D. Burkhardt and W. Ittelson (eds.), pp. 367–374.

Erman, D. C., and E. P. Pister. 1989. "Ethics and the Environmental Biologist." *Fisheries* 14, No. 2 (March/April): 4–7.

Ervin, K. 1989. *Fragile Majesty*. The Mountaineers, Seattle.

Evans, F. C. 1956. "Ecosystem as the Basic Unit in Ecology." *Science* 123: 1127–1128.

Evans, R. A. 1981. "An Introduction to the Case Method." In *Introduction to Philosophy: A Case Method Approach*, J. B. Rogers, and F. E. Baird (eds.). Harper and Row, New York, pp. xv–xxvi.

Farner, D. S., and J. R. King (eds.). 1971. *Avian Biology*. Academic Press, New York.

Feinberg, J. 1973. *Social Philosophy*. Prentice-Hall, Englewood Cliffs, NJ.

Feinberg, J. 1974. "The Rights of Animals and Unborn Generations." In W. T. Blackstone (ed.), pp. 43–68.

Fernald, R. T. 1989. *Coastal Xeric Scrub Communities of the Treasure Coast Region, Florida*. Florida Department of Natural Resources, Nongame Wildlife Program Technical Report 6. Tallahassee, FL.

Ferson, S., P. Downey, P. Klerks, M. Weissburg, I. Kroot, S. Stewart, G. Jacquez, J. Ssemakula, R. Malenky, and K. Anderson, 1986. "Competing Reviews, or Why Do Connell and Schoener Disagree?" *American Naturalist* 127: 571–576.

Fetzer, J. 1971. "Dispositional Probabilities." In *PSA 1970*, R. Buck and R. Cohen (eds.). Reidel, Dordrecht.

Fetzer, J. 1974a. "A Single Case Propensity Theory of Explanation." *Synthese* 28: 171–198.

Fetzer, J. 1974b. "Statistical Probabilities: Single Case Propensities vs. Long-Run Frequencies." In *Developments in the Methodology of Social Science*. W. Leinfellner and E. Köhler (eds.), Reidel, Dordrecht, pp. 387–397.

Fetzer, J. 1975. "On the Historical Explanation of Unique Events." *Theory and Decision* 6: 87–97.

Fine. A., M. Forbes, and L. Wessels (eds.). 1990. *PSA 1990*. Vols. 1, 2. Philosophy of Science Association, East Lansing, MI.

Fisher, A. C. 1981. *Resources and Environmental Economics*. Cambridge University Press, Cambridge.

Fisher, J., and N. Myers. 1986. "What We Must Do to Save Wildlife." *International Wildlife* 16, No. 3 (May–June): 12–15.

Foell, W. 1978. "Assessment of Energy/Environment Systems." In D. Burkhardt and W. Ittelson (eds.), pp. 183–202.

Forbes, S. A. 1880. "On Some Interactions of Organisms." *Bulletin of the Illinois State Laboratory of Natural History* 1: 3–17.

Ford, R. F., and W. E. Hazen (eds.). 1972. *Readings in Aquatic Ecology*. W. B. Saunders, Philadelphia, PA.

Forest Service Southern Region. 1990. *National Forests in Florida, Facts of FY 1989*. USDA, Washington, DC.

Francoeur, R. T. 1984. "A Structured Approach to Teaching Decision-Making Skills in Biomedical Ethics." *Journal of Bioethics* 5 (Fall/Winter): 145–154.

Frankena, W. 1962. "The Concept of Social Justice." In R. Brandt (ed.), pp. 9–15.

Franklin, A. 1986. *The Neglect of Experiment*. Cambridge University Press, New York.

Franklin, K. 1987. "Endangered Species: Where to From Here?" *American Forests* 93, Nos. 11, 12 (November–December): 57, 58, 60, 74–76.

Fretwell, S. D. 1975. "The Impact of Robert MacArthur on Ecology." *Annual Review of Ecology and Systematics* 6: 1–13.

Frost, D. R., and D. M. Hillis. 1990. "Species in Concept and Practice: Herpetological Applications." *Herpetologica* 46: 87–104.

Fuller, K. 1990. "WWF Works to Save Asia's Large Mammals." *Focus* 12, No. 1: 1, 7.

Futuyma, D. 1973. "Community Structure and Stability in Constant Environments." *American Naturalist* 107: 443–446.

Game, M. 1980. "Best Shape for Nature Reserves." *Nature* 287: 630–632.

Geraets, T. (ed.). 1979. *Rationality Today*. University of Ottawa Press, Ottawa.

Gerell, R. 1985. "Habitat Selection and Nest Predation in a Common Eider Population in Southern Sweden." *Ornis Scandinavica* 16: 129–139.

Gewirth, A. 1982. *Human Rights*. University of Chicago, Chicago.

Ghiselin, M. T. 1969. *The Triumph of the Darwinian Method*. University of California Press, Berkeley, CA.

Ghiselin, M. T. 1974. "A Radical Solution to the Species Problem." *Systematic Zoology* 23: 536–544.

Ghiselin, M. T. 1987. "Species Concepts, Individuality, and Objectivity." *Biology and*

Philosophy 2: 127–143.

Giere, R. N. 1988. *Explaining Science: A Cognitive Approach.* University of Chicago Press, Chicago.

Gilbert, F. S. 1980. "The Equilibrium Theory of Island Biogeography." *Journal of Biogeography* 7: 209–235.

Gilbert, F., and J. Owen. 1990. "Size, Shape, Competition, and Community Structure in Hoverflies (Diptera: Syrphidae)." *Journal of Animal Ecology* 59: 21–39.

Gilpin, M. 1991. "The Genetic Effective Size of a Metapopulation." *Biological Journal of the Linnean Society* 42: 165–175.

Gilpin, M., and J. Diamond. 1984. "Are Species Co-Occurrences on Islands Non-Random, and Are Null Hypotheses Useful in Community Ecology?" In D. R. Strong, *et al.* (eds.), pp. 297–315.

Gini, A. R. 1985. "The Case Method." *Journal of Business Ethics* 4: 351–352.

Gleason, H. A. 1926. "The Individualistic Concept of the Plant Association." *Bulletin of the Torrey Botanical Club* 53: 7–26.

Gleason, H. A. 1939. "The Individualistic Concept of the Plant Association." *American Midland Naturalist* 21: 92–110.

Gleason, H. A. 1952, (1975). "Letter to C. H. Muller." *Bulletin of the Ecological Society of America* 56: 7–10.

Glenn, S. M., and T. D. Nudds. 1989. "Insular Biogeography of Mammals in Canadian Parks." *Journals of Biogeography* 16: 261–268.

Glymour, C. 1980. *Theory and Evidence.* Princeton University Press, Princeton, NJ.

Glymour, C. 1983. "Revisions of Bootstrap Testing." *Philosophy of Science* 50: 626–629.

Glymour, C. 1992. "Realism and the Nature of Theories." In *Introduction to the Philosophy of Science.* M. H. Salmon, J. Earman, C. Glymour, J. G. Lennox, P. Machamer, J. McGuire, J. Norton, W. C. Salmon, K. F. Schaffner (eds.). Prentice-Hall, Englewood Cliffs, N.J., pp. 104–131.

Goldman, A. 1977. "Reparations to Individuals or Groups." In B. Gross (ed.), pp. 322–333.

Goldman, E. A. 1946. "Classification of the Races of the Puma." In S. P. Young and E. A. Goldman (eds.), pp. 177–302.

Goldstein, J. H. 1990. "The Prospects for Using Market Incentives for Conservation of Biological Diversity." In G. H. Orians, *et al.* (eds.), pp. 246–265.

Golley, F. B., and E. Medina (eds.). 1974. *Tropical Ecological Systems.* Springer-Verlag, New York.

Good, I. J. 1983. "The Philosophy of Exploratory Data Analysis." *Philosophy of Science* 50: 283–295.

Goodman, D. 1975. "The Theory of Diversity–Stability Relationships in Ecology." *Quarterly Review of Biology* 50, No. 3: 237–266.

Goodman, D. 1987a. "Considerations of Stochastic Demography in the Design and Management of Biological Reserves." *Natural Resource Modeling* 1: 205–234.

Goodman, D. 1987b. "The Demography of Chance Extinction." In M. E. Soulé (ed.), pp. 11–34.

Gorovitz, S., and A. MacIntyre. 1976. "Toward a Theory of Medical Fallability." *The Journal of Medicine and Philosophy* 1: 51–71.

Goudge, T. 1961. *The Ascent of Life.* University of Toronto Press, Toronto.

Gould, S. J. 1981. *The Mismeasure of Man.* Norton, New York.

Gould, S. J. 1982. "Darwinism and the Expansion of Evolutionary Theory." *Science* 216: 380–387.

Gould, S. J. 1990. "The Golden Rule – A Proper Scale for Our Environmental Crisis." *Natural History* 9 (September): 34–90.

Graham, R. W. 1986. "Response of Mammalian Communities to Environmental Changes During the Late Quaternary." In J. Diamond and T. J. Case (eds.), pp. 300–313.

Grant, P. R. 1986. "Interspecific Competition of Fluctuating Environments." In J. Diamond and T. J. Case (eds.), pp. 173–191.

Gregory, R., R. Mendelsohn, and T. Moore. 1989. "Measuring the Benefits of Endangered Species Preservation: From Research to Policy." *Journal of Environmental Management* 29: 399–408.

Grene, M. and E. Mendelsohn. 1976. *Topics in the Philosophy of Biology*. Vol. 27. Boston Studies in the Philosophy of Science, R. S. Cohen and M. W. Wartofsky (eds.). Reidel, Dordrecht.

Gross, B. (ed.). 1977. *Reverse Discrimination*. Prometheus, Buffalo, NY.

Grumbine, R. E. 1990. "Viable Populations, Reserve Size, and Federal Lands Management: A Critique." *Conservation Biology* 4, No. 2 (June): 127–136.

Grunbaum, A. 1984. *The Foundations of Psychoanalysis*. University of California Press, Berkeley.

Grunbaum, A. 1988. "The Role of the Case Study." *Canadian Journal of Philosophy* 18, No. 4 (December): 623–658.

Guba, E. G., and Y. S. Lincoln. 1981. *Effective Evaluation*. Jossey-Bass, San Francisco.

Gutierrez, R. J., and A. B. Carey (eds.). 1985. *Ecology and Management of the Spotted Owl in the Pacific Northwest*. US Department of Agriculture, Forest Service, Pacific Northwest Forest and Range Experimentation Station, Portland, OR.

Gutting, G. 1982. "Can Philosophical Beliefs Be Rationally Justified?" *American Philosophical Quarterly* 19: 315–330.

Haar, C., and L. Liebman. 1977. *Property and Law*. Little, Brown, and Company, Boston.

Haines-Young, R. H., and J. R. Petch. 1980. "The Challenge of Critical Rationalism for Methodology in Physical Geography." *Progress in Physical Geography* 4: 63–77.

Hairston, N. G. 1969. "On the Relative Abundance of Species." *Ecology* 50: 1091–1094.

Hairston, N. G., F. E. Smith, and L. B. Slobodkin. 1960. "Community Structure, Population Control, and Competition." *American Naturalist* 94: 421–425. (Reprinted in W. E. Hazen (ed.), pp. 382–386.)

Hall, D. J., W. F. Cooper, and E. E. Werner. 1970. "An Experimental Approach to the Production Dynamics and Structure of Freshwater Animal Communities." *Limnology and Oceanography* 15: 839–928.

Hall, E. R. 1981. *The Mammals of North America*. 2nd ed. John Wiley and Sons, New York.

Hampshire, S. 1972. *Morality and Pessimism*. Cambridge University Press, New York.

Hanemann, W. M. 1990. "Commentary." In G. H. Orians, et al. (eds.), pp. 233–238.

Hanski, I. 1989. "Metapopulation Dynamics: Does It Help to Have More of the Same?" *Trends in Ecology and Evolution* 4: 113–114.

Hanski, I., and M. Gilpin. 1991. "Metapopulation Dynamics: Brief History and Conceptual Domain." *Biological Journal of the Linnean Society* 42: 3–16.

Hanson, H. C. 1962. *Dictionary of Ecology*. Philosophical Library, New York.

Hanson, N. R. 1958. *Patterns of Discovery*. Cambridge University Press, Cambridge.

Hansson, L. 1991. "Dispersal and Connectivity in Metapopulations." *Biological Journal of the Linnean Society* 42: 89–103.

Hardin, G. 1968. "The Tragedy of the Commons." *Science* 162 (December 13): 1243–1248.

Harris, L. D. 1984. *The Fragmented Forest. Island Biogeography Theory and the Preservation of Biotic Diversity*. University of Chicago Press, Chicago.

Harris, L. D., and P. B. Gallagher. 1989. "New Initiatives for Wildlife Conservation: The Need for Movement Corridors." In G. MacKintosh (ed.), pp. 11–34.

Harrison, S. 1991. "Local Extinction in a Metapopulation Context: An Empirical Evaluation." *Biological Journal of the Linnean Society* 42: 73–88.

Harsanyi, J. 1975. "Can the Maximim Principle Serve as a Basis for Morality . . ." *American Political Science Review* 69, No. 2: 594ff.

Harsanyi, J. 1977. "Advances in Understanding Rational Behavior." In R. Butts and J. Hintikka (eds.), pp. 315–344.

Harsanyi, J. 1986. "Advances in Understanding Rational Behavior." In J. Elster (ed.), pp. 88ff.

Harvell, D. 1990. "Summary of the Discussion." In G. H. Orians, *et al.* (eds.), pp. 198–202.

Hazen, W. E. (ed.). 1970. *Readings in Population and Community Ecology.* 2nd ed. W. B. Saunders, Philadelphia, PA.

Healy, R. G. 1979. "Land Use and the States." In R. Andrews (ed.), pp. 7–23.

Hempel, C. G. 1965. *Aspects of Scientific Explanation.* Free Press, New York.

Hempel, C. G. 1979. "Scientific Rationality." In T. Geraets (ed.), pp. 45–66.

Hempel, C. G. 1982. "Science and Human Values." In E. Klemke, *et al.* (eds.), pp. 254–268.

Hempel, C. G. 1983. "Valuation and Objectivity in Science." In R. Cohen and L. Laudan (eds.), pp. 73–100.

Henderson, L. J. 1913. *The Fitness of the Environment.* Macmillan, New York.

Henderson, L. J. 1917. *The Order of Nature.* Harvard University Press, Cambridge, MA.

Hengeveld, R. 1988. "Mechanisms of Biological Invasions." *Journal of Biogeography* 15: 819–828.

Hengeveld, R. 1989. *Dynamics of Biological Invasions.* Chapman and Hall, London.

Herbold, B., and P. B. Hoyle. 1986. "Introduced Species and Vacant Niches." *American Naturalist* 128: 751–760.

Hoering, W. 1980. "On Judging Rationality." *Studies in History and the Philosophy of Science* 11, No. 2 (June): 123–136.

Hoffman, W. M., and J. V. Fisher. 1984. "Corporate Responsibility: Property and Liability." In L. C. Becker and K. Kipnis (eds.), pp. 211–220.

Holling, C. S. 1973. "Resilience and Stability of Ecological Systems." *Annual Review of Ecology and Systematics* 4: 1–23.

Hon, G. 1987. "H. Hertz . . . A Case Study of an Experimental Error." *Studies in History and Philosophy of Science* 18, No. 3: 367–382.

Howard, L. O. 1931. "Man and Insects." *Smithsonian Reports (1930)*: 395–399.

Hubbell, S P., and R. B. Foster. 1986. "Biology, Chance, and History and the Structure of Tropical Rain Forest Tree Communities." In J. Diamond and T. J. Case (eds.), pp. 314–329.

Hufschmidt, M. M., *et al.* 1983. *Environment, Natural Systems, and Development: An Economic Valuation Guide.* Johns Hopkins University Press, Baltimore, MD.

Hughson, R., and H. Popper. 1983. "Environmental-Ethics Panel Offers Views and Guidelines." In J. Schaub, *et al.* (eds.), pp. 258–272.

Hull, D. 1974. *The Philosophy of Biological Science.* Prentice-Hall, Englewood Cliffs, NJ.

Hull, D. 1976a. "Central Subjects and Historical Narratives." *History and Theory* 14: 253–274.

Hull, D. 1976b. "Are Species Really Individuals?" *Systematic Zoology* 25: 174–191.

Hull, D. 1978. "A Matter of Individuality." *Philosophy of Science* 45: 335–360.

Hull, D. 1988. *Science as a Process.* University of Chicago Press, Chicago.

Humphreys, P. 1981. "Aleatory Explanation." *Synthese* 48: 225–232.

Humphreys, P. 1982. "Aleatory Explanation Expanded." In *PSA 1982*, Vol. 2, P. Asquith and T. Nickles (eds.). Philosophy of Science Association, East Lansing, MI, pp. 208–223.

Humphreys, P. 1989. "Scientific Explanation." In *Scientific Explanation*, P. Kitcher and W. Salmon (eds.), University of Minnesota Press, Minneapolis.

Humphreys, P. 1991. *The Chances of Explanation.* Princeton University Press, Princeton, NJ.

Hutchinson, G. E. 1948. "Circular Causal Systems in Ecology." *Annuals of the New York Academy of Sciences* 50: 221–246.

Hutchinson, G. E. 1959. "Homage to Santa Rosalia, or Why Are There So Many Kinds of Animals?" *American Naturalist* 93: 145–159. (Reprinted in W. E. Hazen (ed.), pp. 338–351.)

Hutchinson, G. E. 1975. "Variations on a Theme by Robert MacArthur." In M. L. Cody and J. M. Diamond (eds.), pp. 492–521.

Innis, G. 1974. "Stability, Sensitivity, Resilience, Persistence. What is of Interest?" In S. Levin (ed.), pp. 131–139.

Irland, L. C. 1976. "Determining the Value of Forests to Communities and the General Public: The Case of Southern Bottomland Hardwoods." In *25th Annual Forestry Symposium:*

Economics of Southern Forest Resources Management, A. C. Main (ed.). School of Forestry and Wildlife Management, Division of Continuing Education. Louisiana State University, Baton Rouge, pp. 17–38.

Jackson, C. I. 1986. *Honor in Science*. Sigma Xi. The Scientific Research Society, New Haven, CT.

Janzen, D. H. 1968. "Host Plants as Islands in Evolutionary and Contemporary Time." *American Naturalist* 102: 592–595.

Janzen, D. H. 1973. "Tropical Agroecosystems." *Science* 182 (December 21): 1212–1219.

Jarvinen, O. 1984. "Dismemberment of Facts: A Reply to Willis on Subdivision of Reserves." *Oikos* 42: 402–403.

Johansson, P-O. 1987. *The Economic Theory and Measurement of Environmental Benefits*. Cambridge University Press, Cambridge.

Johnson, R. F. (ed.). 1983. *Current Orthinology*. Vol. I. Plenum Press, New York.

Johnson, R. N. 1990. "Commentary." In G. H. Orians, *et al.* (eds.), pp. 264–268.

Jonsen, A. 1986. "Casuistry and Medical Ethics." *Theoretical Medicine* 7: 65–74.

Jordan, C. F., J. R. Kline, and D. S. Sasscer. 1972. "The Relative Stability of Mineral Cycles in Forest Ecosystems." *American Naturalist* 106: 237–253.

Jorling, T. C. 1976. "Incorporating Ecological Principles into Public Policy." *Environmental Policy and Law* 2, No. 3: 140–146.

Joseph, G. 1980. "The Many Sciences and the One World." *Journal of Philosophy* 77: 773–791.

Kahneman, D., *et al.* (eds.). 1982. *Judgment Under Uncertainty: Heuristics and Biases*. Cambridge University Press, Cambridge.

Kahneman, D., and A. Tversky. 1982a. "Availability; A Heuristic for Judging Frequency and Probability." In D. Kahneman, *et al.* (eds.), pp. 63–78.

Kahneman, D., and A. Tversky. 1982b. "Judgment Under Uncertainty." In D. Kahneman, *et al.* (eds.), pp. 4–11.

Kangas, P. C. 1986. "A Method for Predicting Extinction Rates Due to Deforestation in Tropical Life Zones." Abstract, IV International Congress of Ecology, Meeting Program, p. 194.

Kangas, P. C. 1987. "On the Use of Species Area Curves to Predict Extinctions." *Bulletin of the Ecological Society of America* 68: 158–162.

Kant, I. 1964. *Groundwork of the Metaphysics of Morals*. H. J. Paton (trans.). Harper and Row, New York.

Kaplan, A. 1964. *The Conduct of Inquiry: Methodology for Behavioral Science*. Chandler, San Francisco.

Kazdin, A. 1980. *Research Design in Clinical Psychology*. Harper and Row, New York.

Kazdin, A. 1981. "Drawing Valid Inferences from Case Studies." *Journal of Consulting and Clinical Psychology* 49: 183–192.

Kazdin, A. 1982. *Single-Case Research Designs*. Oxford University Press, New York.

Kendeigh, S. C. 1961. *Animal Ecology*. Prentice-Hall, Englewood Cliffs, NJ.

Kenny, W. R., and A. D. Grotelueschen. 1980. *Making the Case for Case Study*. Occasional Paper, Office for the Study of Continuing Professional Education. College of Education, University of Illinois, Urbana-Champaign.

Kent, M. 1987. "Island Biogeography and Habitat Conservation." *Progress in Physical Geography* 11: 91–102.

Kidder, T. 1981. *The Soul of a New Machine*. Little, Brown, Boston.

Kiester, A. 1982. "Natural Kinds, Natural History, and Ecology." In E. Saarinen (ed.), pp. 345–356.

Kingsland, S. E. 1985. *Modeling Nature*. University of Chicago Press, Chicago.

Kitcher, P. 1977. "Remarks on Being the Only Philosopher of Science on Campus." *Teaching Philosophy* 2, No. 2: 115–119.

Kitcher, P. 1985a. *Vaulting Ambition: Sociobiology and the Quest for Human Nature*. MIT Press, Cambridge, MA.

Kitcher, P. 1985b. "Two Approaches to Explanation." *Journal of Philosophy* **82**: 632–639.

Kitcher, P. 1985c. *Species*. MIT Press, Cambridge, MA.

Kitcher, P. 1989. "Explanatory Unification and the Causal Structure of the World." In P. Kitcher and W. C. Salmon (eds.), pp. 410–506.

Kitcher, P., and W. C. Salmon (eds.). 1989. *Scientific Explanation*, Vol. 13, *Minnesota Studies in the Philosophy of Science*. University of Minnesota Press, Minneapolis.

Kitts, D. B., and D. J. Kitts. 1979. "Biological Species as Natural Kinds." *Philosophy of Science* **46**: 613–622.

Kleiman, D. 1989. "Reintroduction of Captive Mammals for Conservation." *BioScience* **39**, No. 3 (March): 152–161.

Klemke, E., R. Hollinger, and A. Kline (eds.). 1982. *Introductory Readings in the Philosophy of Science*. Prometheus, Buffalo, NY.

Knight, C. B. 1965. *Basic Concept of Ecology*. Macmillan, New York.

Knight, D. H., and L. L. Wallace. 1989. "The Yellowstone Fires: Issues in Landscape Ecology." *BioScience* **39**, No. 10 (November): 700–706.

Kogan, M. (ed.). 1986. *Ecological Theory and Integrated Pest Management Practices*. John Wiley and Sons, New York.

Kolata, G. B. 1974. "Theoretical Ecology: Beginnings of a Predictive Science." *Science* **183**: 400–401, 450.

Korchmar, M. 1978. "Radiation Hearings Uncover Dust." *Critica Mass Journal* 3, No. 12: 5–6.

Kormandy, E. J. (ed.). 1965. *Readings in Ecology*. Prentice-Hall, Englewood Cliffs, NJ.

Krebs, C. J. 1972, (1985). *Ecology: The Experimental Analysis of Distribution and Abundance*. 2nd ed. (3rd ed.). Harper and Row, New York.

Kripke, S. 1982. "Wittgenstein on Rules and Private Language." In *Perspectives on the Philosophy of Wittgenstein*, I. Black (ed.). Blackwell, Oxford, pp. 239–296.

Krutilla, J. V., and A. C. Fisher. 1975. *The Economics of Natural Environments: Studies in the Valuation of Commodity and Amenities Resources*. Resources for the Future/Johns Hopkins University Press, Baltimore, MD.

Kuhn, T. 1970. *The Structure of Scientific Revolutions*. University of Chicago Press, Chicago.

Kuhn, T. 1977. *The Essential Tension*. University of Chicago Press, Chicago.

Kunreuther, H., *et al.* 1987. "A Decision-Process Perspective on Risk and Policy Analysis." In R. W. Lake (ed.), pp. 260–274.

Lack, D. 1969. "The Numbers of Bird Species on Islands." *Bird Study* **16**: 193–209.

Lack, D. 1976. *Island Biology Illustrated by the Land Birds of Jamaica*. Blackwell, Oxford.

Lahti, T. 1986. "Island Biogeography and Conservation: A Reply to Murphy and Wilcox." *Oikos* **47**: 388–389.

Laikre, L., and N. Ryman. 1991. "Inbreeding Depression in a Captive Wolf (*Canis lupus*) Population." *Conservation Biology* **5**: 33–40.

Lake, R. W. (ed.). 1987. *Resolving Locational Conflict*. Center for Urban Policy Research, Rutgers, NJ.

Lamb, D. 1977. "Conservation and Management of Tropical Rain-Forest: A Dilemma of Development in Papua New Guinea." *Environmental Conservation* **4**: 121–129.

Lederer, R. J. 1984. *Ecology and Field Biology*. Benjamin/Cummings, Menlo Park, CA.

Legendre, P., S. Dallot, and L. Legendre. 1985. "Succession of Species Within a Community: Chromological Clustering, with Applications to Marine and Freshwater Zooplankton." *American Naturalist* **125**: 257–288.

Leopold, A. 1933. *Game Management*. Scribner's, New York.

Leopold, A. 1949. *A Sand County Almanac*. Oxford University Press, New York.

Leopold, A., and L. Leopold. 1953. *Round River: From the Journals of Aldo Leopold*. Oxford University Press, New York.

Levin, S. (ed.). 1974. *Ecosystem Analysis and Prediction*. Society for Industrial and Applied Mathematics, Philadephia, PA.

Levins, R. 1968a. *Evolution in Changing Environments*. Princeton University Press, Princeton, NJ.

Levins, R. 1968b. "Ecological Engineering." *Quarterly Review of Biology* 43: 301–305.

Levins, R. 1974. "The Qualitative Analysis of Partially Specified Systems." *Annals of the New York Academy of Sciences* 231: 123–138.

Levins, R. 1975. "Evolution in Communities Near Equilibrium." In M. L. Cody and J. M. Diamond (eds.), pp. 16–50.

Levins, R., and R. Lewontin. 1985. *The Dialectical Biologist.* Harvard University Press, Cambridge, MA.

Lewin, R. 1984. "Fragile Forests Implied by Pleistocene Data." *Science* 226: 36–37.

Lewin, R. 1986. "In Ecology, Change Brings Stability." *Science* 234: 1071–1073.

Lewontin, R. 1969. "The Meaning of Stability." In G. Woodwell and H. Smith (eds.), pp. 13–24.

Lichtenberg, J. 1981. "National Boundaries and Moral Boundaries." In P. Brown and H. Shue (eds.), pp. 79–100.

Likens, G. E. (ed.). 1989. *Long-Term Studies in Ecology.* Springer-Verlag, New York.

Lincoln, Y. S., and E. G. Guba. 1985. *Naturalistic Inquiry.* Sage, Newbury Park, CA.

Lindgren, B. W. 1968. *Statistical Theory.* Macmillan, New York.

Little, C. E. 1979. "Preservation Policy and Personal Perception." In R. Andrews (ed.), pp. 83–98.

Livingston, R. J. (ed.). 1979. *Ecological Processes in Coastal Marine Systems.* Plenum Press, New York.

Locke, J. 1960, (1967). *Two Treatises of Government.* Cambridge University Press, Cambridge (2nd ed. 1967).

Loehle, C. 1988. "Philosophical Tools: Potential Contributions to Ecology." *Oikos* 51: 97–104.

Lomolino, M. V. 1990. "The Target Area Hypothesis: The Influence of Island Area on Immigration Rates of Non-Volant Mammals." *Oikos* 57: 297–300.

Longino, H. 1982. "Beyond 'Bad Science,' Skeptical Reflections on the Value-Freedom of Scientific Inquiry." Unpublished essay, done with the assistance of National Science Foundation Grant OSS 8018095.

Longino, H. 1990. *Science as Social Knowledge.* Princeton University Press, Princeton, NJ.

Loope, L. L., P. G. Sanchez, P. W. Tarr, W. L. Loope, and R. L. Anderson. 1988. "Biological Invasions of Arid Land Nature Reserves." *Biological Conservation* 44: 95–118.

Lotka, A. J. 1924, (1956). *Elements of Physical Biology.* Williams and Wilkins, New York (reprinted 1956, Dover, New York).

Lovejoy, T. E., *et al.* 1986. "Edge and Other Effects of Isolation on Amazon Forest Fragments." In M. E. Soulé (ed.), pp. 257–285.

Lovins, A. 1977. *Soft Energy Paths.* Ballinger, Cambridge, MA.

Lovins, A., and J. Price. 1975. *Non-Nuclear Futures.* Harper and Row, New York.

Lubchenko, J., *et al.* 1991. "The Sustainable Biosphere Initiative: An Ecological Research Agenda." *Ecology* 72, No. 2: 371–412.

Lynch, J. F., and N. K. Johnson. 1974. "Turnover and Equilibria in Insular Avifaunas with Special Reference to the California Channel Islands." *Condor* 76: 370–384.

MacArthur, R. 1955. "Fluctuations of Animal Populations, and a Measure of Community Stability," *Ecology* 36: 533–536.

MacArthur, R. 1957. "On the Relative Abundance of Bird Species." *Proceedings of the National Academy of Sciences* 43: 293–295.

MacArthur, R. 1966. "Note on Mrs. Pielou's Comments." *Ecology* 47: 1074.

MacArthur, R. 1971. "Patterns of Terrestrial Bird Communities." In D. S. Farner and J. R. King (eds.), pp. 189–221.

MacArthur, R. 1972. *Geographical Ecology.* Harper and Row, New York.

MacArthur, R., and E. O. Wilson. 1963. "An Equilibrium Theory of Insular Zoogeography." *Evolution* 17: 373–387.

MacArthur, R., and E. O. Wilson. 1967. *The Theory of Island Biogeography.* Princeton University Press, Princeton, NJ.

Macdonald, I. A. W., and G. W. Frame. 1988. "The Invasion of Introduced Species into Nature Reserves in Tropical Savannas and Dry Woodlands." *Biological Conservation* 44: 67–93.

Macfadyen, A. 1963. *Animal Ecology. Aims and Methods.* 2nd ed. Pitman, Bath, UK.

MacKintosh, G. (ed.). 1989. *Preserving Communities and Corridors.* Defenders of Wildlife, Washington, DC.

MacPherson, C. B. 1962. *The Political Philosophy of Possessive Individualism.* Clarendon Press, Oxford.

Maehr, D. S. 1990. "The Florida Panther and Private Lands." *Conservation Biology* 4: 167–170.

Maehr, D. S., R. C. Belden, E. D. Land, and L. Wilkins. 1990. "Food Habits of Panthers in Southwest Florida." *Journal of Wildlife Management* 54: 429–423.

Maguire, B. 1963. "The Passive Dispersal of Small Aquatic Organisms and Their Colonization of Isolated Bodies of Water." *Ecological Monographs* 33: 161–185.

Maguire, B. 1971. "Phytotelmata: Biota and Community Structure Determination in Plant-Held Waters." *Annual Review of Ecology and Systematics* 2: 439–464.

Major, J. 1969. "Historical Development of the Ecosystem Concept." In G. M. VanDyne (ed.), pp. 9–22.

Mares, M. A. 1986. "Conservation in South America: Problems, Consequences, and Solutions." *Science* 233, No. 4765 (August 15): 734–739.

Margules, C., A. Higgs, and R. Rafe. 1982. "Modern Biogeographic Theory: Are There Any Lessons for Nature Reserve Design?" *Biological Conservation* 24: 115–128.

Marsh, C. 1988. *Exploring Data.* Polity Press, Cambridge, UK.

Maurer, B. A. 1987. "Scaling of Biological Community Structure: A Systems Approach to Community Complexity." *Journal of Theoretical Biology* 127: 97–110.

May, R. M. 1972. "Will a Large Complex System Be Stable?" *Nature* 238: 413–414.

May, R. M. 1973. *Stability and Complexity in Model Ecosystems.* Princeton University Press, Princeton, NJ.

May, R. M. 1975a. "Island Biogeography and the Design of Wildlife Preserves." *Nature* 254: 177–178.

May, R. M. 1975b. "Patterns of Species Abundance and Diversity." In M. L. Cody and J. M. Diamond (eds.), pp. 81–120.

May, R. M. (ed.). 1976. *Theoretical Ecology.* Blackwell, Oxford.

May, R. M. 1984. "An Overview: Real and Apparent Patterns in Community Structure." In D. R. Strong *et al.* (eds.), pp. 3–18.

May, R. M. 1986. "The Search for Patterns in the Balance of Nature: Advances and Retreats." *Ecology* 67: 1115–1126.

Mayr, E. 1942. *Systematics and the Origin of Species.* Columbia University Press, New York.

Mayr, E. 1963. *Animal Species and Evolution.* Harvard University Press, Cambridge, MA.

Mayr, E. 1969. *Principles of Systematic Zoology.* McGraw-Hill, New York.

Mayr, E. 1982. *The Growth of Biological Thought: Diversity, Evolution, and Inheritance.* Harvard University Press, Cambridge, MA.

Mayr, E. 1987. "The Ontological Status of Species: Scientific Progress and Philosophical Terminology." *Biology and Philosophy* 2: 145–166.

Mayr, E. 1988. *Toward a New Philosophy of Biology: Observations of an Evolutionist.* Belknap Press, Cambridge, MA.

McBride, R. 1985. *Population Status of the Florida Panther in the Everglades National Park and Big Cypress National Preserve.* Unpublished report.

McClure, J. A. 1989. "A View from Congress." *Forum for Applied Research and Public Policy* 4, No. 2 (Summer): 57–61.

McCoy, E. D. 1982. "The Application of Island Biogeography to Forest Tracts; Problems in Determination of Turnover Rates." *Biological Conservation* 22: 217–227.

McCoy, E. D. 1983. "The Application of Island Biogeographic Theory to Patches of Habitat: How Much Land is Enough?" *Biological Conservation* 25: 53–61.

McCoy, E. D. 1987. "Letter to the Editor, July 1987." *Bulletin of the Ecological Society of America* **68**: 535.

McCoy, E. D., S. Bell, and K. Walters. 1986. "Identifying Biotic Boundaries Along Environmental Gradients." *Ecology* **67**: 749–759.

McCoy, E. D., and H. R. Mushinsky. 1992. "Rarity of Organisms in the Sand Pine Scrub Habitat of Florida." *Conservation Biology* **6**: 537–548.

McCoy, E. D., H. R. Mushinsky, and D. S. Wilson. 1993. "The Compass Orientation of Gopher Tortoise Burrows," in press.

McEvoy, A. F. 1986. *The Fisherman's Problem.* Cambridge University Press, Cambridge.

McGuinness, K. A. 1984. "Equations and Explanations in the Study of Species–Area Curves." *Biological Reviews of the Cambridge Philosophical Society* **59**: 423–440.

McIntosh, R. P. 1976. "Ecology Since 1900." In B. J. Taylor and T. J. White (eds.), pp. 353–372.

McIntosh, R. P. 1980. "The Background and Some Current Problems of Theoretical Ecology." *Synthese* **43**: 195–255.

McIntosh, R. P. 1982. "Some Problems of Theoretical Ecology." In E. Saarinen (ed.), pp. 1–62.

McIntosh, R. P. 1985. *The Background of Ecology: Concept and Theory.* Cambridge University Press, Cambridge.

McIntosh, R. P. 1987. "Pluralism in Ecology." *Annual Review of Ecology and Systematics* **18**: 321–341.

McIntosh, R. P. 1989. "Citation Classics of Ecology." *Quarterly Review of Biology* **64**: 31–49.

McMullin, E. 1983. "Values in Science." In *PSA 1982*, Vol. 2, P. Asquith (ed.). Philosophy of Science Association, East Lansing, MI.

McNab, B. K. 1963. "Bioenergetics and the Determination of Home Range Size." *American Naturalist* **97**: 133–140.

McNaughton, S. J., and L. L. Wolf. 1979. *General Ecology.* Holt, Rinehart, and Winston, New York.

McNeeley, J. A., *et al.* 1990. *Conserving the World's Biodiversity.* IUCN, and WRI, WWF-US, and World Bank, Washington, DC.

Meehl, P. E. 1983. "Subjectivity in Psychoanalytic Inference." In *Testing Scientific Theories*, J. Earman (ed.). University of Minnesota Press, Minneapolis, pp. 349–411.

Merriam, S. 1988. *Case Study Research in Education.* Jossey-Bass, San Francisco.

Meyer, G. February 1975. "Maxey Flats Radioactive Waste Burial Site: Status Report," unpublished report, Advanced Science and Technology Branch, US Environmental Protection Agency, Washington, DC.

Mill, J. S. 1986. *On Liberty.* Prometheus, Buffalo, NY.

Miller, S. D., and D. D. Everett (eds.). 1987. *Cats of the World: Biology, Conservation and Management.* National Wildlife Federation. Washington, DC.

Miller, W. D., W. G. Van Name, and D. Quinn. 1929. *A Crisis in Conservation: Serious Danger of Extinction of Many North American Birds.* Published by the authors, New York.

Millikan, R. A. 1930. "Alleged Sins of Science." *Scribner's Magazine* **87**, No. 2: 119–130.

Minshall, G. W., J. T. Brock, and J. D. Varley. 1989. "Wildfires and Yellowstone's Stream Ecosystems." *BioScience* **39**, No. 10 (November): 707–715.

Mitchell, G. C. 1986. "Vampire Bat Control in Latin America." In G. H. Orians, *et al.* (eds.), pp. 151–164.

Mobius, K. 1877. "Die Auster und die Austernwirtshaft." In *Report of the Commissioner for 1880, Part VIII*, H. J. Rice, (trans.). US Commission of Fish and Fisheries, Washington, DC, pp. 683–751.

Mooney, H. A., and J. A. Drake (eds.). 1986. *Ecology of Biological Invasions of North America and Hawaii.* Springer-Verlag, New York.

Moore, J. C., and H. W. Hunt. 1988. "Resource Compartmentation and the Stability of Real Ecosystems." *Nature* **333**: 261–263.

Morris, D. W. 1988. "Habitat-Dependent Population Regulation and Community Structure."

Evolutionary Ecology 2: 253–269.

Moss, C. E. 1910. "The Fundamental Units of Vegetation: Historical Development of the Concepts of the Plant Association and the Plant Formation." *New Phytologist* 9: 18–53.

Moulton, M. P., and S. L. Pimm. 1986. "Species Introductions to Hawaii." In H. A. Mooney and J. A. Drake (eds.), pp. 231–249.

Mowry, B. 1985. "From Galen's Theory to William Harvey's Theory." *Studies in History and Philosophy of Science* 16 (March): 49–82.

Murdoch, W. W. 1966. "'Community Structure, Population Control, and Competition' – A Critique." *American Naturalist* 100: 219–226. (Reprinted in W. E. Hazen (ed.), pp. 387–399.)

Murphy, D. D. 1989. "Conservation and Confusion: Wrong Species, Wrong Scale, Wrong Conclusions." *Conservation Biology* 3: 82–84.

Murphy, D. D., and B. A. Wilcox. 1986. "On Island Biogeography and Conservation." *Oikos* 47: 385–387.

Murray, B. G., Jr. 1979. *Population Dynamic: Alternative Models*. Academic Press, New York.

Murray, B. G., Jr. 1986. "The Structure of Theory, and the Role of Competition in Community Dynamics." *Oikos* 46: 145–158.

Myers, N. 1983. *A Wealth of Wild Species*. Westview press, Boulder, CO.

Nagel, E. 1961. *The Structure of Science*. Hartcourt, Brace and World, New York.

Nagel, T. 1981. "A Defence of Affirmative Action." *Report from the Center for Philosophy and Public Policy* 1, No. 4 (Fall): 7.

Newell, R. 1986. *Objectivity, Empiricism, and Truth*. Routledge and Kegan Paul, New York.

Newmark, W. D. 1987. "A Land-Bridge Island Perspective on Mammalian Extinctions in Western North American Parks." *Nature* 325: 430–432.

Nicholls, A. O., and C. R. Margules. 1991. "The Design of Studies to Demonstrate the Biological Importance of Corridors." In D. A. Saunders and R. J. Hobbs (eds.), pp. 49–61.

Nichols, T. 1989. "U.S. Parks." *Forum for Applied Research and Public Policy* 4, No. 2 (Summer): 50–53.

Nicholson, A. J. 1933. "The Balance of Animal Populations." *Journal of Animal Ecology* 2: 132–178.

Nicholson, A. J., and V. A. Bailey. 1935. "The Balance of Animal Populations." Part I. *Proceedings of the Zoological Society (London) 1935*: 551–598.

Nitecki, M. H. (ed.). 1981. *Biotic Crises in Ecological and Evolutionary Time*. Academic Press, New York.

Nitecki, M. H., and A. Hoffman (eds.). 1987. *Neutral Models in Biology*. Oxford University Press, New York.

Noll, R. G. 1990. "Commentary." In G. H. Orians, *et al.* (eds.), pp. 269–275.

Norse, E. A. (ed.). 1990. *Ancient Forests of the Pacific Northwest*. Island Press, Washington, DC.

Norton, B. G. (ed.). 1986. *The Preservation of Species: The Value of Biological Diversity*. Princeton University Press, Princeton, NJ.

Norton, B. G. 1987. *The Spice of Life: Why Save Natural Variety?* Princeton University Press, Princeton, NJ.

Norton, B. G. 1988. "Avoiding the Triage Question." *Endangered Species Update* 5: 1–4.

Noss, R. F. 1986. "Dangerous Simplifications in Conservation Biology." *Bulletin of the Ecological Society of America* 67: 278–279.

Noss, R. F. 1987a. "Do We Really Want Diversity?" *Whole Earth Review* 55: 126–128.

Noss, R. F. 1987b. "Corridors in Real Landscapes: A Reply to Simberloff and Cox." *Conservation Biology* 1: 159–164.

Noss, R. F. 1988. "Letter to the Editor, 22 September, 1988." *Bulletin of the Ecological Society of America* 69: 4–5.

Noss, R. F., and L. D. Harris, 1986. "Nodes, Networks, and MUMs: Preserving Diversity at All Scales." *Environmental Management* 10: 299–309.

Nyiri, J., and B. Smith (eds.). 1988. *Practical Knowledge*. Croom Helm, London.

O'Brien, S. J., and E. Mayr. 1991. "Bureaucratic Mischief: Recognizing Endangered Species and Subspecies." *Science* **251**: 1187–1188.

O'Brien, S. J., M. E. Roelke, L. Marker, A. Newman, C. A.Winkler, D. Meltzer, L. Colly, J. F. Evermann, M. Bush, and D. E. Wildt. 1985. "Genetic Basis for Species Vulnerability in the Cheetah." *Science* **227**: 1428–1434.

O'Brien, S. J., M. E. Roelke, N. Yuhki, K. W. Richards, W. E. Johnson, W. L. Franklin, A. E. Anderson, O. L. Bass Jr., R. C. Belden, and J. S. Martenson. 1990. "Genetic Introgression within the Florida Panther *Felis concolor coryi.*" *National Geographic Research* **6**: 485–494.

Odum, E. P. 1953. *Fundamentals of Ecology*. Saunders, Philadelphia, PA.

Odum, E. P. 1963. *Ecology*. Holt, Rinehart, and Winston, New York.

Odum, E. P. 1964. "The New Ecology." *BioScience* **14**, No. 7: 14–16.

Odum, E. P. 1969. "The Strategy of Ecosystem Development." *Science* **164**: 262–270.

Odum, E. P. 1977. "The Emergence of Ecology as a New Integrative Discipline." *Science* **195**: 1289–1293.

Odum, E. P. 1989. *Ecology and Our Endangered Life-Support Systems*. Sinauer Associates, Sunderland, MA.

Oksanen, L. 1988. "Ecosystem Organization: Mutualism and Cybernetics or Plain Darwinian Struggle for Existence?" *American Naturalist* **131**: 424–444.

Olding, A. 1978. "A Defence of Evolutionary Laws." *British Journal for the Philosophy of Science* **29**: 131–143.

Omi, P. N. 1989. "Lessons from Fires of 1988." *Forum for Applied Research and Public Policy* **4**, No. 2 (Summer): 41–45.

O'Neill, R. V., D. L. De Angelis, J. B. Waide, and T. F. H. Allen. 1986. *A Hierarchical Concept of Ecosystems*. Princeton University Press, Princeton, NJ.

Oosting, H. J. 1958. *The Study of Plant Communities*. W. H. Freeman and Company, San Francisco.

Orians, G. H. 1975. "Diversity, Stability and Maturity in Natural Ecosystems." In W. H. VanDobben and R. H. Lowe-McConnell (eds.), pp. 139–150.

Orians, G. H. 1986. "Site Characteristics Favoring Invasions." In H. A. Mooney and J. A. Drake (eds.), pp. 133–148.

Orians, G. H., J. Buckley, W. Clark, M. Gilpin, C. Jordan, J. Lehman, R. May, G. Robilliard, D. Simberloff, W. Erckmann, D. Policansky, and N. Grossblatt. 1986. *Ecological Knowledge and Environmental Problem Solving*. National Academy Press, Washington, DC.

Orians, G. H., G. M. Brown, Jr., W. E. Kunin, and J. E. Swierzbinski (eds.). 1990. *The Preservation and Valuation of Biological Resources*. University of Washington Press, Seattle.

Otway, H., and M. Peltu (eds.). 1985. *Regulating Industrial Risks*. Butterworths, London.

Ovington, J. D. 1962. "Quantitative Ecology and the Woodland Ecosystem Concept." *Advances in Ecological Research* **1**: 103–192.

Pahor, S. 1985. "On the $-3/2$ Power Thinning Law in Plant Ecology." *Journal of Theoretical Biology* **112**: 535–537.

Paine, R. T. 1966. "Food Web Complexity and Species Diversity." *American Naturalist* **100**: 65–75.

Paine, R. T. 1969. "A Note on Trophic Complexity and Community Stability." *American Naturalist* **103**: 91–93.

Paine, R. T., and S. A. Levin. 1981. "Intertidal Landscapes: Disturbance and the Dynamics of Pattern." *Ecological Monographs* **51**: 145–178.

Parker, G. G. 1989. "Are Currently Available Statistical Methods Adequate for Long-Term Studies?" In G. E. Likens (ed.), pp. 199–200.

Patten, B. C. 1962. "Species Diversity in Net Phytoplankton of Raritan Bay" *Journal of Marine Research* **20**: 57–75.

Peacocke, C. 1986. "Reply." In J. Canfield (ed.), pp. 274–297.

Pearce, W. D. 1976. *Environmental Economics*. Longmans, London.

Pearsall, S. H. 1984. "*In Absentia* Benefits of Nature Preserves." *Environmental Conservation*

11, No. 1 (Spring): 3–9.

Peltu, M. 1985. "The Role of Communications Media." In H. Otway and M. Peltu (eds.), pp. 132–136.

Peters, R. H. 1982. "Useful Concepts for Predictive Ecology." In E. Saarinen (ed.), pp. 215–228.

Peters, R. H. 1991. *A Critique for Ecology*. Cambridge University Press, Cambridge.

Peterson, G. L., and A. Randall. 1984. *Valuation of Wildlife Resource Benefits*. Westview Press, Boulder, CO.

Petraitis, P. S., R. E. Latham, and R. A. Niesenbaum. 1989. "The Maintenance of Species Diversity by Disturbance." *Quarterly Review of Biology* 64: 393–418.

Phillips, D. C. 1976. *Philosophy, Science, and Social Inquiry*. Pergamon, New York.

Pianka, E. R. 1978, (1988). *Evolutionary Ecology*. 2nd ed. (4th ed.). Harper and Row, New York.

Picardi, E. 1988. "Meaning and Rules." In J. Nyiri and B. Smith (eds.), pp. 90–121.

Pickett, S. T. A., J. Kolasa, J. J. Armesto, and S. L. Collins. 1989. "The Ecological Concept of Dispersal and its Expression at Various Hierarchical Levels." *Oikos* 54: 129–136.

Pickett, S. T. A., and J. N. Thompson. 1978. "Patch Dynamics and the Design of Nature Reserves." *Biological Conservation* 13: 27–37.

Pickett, S. T. A., and P. S. White (eds.). 1985. *The Ecology of Natural Disturbance and Patch Dynamics*. Academic Press, New York.

Pielou, E. C. 1974. *Population and Community Ecology: Principles and Methods*. Gordon and Breach, New York.

Pielou, E. C. 1981. "The Broken-Stick Model: A Common Misunderstanding." *American Naturalist* 117: 609–610.

Pimentel, D. 1961. "Species Diversity and Insect Population Outbreaks." *Annals of the Entomological Society of America* 54: 76–86,

Pimm, S. L. 1982. *Food Webs*. Chapman and Hall, London.

Pimm, S. L. 1984. "The Complexity and Stability of Ecosystems." *Nature* 307: 321–326.

Pimm, S. L. 1991. *The Balance of Nature? Ecological Issues in the Conservation of Species and Communities*. University of Chicago Press, Chicago.

Pimm, S. L., and A. Redfern. 1988. "The Variability of Population Densities." *Nature* 334: 613–614.

Plantinga, A. 1974. *The Nature of Necessity*. Oxford University Press, Oxford.

Poirot, E. M. 1964. *Our Margin of Life*. Vantage Press, New York.

Polanyi, M. 1959. *The Study of Man*. University of Chicago Press, Chicago.

Polanyi, M. 1964. *Personal Knowledge*. Harper and Row, New York.

Poli, C., and P. Timmerman (eds.). 1991. *Ethics and Environmental Policies: First International Conference*. Fondazione, Lanza, Padua.

Popper, H., and R. Hughson. 1983. "How Would You Apply Engineering Ethics to Environmental Problems?" In J. Schaub, *et al.* (eds.), pp. 252–257.

Popper, K. 1950. *The Open Society and Its Enemies*. Princeton University Press, Princeton.

Popper, K. 1965. *The Logic of Scientific Discovery*. Harper and Row, New York.

Post, D. 1986. "Jeffersonian Revisions of Locke." *Journal of the History of Ideas* 47: 147–157.

Potier, M. 1990. "Towards Better Integration of Environmental, Economic, and Other Governmental Policies." In N. Akerman (ed.), pp. 69–81.

Prescott-Allen, R. 1986. *National Conservation Strategies and Biological Diversity*. Report to IUCN, Gland, Switzerland.

Pulliam, R. 1988. "Sources, Sinks, and Population Regulation." *American Naturalist* 132: 653–661.

Pyne, S. J. 1989. "Burning Questions and False Alarms About Wildfires at Yellowstone." *Forum for Applied Research and Public Policy* 4, No.2 (Summer): 31–40.

Quinn, J. F., and A. E. Dunham. 1983. "On Hypothesis Testing in Ecology and Evolution." *American Naturalist* 122: 602–617.

Quinn, J. F., C. L. Wolin, and M. L. Judge. 1989. "An Experimental Analysis of Patch Size,

Habitat Subdivision, and Extinction in a Marine Intertial Snail." *Conservation Biology* 3: 242–251.

Raab, P. V. 1980. "Equilibrium Theory and Paleoecology." *Lethaia* 13: 175–181.

Rabinowitz, D., S. Cairns, and T. Dillon. 1986. "Seven Forms of Rarity and Their Frequency in the Flora of the British Isles." In M. E. Soulé (ed.), pp. 182–204.

Rachels, J. 1980. "Euthanasia." In T. Regan (ed.), pp. 28–66.

Railton, P. 1980. *Explaining Explanation*. Ph.D. Dissertation, Princeton University.

Railton, P. 1981. "Probability, Explanation, and Information." *Synthese* 48: 233–256.

Raloff, J. 1989. "Endangered Species Need More Help." *Science News* 135, No. 5 (February 4): 79.

Raloff, J., and J. Silberner. 1986. "Chernobyl: Emerging Data on Accident." *Science News* 129: 292–293.

Rambler, M., L. Margulis, and R. Fester. 1988. *Global Ecology*. Academic Press, New York.

Ramensky, L. G. 1926. "Die Grundgesetzmassigkeiten im aufbau der Vegetationsdecke." *Botanische Centralblatt N.F.* 7: 453–455.

Rapport, D. J. 1989. "What Constitutes Ecosystem Health?" *Perspectives in Biology and Medicine* 33, No. 1: 120–132.

Rasmussen, N. C. 1981. "Methods of Hazard Analysis and Nuclear Safety Engineering." In *The Three Mile Island Nuclear Accident*, T. Moss and D. Sills (eds.). New York Academy of Sciences, New York.

Raup, D. M., and D. Jablonski (eds.). 1986. *Patterns and Processes in the History of Life*. Springer-Verlag, Berlin.

Rawls, J. 1971. *A Theory of Justice*. Harvard University Press, Cambridge, MA.

Rawls, J. 1974. "Some Reasons for the Maximin Criterion." *American Economic Review* 64 (May): 141–146.

Reddingius, J., and P. J. den Boer. 1970. "Simulation Experiments Illustrating Stabilization of Animal Numbers by Spreading of Risk." *Oecologia* 5: 240–284.

Reed, T. M. 1983. "The Role of Species–Area Relationships in Reserve Choice: A British Example." *Biological Conservation* 25: 263–271.

Regan, T. (ed.). 1980. *Matters of Life and Death*. Random House, New York.

Regan, T. 1983. *The Care for Animal Rights*. University of California Press, Los Angeles.

Reichenbach, H. 1956. *The Direction of Time*. University of California Press, Berkeley.

Rescher, N. (ed.). 1986. *Current Issues in Telology*. University of Pittsburg Press, Pittsburg.

Rescher, N. (ed.). 1990. *Evolution, Cognition, and Realism*. University Press of America, Lanham, MA.

Rey, J. R. 1981. "Ecological Biogeography of Arthropods on *Spartina* Islands in Northwest Florida." *Ecological Monographs* 51: 237–265.

Rey, J. R. 1985. "Insular Ecology of Salt Marsh Arthropods: Species Level Patterns." *Journal of Biogeography* 12: 97–107.

Rey, J. R., and E. D. McCoy. 1979. "The Application of Island Biogeographic Theory to the Pests of Cultivated Crops." *Environmental Entomology* 8: 577–582.

Ricklefs, R. E. 1973. *Ecology*. Chiron Press, Newton, MA.

Ricklefs, R. E. 1987. "Community Diversity: Relative Roles of Local and Regional Processes." *Science* 235: 167–171.

Robinson, E. R., and J. F. Quinn. 1988. "Extinction, Turnover, and Species Diversity in an Experimentally Fragmented California Annual Grassland." *Oecologia* 76: 71–82.

Roelke, M. E., E. R. Jacobsen, G. V. Kollias, and J. Forrester. 1985. *Medical Management and Biomedical Findings on the Florida Panther, Felis concolor coryi, July 1, 1983 to June 30, 1985*. Appendix I, Panther Health and Reproduction Annual Performance Report E-1-9. Florida Game and Fresh Water Fish Commission, Tallahassee, FL.

Rolston, H. 1986. *Philosophy Gone Wild*. Prometheus, Buffalo, NY.

Romesburg, C. 1981. "Wildlife Science: Gaining Reliable Knowledge." *Journal of Wildlife Management* 45: 293–313.

Romme, W. H., and D. G. Despain. 1989a. "The Yellowstone Fires." *Scientific American* **261**: 36–44, 46.

Romme, W. H., and D. G. Despain. 1989b. "Historical Perspective on the Yellowstone Fires of 1988." *BioScience* **39**, No. 10 (November): 695–699.

Rosen, D. E. 1978. "Vicariant Patterns and Historical Explanation in Biogeography." *Systematic Zoology* **27**: 159–188.

Rosen, D. E. 1979. "Fishes from the Uplands and Intermontane Basin of Guatemala: Revisionary Studies and Comparative Geography." *Bulletin of the American Museum of Natural History* **162**: 267–376.

Rosenberg, A. 1978. "Supervenience of Biological Concepts." *Philosophy of Science* **45**: 368–386.

Rosenberg, A. 1985. *The Structure of Biological Science*. Cambridge University Press, Cambridge.

Rosenzweig, M. L. 1976. "Review of: Golley, F. B., K. Petrusekwicz and L. Ryskowski (eds.), *Small Mammals*." *Science* **192**: 778–779.

Roughgarden, J. 1989. "The Structure and Assembly of Communities." In J. Roughgarden, et al. (eds.), pp. 293–326.

Roughgarden, J., and J. Diamond. 1986. "Overview: The Role of Species Interactions in Community Ecology." In J. Diamond and T. J. Case (eds.), pp. 333–343.

Roughgarden, J., R. M. May, and S. A. Levin (eds.). 1989. *Perspectives in Ecological Theory*. Princeton University Press, Princeton, NJ.

Ruse, M. 1971. "Narrative Explanation and the Theory of Evolution." *Canadian Journal of Philosophy* **1**: 59–74.

Ruse, M. 1973. *The Philosophy of Biology*. Hutchinson, London.

Ruse, M. 1984. *Sociobiology: Sense or Nonsense*. Reidel, Boston.

Ruse, M. (ed.). 1989. *What the Philosophy of Biology Is: Essays Dedicated to David Hull*. Kluwer Academic Publishers, Dordrecht, The Netherlands.

Russett, C. E. 1966. *The Concept of Equilibrium in American Social Thought*. Yale University Press, New Haven, CT.

Rutledge, R. W., B. L. Basore, and R. J. Mulholland. 1976. "Ecological Stability: An Information Theory Viewpoint." *Journal of Theoretical Biology* **57**: 355–371.

Saarinen, E. (ed.). 1982. *Conceptual Issues in Ecology*. Reidel, Boston.

Sagoff, M. 1980. "On the Preservation of Species." *Columbia Journal of Environmental Law* **7**: 51ff.

Sagoff, M. 1985a. "Fact and Value in Environmental Science." *Environmental Ethics* **7**, No. 2 (Summer): 99–116.

Sagoff, M. 1985b. "Environmental Science and Environmental Law." College Park, Maryland, Center for Philosophy and Public Policy. Unpublished essay.

Salmon, W. 1984. *Scientific Explanation and the Causal Structure of the World*. Princeton University Press, Princeton, NJ.

Salmon, W. 1989. "Four Decades of Scientific Explanations." In P. Kitcher and W. C. Salmon (eds.), pp. 3–219.

Salt, G. W. 1979. "A Comment on the Use of the Term *Emergent Properties*." *American Naturalist* **113**: 145–148.

Salt, G. W. (ed.). 1984. *Ecology and Evolutionary Biology*. University of Chicago Press, Chicago.

Salwasser, H. 1986. "Conserving a Regional Spotted Owl Population." In G. H. Orians, et al. (eds.), pp. 227–247.

Santos, S. L., and S. A. Bloom. 1980. "Stability in an Annually Defaunated Estuarine Soft-Bottom Community." *Oecologia* **46**: 290–294.

Sattler, R. 1986. *Biophilosophy: Analytic and Holistic Perspectives*. Springer-Verlag, New York.

Saunders, D. A., and R. J. Hobbs (eds.). 1991. *Nature Conservation 2; The Role of Corridors*. Surrey Beatty and Sons, Chipping Norton, Australia.

Savage, H. M. 1983. "The Shape of Evolution." *Biological Journal of the Linnean Society* **20**: 225–244.

Sawyer, J. 1989. "Biodiversity: A Conservation Imperative." *The New World* **8** (January–March): 4–5.

Schaub, J., K. Pavlovic, M. Morris (eds.). 1983. *Engineering Professionalism and Ethics*. John Wiley and Sons, New York.

Schelling, T. 1984. *Choice and Consequence*. Harvard University Press, Cambridge, MA.

Scherer, D., and T. Attig (eds.). 1983. *Ethics and the Environment*. Prentice-Hall, Englewood Cliffs, NJ.

Schlick, M. 1949. "Causality in Everyday Life and in Recent Science." In *Readings in Philosophical Analysis*, H. Feigel and W. Sellars (eds.). Appleton-Century Crafts, NY.

Schoener, A. 1974a. "Experimental Zoogeography: Colonization of Marine Mini-Islands." *American Naturalist* **108**: 715–738.

Schoener, A. 1974b. "Colonization Curves for Planar Marine Islands." *Ecology* **55**: 818–827.

Schoener, T. W. 1972. "Mathematical Ecology and Its Place among the Sciences." *Science* **178**: 389–391.

Schoener, T. W. 1988. "Testing for Non-Randomness in Sizes and Habitats of West Indian Lizards: Choice of Species Pool Affects Conclusions from Null Models." *Evolutionary Ecology* **2**: 1–26.

Schullery, P. 1989. "The Fires and Fire Policy." *BioScience* **39**, No. 10 (November): 686–694.

Scriven, M. 1982. "The Exact Role of Value Judgments in Science." In E. Klemke, *et al.* (eds.), pp. 269–291.

Sellars, W. 1967. *Philosophical Perspectives*. Charles Thomas, Springfield, IL.

Shackle, G. L. S. 1972. *Epistemics and Economics*. Cambridge University Press, Cambridge.

Shaffer, M. L. 1985. "The Metapopulation and Species Conservation: The Special Case of the Northern Spotted Owl." In R. J. Gutierrez and A. B. Carey (eds.), pp. 86–99.

Shea, W. R., and B. Sitter (eds.). 1989. *Scientists and Their Responsibility*. Watson, Canton, MA.

Shelford, V. E. 1963. *The Ecology of North America*. University of Illinois Press, Urbana, IL.

Shrader-Frechette, K. S. 1980. "Recent Changes in the Concept of Matter: How Does 'Elementary Particle' Mean?" In *PSA 1980*, Vol. 1, P. D. Asquith and R. N. Giere (eds.), Philosophy of Science Association, East Lansing, MI, pp. 302–316.

Shrader-Frechette, K. S. 1981. *Environmental Ethics*. Boxwood, Pacific Grove, CA.

Shrader-Frechette, K. S. 1983. *Nuclear Power and Public Policy*. 2nd ed. Reidel, Boston.

Shrader-Frechette, K. S. 1985a. *Science Policy, Ethics, and Economic Methodology*. Reidel, Boston.

Shrader-Frechette, K. S. 1985b. *Risk Analysis and Scientific Method*. Reidel, Boston.

Shrader-Frechette, K. S. 1986. "Organismic Biology and Ecosystems Ecology: Description or Explanation?" In N. Rescher (ed.), pp. 77–92.

Shrader-Frechette, K. S. 1989a. "Idealized Laws, Anti-Realism, and Applied Science: A Case in Hydrogeology." *Synthese* **81**: 329–352.

Shrader-Frechette, K. S. 1989b. "Scientific Method and the Objectivity of Epistemic Value Judgments." In *Logic, Methodology, and the Philosophy of Science* (Series: *Studies in Logic and the Foundations of Mathematics*), J. Fenstad, R. Hilpinen, and I. Frolov (eds.). Elsevier Science Publishers, New York, pp. 373–389.

Shrader-Frechette, K. S. 1989c. "Ecological Theories and Ethical Imperatives." In W. R. Shea and B. Sitter (eds.), pp. 73–104.

Shrader-Frechette, K. S. 1990a. "Island Biogeography, Species–Area Curves, and Statistical Errors: Applied Biology and Scientific Rationality." In *PSA 1990*, Vol. 1, A. Fine, M. Forbes, and. L. Wessels (eds.). Philosophy of Science Association, East Lansing, MI, pp. 447–456.

Shrader-Frechette, K. S. 1990b. "Interspecific Competition, Evolutionary Epistemology, and Ecology." In N. Rescher (ed.), pp. 47–62.

Shrader-Frechette, K. S. 1991. *Risk and Rationality*. University of California Press, Berkeley.

Shrader-Frechette, K. S. 1993. *Burying Uncertainty: Risk and the Case Against Geological Disposal of Nuclear Waste.* University of California Press, Berkeley.

Shrader-Frechette, K. S., and E. D. McCoy. 1990. "Theory Reduction and Explanation in Ecology." *Oikos* **58**: 109–114.

Shrader-Frechette, K. S., and E. D. McCoy. 1992. "Statistics, Costs and Rationality in Ecological Inference." *Trends in Evolution and Ecology* **7**, No. 3 (March): 96–99.

Shue, H. 1981. "Exporting Hazards." In P. Brown and H. Shue (eds.)., pp. 107–145.

Shugart, H. H., Jr., and D. C. West. 1981. "Long-Term Dynamics of Forest Ecosystems." *American Scientist* **69**: 647–652.

Silvertown, J. 1987. "Ecological Stability: A Test Case." *American Naturalist* **130**: 807–810.

Simberloff, D. 1970. "The Taxonomic Diversity of Island Biotas." *Evolution* **24**: 22–47.

Simberloff, D. 1974. "Equilibrium Theory of Island Biogeography and Ecology." *Annual Review of Ecology and Systematics* **5**: 161–182.

Simberloff, D. 1976a. "Species Turnover and Equilibrium Island Biogeography." *Science* **194**: 572–578.

Simberloff, D. 1976b. "Experimental Zoogeography of Islands: Effects of Island Size." *Ecology* **57**: 629–648.

Simberloff, D. 1980. "A Succession of Paradigms in Ecology: Essentialism to Materialism and Probabilism." *Synthese* **43**: 3–39.

Simberloff, D. 1981. "Community Effects of Introduced Species." In M. H. Nitecki (ed.), pp. 53–81.

Simberloff, D. 1982. "A Succession of Paradigms in Ecology: Essentialism to Materialism and Probabilism." In E. Saarinen (ed.), pp. 62–100.

Simberloff, D. 1983. "Competition Theory, Hypothesis Testing, and Other Community Ecological Buzzwords." *American Naturalist* **122**: 626–635.

Simberloff, D. 1986a. "Introduced Insects: A Biogeographic and Systematic Perspective." In H. A. Mooney and J. A. Drake (eds.), pp. 3–26.

Simberloff, D. 1986b. "Design of Nature Reserves." In M. B. Usher (ed.), pp. 315–337.

Simberloff, D. 1986c. "Island Biogeographic Theory and Integrated Pest Management." In *Ecological Theory and Integrated Pest Management Practice*, M. Cogan, (ed.). John Wiley and Sons, New York, pp. 19–35.

Simberloff, D. 1986d. "The Proximate Causes of Extinction." In D. M. Raup and D. Jablonski (eds.), pp. 259–276.

Simberloff, D. 1987. "Simplification, Danger, and Ethics in Conservation Biology." *Bulletin of the Ecological Society of America* **68**: 156–157.

Simberloff, D., and L. G. Abele. 1976. "Island Biogeography Theory and Conservation Practice." *Science* **191**: 285–286.

Simberloff, D., and L. G. Abele. 1982. "Refuge Design and Island Biogeographic Theory: Effects of Fragmentation." *American Naturalist* **120**: 41–50.

Simberloff, D., and L. G. Abele. 1984. "Conservation and Obfuscation: Subdivision of Reserves." *Oikos* **42**: 399–401.

Simberloff, D., and J. Cox. 1987. "Consequences and Costs of Conservation Corridors." *Conservation Biology* **1**: 63–71.

Simberloff, D., J. A. Farr, J. Cox, and D. W. Mehlman. 1992. "Movement Corridors: Conservation Bargains or Poor Investments?" *Conservation Biology* **6**: 493–504.

Simberloff, D., and N. Gotelli. 1984. "Effects of Insularization on Plant Species Richness in the Prairie-Forest Ecotone." *Biological Conservation* **29**: 27–46.

Simberloff, D., K. L. Heck, E. D. McCoy, and E. F. Connor. 1981. "There Have Been No Statistical Tests of Cladistic Biogeographical Hypotheses." In *Vicariance Biogeography: A Critique*, G. Nelson and D. Rosen (eds.). Columbia University Press, NY, pp. 40–63.

Simberloff, D., and E. O. Wilson. 1969. "Experimental Zoogeography of Islands: The Colonization of Empty Islands." *Ecology* **50**: 278–296.

Simberloff, D., and E. O. Wilson. 1970. "Experimental Zoogeography of Islands: A Two-year Record of Colonization." *Ecology* **51**: 934–937.

Simpson, G. G. 1961. *The Principles of Animal Taxonomy.* Columbia University Press, New York.

Simpson, G. G. 1964. *This View of Life. The World of an Evolutionist.* Harcourt, Brace and World, New York.

Sinden, J., and A. Worrell. 1979. *Unpriced Values: Decisions without Market Prices.* John Wiley and Sons, New York.

Singer, F. J., *et al.* 1989. "Drought, Fires, and Large Mammals." *BioScience* 39, No. 10 (November): 716–722.

Sjogren, P. 1991. "Extinction and Isolation Gradients in Metapopulations: The Case of the Pool Frog (*Rana lessonae*)." *Biological Journal of the Linnean Society* 42: 135–147.

Skolimowski, H. 1974. "Problems of Rationality in Biology." In F. Ayala and T. Dobzhansky (eds.), pp. 205–224.

Sloep, P. B. 1990. "Methodology Revitalized?" Unpublished manuscript.

Slovic, P., *et al.* 1982. "Facts Versus Fears." In D. Kahneman, *et al.* (eds.), pp. 463–489.

Smart, J. J. C. 1963. *Philosophy and Scientific Realism.* Routledge and Kegan Paul, London.

Smith, B. 1988. "Knowing How Vs. Knowing That." In J. Nyiri and B. Smith (eds.), pp. 1–16.

Smith, H. M. 1990. "The Universal Species Concept." *Herpetologica* 46: 122–124.

Smith, R. L. 1980. *Ecology and Field Biology.* 3rd ed. Harper and Row, New York.

Smith, R. L. 1986. *Elements of Ecology.* 2nd ed. Harper and Row, New York.

Sneed, J. D. 1971. *The Logical Structure of Mathematical Physics.* Reidel, Dordrecht.

Sober, E. 1981. "Revisability, A Priori Truth, and Evaluation." *Australasian Journal of Philosophy* 59: 68–85.

Sober, E. 1986. "Philosophical Problems for Environmentalism." In B. G. Norton (ed.), pp. 173–194.

Sober, E. 1987. "Parsimony, Likelihood, and the Principle of the Common Cause." *Philosophy of Science* 54: 465–469.

Sober, E. 1988a. *Reconstructing the Past: Parsimony, Evolution, and Inference.* MIT Press, Cambridge, MA.

Sober. E. 1988b. "The Principle of the Common Cause." In *Probability and Causality*, J. Fetzer (ed.). Reidel, Boston, pp. 211–228.

Sobetzer, J. G. 1979. "American Land and Law." In R. Andrews (ed.), pp. 213–218.

Sokal, P., and P. Sneath. 1963. *Principles of Numerical Taxonomy.* Freeman, San Francisco.

Soper, P. 1983. "'Taking' Issues." In D. Scherer and T. Attig (eds.), pp. 113–129.

Soulé, M. E. 1980. "Thresholds for Survival: Maintaining Fitness and Evolutionary Potential." In M. Soulé and B. Wilcox (eds.), pp. 151–169.

Soulé, M. E. 1986a. "Conservation Biology and the 'Real World'." In M. E. Soulé (ed.), pp. 1–12.

Soulé, M. E. (ed.). 1986b. *Conservation Biology: The Science of Scarcity and Diversty.* Sinauer, Sunderland, MA.

Soulé, M. E. (ed.). 1987. *Viable Populations for Conservation.* Cambridge University Press, Cambridge, UK.

Soulé, M. E. 1989. "Conservation Biology in the Twenty-First Century: Summary and Outlook." In D. Western and M. C. pearl (eds.), pp. 297–303.

Soulé, M. E. and K. A. Kohm (eds.). 1989. *Research Priorities for Conservation Biology.* The Society for Conservation Biology, Island Press, Washington, DC.

Soulé, M. E., and D. Simberloff. 1986. "What Do Genetics and Ecology Tell Us About the Design of Nature Reserves?" *Biological Conservation* 35: 19–40.

Soulé, M. E., and B. A. Wilcox (eds.). 1980. *Conservation Biology.* Sinauer, Sunderland, MA.

Starr, C. 1976. "General Philosophy of Risk-Benefit Analysis." In H. Ashley, *et al.* (eds.), pp. 15ff.

Steele, J. H. 1985. "A Comparison of Terrestrial and Marine Ecological Systems." *Nature* 313: 355–358.

Stent, G. S. 1978. *The Coming of the Golden Age: A View of the End of Progress.* Natural History, Garden City, NJ.

Stone, C. D. 1974. *Should Trees Have Standing?* William Kaufmann, Los Altos, CA.

Strang, W. J. 1990. "Summary of the Discussion." In G. H. Orians, *et al.* (eds.), pp. 240–245.

Strauss, L. 1953. *Natural Right and History.* University of Chicago Press, Chicago.

Strong, D. R., 1979. "Biogeographic Dynamics of Insect–Host Plant Communities." *Annual Review of Entomology* 24: 89–119.

Strong, D. R. 1982a. "Null Hypotheses in Ecology." In E. Saarinen (ed.), pp. 245–260.

Strong, D. R. 1982b. "Harmonious Coexistence of Hispine Beetles on *Heliconia* in Experimental and Natural Communities." *Ecology* 63: 1039–1049.

Strong, D. R. 1983. "Natural Variability and the Manifold Mechanisms of Ecological Communities." *American Naturalist* 122: 636–660.

Strong, D. R. 1986a. "Population Theory and Understanding Pest Outbreaks." In M. Kogan (ed.), pp. 37–58.

Strong, D. R. 1986b. "Density Vagueness: Abiding the Variance in the Demography of Real Populations." In J. Diamond and T. J. Case (eds.), pp. 257–268.

Strong, D. R., *et al.* 1979. "Tests of Community-Wide Character Displacement Against Null Hypotheses." *Evolution* 33: 897–913.

Strong, D. R., D. Simberloff, L. G. Abele, and A. B. Thistle (eds.). 1984. *Ecological Communities: Conceptual Issues and the Evidence.* Princeton University Press, Princeton, NJ.

Suppe, F. 1989. *The Semantic Conception of Theories and Scientific Realism.* University of Chicago Press, Chicago.

Tansley, A. G. 1935. "The Use and Abuse of Vegetational Concepts and Terms." *Ecology* 16: 284–307.

Taylor, B. J., and T. J. White (eds.). 1976. *Issues and Ideas in America.* University of Oklahoma Press, Norman, OK.

Taylor, P. J. 1988. "Technocratic Optimism. H. T. Odum, and the Partial Transformation of Ecological Metaphor after World War II." *Journal of the History of Biology* 21: 213–244.

Taylor, P. W. 1986. *Respect for Nature.* Princeton University Press, Princeton, NJ.

Terborgh, J. 1974. "Faunal Equilibria and the Design of Wildlife Preserves." In F. B. Golley and E. Medina (eds.), pp. 369–380.

Terborgh, J. 1976. (Letter to the editor). *Science* 193: 1029–1030.

Thomas, J. W., E. D. Forsman, J. B. Lint, E. C. Meslow, B. R. Moon, and J. Verner. 1990. *A Conservation Strategy for the Northern Spotted Owl.* USDA, Forest Service; USDI, Bureau of Land Management; USDI, Fish and Wildlife Service; USDI, National Park Service; Portland, OR.

Thomson, J. 1986. *Rights, Restitution, and Risk.* Harvard University Press, Cambridge, MA.

Thorpe, J. H. 1986. "Two Distinct Roles for Predators in Freshwater Assemblages." *Oikos* 47: 75–82.

Tolba, M. K. 1989. "AIBS News: Our Biological Heritage Under Siege." *BioScience* 39, No. 10 (November): 725–728.

Tool, M. C. 1979. *The Discretionary Economy: A Normative Theory of Political Economy.* Goodyear, Santa Monica, CA.

Toulmin, S. 1961. *Foresight and Understanding.* Harper and Row, New York.

Tukey, J. W. 1977. *Exploratory Data Analysis.* Addison-Wesley, Reading, MA.

Ulanowicz, R. E. 1990. "Aristotelean Causalities in Ecosystem Development." *Oikos* 57: 42–48.

Underwood, A. J. 1986. "What Is a Community?" In D. M. Raup and D. Jablonski (eds.), pp. 351–367.

Underwood, A. J. 1990. "Experiments in Ecology and Management: Their Logics, Functions, and Interpretations." *Australian Journal of Ecology* 15: 365–389.

Underwood, A. J., and E. Denley. 1984. "Paradigms, Explanations, and Generalizations in Models for the Structure of Intertidal Communities on Rocky Shores." In D. R. Strong, *et al.* (eds.), pp. 151–180.

US Congress. (Senate) 1973a. *Congressional Record*, 93rd Congress, First Session, 119 (July 24): 25668.

US Congress. 1973b (28 December). *US Code*, Public Law 93–205, "The Endangered Species Act of 1973." Pp. 884–903.

US Congress. 1973c. *Endangered Species Act of 1973*, Sec. 2(a) (1) (Public Law 93–205).

US Congress. 1976. *Technology Assessment Activities in the Industrial, Academic, and Governmental Communities*. Hearings Before the Technology Assessment Board of the Office of Technology Assessment, 94th Congress, Second Session, June 8–10 and 14, 1976, US Government Printing Office, Washington, DC.

US Congress. 1990. *Report of the Interagency Scientific Committee to Address the Conservation of the Northern Spotted Owl*. Senate Hearings, 101–850, US Government Printing Office, Washington, DC.

US Fish and Wildlife Service. 1981. *Endangered Means There's Still Time*. US Fish and Wildlife Service, Washington, DC.

US Fish and Wildlife Service. 1986. *Endangered and Threatened Wildlife and Plants*. 50 CFR 17.11 and 17.12. Washington, DC.

US Fish and Wildlife Service. 1987. *Florida Panther (Felis concolor coryi) Recovery Plan*. Atlanta, GA.

US Nuclear Regulatory Commission (NRC). 1975. *Reactor Safety Study*. (NUREG-75/014), WASH 1400, US Government Printing Office, Washington, DC.

Usher, M. B. (ed.). 1986a. *Wildlife Conservation Evaluation*. Chapman and Hall, London.

Usher, M. B. 1986b. "Wildlife Conservation Evaluation: Attributes, Criteria and Values." In M. B. Usher, (ed.), pp. 3–44.

Usher, M. B. 1988. "Biological Invasions of Nature Reserves: A Search for Generalisations." *Biological Conservation* 44: 119–135.

Usher, M. B. 1991. "Habitat Structure and the Design of Nature Reserves." In S. S. Bell, E. D. McCoy, and H. R. Mushinsky (eds.), pp. 373–391.

Vadas, R. L., Jr. 1989. "Food Web Patterns in Ecosystems: A Reply to Fretwell and Oksanen." *Oikos* 56: 339–343.

Vandermeer, J. 1981. *Elementary Mathematical Ecology*. John Wiley and Sons, New York.

Van Der Steen, W., and H. Kamminga. 1991. "Laws and Natural History in Biology." *British Journal for the Philosophy of Science* 42: 445–467.

VanDobben, W. H., and R. H. Lowe-McConnell (eds.). 1975. *Unifying Concepts in Ecology*. W. Junk, The Hague, The Netherlands.

VanDyne, G. M. (ed.). 1969. *The Ecosystem Concept in Natural Resource Management*. Academic Press, New York.

van Fraassen, B. C. 1980. *The Scientific Image*. Clarendon Press, Oxford.

Van Valen, L. 1976. "Ecological Species, Multispecies, and Oaks." *Taxon* 25: 233–239.

Van Valen, L., and F. Pitelka. 1974. "Intellectual Censorship in Ecology." *Ecology* 55: 925–926.

Varner, G. 1987. "Do Species Have Standing?" *Environmental Ethics* 9, No. 1 (Spring): 57–67.

Vining, J. (ed.). 1990. *Social Science and Natural Resource Recreation Management*. Westview Press, Boulder, CO.

Vrijenhock, R. C. 1989. "Population Genetics and Conservation." In D. Western and M. C. Pearl (eds.), pp. 89–98.

Waide, R. B. 1987. "Letter to the Editor, April 1987." *Bulletin of the Ecological Society of America* 68: 485.

Walker, B. 1989. "Diversity and Stability in Ecosystem Conservation." In D. Western and M. C. Pearl (eds.), pp. 121–130.

Walker, R. L., J. S. Medeiros, R. S. Saito, P. Sekora, G. Swedberg, T. Telfer, D. H. Woodside, and F. Zeillemaker. 1977. *Hawaiian Waterbirds Recovery Plan*. US Fish and Wildlife Service, Portland, OR.

Walters, J. R. 1991. "Application of Ecological Principles to the Management of Endangered

Species: The Case of the Red-Cockaded Woodpecker." *Annual Review of Ecology and Systematics* **22**: 505–523.

Warming, E. 1909. *Oecology of Plants, An Introduction to the Study of Plant Communities.* Clarendon Press, Oxford.

Watt, K. E. F. 1968. *Ecology and Resource Management.* McGraw-Hill, New York.

Wayne, R. K., *et al.* 1991. "Conservation Genetics of the Endangered Isle Royale Gray Wolf." *Conservation Biology* **5**: 41–51.

Western, D. 1989. "Conservation Biology." In D. Western and M. C. Pearl (eds.), p. 31–36.

Western, D., and M. C. Pearl (eds.). 1989. *Conservation for the Twenty-First Century.* Oxford University Press, New York.

Westman, W. E. 1977. "How Much Are Nature's Services Worth?" *Science* **197**: 960–964.

Whitcomb, R. F., J. F. Lynch, P. A. Opler, and C. S. Robbins. 1976. Letter to the Editor. *Science* **193**: 1030–1032.

White, P. S., and S. P. Bratton. 1980. "After Preservation: Philosophical and Practical Problems of Change." *Biological Conservation* **18**: 241–255.

Whitehead, D. R., and C. E. Jones. 1969. "Small Islands and the Equilibrium Theory of Insular Biogeography." *Evolution* **23**: 171–179.

Whittaker, R. H. 1951. "A Criticism of the Plant Association and Climatic Climax Concepts." *Northwest Science* **25**: 17–31.

Whittaker, R. H. 1953. "A Consideration of Climax Theory: The Climax as a Population and Pattern." *Ecological Monographs* **23**: 41–78.

Whittaker, R. H. 1957. "Recent Evolution of Ecological Concepts in Relation to the Eastern Forests of North America." *American Journal of Botany* **44**: 197–206.

Whittaker, R. H. 1962. "Classification of Natural Communities." *Botanical Review* **28**: 1–239.

Whittaker, R. H. 1967. "Gradient Analysis of Vegetation." *Biological Reviews of the Cambridge Philosophical Society* **42**: 207–264.

Whittaker, R. H. 1970. *Communities and Ecosystems.* Macmillan, New York.

Whittaker, R. H. (ed.). 1973. *Ordination and Classification of Communities.* W. Junk, The Hague, The Netherlands.

Whittaker, R. H., S. Lovin, and R. Root. 1973. "Niche, Habitat and Ecotope." *American Naturalist* **107**: 321–338.

Wicke, L. 1990. "Environmental Damage Balance Sheets." In N. Akerman (ed.), pp. 34–53.

Wiens, J. A. 1984. "On Understanding a Non-Equilibrium World: Myth and Reality in Community Patterns and Processes." In D. R. Strong, *et al.* (eds.), pp. 439-457.

Wiens, J. A., and J. T. Rotenberry. 1981. "Censusing and the Evaluation of Avian Habitat Occupancy." *Studies in Avian Biology* **6**: 522–532.

Wilcove, D. S. 1990. "Of Owls and Ancient Forests." In E. A. Norse (ed.), pp. 76–83.

Wildt, D. E., J. G. Howard, L. L. Hall, and M. Bush. 1987. "The Reproductive Physiology of the Clouded Leopard [*Neotelis nebulosa*]: I. Electroejaculates Contain High Proportions of Pleiomorphic Spermatozoa throughout the Year." *Biology of Reproduction* **34**: 937–948.

Wiley, E. O. 1978. "The Evolutionary Species Concept Reconsidered." *Systematic Zoology* **27**: 17–26.

Wilhm, J. L., and T. C. Dorris. 1968. "Biological Parameters for Water Quality Criteria." *BioScience* **18**: 477–481.

Williams, C. B. 1964. *Patterns in the Balance of Nature.* Academic Press, London.

Williams, G. C. 1966a. "On Group Selection and Wynne-Edwards' Hypothesis." *American Scientist* **54**: 273–287.

Williams, G. C. 1966b. *Adaptation and Natural Selection.* Princeton University Press, Princeton, NJ.

Williamson, M. 1981. *Island Populations.* Oxford University Press, New York.

Williamson, M. 1987. "Are Communities Ever Stable?" *Symposium of the British Ecological Society* **26**: 353–370.

Willis, E. O. 1984. "Conservation, Subdivision of Reserves, and the Anti-Dismemberment Hypothesis." *Oikos* **42**: 396–398.

Wilson, E. O. (ed.). 1988. *Biodiversity.* National Academy Press, Washington, DC.

Wilson, E. O., and W. H. Bossert. 1971. *A Primer of Population Biology*. Sinauer, Stamford, CT.

Wilson, E. O., and D. S. Simberloff. 1969. "Experimental Zoogeography of Islands: Defaunation and Monitoring Techniques." *Ecology* 50: 267–278.

Wilson, E. O., and E. O. Willis. 1975. "Applied Biogeography." In M. L. Cody and J. M. Diamond (eds.), pp. 523–534.

Wilson, M. 1979. "Maxwell's Condition – Goodman's Problem." *British Journal for the Philosophy of Science* 30: 107–123.

Wimsatt, W. 1980. "Randomness and Perceived-Randomness in Evolutionary Biology." *Synthese* 43: 287–329.

Wimsatt, W. 1987. "False Models and Means to Truer Theories." In M. H. Nitecki and A. Hoffman (eds.), pp. 23–55.

Winemiller, K. O. 1989. "Must Connectance Decrease with Species Richness?" *American Naturalist* 134: 960–968.

Wisdom, J. 1965. *Paradox and Discovery*. Blackwell, Oxford.

Wittgenstein, L. 1969. *On Certainty*. Blackwell, Oxford.

Wittgenstein, L. 1973. *Philosophical Investigations*. G. E. M. Anscombe (trans.), G. E. M. Anscombe and R. Rhees (eds.), Blackwell, Oxford.

Wittgenstein, L. 1979. "Remarks on Frazer's *The Golden Bough*." J. Beversluis (trans.). In *Wittgenstein*, C. Luckhardt (ed.). Cornell University Press, Ithica, NY, pp. 61–81.

Wood, D. A. 1991. *Official Lists of Endangered and Potentially Endangered Fauna and Flora in Florida*. Florida Game and Fresh Water Fish Commission, Tallahassee, FL.

Woodruff, O. S. 1989. "The Problems of Conserving Genes and Species." In D. Western and M. C. Pearl (eds.), pp. 76–88.

Woodwell, G. 1978. "Paradigms Lost." *Bulletin of the Ecological Society of America*, **59**: 136–140.

Woodwell, G., and H. Smith (eds.). 1969. *Diversity and Stability in Ecological Systems*. Brookhaven Laboratory Publication No. 22, Brookhaven, NY.

Worster, D. 1977. *Nature's Economy: The Roots of Ecology*. Sierra Club Books, San Francisco.

Worster, D. 1990. "The Ecology of Order and Chaos." *Environmental History Review* 14: 1–18.

Worthington, E. B. 1975. *The Evolution of IBP*. Cambridge University Press, Cambridge.

Wu, L. 1974. "On the Stability of Ecosystems." In S. Levin (ed.), pp. 155–165.

Wu, L. 1977. "The Stability of Ecosystems – A Finite-Time Approach." *Journal of Theoretical Biology* 66: 345–359.

Yin, R. K. 1981a. "The Case Study as a Serious Research Strategy." *Knowledge: Creation, Diffusion, Utilization* 3: 97–114.

Yin, R. K. 1981b. "The Case Study Crisis: Some Answers." *Administrative Science Quarterly* 26: 58–65.

Yin, R. K. (ed.) 1984. *Case Study Research*. Sage, Beverly Hills, CA.

Young, S. P., and E. A. Goldman. 1946. *The Puma, Mysterious American Cat*. National Wildlife Federation. Washington, DC.

Zimmerman, B., and R. Bierregaard. 1986. "Relevance of the Equilibrium Theory of Island Biogeography and Species–Area Relations to Conservation with a Case from Amazonia." *Journal of Biogeography* 13: 133–143.

Name Index

Subject Index

Revisions (1993 printing)

Replace lines 9–16, p. 13, with: 'changed and developed through-out the twentieth century. We argue that (1) ecologists first con-ceived of communities as interactive groups defined in a *typological* way, i.e., largely through *phenomenological descriptions* of co-occurring species. Later in the century, (2) ecologists thought of communities as interactive groups defined in a *functional* way, i.e., largely through *mathematical processes* of co-occurring species. In most recent days, (3) ecologists have understood communities as groups of species defined primarily through the *statistical frequency* of their co-occurrence in certain environments. Because our focus is on applying community concepts to environmental problems, we shall not discuss whether communities are natural kinds. Nor shall we investigate any purely stipulative'.

Replace heading on p. 13 with: '2.1.1 The early community con-cept: "Types" composed of interacting species'.

Replace last four lines on p. 15 and first line on p. 16 with: 'As these definitions of various community terms suggest, Clements and his contemporaries tended to think of communities as interac-tive groups defined in a *typological* way, i.e., largely through *phenomenological* descriptions of co-occurring species. By the 1930s, however, ecologists recognized that the broad variety of kinds of'.

Replace the word 'environment' with the word 'community' so that line 17 on p. 16 reads: 'community as a scaled-up organism seems to have fostered a tendency'.

Replace heading on p. 16 with: '2.1.2 Community concepts: From an idealized interactive "type" to a functionally interacting "group" '.

Replace line 9 on p. 19 with: 'communities, one focused on a functionally interacting group, had begun to gain'.

Replace lines 23–24 on p. 22 with: 'were rarely mentioned in the ecological literature written in the middle of the twentieth century. Attacks on group selection during the'.

Replace the heading on p. 24 with: '2.1.3 Community concepts: From a functionally interacting group to a statistically co-occurring group of species'.

Delete the word 'simple' in three places: in line 9, p. 25, in 'simple "mixture of individuals" '; in line 14, p. 25, in 'simple co-occurrence of species'; and in line 26, p. 25, in 'simple co-occurrence as one'.

Insert the word 'partial' before the word 'return' in line 7, p. 25 and in line 13, p. 25.

Replace all seven lines of the last paragraph on p. 27 with: 'Based on an analysis of wording used in the definitions (Table 2.1), we suggest that twentieth-century ecologists have had two basic ways of thinking about communities. These are as types or kinds (representing co-occurring and interacting species) without precise specification of boundaries or interactions among components ("type" way represented in the earliest historical stage of ecological concepts), and as groups of species with quantitative boundaries and/or interactive components ("group" way represented in the second and third historical stages of ecological concepts) (see Figure 2.2). Definitions'.

Remove the word 'mere' from two places: from line 3, paragraph 3 of p. 58 and from line 2, paragraph 2 of p. 59.

Insert the words 'and interacting' in five different places: in the last line of p. 16; in line 4 of p. 19; in the second line from the bottom of p. 20; in the third line on p. 22; and in the tenth line from the bottom of p. 31, so that the parenthetical remark at each of these five places reads: '(representing co-occurring and interacting species)'.